# Nigeria and World War II

*Colonialism, Empire, and Global Conflict*

Chima J. Korieh

*Marquette University*

**CAMBRIDGE**
UNIVERSITY PRESS

# CAMBRIDGE
## UNIVERSITY PRESS

University Printing House, Cambridge CB2 8BS, United Kingdom

One Liberty Plaza, 20th Floor, New York, NY 10006, USA

477 Williamstown Road, Port Melbourne, VIC 3207, Australia

314–321, 3rd Floor, Plot 3, Splendor Forum, Jasola District Centre, New Delhi – 110025, India

79 Anson Road, #06–04/06, Singapore 079906

Cambridge University Press is part of the University of Cambridge.

It furthers the University's mission by disseminating knowledge in the pursuit of education, learning, and research at the highest international levels of excellence.

www.cambridge.org
Information on this title: www.cambridge.org/9781108425803
DOI: 10.1017/9781108579650

First published 2020

Printed in the United Kingdom by TJ International Ltd, Padstow Cornwall

*A catalogue record for this publication is available from the British Library.*

*Library of Congress Cataloging-in-Publication Data*
Names: Korieh, Chima J. (Chima Jacob), 1962– author.
Title: Nigeria and World War II : colonialism, empire, and global conflict / Chima J. Korieh, Marquette University, Wisconsin.
Description: Cambridge, United Kingdom ; New York : Cambridge University Press, 2020. | Includes bibliographical references and index.
Identifiers: LCCN 2019037672 (print) | LCCN 2019037673 (ebook) | ISBN 9781108425803 (hardback) | ISBN 9781108579650 (epub)
Subjects: LCSH: World War, 1939–1945 – Nigeria. | World War, 1939–1945 – Participation, Nigerian. | World War, 1939–1945 – Economic aspects – Nigeria. | Nigeria – Colonial influence. | Nigeria – Politics and government – To 1960.
Classification: LCC D766.99.N6 K67 2020 (print) | LCC D766.99.N6 (ebook) | DDC 940.53/669–dc23
LC record available at https://lccn.loc.gov/2019037672
LC ebook record available at https://lccn.loc.gov/2019037673

ISBN 978-1-108-42580-3 Hardback

# Contents

# Figures

# Maps

# Tables

# Acknowledgments

The idea for writing this book emerged after I had published a collection of petitions written by Nigerians during the Second World War. The letters were a reaction to several regulations and measures implemented by the British colonial authorities during World War II to channel colonial resources toward the war effort. The role that African soldiers played has become emblematic of colonial contributions to the war effort. However, these petitions and supplications were unprecedented in placing the civilian population in Nigeria at the intersection of colonial overrule, wartime economics, and management of wartime crisis. This book attempts to tell these other stories: of farmers, who produced the goods that supported the war; of market men and women, whose activities and roles were of no lesser value; and of many others, who labored at home and in the mines in the name of the empire. The stories of the rising cost of living that became more pronounced as the war raged on, labor shortages, the policies implemented to ameliorate these conditions, and their impact on those who experienced these conditions as colonial subjects helps to capture the complex histories of the era. Thus, if World War II is to be understood in its global context, it is important to understand different historical actors, regional experiences, and the concomitant effect of the global capitalist system on African colonial societies and economies. For the African men and women who participated in this global conflict as soldiers and those who engaged in a different array of work at home, their stories of heroism, suffering, stress, and growing dissatisfaction with the colonial order redefined imperial relations.

I have incurred debts from so many individuals and institutions in the process of writing this book. I am grateful to a number of institutions that provided me the logistical and financial support for this project. Marquette University provided me a number of funds that supported my fieldwork and writing. I am particularly grateful to Marquette University's Department of History, Office of Research and Sponsored Projects, Klingler College of Arts and Sciences, and the Office of the Provost for these crucial supports. Jim Marten, the chair and head of the

Department of History at Marquette, has been an exceptional colleague and a fine administrator. His support has been most generous. My colleagues at the Department of History, Marquette University, provide the kind of collegiality that is rare. I thank them for their friendship. I thank the University of Nigeria, Nsukka, for providing me the time and space to work on this project. I thank the staff of the National Archive in Enugu, Calabar, Kaduna, and Ibadan for their help. The same goes for the Rhodes Library at the University of Oxford, where I had collected materials that proved very useful in this project.

I am indebted to my Nigerian colleagues, Reginald Okeke and Cajetan Nnaocha, for offering me research assistance at the National Archive, Ibadan, and the National Archive, Kaduna. My friends, Raph Njoku, Saheed Adeirnto, Cajetan Iheka, Elizabeth Onogwu, Oliver Coates, and Okwuchi Nwauwa, I remain grateful for your friendship and stimulating intellectual discussions as we try to address old and new challenges in presenting African voices in the historiography of African colonial experience. Elizabeth Dillenburg, Cory Haala, Jeremy Alt, and Kelly Smale, you deserve special thanks for your generosity and for comments on early drafts. I am grateful to Sylvester Ogbechie for permission to reproduce the photograph of his family member who served in the Second World War.

Ijeoma Nwajiaku opened her home to me whenever I was in Enugu. I am very grateful for the hospitality she and her family graciously offered me. I am grateful to Uncle Toba and his wife, Kate, and to Chris and his wife, Ada, for being a pillar of support during my many research trips to Nigeria. I salute Isac Iwuh, my homeboy, who shared the stories of his father, an ex-soldier of World War II, with me. Our discussion provided me information one could not find in the archives; for that I remain grateful. Many thanks to my mentor, Matty Klein, who continues to be a pillar of support more than a decade after he shepherded me through the doctoral program at the University of Toronto. He bid me farewell with the expectation that I was to be "a fine historian." Thank you for all you did for me and other African students at the University of Toronto.

Cambridge University Press gave me the opportunity to bring to life the hidden voices of Nigerians who labored in the name of the empire. Maria Marsh, my commissioning editor; Dan Brown, my editor; Stephanie Taylor, Atifa Jiwa, Sunantha Ramamoorthy, Ami Naramor, and other members of the editorial and production team are the best in what they do. Their professionalism is unmatched. It has been a privilege working with you all on this project.

I cannot thank my family enough for what they have endured and contributed to the success of this project. Akunna (*Nnem*), you have taught me to look forward. I have learned so much from you and I cherish your unconditional love and generosity of heart. Ezenwa, I remain eternally indebted to you for all the time, holidays, and celebrations I have missed as a result of separation. You epitomize resilience. Mom (*Amara-ahia-ugwu*) and the rest of the Onyegbule Osueke Korieh clan have been a pillar of support. I can't trade you for anything. Dad, this is another one in your memory.

# Abbreviations

CO     Colonial Office

IWM   Imperial War Museum, London

NA     National Archives, London

NAC   National Archives of Nigeria, Calabar

NAE   National Archives of Nigeria, Enugu

NAI    National Archives of Nigeria, Ibadan

NAK   National Archives of Nigeria, Kaduna

RH     Rhodes House

# Introduction
## Colonialism, Imperialism, and Global Conflict

There was so little compulsion, so much voluntary effort, and so great an enthusiasm that it makes one rather humble, too.

*A Colony's Effort*, compiled by the Nigerian government[1]

That the African war experience remains just a footnote in European – and especially in German – history books is partly due to the fact that the countries of Europe are reluctant to see any need to draw consequences.

German journalist Karl Rössel[2]

On September 3, 1939, the day the British prime minister, Neville Chamberlain, declared war on Germany during the Second World War, members of the Ututu Clan Executive Committee in southeastern Nigeria wrote a letter pledging loyalty and support to the king of the United Kingdom and the British Empire. The committee wrote: "Though we are but poor farmers by trade, we are quite prepared to render any assistance which may come to our reach to our British Government who is fighting for world peace."[3] Local regional leaders called for national unity and a common goal to defeat Hitler. A week after the British declared war on Germany, the Oba of Benin, Omonoba Akinzua II, called on Nigerians to "bury all our differences and use our strength, our money and everything in defence of our country and Britain."[4] Nigerian newspapers threw their full support behind the British war effort through their editorials and articles. In the editorial of August 26, 1939, the *West African Pilot* called on all Nigerians to render necessary assistance to the government in any form whatsoever, whenever

---

[1] Nigeria, *A Colony's Effort* (Lagos: Government Printing Department, 1939).

[2] "Africa in World War II: The Forgotten Veterans," accessed September 13, 2019, www.dw.com/en/africa-in-world-war-ii-the-forgotten-veterans/a-18437531.

[3] National Archives of Nigeria, Calabar (hereafter NAC), CALPROF, 3/1/2353, "Loyalty to the King and Government."

[4] *West African Pilot*, September 11, 1939. Cited in Onwuka N. Njoku, "Burden of Imperialism: Nigeria War Relief Fund, 1939–1945," *Transafrican Journal of History* 6, no. 7 (1977–1978): 79–99, at 82.

it was demanded, with a view to strengthening the defense of the country against attack either from within or from without.[5] The *Nigerian Daily Times* in two separate editorials emphasized the historic importance of the British government's declaration of war as a commitment to uphold fair and free negotiations.[6] About four years later, on January 2, 1944, the chiefs of Idomi, a small town in the Obura Division in southeastern Nigeria, wrote a letter in support of the British war effort. They pledged their readiness to help in the war by giving full attention to kernel production.[7] The general population in Nigeria would devote considerable resources and funds to the war effort. Later, in 1948, Baron Milverton, the governor of Nigeria (1943–1948), recalled the effort of Nigerians and how much they contributed in both men and material goods.[8] The spontaneous reaction and support for Britain from men and women and from local newspapers was widespread across Nigeria.

In the months following the beginning of the Second World War, increasing numbers of Nigerians offered moral support to Britain. But they did much more, including producing needed agricultural and mineral products, entering the army, and meeting labor needs in several other areas. While Nigeria did not directly experience the conflict on its soil, the war nevertheless had a knock-on effect on its population and on every small village and hamlet in Nigeria.

Oddly enough, Nigerians wrote passionate letters in support of a faraway king and agonized over a war far beyond their borders. Their letters reveal the fascinating attention they paid to the events leading to the outbreak of the Second World War, the most devastating and widespread conflict known to humanity. Like their counterparts in so many other regions of the British Empire, Nigerians appropriated and localized the war itself and expressed their readiness to make sacrifices in order to defeat Hitler. Although dominion autonomy was not extended to the empire's colonies, Nigerian reactions and responses illustrate the necessary cooperation between the British Empire and its colonies and the apparent roles the colony was expected to play in supporting the war effort, and reflect the deep commitment of ordinary Nigerians to the

[5] The *West African Pilot* was a newspaper founded by Nnamdi Azikiwe ("Zik") in 1937. Its mission was to fight for independence from British colonial rule, but it became an ally of the empire during the war. For an analysis of the Nigerian response, see Levi Onyemuche Amadi, "Political Integration in Nigeria, 1939–1945: The Role of Economic Development during the Second World War," *Transafrican Journal of History* 6, no. 7 (1977–1978): 142–153, at 144.
[6] "Up against Habits of the Jungle" and "A Stand for Fair and Free Negotiation," *Nigerian Daily Times*, April 1, 1939, 1.
[7] "Up against Habits of the Jungle," 1.
[8] Lord Milverton, "Nigeria," *African Affairs* 47 (1948): 80–89, at 82.

Allied Powers' objectives and vision. These Nigerian accounts also present the history of the war less as a European war and more as a global conflict.

Yet most studies on the Second World War have given scant attention to the contributions of ordinary Africans or the impact of the war on their lives. Such pervasive neglect of the significant role played by Africans on behalf of the Allies is not only historically problematic but limits our full understanding of the war and its general impact on all humanity. The Second World War, as Paul Mulvey has pointed out, "was truly a global imperial war for Britain, with British and imperial soldiers, sailors and airmen seeing action in far more locations around the world than ever before."[9] Throughout these campaigns, "the contribution of the Empire's Dominions, Colonies and Territories was anything but nominal."[10] And the British colonies contributed more than half of the troops and provided even greater contributions in material resources.[11] Thus, the contributions of small villages and hamlets in Nigeria during the war must also be considered, like the "great cities of England and the United States to get a complete picture of the efforts put out by the United Nations in this war."[12] While historians of the Second World War have raised some important questions in recent years that are significant in grasping a holistic understanding of the event, a particular version of the war narrative has prevailed. That is a tendency, as Keith Lowe rightly argues, to imagine the Second World War as a single, unambiguous conflict between the Allies on one side and the Axis on the other.[13] As Ashley Jackson reminds us, the role of the African colonies in imperial warfare has been consistently undervalued by historians, and their histories are less well developed than those of India and former "white" dominions such as Canada, Australia, South Africa, and New Zealand.[14] As Nicholas Manserg outlines in his book *Survey of British Commonwealth*

---

[9] Throughout the war, Briton, colonial, and dominion armies fought around the world – in Europe, West Africa, the Middle East, and Asia. Paul Mulvey, "The British Empire in World War Two (Lecture)," Academia.edu, accessed January 1, 2019, www.academia.edu/444982/The_British_Empire_in_World_War_Two_lecture.

[10] Ibid.

[11] The numbers of troops who came from the colonies and dominions vary. On the figures, see Ashley Jackson, *The British Empire and the Second World War* (New York: Bloomsbury Academic, 2006), which suggests a figure of 47.6 percent from the United Kingdom (p. 38). In *The Rise and Fall of the British Empire*, 3rd edn. (New York: St. Martin's Press, 1997), Lawrence James has the figures slightly above 50 percent (p. 489).

[12] Nigeria, *A Colony's Effort*, 6.

[13] Keith Lowe, *Savage Continent: Europe in the Aftermath of World War II* (New York: St. Martin's Press, 2012), 272.

[14] Ashley Jackson, cited in Kwei Quartey, "How West Africa Helped Win World War II," Foreign Policy in Focus, June 6, 2012, accessed January 22, 2019, http://fpif.org/how_west_africa_helped_win_world_war_ii/. See also John H. Morrow Jr., "Black Africans in

*Affairs,* there was no ambiguity – these dominions were self-governing and only themselves decided "whether to remain at peace or go to war."[15] The colonial empire, on the other hand, as Onwuka Njoku has correctly observed, was "involuntarily sucked into World War II."[16] The participation of Nigerians in this global war as part of a colonial empire raises a number of broad questions: What roles did European colonial possessions such as Nigeria play in the Second World War? How did the war redefine the relationship between African colonies and European empires in the most important global conflict of the twentieth century? What do we know about the daily lives and wartime experiences of colonial subjects during the war, and how were they shaped by colonial policies, propaganda, and local economic regulations? These questions, among others, and their intersection with empire, colonialism, and global conflagrations lie at the heart of this book.[17]

In this book, I focus on one of Britain's most important colonial possessions and its most prosperous West African colony. The wider aim is to explore the lives of the Nigerian population during the Second World War and the extraordinary roles Nigerians played as part of the British Empire. Our knowledge of World War II will look different if we focus on the ways in which Nigerians of all classes, genders, and ages were drawn into a global conflict as part of the British Empire and on the enormous burden they carried as colonial subjects. This book pays attention to the service of large numbers of Nigerian men overseas, the resultant lack of men on the home front, and the enormous implications it had for production and gender as women took up new and increased roles in production, trade, and marketing. Additionally, I examine the different responses to wartime mobilization by Nigerian producers, workers, merchants, children, women, traditional leaders, and colonial authorities.

I unpack how Nigerians, like other Africans, were forced not only to fight in the war and to feed its participants but to pay for it as well.

---

World War II: The Soldiers' Stories," *ANNALS of the American Academy of Political and Social Science* 632 (2010): 12–25.

[15] While each of these dominions joined the war to support the British Commonwealth, they were not compelled, as was the case with Nigeria and other colonies of Britain. Nicholas Manserg, *Survey of British Commonwealth Affairs: Problems of Wartime Cooperation and Post-War Change, 1939–52* (London: Frank Cass, 1968), 3.

[16] Onwuka N. Njoku, "Nigeria: World War II," Worldhistory.biz, August 21, 2015, accessed December 1, 2018, www.worldhistory.biz/sundries/44822-nigeria-world-war-ii.html.

[17] I use the terms *empire* and *colonial power* interchangeably here. For most of the period of the war, Nigeria was treated as part of the empire in terms of the British ideology of a commonwealth of British territories. At the same time, the territory and colony of Nigeria was specifically influenced by this ideology of cooperation, and was a source for extraction, as evidenced in British policies during the war.

I reconstruct what Nigerian men, women, and children from all walks of life were "doing and thinking on the home front and abroad," to use Emily Yellin's expression, in service to the empire.[18] Given the enormous financial need during the war, Nigeria, like other British colonial possessions, was forced to invest funds in the war effort abroad at the expense of their own budgets and with little recompense after the war was over. By examining Nigeria's participation through the lens of wartime regulations, restrictions, food, rationing, and supplies, I reveal the extent to which everyday life on the Nigerian home front was affected by the Second World War. By investigating the multifaceted relationships between Britain and the colony of Nigeria, and by demonstrating how an elaborate system of media control and the dissemination of propaganda designed to promote particular views about the war, fostered engagement, cooperation, and self-determination, I illustrate the complexity of colonial participation in the war. In doing so, I challenge the dominant perception of historians that the Second World War was mainly a European conflict (at least in terms of the contributions of ordinary people), and I examine the preponderant role noncombatants played to support the war effort and their impact globally. This situation underscores the complexity and diversity of the global experiences of the Second World War, illustrating that there is no single societal experience, but many experiences.[19] The portrait of the empire's ambivalent war goals, the cooperation of colonial subjects and the notion of a commonwealth in which the empire and its constituent parts shared a common goal, and a multidimensional account of the nature and enduring significance of Nigeria's role as a colony offers a unique glimpse into the complexities and contradictions of the British Empire and the colony's participation in the war. *Nigeria and World War II* offers a case study through which to investigate the intertwined histories of colonialism, imperialism, and the most enduring global conflict in the modern era.

Those who write history from below – the history of ordinary people and everyday life – face a particular problem. In most cases, these lives are often nothing but ordinary as in a colonial context or during a period of

---

[18] Emily Yellin, *Our Mothers' War: American Women at Home and at the Front during World War II* (New York: Free Press, 2005).

[19] Ashley Jackson has called for attention to be given to case studies in order to capture specific experiences. See Ashley Jackson, "Motivation and Mobilization for War: Recruitment for the British Army in the Bechuanaland Protectorate, 1941–42," *African Affairs* 96, no. 384 (1997): 399–417. For an exploration of the local economy during the war, see Toyin Falola, "'Salt Is Gold': The Management of Salt Scarcity in Nigeria during World War II," *Canadian Journal of African Studies* 26, no. 3 (1992): 412–436.

war. My intervention and methodological frame are informed and situated within multiple contextual and theoretical frames – colonialism, local agency, race, gender, identity, labor, children's experiences, and intellectual and social history. As Sheila Fitzpatrick has highlighted, there are several theories of writing social history. One trend is the focus on everyday dynamics of private life as they relate to family, home, raising of children, leisure, friendship, and sociability. The other is the world of work.[20] In a colonial context and during a period of mass mobilization for war, as was the case during the Second World War, everyday life transcended both the home and the workplace, and it was mediated by the state and other political entities. People in subordinate positions or under state control have been explored by scholars often focusing on the forms of response that James Scott popularized as "everyday."[21] But I am more interested in interpreting the actions and reactions of ordinary people as a "practice" through which I analyze the strategies of survival and advancement that people develop to cope with particular social and political situations.[22]

Focusing on the role of the civilian population and the enormous burden placed on the colony, I emphasize the unparalleled demands on local manpower, minerals, and agricultural goods amidst new forms of colonial control and regulations. These demands, however, offered Nigerian men and women an opportunity to make sense of their place within the British Empire and to assert both their colonial and individual identities as citizens of both the empire and Nigeria. Nigerians invoked imperialist discourse and ideals such as freedom and liberty in service to the empire despite the contradictions such discourse posed in the colonial context. Indeed, the empire and innumerable colonial subjects inspired by the promise of freedom, liberty, and self-determination worked together to defeat totalitarianism. Nigeria's critical role through the agency of its civil populations in the war and their place in the empire's war effort make a macro- and micro-level historical analysis of a single country a welcome one. Thus, I contribute to a better understanding of the themes of society, war, and economy in general, and of the response of traders and local producers to new war-induced policies and demands from Nigerians in particular.

---

[20] Sheila Fitzpatrick, *Everyday Stalinism: Ordinary Life in Extraordinary Times: Soviet Russia in the 1930s* (New York: Oxford University Press, 2000), 1.

[21] These include the subtle and mundane ways in which dependent populations express dissatisfaction with their conditions. James Scott, *Weapons of the Weak: Everyday Forms of Peasant Resistance* (New Haven, CT: Yale University Press, 1985).

[22] Fitzpatrick, *Everyday Stalinism*, 2.

Map 0.1  Map of colonial Nigeria

## A Global War

The Second World War elicited a profound and haunting response on a global scale, drawing in people who are often forgotten in the traditional Eurocentric narrative.[23] In his recent book on the Second World War, military historian Victor Davis Hanson chose "Wars" in his title in order to capture the many diverse landscapes, peoples, strategies, and ideologies that drove this particular war like no other.[24] Britain and France, more than the lesser colonial players in Africa, relied heavily on their African colonies to help fund the war effort and to provide other forms of support for "the common cause."[25] Britain sought and received the commitment of its citizens at home and its colonial subjects abroad to

[23] General histories of the war include: Gerhard L. Weinberg, *A World at Arms: A Global History of World War II*, 2nd edn. (New York: Cambridge University Press, 2005); Martin Kitchen, *A World in Flames: A Short History of the Second World War in Europe and Asia, 1939–1945* (London: Longman, 1990); H. P. Willmott, *The Great Crusade: A New Complete History of the Second World War* (New York: Free Press, 1989); Robert Alexander Clarke Parker, *Struggle for Survival: The History of the Second World War* (Oxford: Oxford University Press, 1990); John Keegan, *The Second World War* (Sydney: Hutchinson, 1989).

[24] Victor Davis Hanson, *The Second World Wars: How the First Global Conflict Was Fought and Won* (New York: Basic Books, 2017).

[25] The National Archives (hereafter NA), London, CAB/66/34/45 – Swinton. Resident minister, West Africa, dated January 30, 1943, reporting on his recent conversations with the governor-general of French West Africa, and later with President Roosevelt.

support the war effort.[26] In reality, Nigeria became an integral part of the global conflicts that defined the twentieth century on account of being a colony of Britain.

The war had important spatial aspects – the intensive deepening of colonial extraction went hand in hand with the extensive spread of the war beyond European borders. The forms of this spatial integration and the connections between metropole, colony, and the global reach of the European empires shaped relations significantly. During the war, as Ashley Jackson has shown, all parts of the British Empire joined the struggle from the outset – an adventure that led to huge changes and sometimes to great losses on the part of the colonies.[27] Nonetheless, the empire and its countless colonial subjects largely worked together to defeat totalitarianism. Indeed, Britain devoted considerable resources to "sell" the war at home and to win the hearts and minds of colonial peoples. But the surge in identifying with the empire occurred within a specific context and at a historical moment of global importance. This conflicting parallel of a morally superior empire at war with an evil empire epitomized by Germany forced colonial subjects to downplay the differences between empire and colony and to seek new engagements in a pivotal battle between good and evil.

In this context, Britain's declaration of war on Germany on September 3, 1939, made the African colonies active participants in the war against the Axis. The demands of the war forced British officials to initiate a vigorous propaganda campaign and to restructure the local economy to ensure that Nigerians produced the necessary commodities to support the war effort. In addition to the unprecedented mobilization of the local population, the government introduced new regulations and laws to effectively control the production, marketing, and distribution of local products and imported items. These regulations sought to address the crisis that emerged during the war. But drawing Nigeria into the conflict took an enormous toll on the population. Across Nigeria, communities mobilized and contributed financially in both direct and indirect ways. They supplied soldiers in a variety of capacities and provided material resources, including food items, for the troops.[28] The demands Britain made on African manpower, minerals, and agricultural goods

---

[26] Jackson, *The British Empire and the Second World War*. Judith A. Byfield, Carolyn A. Brown, Timothy Parsons, and Ahmad Alawad Sikaing, eds., *Africa and World War II* (New York: Cambridge University Press, 2015).

[27] Jackson, *The British Empire and the Second World War*. Chima J. Korieh, "Urban Food Supply and Vulnerability in Nigeria during the Second World War," in *Nigeria Cities*, ed. Toyin Falola and Steven J. Salm (Trenton, NJ: Africa World Press, 2003), 127–152.

[28] See David Killingray with Martin Plaut, *Fighting for Britain: African Soldiers in the Second World War* (London: James Currey, 2010); Byfield et al., *Africa and World War II*;

because of the war were unparalleled. The production of resources of such magnitude proved taxing to Nigerians, who endured demand on their labor and suffered food shortages amid new colonial regulations and restrictions and severe economic dislocation.

## Nigeria in the Empire and War

The recurring themes in this book – colonialism, empire, and global war – are used in relationship to their intersection with Nigerian colonial subjects as both instruments of colonial exploitation and collaborators in pursuit of imperial goals during wartime. Colonialism was a critical determinant of the place and role of Africans in the Second World War and of the exploitation of human and natural resources to provision the war. As a colonial project, and for war purposes, Britain continued converting natural resources, land, and people into effective units of commodity production.[29] Nigeria was a consequential part of the British Empire before the war. It was an important source of materials for British industries and an important trading link in British West Africa. In fact, Nigerian trade with Britain was already at a peak a decade before the war began. By 1927, 62 percent of goods imported to Nigeria came from Britain and 45.6 percent of Nigeria's exports went to Britain.[30] So Nigeria was destined to play a key role from the beginning of the war. Nigeria's role varied but remained significant throughout the war.

There were at least two reasons why Britain and the Allies co-opted Africans into the war. The first reason was the Allies' priority in garnering the resources necessary to prosecute the war.[31] This was a pragmatic bid to shore up the number of soldiers as well as necessary products,

UNESCO, *Africa and the Second World War: Report and Papers of the Symposium Organized by UNESCO at Benghazi, Libyan Aram Jamahiriya, from 10 to 13 November 1980* (Paris: UNESCO, 1985). Falola, "Salt Is Gold"; David Killingray and Richard Rathbone, eds., *Africa and the Second World War* (Basingstoke: Palgrave Macmillan, 1986).

[29] Sven Beckert has used this expression in discussing capitalism. See Sven Beckert, "American Danger: United States Empire, Eurafrica, and the Territorialization of Industrial Capitalism, 1870–1950," *American Historical Review* 122, no. 4 (2017): 1137–1170.

[30] Brian Gardiner, *The African Dream* (New York: Putnam, 1970), 257. See also Christian C. Opata and Apex A. Apeh, "In Search of Honour: Eya Ebule As a Legacy of Igbo Resistance and Food Security from World War II," *International Journal of Intangible Heritage* 13 (2018): 114–127, at 115.

[31] On Nigeria, see Judith A. Byfield, "Producing for the War," in *Africa and World War II*, ed. Judith A. Byfield, Carolyn A. Brown, Timothy Parsons, and Ahmad Alawad Sikaing (New York: Cambridge University Press, 2015), 24–42; Carolyn A. Brown, "African Labor in the Making of World War II," in *Africa and World War II*, ed. Judith A. Byfield, Carolyn A. Brown, Timothy Parsons, and Ahmad Alawad Sikaing (New York: Cambridge University Press, 2015), 43–67.

including food, to support the metropolis and the colonial population. The move allowed the colonial government to continue to capitalize on the economic structures that already existed in the colonies. West Africa, especially Nigeria, provided "staging bases for British, American and other Allied soldiers and their supplies and equipment en route to the Middle and Far East."[32] As a strategic colonial territory, Nigeria became the hub of wartime activities in West Africa and the locus of British colonial initiatives to promote production and other forms of support for the Allies. The country was the source of more than 140,000 soldiers and of agricultural produce, minerals, and timber from West Africa. The importance of Nigeria to the British war effort increased after the Japanese overran the British Far Eastern colonies. Nigerians were then called upon to maximize production in the country's main export goods such as palm oil, palm kernels, rubber, and timber. Some of these products were already being exported in peacetime, while the exports of others were new developments derived directly from the war and the Axis occupation of areas in the Far East.[33] Thus, agricultural and war policies were closely intertwined and linked many existing colonial departments in pursuit of the war goals.

The second reason for partnering with Africans was ideological. Britain presented a different perception of race and race relations unlike that of Nazi Germany. Its liberal ideology in regards to race relations, although forged within a colonial context, contrasted intensely with Nazism. For most of the prewar period, the dominant colonial ideology had been white superiority and the notion of the "White Man's burden," but this changed during the war when African support became critical to the war effort. For Nigeria and other colonial territories, however, their peculiar experiences were influenced by the imperatives of colonialism as a source of identification with what President Dwight Eisenhower called "the Great Crusade."[34] As the *Nigerian Daily Times* proclaimed in an editorial, the Nazi strategy of violence "has created an intense conviction, particularly among democratic countries, that international dealings will penetrate into the habits of the jungle if differences between larger and smaller nations continue to be settled by reliance on threat or use of brute force."[35]

---

[32] Peter B. Clarke, *West Africans at War 1914–18, 1939–45: Colonial Propaganda and Its Cultural Aftermath* (London: Ethnographica, 1986), 19.

[33] Nigeria, *A Colony's Effort*, 5.

[34] Dwight Eisenhower, *Crusade in Europe* (Baltimore, MD: Johns Hopkins University Press, 1997).

[35] *Nigerian Daily Times*, April 1, 1939, 3.

The intersection of imperial citizenship and colonial subjecthood, as much as they overlapped in times of war, were by no means conterminous. Colonial societies were often the sites of different layers of interactions, contestations, and collaborations. In Nigeria, like in other colonial territories, imperialist goals, race, identity, and local responses played important roles in the structures that guided the interaction between imperial citizens and colonial subjects. As Santanu Das has noted in an exploration of race and empire in the First World War, the experience of being colonized was "substantially different from being a subjugated race within a self-governing dominion (like Aboriginal Australians) or within an independent nation (like African Americans)."[36] Ideologically, Nigerians perceived the war as their own, taking inspiration and legitimacy from the rhetoric of empire – particularly the propaganda of the British and local African elite – when organizing the war effort. Similarly, discourse affirming the legitimacy of the war against Nazi Germany helped to break down previous divisions between the "empire" and its "subject" peoples, forcing each side to organize around a common goal of defeating totalitarianism. For the African population, the threat to Europe was a threat to the world, and many ordinary people around the British Empire "viewed the war as an imperial struggle."[37]

## Historiography

The role British colonial possessions played during the Second World War has received greater attention in the past two decades. Such scholarship has increasingly adopted transnational perspectives to rewrite the history of empire and its relationship with colonial subjects.[38] Some perspectives have sought to deconstruct the Eurocentric visions of the imperial project and the significant events that defined that relationship, including major global episodes such as the two world wars.[39] David Killingray and Richard Rathbone's edited volume *Africa and the Second World War*, the first continental overview of Africa's participation in

[36] Santanu Das, ed., *Race, Empire and the First World War Writing* (Cambridge: Cambridge University Press, 2011), 8.
[37] Jackson, cited in Quartey, "How West Africa Helped Win World War II."
[38] See Jackson, *The British Empire and the Second World War*; Killingray and Plaut, *Fighting for Britain*.
[39] See, for example, F. A. S. Clark, "The Development of the West African Forces in the Second World War," *Army Quarterly* 55 (1947): 58–72; Michael Crowder, "The Second World War: Prelude to Decolonization in Africa," in *History of West Africa II*, ed. J. F. Ade Ajayi and M. Crowder (London: Longman, 1974), 8–50; Trevor R. Kerslake, *Time and the Hour: Nigeria, East Africa, and the Second World War* (London: Radcliffe Press, 1997); and G. O. Olusanya, *The Second World War and Politics in Nigeria, 1939–1945* (Lagos: University of Lagos, 1973).

the Second World War, was published in 1986 and is now more than three decades old. Although the book was well received critically and it was commercially successful, it is a less than comprehensive survey of any African society. The volume's geographical focus on the whole continent, its concentration on combat experience, and its broad thematic approach means that the book lacks an intensive analysis of the war and its impact on a specific society.

As the reevaluation of Africa's participation in the war continues, new scholarship broadens our perspectives and understanding of the war and of the complex relationship between the British Empire and its colonial subjects. A recent edited volume by Judith A. Byfield, Carolyn A. Brown, Timothy Parsons, and Ahmad Alawad Sikaing, *Africa and World War II*, offers a wider overview of the military, economic, and political significance of Africa during the Second World War. The historiographic overview and the case studies that examine themes such as the combatant and noncombatant roles of Africans and the consequences of the war on their lives are welcome. Like *Africa and World War II*, Richard E. Osborne's work *World War II in Colonial Africa: The Death Knell of Colonialism* is a continental overview of Africa during World War II. This book provides a sweeping survey of all aspects of the Second World War in Africa, but it lacks an in-depth analysis of the war's impact on any particular African country.[40]

Some firsthand accounts focus specifically on wartime experiences in Nigeria. In a trenchant critique of previous historical accounts of the Asiatic theater, which grossly ignored the role of Nigerian soldiers who fought alongside their British counterparts, John Igbino sets out to recover the contributions and experiences of Nigerian soldiers. He argues:

It is not only historians of Operation Thursday who forgot that the so-called backward and primitive Nigerian soldiers of the Spider Brigade were Chindits.[41] Instead there is, in Britain, a collective intentional amnesia about Nigeria's human, military, material and financial resource contributions to Britain and Britain's wars throughout the ages, from the Ashanti Wars through the First and Second World Wars to Post-War reconstruction of Britain.[42]

The amnesia, he contends, "has ensured that the myth that Britain stood alone against Germany until the United States of America entered the war

[40] Richard E. Osborne, *World War II in Colonial Africa: The Death Knell of Colonialism* (Indianapolis, IN: Riebel-Roque, 2001).
[41] The Chindits were a special operations unit of the British army, which saw action in 1943 and 1944, during the Burma campaign in World War II.
[42] John Igbino, *Spidermen: Nigerian Chindits and Wingate's Operation Thursday Burma 1943–1944* (London: Author House, 2018).

following the Japanese attacks on Pearl Harbor in 1942 is perpetuated." On the contrary, "at no time did Britain stand alone because by October 1939 Nigeria's human, financial and physical resources were already being mobilized for war in support of Britain."[43] Trevor R. Kerslake's *Time and the Hour: Nigeria, East Africa, and the Second World War* is a memoir of a British officer in the Colonial Service in Nigeria from 1937 to 1946 and covers his service with the Nigeria Regiment. However, his account is about neither Africans nor African societies. John A. L. Hamilton's memoir about the role of the 81 (West African) Division to which Nigeria belonged foregrounds Nigerians' experiences in the war.[44] He details what has often been a forgotten army, which has been ignored and even belittled over the years in accounts of the war. Along the same lines, David Killingray and Martin Plaut draw from oral accounts and personal testimonies from African soldiers to recount the latter's combat experiences, the impact of the war on them and their families, and how the combat experience shaped postwar society.[45]

A growing body of secondary scholarship on the impact of the war includes the experiences of Africans at home.[46] As Allan Winkler has observed, historians have looked at the impact of the war even more closely than before in their attempt to capture the entire wartime experience.[47] While some attention has been given to the role of African combatants and other forms of labor on the war fronts, I contend that little attention has focused on the "home front," the role of the civilian population, the systematic extraction of local resources in both agriculture and mining during the war, and the ambivalences that marked the Nigerian population's response to colonial wartime policies.[48] Indeed

---

[43] Ibid.

[44] John A. L. Hamilton, *War Bush: 81 (West African) Division in Burma 1943–1945* (Norwich: Michael Russell, 2001).

[45] Killingray and Plaut, *Fighting for Britain*.

[46] Allan M. Winkler, "World War II Homefront: A Historiography," *OAH Magazine of History* 16, no. 3 (Spring 2002): 5–8. On Nigeria, see Njoku, "Burden of Imperialism"; Onwuka N. Njoku, "Export Production Drive in Nigeria during World War II," *Trans-African Journal of History* 10, nos. 1–2 (1981): 11–22; Falola, "Salt Is Gold"; Korieh, "Urban Food Supply and Vulnerability in Nigeria"; Chima J. Korieh, *"Life Not Worth Living": Nigerian Petitions Reflecting an African Society's Experiences during World War II* (Durham, NC: Carolina Academic Press, 2014).

[47] Winkler, "World War II Homefront," 5. See also Allan M. Winkler, *Home Front, U.S.A.: America during World War II*, 2nd edn. (Wheeling, IL: Harlan Davidson, 2000); John W. Jeffries, *Wartime America: The World War II Home Front* (Chicago: Ivan R. Dee, 1996); William L. O'Neill, *A Democracy at War: America's Fight at Home and Abroad in World War II* (New York: Free Press, 1993).

[48] Surveying recent literature on the Second World War reveals few references to the African perspective of the war. One exception is A. Olorunfemi, who details the

a major conceptual problem pervades the history of the Second World War. While the war has often been imagined in terms of European geopolitical dynamics and examination of its effects has extensively focused on the European population and societies, this historiographical focus underestimates the complex nature of the war and the strategically significant role played by European colonial possessions as well as the consequences of the war for their societies. Our histories of the war are incomplete without a comprehensive analysis of African participation and engagement, and the pervasive neglect of the key role played by Africans on behalf of the Allies limits our holistic understanding of the war and its monumental impact on humanity.[49] Most importantly, it neglects African initiatives and the changing power dynamics between empire and subject peoples that significantly influenced the outcome of the war and the transformation of Europe's relationship with its vast colonial possessions. Thus, although the war is often perceived as a conglomeration of European conflicts, Africans played an active role in them and their societies were consequently greatly affected. But the ways these colonial subjects perceived the war and encountered colonial policies were central to the forms of intellectualism that emerged within the colony and the framing strategies through which Nigerians articulated their views of events.

Our understanding of the home front, as reflected in the contributions of the civilian population and the impact of the war at home, is characterized by state and civilian undertakings during the war. While the Second World War had a profound impact on participating societies across the globe, the concept of the home front has mostly been applied to the European experience. But we can speak of many home fronts as they were influenced or transformed in terms of gender ideology, race and ethnicity, and colonialism. All these provide a framework for analysis that captures similarities and differences across regions and local contexts. On a comparative level, most of the societies involved in the global conflict

significant disruption that local economies in British West Africa faced during the war. His exploration of the impact of the war on cocoa traders and producers in southwestern Nigeria clearly illustrates the predicament of cocoa farmers, "most of whom had concentrated solely on cocoa production since the 1920s to the almost total neglect of other cash crops." See A. Olorunfemi, "Effects of War-Time Trade Control on Nigerian Cocoa Traders and Producers, 1939–1945: A Case Study of the Hazards of a Dependent Economy," *International Journal of African Historical Studies* 13, no. 4 (1980): 672–687, at 672. For more recent focus on the civilian population elsewhere, see Aaron William Moore, *Bombing the City: Civilian Accounts of the Air War in Britain and Japan, 1939–1945*. Studies in the Social and Cultural History of Modern Warfare (Cambridge: Cambridge University Press, 2018).

[49] Frans Coetzee and Marilyn Shevin-Coetzee's *The World in Flames: A World War II Sourcebook* has only a peripheral reference to African participation (Oxford: Oxford University Press, 2011).

across Europe, America, Asia, and Africa experienced mass mobilization, greater state intervention, and tighter control of the local economy and population. Indeed, Paul Einzig, in *Economic Problems of the Next War*, written in early 1939, has argued that war economies required "a certain degree of Government control in production and trade" in order to ensure the maximum output of armaments, a condition lacking in Britain and France before the war.[50]

In the American context, the structural changes that occurred in society as the government prepared for conflict, including the creation of a much more complex bureaucratic structure, affected all aspects of American life.[51] There was a massive growth in the labor forces, and women joined the workforce laboring in factories, as symbolized by "Rosie the Riveter," and took new roles in a variety of industries, from factories and shipyards to sports and entertainment.[52] Yet mobilization on the home front was characterized by sacrifice and civilian effort toward winning the war. Some Americans faced discrimination at home because of their race or ethnicity. Driven by national security concerns, the US government rounded up people of Japanese ancestry and placed them in internment camps after the Japanese attack on the American naval fleet at Pearl Harbor on December 7, 1941. Similarly, Italian citizens were removed from strategic coastal areas in California and forced to relocate due to concerns about Fascist Italy. The mass migration of people from the poor South into munition industries in large cities such as Chicago, Detroit, and New York tapped into the contributions of African Americans at a time of great need, but their movement into these cities exacerbated racial tensions that resulted in race riots in 1943. Thus, African Americans faced the dilemma of fighting fascism abroad or racial discrimination at home.

In Europe, the home front was influenced by state institutions and the structure of the state. Like the United States, Britain and France witnessed the mass mobilization of the civilian population, but they also witnessed some of the realities of German aggression and the devastating

---

[50] Paul Einzig, *Economic Problems of the Next War* (London: Macmillan, 1939). Cited in Talbot Imlay, "Democracy and War: Political Regime, Industrial Relations, and Economic Preparations for War in France and Britain up to 1940," *Journal of Modern History* 79, no. 1 (2007): 1–47.

[51] Winkler, *Home Front, U.S.A.* See also Jeffries, *Wartime America*, and Robert G. Spinney, *World War II in Nashville: Transformation of the Homefront* (Knoxville: University of Tennessee Press, 1998).

[52] See Karen Anderson, *Wartime Women: Sex Roles, Family Relations, and the Status of Women during World War II*. Contributions in Women's Studies 20 (Westport, CT: Praeger, 1981). See also Pauline E. Parker, ed., *Women of the Homefront: World War II Recollections of 55 Americans* (Jefferson, NC: McFarland, 2002).

impact it had on their cities and civilian population. In addition to the rationing of food and other household items, which began in January 1940, British civilians endured the bombing of their towns and cities in the Blitz, as well as attacks from flying bombs and rockets.[53] An estimated 60,595 civilians were killed and 86,182 seriously injured.[54] In totalitarian states such as Nazi Germany and Fascist Italy, the home front, as Earl R. Beck notes, was shaped by the capacity of these states to enforce "compliance of their citizens by a combination of propaganda and police action."[55] This tactic applies to Japan, where the state used its powers to compel citizens to aid the war effort.[56]

It may often be tempting to generalize the home front experience, but not certainly for colonial territories that fought on behalf of the imperial powers, especially Britain and France. If we agree that European colonialism was a factor in World War II, then the Second World War was a war for empire and its impact on colonized societies was quite different from the experiences of imperial powers and the United States. British and French colonies increased the resources available to fight the war on the side of the Allies. Yet colonial subjects across these empires had quite distinct experiences at home. In Nigeria, as I recount in this book, the local population engaged in the war both as subjects of the British Empire and as people whose individual assertions and engagement in the war effort were mediated by colonialism and colonial regulations. It is from this perspective that the impact of the war on the Nigerian home front and the contributions of the Nigerian people toward the British war effort can be assessed.

As the war progressed, the participation of combative Africans, especially in Asia, made places like Burma a crossroads where peoples of different races, cultures, and beliefs interacted. These distinct cultures brought contrasting notions of "liberty" and "freedom." For Africans, these experiences on the war front had unparalleled consequences that became entwined with nationalist agitation in the postwar period. Questions of personal liberty, affirmation of African personhood, and freedom from colonial rule were all brought to the forefront when the

---

[53] On dealing with rationing, price control, and the development of Britain's underground economy during the war, see Mark Roodhouse, *Black Market Britain: 1939–1955* (Oxford: Oxford University Press, 2013).

[54] Terry Charman, "What Life Was Like in Britain during the Second World War," Imperial War Museum, January 8, 2018, accessed February 2, 2019, www.iwm.org.uk/history/what-life-was-like-in-britain-during-the-second-world-war.

[55] Earl R. Beck, *The European Home Fronts, 1939–1945* (Wheeling, IL: Harlan Davidson, 1993).

[56] Thomas R. H. Havens, *Valley of Darkness: The Japanese People and World War Two* (New York: University Press of America, 1986).

war ended and African soldiers returned to their homeland from 1945. The war in Burma played some part in breaking down the race barriers of the era for as former infantryman Dauda Kafanchan recalls, "Initially I saw the white man as someone better than me. But after the war, I considered him an equal."[57] Thus, the discriminatory attitude of the British toward colonial soldiers became a source of increasing conflict between the two.

An important but often neglected part of the dynamics of imperial relations with colonized peoples is the question of free and unfree labor. The use of forced labor in building early colonial systems and infrastructure is well documented.[58] Such traditional practices of correlating African labor with "free" labor were increasingly revived to satisfy British wartime needs. The ambiguities of the colonial policies and practices regarding the concepts of "free" and "unfree" labor or their "blurred character" contradict the philosophical discourse of liberty and self-determination increasingly espoused by Britain and other Allies. The historical trend of the massive use of forced labor had reduced by the 1930s in many parts of the British West African colonies due to the significant rise in revenue generated in the colonies and the rise in African production for the international market. This course would significantly change because of the war. As Carolyn Brown explains, "World War II brought contradictory experiences of 'progressive' reform within authoritarian labor systems and the preservation of archaic oppressive systems of labor mobilization."[59] The war created labor shortages and Britain's actions to garner support and elicit a greater Nigerian commitment to the Allied war effort led to intense demands on local labor and resources. However, new labor policies sought to ameliorate local conditions of colonial workers in order to stabilize the atmosphere for maximum production during the war.

An interesting aspect of the Second World War is the role and experiences of women and children. They lived, worked, and contributed to the war effort. Some excellent works have appeared over the years that capture the experiences of European and American women during the

---

[57] "Africa's Forgotten Wartime Heroes," BBC News, August 14, 2009, accessed September 12, 2018, http://news.bbc.co.uk/go/pr/fr/-/2/hi/africa/8201717.stm.

[58] Catherine Mornane Bogosian, "Forced Labor, Resistance and Memory: The Deuxième Portion in the French Soudan, 1926–1950" (Unpublished PhD dissertation, University of Pennsylvania, 2002); Frederick Cooper, *Decolonization and African Society: The Labor Question in French and British Africa* (Cambridge: Cambridge University Press, 1996); Myron Echenberg, *Colonial Conscripts: The Tirailleurs Sénégalais in French West Africa, 1857–1960* (Portsmouth, NH: Heinemann, 1991).

[59] Brown, "African Labor in the Making of World War II," 43.

war.[60] The service of large numbers of African men overseas, and the consequent lack of men on the home front, had enormous implications for production and gender as women took up new and increased roles in production, trade, and marketing. Wartime mobilization of men in Nigeria challenged existing gender relations and placed significant burdens on the women left at home. Masculinity and farm work, cultural conception of gender roles, and the practice of power witnessed significant transformation. Children were drawn into the war just as adults were. Imperial propaganda focused on Nigerian children as an important part of the empire's global citizenry. Nigerian children wrote letters of support to the British king and contributed to win-the-war funds. Pupils at the Hope Waddell Institute contributed items to the war effort and altogether the institution raised a sum of £80 toward the War Charities Fund of the Calabar District.[61] Chinua Achebe recalls how he and his contemporaries proudly sang anti-German war songs and believed their headmaster's order that every palm kernel they collected would be used to buy a nail for Hitler's coffin.[62]

Several important and related claims are at the core of this book. First, the Second World War as a major aspect of Africa's relationship with European empires cannot be understood in isolation from the broader hegemonic structures of European colonialism. This argument is underscored by the fact that the administrative agents of the empire, formulators of wartime policies, did not lose sight of the far-reaching effects of the symbiotic relationship between Europe and Africa and the impact of colonial possessions on British society and psyche. As British Secretary of State for Dominion Affairs Thomas Inskip noted on June 28, 1940, regarding the British Empire and its dominions: "The risk is that England, dominated by danger at home, which she will overcome, may lose sight of the larger situation which makes her the great world power which she is, and which is so essential to the future of the world."[63] Inskip

---

[60] Anderson, *Wartime Women*; Susan M. Hartmann, *The Home Front and Beyond: American Women in the 1940s* (Boston: Twayne Publishers, 1982). See also a perceptive study by Dan Campbell, *Women at War with America: Private Lives in a Patriotic Era* (Cambridge, MA: Harvard University Press, 1984). For women's own voices, see Judy Barrett Liftoff and David C. Smith, eds., *Since You Went Away: World War II Letters from American Women on the Home Front* (Lawrence: University Press of Kansas, 1991); and *American Women in a World at War: Contemporary Accounts from World War II* (Wilmington, DE: SR Books, 1997).

[61] Efiong U. Aye, *Hope Waddell Training Institution: Life and Work, 1894–1978* (Calabar: Paico, 2012), 154.

[62] Chinua Achebe, *The Education of a British-Protected Child: Essays* (New York: Penguin Books, 2009), 18.

[63] NA, CAB/66/9/9, Memorandum by the Secretary of State for Dominion Affairs, June 28, 1940, 2.

was well aware that "Great Britain herself may win through but lose her Empire and Commonwealth." Drawing upon historical experiences, he rhetorically asked if what happened to the French Empire in the eighteenth century, when France won on the home front but lost its empire in Asia and America to Britain, would be "repeated in the case of Britain."[64] To save empire and commonwealth, Inskip concluded, "it is therefore necessary to hold Africa south of the equator at all cost in this war. It is very rich in tropical and mineral resources apart from its strategic position."[65] The possibility that Great Britain could win on the domestic front but lose the empire on the world front was a concern to Inskip and other imperial officials.

Second, like previous outcomes of the encounter with Europe, the outcomes for colonial and imperial polices in this period were not the making of imperial Britain alone but were also shaped by African responses. At home, the Nigerian population contested colonial war policies, regulations, and restrictions. Nigerians' struggles to survive the depressed wartime economy and their strategies for coping with the crisis engendered by the war were reflected in petitions and supplications, which evoke a feeling of what it was like to live through that era and offer a key connection between the war and the Nigerian people.[66] Nigerians challenged the ever-expanding power of the colonial state as it mitigated their lives and livelihood through petitions and other forms of social movement. Letters of petition as a form of local protest provide alternative sources of information for exploring and understanding Nigerian agency, how Nigerians perceived the war, and how they drew from their experiences – vital details about the impact of the war on their lives. The richness of these petitions has allowed for a better understanding of the impacts of the war on African families and communities as they struggled with colonial regulations and control. These accounts situate Nigerian civilian experience in the larger context of the war and the colonial society

---

[64] Ibid.

[65] NA, CAB/66/9/9, "The Strategical Outlook," Memorandum of Secretary of State for Dominion Affairs to War Cabinet, June 28, 1940.

[66] For a recent examination of World War II–related petitions, see Oliver Coates, "'The War, Like the Wicked Wand of a Wizard, Strikes Me and Carries Away All That I Have Loved': Soldiers' Family Lives and Petition Writing in Ijebu, Southwestern Nigeria, 1943–1945," *History in Africa* 45 (2018): 1–27. See also Catherine Burns, "The Letters of Louisa Mvemve," in *Africa's Hidden Histories: Everyday Literacy and Making the Self*, ed. Karin Barber (Bloomington: Indiana University Press, 2006), 78–112; Vukile Khumalo, "Ekukhanyeni Letter-Writers: A Historical Inquiry into Epistolary Network(s) and Political Imagination in Kwazulu-Natal South Africa," in *Africa's Hidden Histories: Everyday Literacy and Making the Self*, ed. Karin Barber (Bloomington: Indiana University Press, 2006), 113–142.

and reveal much about the changing nature of imperial policy during the war and the immediate postwar period.

By using petitions to address their own personal concerns, Nigerian men and women were also creating a space to participate in the larger discourse that went beyond their immediate need for survival. They were, by extension, moving into the realm of public discourse on war and economic policy, imperial subjects, and race relations within the boundaries of the empire. The content and context in which these petitions were written suggest that the impacts of the war were felt within both urban and rural areas and across classes and genders. Petitions linked local economic conditions and production systems to a broad range of ethnicities, classes, and spatial categories – systems that became even more connected at the time of the war. Thus, the war was fought in the spaces of everyday life, where many ordinary people, like the authors of the petitions, worked to achieve the goals of the empire abroad and to give meaning to their daily lives at home. Local people's engagement with the politics of colonial control, especially on matters of everyday subsistence, drove a potential wedge between Nigerian men and women's right to engage freely in economic enterprises and the colony's support for the war effort.

The Second World War had important consequences for the sociopolitical developments in the postwar period, ushering in two differing ideologies: a paternalistic ideology of "co-option" of Africa by the empire, and the African commitment to human rights and self-preservation as ultimate rewards. Ideologically, colonial leaders viewed their policies in this period as key to increasing the production of much-needed raw materials and food, which were essential in winning the war. Although the African response was marred by ambivalence, colonial officials encouraged Africans not only to appropriate the notions of "liberty and self-determination" as universal human rights but also to perceive the war as a global effort to stop Germany's tyrannical desire to control the world and ultimately to enslave Africans. According to Keith Lowe, "In our collective memory the motives and allegiances of each side are transparent: The Nazis and their accomplices fought for the domination of Europe, while the Allies fought for a 'free world.' It was a war of right against wrong or, even more simplistically, good against evil."[67] The African population collaborated with the Allies in this regard.

The Allied war effort was multidimensional – that is, the British Empire relied on its colonial subjects as partners in the war effort, expressing ideas

---

[67] Lowe, *Savage Continent*, 272.

of universal commonwealth citizenship, liberty, and self-determination, and at the same time imposed hegemonic ideology upon the colony in line with colonial objectives. Indeed, Britain and its colonial subjects grappled with the challenges of fighting a common enemy within an ambivalent colonial hierarchical order and context that perceived Africans as inferior but inevitable in implementing the ideals for which the war was fought. Thus, Britain relied on colonial human and material resources to feed the war demands and to give a semblance of the universal brotherhood of man in the fight against tyranny and oppression. Additionally, the British drew upon the notions of "liberty and equality" and the "history of race and racism" to garner African support. Allied leaders viewed their war effort as the preservation of Western civilization and global liberty. Their cultural self-justification is reflected in the tone and content of the wartime intellectual production. Yet the contradiction between imperial policy and the ideals of liberty, self-determination, and freedom was evident.

Colonial subjects gave meanings to European propaganda and the differing notions of rights, liberty, and self-determination. As the war unfolded, Nigerians appropriated the war as their own and became involved in the intellectual propaganda that sought to enlist local support. The new discourse around the notion of imperial citizenship that emerged in this period in response to the changing political and economic land-scape both within and outside of Nigeria created new, unique roles for colonial subjects and enabled both the metropole and the colony to forge common ground in the war against Germany. The war redefined the relationship between the British Empire and the people of its Nigerian colony, enabling the emergence of a new notion of imperial citizenship. This notion of a global commonwealth linking the empire was central to how both the British government and its colonial subjects articulated the global response to Germany in World War II.

The Second World War provided the impetus for changing political and social dynamics. The war shaped colonial history from the 1940s and redefined the relationship between the empire and its subjects. The war and its outcome were very important means by which the gains of the Allied victory were transmitted to the colonies. The end of the war was the impetus for the emergence of a new kind of discourse of self-determination in colonial societies and a reexamination of the imperial project. In addition, the end of the conflict witnessed the demobilization of thousands of African men who had been employed as soldiers or in auxiliary services as drivers or hospital orderlies and had enjoyed a higher pay than the environment of postwar demobilization could afford them. The returning soldiers created a labor reserve cadre desperate to find work. While many had been employed in auxiliary services, as mentioned earlier, with a higher standard of living, acute unemployment rose at the end of the war from the dismantling of the elaborate system of controls that constricted the economy. The postwar economic problems constituted greater chaos and confusion than the war itself. This became a potential source of trouble in the postwar period.

Wartime intellectualism had a long-term impact on political developments in Nigeria and the rest of the continent. Bonny Ibhawoh has shown that the role of Africans in the making of colonial war propaganda "is particularly evident in the paradoxical effect that war propaganda had on the politics of decolonization in British West Africa" in both providing "an opportunity for Britain to rally the support of her West African subjects against what was presented as a dreaded common enemy" and strengthening "the African sense of belonging to the British Empire and fostered some form of imperial idealism at a time of growing local opposition to colonial rule."[68] In the years following the Second World War, Africans would draw on the same rhetoric propagated by the empire to articulate their nationalist agenda and to demand independence from colonial rule. The demand for self-determination that underlined imperial war propaganda would ironically be used to "strengthen an anti-colonial nationalist movement that envisioned Africans not merely as subjects of Empire but also as autonomous citizens of the world."[69]

This book advances our understanding of the Second World War in several other ways. It reaches deep into an African society to uncover its engagement with the war and the impact of the war on the lives of a broader spectrum of citizens – men, women, and children at home – than have previous studies. Additionally, this book moves beyond a generalized approach that has resulted in the mistaken assumption that only African combatants reflect African participation in the war and that the engagement of others at home (as producers, laborers, and wartime protestors) did not contribute to Allied success. In this respect, this is neither another book about the military in the Second World War nor a work exclusively focused on the military aspects of the war in the African context. Rather, this book is about the actions taken by the British Empire to garner sympathizers and to elicit the commitment of Nigerians at home to support the Allied war effort. As such, it offers an alternative perspective to the voluminous history of the Second World War and challenges the assumption of the dominant literature that focuses on the

---

[68] Bonny Ibhawoh, "Second World War Propaganda, Imperial Idealism and Anti-colonial Nationalism in British West Africa," *Nordic Journal of African Studies* 16, no. 2 (2007): 221–243. See also Suryakanthie Chetty, "Imagining National Unity: South African Propaganda Efforts during the Second World War," *Kronos* 38 (2012): 106–130.

[69] Ibhawoh, "Second World War Propaganda," 222–223.

European experience and African soldiers. Shifting the focus to the agency of non-Europeans in the British colony of Nigeria and the shared responsibility between empire and ordinary colonial subjects reveals the possibilities for articulating how notions of an imagined British imperial commonwealth emerged. Thus, this work is much more holistic in its approach by putting the experiences of a wider group of peoples (across gender, generation, location, and ethnicity) into conversation with one another.

This book answers several questions about how the war influenced colonial relations and public policy in a country like Nigeria. How did colonial authorities compel Nigerian men and women to confront the economic questions raised by the war? What were the economic and political consequences of the Nigerian population's participation in the war as soldiers and as civilians? And finally, how did the population respond to wartime policies imposed by colonial authorities on the home front? This book is one of the first to use micro-history, intellectual history, and gender to analyze exclusively the significance of the Nigerian population to the British war effort. This study challenges the "over-masculinization" of the historical literature on Africans and the Second World War. Although comparable situations happened in the United States and Europe during World War II, what is unique about men's wartime mobilization and gender transformation in Nigeria is the impact it had on notions of masculinity and farm work, cultural conceptions of gender roles, and the practice of power.

For expert and general readers alike, this book is an instructive experience that reveals the tortured path of Nigeria's experience of World War II. Much of the history of the war is written from the European perspective, but African sources offer alternative perspectives and a counter-narrative account of the darker sides of colonial policy and African experiences during the war period. Here, one learns how a colonial government, through its own ideological motif, tried to convince Africans that their actions and support for the war against Germany were consistent with the intellectual trajectory of Western civilization and the notions of freedom and liberty for all. A comparative approach to the ways in which the war was presented to Western and African populations respectively provides important lessons about the power of propaganda in shaping ideologies and altering perceptions of the supposedly "fixed" canons of colonial history. Allied leaders viewed their war effort as a defense of civilization. Their cultural self-justification is reflected in the tone and content of wartime propaganda. Yet the contradiction between imperial policy and the ideals of liberty, self-determination, and freedom was evident. The meanings that colonial subjects associated with European propaganda and the differing notions of rights, liberty, and self-determination redefined relations between colonial powers and Africans in the twentieth century.

This work contributes to all areas of colonial studies including cultural studies, histories of cultural encounters, indigenous literary traditions that are marred by and rooted in the colonial experience, and discourses on colonialism from diverse viewpoints. It draws attention beyond academic audiences, to anyone intrigued by how certain ideologies can be appropriated by a totalitarian colonial regime. While the ideals of freedom and self-determination formed an important philosophical and moral ground for the Allies in their prosecution of the war against Nazi Germany, colonial subjects, whose freedom and self-determination were disintegrating under the hegemonic force of colonialism, were encouraged to support these ideals.

This study challenges the dominant perception of historians that the Second World War was mainly a European conflict, at least in terms of the contribution of ordinary people, the preponderant role played by these noncombatants to support the war effort, its intersection with colonialism, and the war's global impact. The experience of rural and urban communities in Nigeria, a region that was central to the British and Allied war effort, is further useful to illustrate the forces that gave rise to the imperial discourse of a common global British commonwealth. In this study, I illustrate how the hegemonic ideology upon which colonial relations were built before the war changed as both colonizer and colonized became partners during the war and enabled colonial subjects to seek self-determination after the war. The contribution of the colony and its people, as Andrekos Varnava observed in the case of Cyprus, says much about imperial loyalty and, in the case of Nigeria in particular, the influence of British modernity and colonial ideology.[70]

## Methods and Sources

Few accounts exist reflecting the reactions and impact of the war on the Nigerian population. The available scholarship has focused almost exclusively on the military records. This is partly a problem of historical sources. The experiences of the general populace appear infrequently in existing records despite their enormous contributions to the war effort and the significant ways the war affected their lives. However, the rich archival and journalistic sources generated by Nigerians offer the

---

[70] Andrekos Varnava, "The Impact of the Cypriot Contribution during the Great War on Colonial Society and Loyalties/Disloyalties to the British Empire," *First World War Studies* 8, no. 1 (2017): 17–36.

opportunity for the first comprehensive overview of the Nigerian experience that extends the discourse beyond the military role of Nigeria. Petitions and supplications written by ordinary Nigerians, including traders and farmers, reveal that Britain, through its wartime policy, initiated subtle forms of resistance that increasingly questioned the legitimacy of colonial policies and the ideals for which the war was fought.

This study is unique in its focus on noncombatants and the sources used to recount their experiences. This book relies mainly on one often overlooked but critically important source left by the Nigerian population: petitions and supplications to British officials. I explored approximately 300 correspondences and petitions written by individuals, including women and children, living in rural and urban areas in Nigeria during the Second World War. These documentary sources, housed at the National Archives of Nigeria, have never been examined thoroughly by scholars. This distinctive mode of communication between colonial officials and colonial subjects spread rapidly during the war, and by the war's cessation, locals wrote hundreds of such petitions.

Petitioning became a tool for everyday Nigerian people and groups to channel political expression and to communicate with the colonial authorities about their concerns. As Andrew Verner has argued in his examination of peasants' petitions during the Russian Revolution, "instead of simply looking at the petitions as another, if unusual, set of documents, by which peasant thoughts and desires are transparently revealed," they should be treated as an "integral part of the complex negotiations among as well as between the peasants and the outside" and their contents regarded as the "results of strategic choices made by their authors in the context of their surroundings."[71] The personal and often intimate petitions of Nigerians paint a unique portrait of a rough-and-tumble time. They reflect local reactions and responses to imperial war policies and provide insights into how Africans perceived the war and what happened to ordinary people as a result of British wartime policies in Nigeria. They thus provide unparalleled perspectives on the war and its impact on Nigerians' lives in both urban and rural settings. Most of those who petitioned officials during the war were small traders and rural farmers. Their petitions and the economic, cultural, and social conditions that gave rise to them reveal the conditions faced by Nigerian societies, especially lower classes. They correct the skewed impression that the effects of the war on the "home front" only applied to European societies. Despite the constraints imposed on the local population by colonial restrictions,

---

[71] Andrew Verner, "Discursive Strategies in the 1905 Revolution: Peasant Petitions from Vladimir Province," *Russian Review* 54, no. 1 (1995): 65–90.

the petitions written by Nigerians reveal a surprisingly flexible power dynamic within colonial societies. Africans, though subject to colonial control, deployed colonial institutions to address individual and group concerns to their benefit, gaining reprieve in some cases and the opportunity to influence policy in others. These local voices place the colonized population at the center and recognize the constituents as historical actors with pliable cultures and communities.

This genre is also important for understanding colonialism, the development of infra politics, and self-determination. We can read these sources in terms of both individual and community organizing. As Kent Lightfoot argues, "any perspective that attempts to understand the diverse outcomes of colonial encounters must consider not only the native viewpoint – the natives' cultural values, practices, families, tribal organization, and histories – but also the nature of the dominant hierarchies and colonial contexts that engaged them."[72] Nigerian petitions provide valuable sources for evaluating the impact of the war on the lives of local people and gauging public opinion. Indeed, petitions were a perfect vehicle for counter-hegemonic discourse from colonial subjects because colonial authorities accepted them as a legitimate means of addressing individual and group concerns. A critical difference, however, existed between how men and women presented their petitions and situated themselves within the war discourse and the ideology that sustained it. While men and women shared the same orientation to the fact that their support was essential to the war effort and appreciated the wartime experience, men and women experienced these trends in similar and dissimilar ways. Their letters reflected these differences in both tone and framing. The petitions indicate that, although men and women were part of a common social and economic context, they indeed viewed their contributions to the war through a gendered lens.

I have argued elsewhere that these correspondences – often the only form of public expression allowed by colonial officials – offer fresh insight into the precarious nature of life under colonialism and reveal the extraordinary steps taken to confront colonial rule and forms of crisis at different historical times.[73] They exemplify the way Nigerian men and women negotiated the varied policies and practices that were introduced during the war. They offer insight into the implications, effects, and results of local people's confrontation with different colonial agencies

[72] Kent G. Lightfoot, *Indians, Missionaries, and Merchants: The Legacy of Colonial Encounters on the California Frontiers* (Los Angeles: University of California Press, 2004).
[73] Chima J. Korieh, "'May It Please Your Honor': Letters of Petition As Historical Evidence in an African Colonial Context," *History in Africa* 37 (2010): 83–106.

and their attempt to halt the optimum control over colonial societies. We can read these letters as strategies and tactics employed to negotiate the power structures designed to subjugate and control the local population for the greater good of the empire.[74]

While men wrote most of the petitions, some women did in fact participate in writing petitions. The occasional moments when voices of women do appear reveal their particular concerns over price and control of local food items by government and illuminate the unique role Nigerian women played during the war. Letters by women for the most part discussed the general trend of events, but they also focused on issues specific to women. The few available letters written by women were set against the backdrop of women's roles, giving the reader a compelling glimpse into their perceptions of themselves and issues of female identity. Women drew upon their femininity in structuring their appeal. For instance, Agnes Garuba, whose husband had gone off to war, metaphorically referred to herself as a "widow" who needed the support of the government to provide for her family. Agnes expressed that "the Government only is my husband" since the family breadwinner had joined the army to fight in the name of the empire.[75]

Overall, petitions reveal diverse voices and multiple layers of authenticity. Who drafted the petitions? Whose voices are represented? To what extent did petition writers successfully express the desires and intents of the petitioner? Did they express the voices and feelings of the victims or use the occasion to parade their own literary genius? A broad range of educated people apparently wrote these petitions: schoolchildren, village teachers, and government employees, especially court clerks who subverted their employers because they distinguished between themselves and the "white man's work." Some court clerks earned extra income moonlighting as petition writers. Indeed, a cadre of professional letter writers emerged from this trend. In the rivalry within the profession, they honed an art. However, some may consider their vocabulary bombastic, tending to exaggerate and indeed to develop a stylized vocabulary of protest. Petition writers, most of whom had some professional training as lawyers, used the petitions of their clients to challenge the ideological underpinnings of colonialism. These indirect attacks on the colonial state concerning the contradictions of colonialism were often beyond what was mandated by clients. Others with some level of education wrote their own petitions, frequently in their own hand. Although often written to attract

---

[74] Korieh, *"Life Not Worth Living."*
[75] National Archives of Nigeria, Enugu (hereafter NAE), ABADIST 14/1/873, File No. 1646.

sympathy, many petitions were intimate expressions of individual conditions but also showed a clear understanding of the larger context that gave rise to the conditions.[76] In addition to archival sources, I rely on local newspapers published during the war to gauge public opinion and local perspectives with reference to Nigeria. Nigerian newspapers took an activist role that was hugely different from their prewar combative stance against colonial polices. Several editorials and articles focused on the war and reflected the general mood. Newspaper articles and opinion pieces in the *West African Pilot* and other local newspapers, including the *Eastern Nigeria Guardian* and *The Daily Service*, reported frequently on the war and the conditions of the Nigerian population.

This book and the sources that gave rise to it highlight the extent to which the interpretation of Western colonization of Africa remains a contested or unsettled terrain. As such, the greatest strength of historical analyses that take African perspective into account is their ability to complicate and, consequently, to transcend the myth of colonial hegemony that emerged out of Western-informed discourses on imperialism.

### Outline of This Book

The following chapters approach the British Empire's prosecution of the Second World War and the progression of Nigeria, with an estimated population of 22 million at the time of the war, from a colonial backwater into a strategic part of the British Empire as not mutually exclusive. I develop a history of Nigeria's role in World War II that allows for a meaningful understanding of the conflict as multidimensional and instrumental to critical transformations in empire–colony relations nationally, transnationally, and internationally. I show how Nigeria's participation in the war as a colony of the British Empire profoundly transformed the relationship between metropole, empire, and colony, created a new sense of shared views and ideology, and shaped new cultural and political ideas in the postwar period. I begin by recounting the extraordinary and often neglected story of the Nigerian population who were drawn into the war, the intense demands made on Nigeria's resources, and how the war transformed their lives. This perspective draws upon a vast range of Nigerian experiences – including rural and urban dwellers – during this pivotal era in the British Empire's relationship with its colonial subjects to provide a broad overview of an African society's participation in imperial global warfare and the historical amnesia that has plagued the analysis of the Second World War. This

[76] For an assessment of Nigerian perceptions, see Korieh, *"Life Not Worth Living."*

introductory chapter addresses a major gap in the historical literature, including the dearth of information on the historical contributions of Africans in the Nigerian colony as participants and victims. The chapter presents the thrust of this book: as a significant contribution to the history of the Second World War in general that explores in detail the contributions of an African society and the impact of the war on their lives. It surveys the history of the war by laying out the key features of local conditions (especially on the eve of the war), the war's impact, and local responses. The historical data – colonial documents, including but not limited to reports, official dispatches, and government reports, newspapers, and oral histories – indicate that a complex and multidimensional relationship existed between the metropole and this important British overseas colony. This chapter concludes that the impact of the Second World War cannot be generalized or the European experience equated with the experiences of Africans in European colonies.

Chapter 1 proceeds with an understanding, as Daniel Travers and Stephen Heathorn have noted, that the Second World War holds a special place in the British national narrative in which the large-scale mobilization of the civilian population transformed the Second World War into a "people's war." The chapter critically analyzes the status of Nigeria as one of Britain's imperial possessions and her strategic importance during the war. The mantra of the "people's war" was effectuated through the systematic implementation of new policies and regulations, changes in existing economic policy, and specific regulations introduced to garner support for the war. This chapter demonstrates how Nigerians were subjected to even greater demands to fight in what was seen as a glorious defense of civilization against barbarism. It presents how Nigeria was woven "into the tapestry of British warfare and Britain's presence on the world stage as the foremost power," to use Ashley Jackson's expression.[77] The government policies during the war conveyed a highly paradoxical attitude toward colonized peoples: consistent on one hand with the goals of imperialism as an economic venture, and on the other, with the Allies' commitment to the preservations of liberty and self-determination through specific wartime colonial policies.

As I argue in Chapter 2, propaganda was used on a massive scale by both sides of the conflict during World War II. The creation of propaganda in World War II was designed to get the public behind the war effort, to unite the country, and to curb disillusionment at home. The main focus of this chapter is the role of propaganda in influencing

[77] Ashley Jackson, *Distant Drums: The Role of Colonies in British Imperial Warfare* (Eastbourne: Sussex Academic Press, 2010), 3.

participation and opinions in the war. Analyzing how the British extensively used wartime propaganda to draw the support of the Nigerian
people, I explore the critical role propaganda played in Nigeria's appropriation of the war and the enthusiastic support different sections of the
population provided Britain during its hour of greatest need. The chapter
illustrates how the propaganda intended for African audiences reiterated
the idea of the "interdependency" of the empire by stressing the unity of
the British Commonwealth of Nations. The call on Africans to produce
goods and to conserve resources during the war was seen by the colonial
government as an extension of their patriotism toward the empire. By
creating space for the local population to consume a particular form of
propaganda, the empire made Nigerians active participants in the creation of propaganda. Their intellectual contribution to this mission was
largely based upon their appropriation of a new status and identity as
"citizens of the empire." Despite the contradictions imposed by fighting
a war for a colonizing power, propaganda oddly enough provided an
effective avenue for expressions of imperial unity and acceptance of
Britain's self-image as a "virtuous imperial power."[78]

Chapter 3 investigates the Nigerian home front. Nigeria, with its huge
reserves of men, food, and raw materials, was critical to the Allied war
effort. Nigerians from all walks of life, diverse regions, and various ethnicities were involved in the struggle to win the war. They were deployed as
soldiers and workers on a large scale, to theaters of war in Europe, Asia
and the Middle East. The optimism expressed by colonial officials regarding support from the dominion and colonies, and the confidence that they
would join the empire in the war with Germany, were not in vain. The
notion that all people, including colonial subjects, were united by
a common cause and a moral war fought against a common enemy
drew Nigerians of all classes into a global fight against tyranny. Yet
Britain embarked on a systematic extraction of human and material
resources on an unprecedented scale. The drive to produce and the
regulations put in place to control the local economy and to meet wartime
requirements created economic crises that the authorities often ignored.
I analyze in detail the significant role played by Nigerians at home and the
impact of the war in transforming their lives and societies in very fundamental ways.

Chapter 4 uncovers African voices and responses to imperial wartime
policies. Nigerian men and women were by no means passive victims of
colonial violence and hegemony. This chapter analyzes the local

[78] Sonya A. Rose, "Race, Empire and British Wartime National Identity, 1939–1945,"
*Historical Research* 74, no. 184 (2001): 220–237.

engagement with British policy and the recurrent protests against wartime regulations. The chapter specifically explores the medium through which the Nigerian population addressed and contested the series of rules, restrictions, and regulations imposed by the British to address the crisis generated by the war. In this context, the letters and petitions Nigerians wrote provide opportunities to locate African voices, as they confronted the new political and economic systems introduced during the war. A critical distinguishing character of these petitions is the social class of the people who wrote them. Most were written by the lower class of petty traders and farmers. Although support for the war cut across class lines, most of the upper class and political elite were less concerned with the issues of daily survival, such as food insecurity and matters of daily subsistence, that lay at the root of these petitions. Yet the richness of these petitions allows for a better understanding of the impacts of the war on rural families and urban communities and situates the civilian experience within the larger context of the war and colonial society while creating a space for petitioners to participate in the larger discourse. These petitions reveal how local economic conditions and production systems linked a broad range of people, classes, and spatial categories and allowed them to move into the realm of public discourses on war, colonialism, and policy.

Chapter 5 explores the sociopolitical and economic changes that consumed Nigeria during the critical postwar years and situates these developments within its different contexts. Foremost on the minds of colonial officials was the anticipated effects of the demobilization of thousands of African men who had been employed as soldiers and in auxiliary services, who had enjoyed a higher pay, and the concomitant unemployment that would be experienced by many who had once been employed in the military. Besides, there were general economic problems beyond resettlement or demobilization after the war. The postwar period was characterized by continuing shortage of food and other essential items. These conditions were exacerbated by ongoing labor strikes in many parts of the country, causing disruptions in shipping and manufacturing. However, the significant amounts of cash that entered the economy as a result of the war became the impetus for new social formations. Exservicemen, who had experienced an increase in income and severance payments, returned to their villages with a substantial amount of money. Army allotments, separation allowances, and money from military contracts for buildings and food flowed steadily into the hands of all classes, particularly the peasants. Trading firms paid higher prices for palm oil and nuts, groundnuts, cocoa, and rubber than in prewar times. Government employees, including those of the mercantile and missionary institutions, were receiving cost-of-living allowances. With this influx of money during the war years, cultural practices were also affected, including local marriage rituals and the bride-price paid for a wife. The political changes that ultimately led to the independence of Nigeria from colonial rule are also examined in this chapter.

The concluding chapter returns to the main themes and highlights the issues analyzed in this book. The entanglements of grassroots action with the world of European colonialism, politics, and economics during the Second World War forced rural and urban classes alike to seek a role in shaping both the economic and political worlds of which they were a part. The demand for agricultural products drew a sizable portion of the population directly into the politics of war production and the ideological debates upon which the Allied Powers fought Germany and Nazism. By supplying needed manpower, producing essential goods, and participating in the vigorous intellectual debates of the period, Nigerians generated new discourses about self-determination and equal rights, and experimented with postwar reforms. Situating Nigeria's participation in a global conflict through the lens of colonialism and ties to the British Empire, this book demonstrates the significance of Nigeria's colonial subjects in one of the moments of greatest global historical significance. Reflecting on the position of Nigeria in this moment in world history, the conclusion draws attention to the entangled webs of relationships and connections between the metropole and colony and how the war ultimately created opportunities for self-determination during the turbulent years of its aftermath.

# 1 Fighting for the World
## Imperialism, Wartime Policy, and Colonial Subjects

> Every day that passes by brings to the people of Nigeria ... the reality
> that confronts the people of the British Empire in this war which is being
> waged against "bad faith, injustice, oppression and suppression," the
> evil things of Nazism.
>
> *West African Pilot*, May 12, 1941, 2

On December 4, 1939, Sir Bernard Henry Bourdillon, the British governor
of Nigeria, addressed the Legislative Council in an extraordinary session. It
was hitherto the custom to address the Council formally only at the opening of each session when the estimates for the forthcoming year were to be
laid before the Council for approval. This address marked a departure from
custom because of what was described as "exceptional circumstances."[1] In
his speech, Bourdillon justified conspicuously introducing fresh taxation in
the middle of a fiscal year. The address drew attention to Nigeria's
expected role as part of the British Empire during the war:

This war will not be won solely by the efforts of the [A]llied navies, armies and air
forces. Its winning demands a determined, coordinated and sustained effort on
the part of the whole civil population of the British Empire, and we in Nigeria
must take to the full our share in that effort ... providing men for the fighting
forces ... placing at the disposal of Great Britain the whole of the natural resources
of this country.[2]

Bourdillon's address carried a clear association between the "war with
Nazi Germany" and the demands the empire would make upon Nigeria.[3]

Bourdillon, who officiated as governor for most of the war period
(1935–1943), arrived in Nigeria during a time of great economic uncertainty. Thus, his policy of increasing taxes and enjoining Nigerians to
partly bear the burden of prosecuting the war was not necessarily
a departure from the past. Nigeria, like other colonial territories, had
borne the burden of supporting the empire throughout the prewar period.

---

[1] Nigeria, *An Address by His Excellency the Governor, Sir Bernard Bourdillon to the Legislative Council, 4 December 1939*. Lagos: Government Printer, 1939. Reproduced in the *Nigerian Eastern Mail*, January 6, 1940, 9.
[2] *Nigerian Eastern Mail*, January 6, 1940, 9.  [3] Ibid.

The introduction of taxation had already led to violent rebellions in parts of the country five years earlier.[4] Although the war indirectly affected colonial subjects, the colonial government embarked on an aggressive policy of extracting more resources and cash from the local population. The programs and regulations implemented during the war show an undeniable continuity between prewar expectations about supporting the empire and wartime attitudes and actions toward Nigerians. This chapter focuses on the changing nature of colonial policy and the specific regulations introduced to garner support for the war, the optimism expressed by colonial officials, and how ordinary Nigerians perceived their roles as subjects of the empire and as participants in the war against tyranny.

As they had in the Great War, the most global war of its time, Nigerians from all walks of life, diverse regions, and various ethnicities were involved in the struggle to win the Second World War. Daniel Travers and Stephen Heathorn have noted that the Second World War "holds a special place in the British national narrative."[5] With significant reliance on a large-scale mobilization of the civilian population, the Second World War was viewed as the "'People's War' – a term that connotes both a war of the whole people, united in common cause, and a moral war, fought by decent people for decent values against an indecent enemy."[6] Nigerians, like other colonial subjects, were required to contribute to what Raphael Samuel has characterized as a "glorious defense of civilization against barbarism."[7] Thus, wartime policies developed from the prior foundations of the colonial relationship, rather than a moment induced by the war. British colonies, historian Ashley Jackson has remarked, were "woven into the tapestry of British warfare and Britain's presence on the world stage as the foremost power."[8] Nigeria's status as one of Britain's prized imperial possessions (colonies of commerce and

---

[4] Chima J. Korieh, *The Land Has Changed: History, Society, and Gender in Colonial Eastern Nigeria* (Calgary: University of Calgary Press, 2010). See also NA, CO, 589/159/12, "Petition by Ezzi Chiefs against Taxation," RHJ Sasse to Secretary, Southern Provinces, Lagos, March 11, 1928. Taxation was an important instrument of colonial control and defined the relationship between colonialists and Africans, and the potential for effective administration.

[5] Daniel Travers and Stephen Heathorn, "Collective Remembrance, Second World War Mythology and National Heritage on the Isle of Man," *National Identities* 10, no. 4 (2008): 433–448, at 435.

[6] Ibid. See also Angus Calder, *The People's War: Britain 1939–45* (New York: Pantheon Books, 1969).

[7] Raphael Samuel, *Theatres of Memory, vol. I: Past and Present in Contemporary Culture* (London: Verso, 1994). Cited in Travers and Heathorn, "Collective Remembrance," 435.

[8] Jackson, *Distant Drums*, 3.

conquest) in a vast mass of territories spread across tropical Africa, Asia, and the Pacific positioned it as a strategic resource during the war. Nigerians were deployed as soldiers, workers, and suppliers to theaters of war in Europe and the Middle East on a large scale. But as Indivar Kamtekar describes in the case of India during the same period, "states inaugurate wars and then try to make them the business of the peoples over whom they govern."[9] This premise is reflected in how Britain and colonial Nigeria intersected and complemented each other during the Second World War, and the harmony and contradictions that defined their relationship in this period. It would be fruitful, however, to briefly explore the socioeconomic and political conditions in Nigeria in the interwar years as an era of significant change when disparate ideologies created a level of economic and political crisis and agitation.

## Nigeria and Britain during the Interwar Years

The Colony and Protectorate of Nigeria, including the Mandated Territory of the Cameroons, had an estimated population of more than 22 million people and covered an area of 373 square miles, exceeding the combined sizes of Belgium, Holland, France, and Italy.[10] With a population greater than Canada, Australia, and New Zealand put together, Nigeria was a tremendous potential source of human and material support for Britain. With the conclusion of World War I and the acquisition of new territories under the Treaty of Versailles, the British Empire reached its height geographically and in terms of population. The new territories given under the treaty added 1,800,000 square miles (4,700,000 km$^2$) and 13 million new subjects to the empire, but despite this growth, cracks within the imperial façade were growing – and not without significant consequences for the colonies. As part of a global conglomerate, British colonies faced economic difficulties from the end of World War I. The colonial economy in Nigeria remained largely agrarian with the local population laboriously working the land to survive. But for most of the years before World War II, British policy had favored noninterference with agricultural production. Rural farmers sought to raise the standard of living and to expand export production through the monetized economy, which was stimulated by strong demand in Europe. In 1903, for example, Nigeria exported 131,898 tons of palm

---

[9] Indivar Kamtekar, "A Different War Dance: State and Class in India 1939–1945," *Past & Present* 176, no. 1 (2002): 187–221, at 180.

[10] Milverton, "Nigeria," 81.

kernels and 54,257 tons of palm oil to Europe.[11] Revenue from palm kernels exported in 1921 amounted to £3,189,000 and by 1930 had reached £4,429,000. The value of exports had increased more than sevenfold and export volume fivefold, representing an annual growth rate of 7 percent and 5.5 percent respectively, as well as an increase from 5 percent to 7 percent of the gross domestic product.[12] The growth in oil palm planting and rehabilitation was more dramatic, beginning in the late 1920s. By 1932, there were about 200 native-owned new oil palm plots and 54 extensions of old plots in the southern provinces.[13] Most of these oil palm plots were locate in Owerri and Onitsha Provinces.[14] In the western and northern provinces, farmers made significant investments in cocoa, cotton, and groundnut production.

Yet the overall economic conditions in Nigeria toward the late 1930s were less than ideal for the local population. The worldwide depression that occurred before the war also began to affect the economic fortunes of the colonial state and the native population.[15] By the mid-1920s, farmers were already facing challenging times financially due to the low prices of produce and the prohibitive cost of imported goods. The low cash flow within the local economy exacerbated the effects of the depression.[16] Between 1929 and 1935, the value of the palm produce trade dropped by more than 70 percent, causing a substantial fall in farmers' incomes and in government revenue.[17] Nigel Cookes, a colonial administrative officer, recalled in his memoir of service in Nigeria from 1938: "No economic depression in my lifetime is in any way comparable to that of the early thirties. All countries and every class were affected. Britain fared somewhat better than some countries, such as, particularly, Germany and countries like Nigeria and the West Indies which were dependent on primary products."[18] Historian Moses Ochono has rightly noted that the drastic fall in the price of Nigeria's major agricultural exports

[11] Gerald K. Helleiner, *Peasant Agriculture, Government, and Economic Growth in Nigeria* (Homewood, IL: Richard D. Irwin, 1966), 500.

[12] Ibid. See also Nigeria, *Annual Report of the Agricultural Department, 1932* (Lagos, Government Printer, 1932), 22; I. E. S. Amdii, "Revenue Generating Capacity of the Nigerian Customs and Excise: 1875–1960," in *100 Years of the Nigerian Customs and Excise: 1891–1991*, ed. I. E. S. Amdii (Abuja: Department of Customs and Excise, 1991), 12–47.

[13] Nigeria, *Annual Report of the Agricultural Department, 1932*, 22.    [14] Ibid.

[15] I have dealt with aspects of the economic problems associated with the Second World War elsewhere. See Korieh, "Urban Food Supply."

[16] On the Depression and its intersection with British policies in the era, see Moses E. Ochono, "Conjoined to Empire: The Great Depression and Nigeria," *African Economic History* 34 (2006): 103–145.

[17] Korieh, "Urban Food Supply." See also Gloria Chuku, *Igbo Women and Economic Transformation in Southeastern Nigeria, 1900–1960* (New York: Routledge, 2005).

[18] RH, Mss Afr. s. 2426, Nigel Cookes, Empire in Decline: A Personal Experience.

"undermined the personal economies of peasant producers, diminishing their ability to pay taxes and their capacity to produce more."[19]

The Great Depression in the late 1920s and early 1930s made control of the colonies more challenging and highlighted the inadequacies of government policies. Yet British colonial policy in this period tended to support metropolitan interests rather than colonial interests.[20] The economic challenges of the Depression era created ideal conditions for protests.[21] The most important protest against direct taxation was the 1929 women's revolt in eastern Nigeria, in which women protested against the perceived extension of direct taxation to them.[22] In his diary, J. C. Bull recorded in his entry for December 12, 1929:

> News from Aba that there is struggle by the way. The women of that locality have engaged in fighting with Europeans. The soldiers and policemen are up there. (This is a reference to the famous Aba riots by women.) It was due to a misunderstanding. The women had been counted and they thought that they were now going to be taxed as well as the men, so they organized themselves and rioted in large numbers.[23]

Women used the opportunity offered by the tax incident to articulate other matters of economic concern. On December 4, 1929, for example, women gathered at Umuahia in the Eastern Region to discuss the low price of produce. At a meeting with agents of European trading companies at Umuahia, one of the women leaders, Nwanwanyi, said: "We wish to discuss the price of produce. We have no desire or intention of making any trouble, but we have fixed a certain price for palm oil and kernels and if we get that we will bring them in. We want 10 shillings a tin [4 gallons] for oil and 9 shillings a bushel for kernels."[24] By that time, the price of a four-gallon tin of palm oil in Umuahia District had fallen to five shillings from six shillings and eight pence.[25]

---

[19] Ochono, "Conjoined to Empire," 110–111. For the impact of the Depression on northern Nigeria, see Moses E. Ochono, *Colonial Meltdown: Northern Nigeria in the Great Depression* (Athens: Ohio University Press, 2009).

[20] David Meredith, "The British Government and Colonial Economic Policy, 1919–39," *Economic History Review* 28, no. 3 (1975): 484–499, at 485.

[21] Oliver Coates, "Nigeria and the World: War, Nationalism, and Politics, 1914–60," in *The Oxford Handbook of Nigerian Politics*, ed. Carl Levan and Patrick Ukata (Oxford: Oxford University Press, 2018).

[22] On the women's tax revolt, see Marc Matera, Misty L. Bastian, and Susan Kingsley Kent, *The Women's War of 1929: Gender and Violence in Colonial Nigeria* (New York: Palgrave Macmillan, 2011).

[23] RH, Mss Afr. s. 1221 J. C. Bull – Part of the diary of J. C. Bull, an African who worked for the Methodist minister in charge of the Oron Circuit, Calabar Province, Nigeria.

[24] Ibid.

[25] See Nina Mba, *Nigerian Women Mobilized: Women's Political Activity in Southern Nigeria, 1900–1965*. University of California Institute of International Studies, Research Series No. 48 (Berkeley: University of California, 1982), 75.

Other districts in the Eastern Region were experiencing this wave of protest by rural women. The district officer for Owerri Province reported in December 1929 that the women in the district demanded the abolition of male taxation, an increase in the price of produce (particularly palm oil and kernels), and a decrease in the price of imported goods.[26] The women of Obowo in Okigwe District in eastern Nigeria petitioned the district officer regarding the falling prices of produce and demanded ten shillings for a tin of palm oil and seven shillings for a bushel of palm kernels.[27] Considerable unrest and discontent continued in the poorer areas of Owerri. F. W. Tristram, the assistant commissioner of police at Okpala, noted that "the slump in the price of oil and kernels, coupled with the fact that the demand for these commodities has decreased, has hit them [the farmers] very hard."[28] At Oron in Calabar Province, about 1,500 market women demanding an increase in the price of palm oil from the United African Company staged a trade boycott and broke up markets to enforce an embargo in 1933.[29]

Rural protests relating mainly to taxation on the local population continued intermittently throughout the 1930s and 1940s in various parts of Nigeria.[30] In April 1927, the colonial government enforced the Native Revenue (Amendment) Ordinance. Direct taxation was introduced in the Eastern Region in 1928 without major incidents due to widespread and careful propaganda during the preceding twelve months.[31] Deputy Governor Baddeley noted considerable "agitation against the tax" from Awka District in the Eastern Region in 1928.[32] In addition, the assistant commissioner of police at Okpala, C. H. Ward, remembered: "Every inhabitant of the Division is against both the rate and principles of tax and in my opinion it will take years of propaganda before the people are convinced of its benefits."[33] Mass protests against taxation by both men and women in Okigwe and Bende Divisions of Owerri Province broke out a decade after the women's revolt in 1939.[34] The prices of palm products,

---

[26] *Aba Commission of Inquiry*, Appendix III (1), 32.     [27] Ibid., 75.

[28] NAE, UMUPROF 1/5/24, File No. C 53/1929/vol. 26 – F. W. Tristram (ACP) at Okpala, April 2, 1931.

[29] Mba, *Nigerian Women Mobilized*, 47.     [30] Korieh, *The Land Has Changed*.

[31] See *Aba Commission of Inquiry*, 8.

[32] PRO CO, 589/159/12, "Deputy Governor Baddeley to CMS Amery, Secretary of State for Colonies," April 16, 1928.

[33] NAE, UMUPROF, 1/5/24, File No. C 53/1929/vol. 26 – C. H. Ward (ACP) at Okpala, January 22, 1931.

[34] The disturbance involved the Isuikwuato, Uturu, Nneato, Isuochi, Umuchieze, Otanzu, and Otanchara clans of Okigwe Division, and the Alayi, Item, and Umuimenyi clans of Bende Division. The acting secretary of the southern provinces conceded that the administration had not made a proper allowance for the effects of trade decline in adjusting taxes.

the main source of trade and revenue for these areas, had fallen sharply and farmers' purchasing power continued to decline up to the end of World War II.[35] As the colonial government acknowledged, the low prices of oil and kernels in recent years had not made the work of governance easier.[36] Conditions in other parts of the country were not much better. British colonial officer H. P. Elliot blamed the Great Depression and its effect on farmers' income for what he called "the embarrassing condition of British colonialism in Northern Nigeria."[37]

Urban unemployment increased significantly in the wake of mass movements from the rural areas. Cities like Lagos were affected by joblessness and the declining income due to the Great Depression. The fall in the price of cocoa, the mainstay of the economy of the Western Region, did not help the joblessness that Lagosians faced due to European and Levantine domination of commercial firms.[38] As historian Oliver Coates has reported, "whereas 1,000 jobless individuals were recorded in Lagos in 1920, as many as 27,000 traders alone had lost their jobs in the city by 1929, in addition to the 20,104 railway workers who were also unemployed."[39] Indeed, toward the end of the 1930s, food shortages were more evident, prompting the Nigerian press to criticize the colonial authority for its failure to curb inflation and for its pursuit of an unbalanced economic policy.[40]

Nigeria faced political challenges related to the nature of colonial administration in the late 1930s. Although pacification seemed a conclusive part of the imperial mission, the political reorganization of the local polity harbored lingering mistrust and anger against the British. British colonial administration was generally guided by the ideology of indirect rule and was conceptualized as an indigenization of the colonial administration – a process by which the British imposed colonial rule through African social and political institutions.[41] Indirect rule was based

---

[35] See *Aba Commission of Inquiry Report and Notes of Evidence Taken by the Commission of Inquiry Appointed to Inquire into the Disturbances in the Calabar and Owerri Provinces, December 1929* (Lagos, 1929).

[36] Nigeria, *Annual Report of the Agricultural Department, 1932*, 29.

[37] Ochono, *Colonial Meltdown*, 1.    [38] Coates, "Nigeria and the World."

[39] Ibid. See also Laurent Fourchard, "Lagos and the Invention of Juvenile Delinquency in Nigeria, 1920–1960," *Journal of African History* 47 (2006): 115–137.

[40] O. Uwakwe Esse, "The Second World War and Resource Management in Eastern Nigeria, 1939–1945" (Unpublished MA thesis, University of Nigeria, 1997), 148.

[41] See the discussion in Adiele Afigbo, *The Warrant Chiefs: Indirect Rule in Southeastern Nigeria, 1891–1929* (London: Longman, 1972); Michael Crowder, *West Africa under Colonial Rule* (Evanston, IL: Northwestern University Press, 1968); and Michael Crowder, *Colonial West Africa: Collected Essays* (London: Frank Cass, 1978).

on the Lugardian Doctrine, which argued that African institutions were best suited for colonial governance, except where they were repugnant to European ideas.[42] Frederick Lugard expounded his theory in his classic *The Dual Mandate in British Tropical Africa*, where he emphasized the need for "collaboration" between natives and colonial masters. Yet the appointment of a chief over peoples whose traditional institutions were largely egalitarian was a challenge to both the colonial authorities and the indigenous peoples. So the new administrative and economic system, which was still on trial in some parts of Nigeria on the eve of the war, had not improved the lives of the Nigerian population.[43] Although pacification seemed to be a settled part of the imperial mission by the 1920s, the reorganization of the local societies generated lingering mistrust and anger toward the British.

F. B. Carr, the resident for Owerri Province and later the chief commissioner in charge of the eastern provinces in 1943, noted that the conditions of rural life in the Eastern Region, for example, were less than satisfactory on many fronts before the war began.[44] As Carr observed, there were "many problems of more material nature which had to be tackled," and many demands for "improved material conditions many of which though far beyond resources led to heightened interest in progress and highlighted the urgent need for development on a vast scale."[45] Carr's statement aptly captures the general conditions in many parts of Nigeria when the war began. Despite the prevailing economic depression and unrest in the 1930s, however, there was public clamor and enthusiasm in Nigeria to join Britain in the fight against Germany.

### The Politics of Wartime Control

Between 1939 and 1945, Nigeria's population was drawn into the Second World War. The involvement of the colonial state in Nigeria, the imperial authority in London, the human and material resources of the Nigerian societies, and the financial support from all classes of Nigerians aided the war effort. Nigerians volunteered for the army, and the population at home produced agricultural goods, provided labor in the mines, and constructed infrastructure. Others contributed to the intellectual production that was essential in selling the war at home, generating moral support abroad, and explicating the conditions that gave rise to the war, including Germany's threat to world order. Nigerians of all classes, from

---

[42] See Frederick Lugard, *The Dual Mandate in British Tropical Africa* (London: Frank Cass, 1965).
[43] RH, Mss Afr. s. 546, F. B. Carr Papers.
[44] Ibid. See Korieh, *The Land Has Changed.*    [45] RH, Mss Afr. s. 546, F. B. Carr Papers.

schoolchildren to native authorities to women's organizations and groups, bolstered by new notions of imperial citizenship and membership in the free world, turned their attention to the task of supporting the British Empire in the war against Germany and its allies.

As a imperial power, Britain had a reputation for establishing a model colonial policy with its indirect rule system. The strategy of achieving economic and political transformations through the encouragement of local production, especially of agricultural goods, had laid a solid foundation that colonial Britain could draw upon when the war broke out. Nigeria was particularly important because the agricultural sector had been significantly developed by the 1930s. By the start of the war, Nigeria had become a major producer of palm oil and kernels, cocoa, peanuts, and a significant quantity of rubber. Britain understood the vital role that Nigerian producers would play in the prosecution of the war. The British laissez-faire policy toward the production and marketing of agricultural goods changed dramatically because of the war. The colonial authorities used all the means at their disposal, including the introduction of new regulations and control policies, to encourage more production as well as methods to systematically reduce the ability of local producers to control their own lives.[46]

In the war with Germany, all parts of the British Empire and its dominions were regarded as integral to the empire. Apart from South Africa, where the Afrikaner position vigorously contested and opposed South Africa's support for Britain, all other British colonial possessions and dominions regarded the war as theirs. British colonial subjects saw themselves as part of the empire and believed they were fighting for a noble cause. Demonstration of loyalty and solidarity across the British Empire began as soon as the war did, even among those who in peacetime "ha[d] been the most relentless critics of the British Imperial Government."[47] As a British wartime bulletin noted, the subjects of the British Empire, from India, Palestine, and Jamaica, among others, have all "spontaneously and unreservedly placed their services at the disposal of [the] Government and pledged themselves to loyal cooperation."[48] From Australia to New Zealand and India to the colonies in Africa, colonial subjects expressed their support for Britain as the empire sought the human and material support of its subjects. Indeed, the notion of the British Commonwealth was not just an abstraction. Joe Culverwell of Zimbabwe, who volunteered as a soldier the day the war began in 1939, reflected: "Don't forget in those days we were very loyal Brits – stupid as

[46] Korieh, *The Land Has Changed.*
[47] NAK, KANOPROF, 4494, "The Solidarity of the British Empire."     [48] Ibid.

that may sound now. ... We were brainwashed into being little brown Britishers."[49] And in an address to the Canadian people after the 1940 elections, William Lyon Mackenzie King, who had been reelected as prime minister, said: "The result is the proof that you felt that a vigorous united war effort by a united Canada was necessary above all things not only effectively to aid Britain and France in the struggle to preserve freedom in Europe, but also to preserve true freedom in our own land."[50] Remarkably though, the colonies were treated differently from the "white" dominions, where the emphasis was on the internal defense of their territories. The colonies, on the other hand, were valued for the significant logistical support they provided to Britain's war effort.

Nigerian young men consistently reminded British officials of their eagerness to join the war in order to prove their place as citizens of the empire. In a meeting with H. P. James, the British resident for Calabar Province, on June 3, 1940, a delegation of the Calabar branch of the Nigerian Youth Movement protested that Nigerians' manpower had not been called to service in the war. They told James that they were as loyal as any people in the empire and, if they could not give much financial aid, they could give men. They felt that they had not been called to service because of color prejudice and argued that the color bar should not be considered at a critical time such as this. They further drew attention to the large number of Africans from the French dependencies who were fighting in France and felt disgraced for not being allowed to give their service and for being treated like women.[51] The group also raised the issue of the apparent imminence of Italy's entry into the war and the possibility of Spain's; the proximity of Fernando Po, a Spanish colony, to Calabar had to be considered. This in their view made it even more urgent to form a territorial battalion in Calabar, along the lines of the Lagos battalion, to be trained in the event of an emergency.[52] H. P. James's assurance that the group should dismiss from their minds any question of color prejudice or any doubt about their loyalty was betrayed by his claim:

So far, the war on land had been confined to Europe where climatic conditions were not suitable for the employment of West Africans. The physique of the people was not as high as it should be owing to nutritive deficiencies. If they

[49] Interview with Joe Culverwell, Zimbabwean veteran of the Second World War. Cited by Martin Plaut, "The Africans Who Fought in WWII," BBC News, November 9, 2009, accessed December 6, 2018, http://news.bbc.co.uk/go/pr/fr/-/2/hi/africa/8344170.stm.
[50] NA, CAB/68/6/17, "Report for the Month of April 1940, for the Dominions, India, Burma and the Colonies, Protectorates and Mandated Territories," War Cabinet Records, May 1940.
[51] NAE, CALPROF, 3/1/2496, File No. CP 50/2, "Anglo-German War 1939: Voluntary National Service."
[52] Ibid.

were employed and could not stand up to the hardships and climate they would become a serious liability. In my opinion there was plenty of time for Nigerians to have a chance to prove their loyalty and manhood.[53]

However, change was difficult to enact until the exigencies of the war forced the British to enlist Nigerian troops.

The British administration in Nigeria had begun to prepare in earnest to assist the motherland before the war began.[54] Nazi Germany did not have the same fortune. Its colonies had been lost at the end of the Great War and German nationals across the British Empire, including those in Africa, did not show any "inclination to give Hitler any long-distance help in his war," according to the British Official Press.[55] German nationals in places such as Tanganyika, Northern Rhodesia, and Kenya submitted to internment without incident. By the time the war began, men, women, and perhaps children were at the service of the empire. British colonial subjects were essential in the endeavor to provide material support for the war. The changing nature of colonial policy and specific regulations introduced to garner African support for the war are reflected in the fervent desire of ordinary people as well as African chiefs and the local elite to support recruitment into the army and the production of other resources needed to support the empire.

The first few months of the war were followed by systematic attempts to organize colonial subjects, production, and needed resources in support of the war effort through laws, regulations, and prohibitions. Colonial policies were revised to meet the wartime demands in Britain by increasing the production of traditional agricultural goods and expanding into other areas such as mining. New regulations and controls ensured that more quantities were produced and channeled properly where they were needed most. Colonial officials were empowered to reorganize public institutions to facilitate the extraction of needed goods and services. In 1940, Norman Herington, a colonial agricultural officer in Nigeria, noted that officials of the Department of Agriculture were becoming "fully occupied by their efforts to increase food production and commodities such as palm oil, kernels, wild rubber and other products."[56] The war ushered in a new phase of British imperialism. Demands for increased

---

[53] Ibid.
[54] Judith A. Byfield, "Women, Rice, and War: Political and Economic Crisis in Wartime Abeokuta (Nigeria)," in *Africa and World War II*, ed. Judith A. Byfield, Carolyn A. Brown, Timothy Parsons, and Ahmad Alawad Sikaing (New York: Cambridge University Press, 2015), 147–165.
[55] NAK, KANOPROF, 4494, "The Solidarity of the British Empire."
[56] RH, Mss Afr. s. 1779, Norman Herington, papers, photos, agriculture education officer, 1944.

production of food for the country and the army, and for exports for
Europe, required an enormous restructuring of the local labor force.

The optimism and confidence expressed by colonial officials that the
dominions and colonies would join the empire in the war against
Germany were not in vain. Imperial strategies of drawing Nigeria and
other parts of the empire into the war worked. A degree of cooperation
developed between Nigeria and Britain. A Nigerian chief offered to send
his three strongest sons to Germany to kill Adolf Hitler. Sir Bernard
Bourdillon, governor and commander in chief of the Nigerian forces,
reported during a visit to England that the chief stated: "I have many
sons. I can easily spare three of them to put an end to the man causing so
much trouble. They will stalk and kill him like any jungle beast."[57]
Likewise, when the chiefs of Idomi, a small town in the Obura Division
in southeastern Nigeria, wrote to the British district officer on January 2,
1944, they pledged their readiness "to help in the war business, by giving
full attention to kernel production."[58] "Since we have no rubber in our
area," they wrote, "we have agreed to pay our full attention to kernel
production . . . to help in winning the war."[59] Similar letters offering help
and support had been written by Nigerians of different classes when the
war began.[60]

## Organization and Control of Wartime Trade and Production

The beginning of the war in Europe prompted the colonial government to
begin a massive reorganization of Nigerian society. The government
began centralizing several aspects of the economy, including the production and marketing of agricultural goods, which had previously been
undertaken by the local population. The establishment of closer economic ties between Great Britain and its West African colonies during
the war led to increased control of colonial subjects in all aspects –
political, economic, and social.[61] The new steps taken by the colonial
government would have fundamental repercussions for the Nigerian

---

[57] Associated Press London, June 23, 1942, accessed December 2, 2017, www
.africanmilitaryblog.com/2017/10/did-you-know-nigerian-chief-offers-his.html.
[58] NAE, ABADIST 14/1/875, Vol IV. Idomi Chiefs to the District Officer, Obura Division,
January 2, 1944.
[59] Ibid.    [60] See NAE, CALPROF, 3/1/2353, "Loyalty to the King and Government."
[61] For more on this, see David Meredith, "State Controlled Marketing and Economic
'Development': The Case of West African Produce during the Second World War,"
*Economic History Review* 39, no. 1 (1986): 77–91. As David Killingray notes, discussion
began "on future economic and social consequences of belligerence" (Killingray and
Plaut, *Fighting for Britain*, 11).

population. Over the three years after 1939, the colonial governments introduced new laws to regulate production, distribution, and trade in Nigeria, increasingly centralizing the economy as a systematic and consistent policy of extraction.

Britain's wartime policy in Nigeria and its other West African colonial territories was informed by two imperatives. First, Britain stood as the dominant colonial power and proxy representative of the Allies, especially after the fall of France in 1940. Second, as an influential political and economic power, Britain sought to assert its influence and to limit the possible influence that France and particularly the United States might obtain at the end of the war.

Overall, however, Britain's wartime policy was entwined with its broader goals as a leading imperial power. The war stimulated major changes in the organization of the production and utilization of goods produced by colonial subjects. As O. U. Esse has noted, the innovative aspect of the Second World War "brought about extensive exploitation of resources among the belligerent nations and their allies and supporters."[62] As the Allies lost important sources of raw materials and other trade goods in Asia, the extensive extraction of raw materials from West African territories became a major objective. This was particularly so in Nigeria, where its vast territories provided a variety of crucially needed raw materials – namely, agricultural products and minerals.[63] The period of the Second World War thus witnessed a major change in British colonial policy and economic development strategy in Nigeria, which in turn stimulated the introduction of new processes and new products. Yet government priorities did not change drastically. Rather, under the war conditions, there was an expansion of government control and regulation of the local economy.

To provide better coordination, the government established the Nigeria Supply Board. The board consisted of the director of supplies, a secretary, and controllers or assistant secretaries in charge of the various sections, including imports, indents, exports, food control, price control, transport control, finance, stores and accounts, and general (shipping, mineral oil, etc.).[64] The Nigeria Supply Board brought together and directed the duties of those departments, created for special wartime

[62] Esse, "The Second World War and Resource Management in Eastern Nigeria," 3.
[63] E. N. Mordi, "The Nigeria Win the War Fund: An Unsung Episode in Government–Press Collaboration in Nigeria during the Second World War," *Journal of Social Science* 24, no. 2 (2010): 87–100, at 88.
[64] *Memorandum on the Organisation and Control of War Time Trade and Production* (Lagos: Government Printer, 1943), 1.

functions. The board also included other existing departments closely concerned with economic aspects of the war effort.[65]

The power of various controlling authorities derived from the Emergency Power (Defence) Acts of 1939 and 1940 and the Nigeria General Defence Regulations of 1941. Those regulations gave the colonial authorities enormous power to control the local economy and society. They put this power to full use as the war progressed to harness the resources needed to execute the war. European enterprises, especially trading companies, played an essential role in promoting the production goals of the government. These enterprises were also expected to offer instruction to and encourage government agricultural and administrative officers, to inspect and grade produce at centers established for the marketing of crops, to purchase produce at government-controlled prices, and to organize the collection and transportation of produce to ports for shipment overseas.[66] The drive for export production focused on vegetable oil, including palm oil, palm kernels, groundnuts, and beniseed. A carefully considered price increase was designed to provide incentives for farmers in addition to transport subsidies for producers in very distant areas as part of an overall strategy.[67]

## Imposition of Emergency Powers

As soon as war became imminent, colonial officials enacted laws circumscribing trade relations and the exportation of agricultural products that were essential to the war effort and internal and external food supply and distribution. Administrative departments and officials in Nigeria witnessed a steady expansion of power over the local population beginning with the 1939 Emergency Powers (Defence) Act. The act, passed by the UK Parliament prior to the outbreak of World War II, gave the king authority to exercise certain powers in defence of the empire.[68] He secured the power to make regulations "necessary or expedient for securing the public safety, the defence of the realm, the maintenance of public order and the efficient prosecution of any war in which His Majesty may be engaged, and for maintaining supplies and services essential to the life of the community."[69] The act also gave wide-ranging powers to colonial authorities and empowered them to make regulations, orders, and bylaws necessary to achieve the goals of the act, including emergency powers to prosecute the war effectively. By this act, colonial governors were given

---

[65] Ibid.    [66] Nigeria Supply Board, "Memorandum, Economic Position in Nigeria."
[67] Ibid.
[68] *Nigeria General Defence Regulation, 1941* (Lagos: Government Printer, 1941), 1.
[69] Ibid.

supplementary powers over their territories to impose regulation and restrictions to meet the goal of prosecuting the war. The Emergency Powers (Defence) Acts of 1939 and 1940, which extended the original 1939 act, conferred on the colonial governor the power to implement the provisions of the acts. These acts, which came into effect on September 24, 1941, were adapted and modified in their application to Nigeria as the 1941 Nigeria General Defence Regulation.

The intensification of hostilities in 1940 led to the enactment of another piece of legislation that extended the emergency powers stipulated in the Defence Act of 1939. The 1940 Emergency Powers (Defence) Act put at the king's disposal "the whole resources of the community" that may be "rendered immediately available when required for purposes connected with the defence of the Realm."[70] In particular, the 1940 Emergency Act empowered His Majesty to make defense regulations, including provisions that placed persons, their services, and their property at the disposal of the king. Such powers were necessary or expedient for the efficient prosecution of any war in which His Majesty may be engaged.[71] These acts covered a wide range of activities that channeled the human and material resources of the colony toward the war effort.

By 1941, the Emergency Powers (Defence) Act included censorship, control, and suppression of publications, writings, plans, photographs, communications, and means of communication in order to regulate and control a varied media outlet. The law allowed for the monitoring of the movements and activities of people who could be conceived as "enemy aliens." Effective monitoring of ports and movements of vessels and aircrafts was included to secure the realm. The acts gave the authorities wide powers to control transport, food, and propaganda as well as compensation for expenses incurred through the exercising of the emergency power. Moreover, the acts limited individual liberty by giving the authorities power to arrest people for war offenses without a warrant. Indeed, coercion, instead of persuasion, coupled with a deliberate low-cost strategy, was employed to achieve this objective.

Reorganizing the local economy to address war needs was often not easy and, in Nigeria's experience, resulted in local agitation, largely due to the ambivalent nature of British war policy. While Britain viewed its directives to increase production of much-needed food items and raw materials, such as palm oil, as essential to winning the war, the Nigerian population was more ambivalent. Inflation was perhaps the most difficult

[70] Ibid., 11.    [71] Ibid.

problem faced by the government and the population, as the rise in the price of essential goods received close attention from the government and the local press. Frugality was expected of the Nigerian population, much like other societies at war. As Terrence H. Witkowski has argued in the case of America, "frugality received official sanction during World War II when the U.S. government, to mobilize the home front, launched poster campaigns that preached being thrifty with goods and services, recycling metals and other materials, growing and storing of food at home, obeying price and ration controls, and buying war bonds."[72]

As already stated, the colonial government had enacted new regulations and laws, especially the so-called Nigeria General Defence Regulations of 1941, to effectively control peasants' production and to direct their energies toward the war effort.[73] By 1941, the colonial government was forced to impose price controls to deal with the looming food crisis.[74] Under the Nigeria General Defence Regulations, several policies were enacted to control various food items and other goods, including the Control of Bicycle Spare Parts and Accessories (Eastern Provinces) Order and the Control of Pedal Bicycle Accessories and Spare Parts (Eastern Transport Zone) Order of 1943.[75] Among other provisions, the Control of Bicycle Spare Parts and Accessories Order required all dealers in new spare bicycle parts to obtain the written permission of the Controller of Pedal Bicycle Accessories and Spare Parts for the Eastern Transport Zone in Aba or any other officer authorized to act on his behalf.[76] Under the Garri Non-removal Revocation (Owerri Province) Order of 1944, persons could not remove garri (a local foodstuff made from cassava) by rail from Owerri Province to any station north of Enugu without a permit signed by a competent authority.[77] From 1943, a permit from the district officer was required to transport garri to northern Nigerian towns for commercial purposes. The

---

[72] Terrence H. Witkowski, "World War II Poster Campaigns: Preaching Frugality to American Consumers," *Journal of Advertising* 32, no. 1 (2003): 69–82, at 69.

[73] See NAE, ABADIST 14/1/876, vol. V.

[74] NAE, EP, OPC, 122, vol. vii, ONDIST, 13/1/2, "Public Notice," B. W. Walter, Local Authority, Enugu, October 28, 1942; NAE, CALPROF, 3/1/2329, District Officer Abakiliki, November 9, 1942.

[75] NAE, CALPROF, 3/1/2329, District Officer Abakiliki, November 9, 1942.

[76] On the Control of Pedal Bicycle Accessories and Spare Parts (Eastern Transport Zone) Order of 1943, see Gazette N. 50 of October 7, 1943. "Govt. Notice No. 1155 authorizes Mr. J. W. Wallace to act on my behalf as a competent authority to be known as the Controller of Pedal Bicycle Accessories and Spare Parts in respect of the area known as the Eastern Transport Zone and defined in the schedule to Public Notice no. 271 of 1943." See also NAE, CSE 1/85/8614, vol. III. See *Memorandum on the Organisation and Control of War Time Trade and Production*, 14.

[77] See NAE, CSE 1/85/8614, vol. III.

regulation required that only the traders who had operated in 1942 would be proportionally allotted quotas from 1943. This was a striking departure from previous economic planning. As war became inevitable, the government's leadership in the realm of "preparedness" involved direct control of local economic structures to produce food and other materials. Such direct intervention in the local economy was a departure from prewar laissez-faire doctrine that characterised colonial economic planning before the war. As Helen Chapin Metz explains:

Once the wartime colonial government assumed complete control of the local economy, it would issue trade licenses only to established firms, a practice that formalized the competitive advantage of foreign companies . . . wartime marketing boards pegged the prices of agricultural commodities below the world market rate, workers faced wage ceilings, traders encountered price controls, and Nigerian consumers experienced shortages of import goods.[78]

Furthermore, coercive measures were extensively used to force rural peoples to produce crops and satisfy metropolitan demands for other forest products and minerals. Thus, the Nigeria Defence [Oil Palm Production] Regulation No. 55 of 1943 directed farmers to harvest, process, and market palm produce or face incarceration. The regulation also empowered the deputy controller of oil palm production to order the harvesting, processing, and marketing of palm produce. Furthermore, Defence Regulation No. 89 of 1945 compelled native authorities to ensure the implementation of Regulation No. 55. Failure to comply with these rules resulted in prosecutions, fines, and imprisonment.[79] For instance, in Owerri Province, where the regulation resulted in prosecutions, palm production officer P. L. Allpress explained that "palm production has greatly fallen off, and from the unharvested areas I have found in the Aba Division one must conclude that this is to some extent due to the dilatoriness of the people." In his view, "no amount of talk has any effect on the people unless one's threats are backed by action now and then."[80] In other parts of the Eastern Region such as the Obudu District, hundreds of people were prosecuted, fined, or imprisoned for failing to harvest oil palm, crack kernels, or tap wide rubber.[81]

[78] Helen Chapin Metz, ed., *Nigeria: A Country Study* (Washington, DC: Government Printing Office for the Library of Congress, 1991).
[79] NAE, EP, 19919, CSE 1/85/9915 "Prosecutions under the Oil Palm Production Regulation 89 of 1994," 1.
[80] NAE, ABADIST 1/26/907, File No. 1642, "Palm Produce Production," and P. L. Allpress to Resident, Owerri Province, October 4, 1945.
[81] NAE File No. OB 699/Vol. II, OBUDIST 4/1/309, "Produce Drive: Kernel and Rubber Return Prosecutions."

Reactions and responses to the war and the demands made upon the local population took many forms across Nigeria. Generally, the Nigerian population was visibly distressed by these regulations that fixed prices either by prescribing maximum percentages of profit on cost or by fixing specific selling prices. On May 25, 1943, one Madam Victoria of Ndom Ebom, who lived fifty-seven miles from Aba, the administrative seat of District Officer J. V. Dewhurst, wrote a letter to Dewhurst requesting a permit to engage in the garri trade. The buying and selling of garri had been restricted to those with a permit issued by the district officer as part of the war measures. Madam Victoria requested "a little chance to do my bit towards the winning of the present war."[82] She entreated:

I have noticed that the cost of garri (the staple food in Nigeria) is high in big towns all over Nigeria today. There might be money adequate for the purchase of garri but there may not be sufficient garri to be had for the feeding of His Majesty's troops in the area. I have then ask[ed] if I can be given some contract to help on buying garri for the Military Department of this area. The garri would be carried in bags by any convenient means His Majesty's government might find at their disposal. Such would at least alleviate some of the previous difficulties experienced in the purchase of this important food stuff. I would be thankful if your worship could let the authorities concerned know of this application.[83]

Madame Victoria's letter reveals one aspect of the critical roles that women played in household and local economies. In her study of Abeokuta and other provinces in western Nigeria, Judith Byfield similarly found that most economic decisions taken during the war impacted women's lives as producers and traders.[84]

Still support for the British found expression in a wide variety of offers of spontaneous services and donations in cash and kind from several sections of the Nigerian community.[85] The enthusiasm was also motivated by the quick profit made from the foodstuff trade. Many new traders entered what had become a lucrative business of buying and transporting foodstuffs to northern Nigerian cities and towns. By 1944, the price of garri had increased from about one shilling and six pennies to about nine shillings in urban markets. In a report to the district officer in May 1944, the Nigerian police wrote that garri producers "are making an exorbitant profit when one considers that they found it worthwhile to make garri up

---

[82] NAE, ABADIST 14/1/875, File No. 1646 Vol. IV, "Garri Control," Nigerian Police, Aba to District Officer.
[83] Ibid.    [84] Byfield, "Women, Rice and War," 155.
[85] Esse, "The Second World War and Resource Management in Eastern Nigeria," 29.

to 1940 and sell at 1/6d -2/- a bag."[86] The lucrative trade for foodstuffs that developed in Spanish Fernando Po, where many Igbo and Ibibio migrant laborers were working on plantations, contributed to higher prices in places like Uyo and other parts of Calabar Province.[87]

Plans for food control and price restrictions had been imposed previously as war loomed. Some food items, except milk and flour, were already rationed in Lagos, Nigeria's largest city. Although the availability of many other food items was not seriously threatened by the war, the government did make plans to ensure that the rationing of these items would follow periods of severe shortfall.[88] Importing firms in Lagos were requested to ensure that consumers purchased all their supplies from a particular source in order to regulate the distribution of essential commodities. This helped the government compile a list of customers, which was then circulated among the importing firms.[89] Wartime regulations and restrictions was not just a means of ameliorating the deteriorating food conditions, but it also served to reinforce colonial control in the face of threats to order. Thus, the power of local administrators to determine who had access to trading permits enabled them to impose control, to effectively regulate available resources, and to limit the freedom of the local population.

By 1939, a general shift in policy began in the form of new regulations to curb the food problems caused by the war. Reports of shortages and rationing came from all regions in the country. Consumer items such as alcoholic beverages were severely affected. The deputy food controller for Kano Province for example, noted that the continued delay in the arrival of liquor stocks for the Expeditionary Force Institute, coupled with the opening of new and the expansion of existing military messes throughout the country, led to a "heavy drain on the limited stock of liquor available and rendered equitable distribution extremely difficult."[90] Salt importation fell from a prewar consumption of approximately 50,000 tons to 12,000 tons in the first half of 1941 thus creating a major problem in the availability of the product in the market.[91]

The rising rate of inflation and increases in the price of foodstuffs and other local and imported goods led to more regulation of local consumer habits, trade goods, and prices. A central food committee was busy devising schemes for developing Nigerian industries and for supplementing supplies

[86] NAE, ABADIST 14/1/875, File No. 1646 Vol. IV, "Garri Control."      [87] Ibid.
[88] NAE, ONDIST, 12//92, file OP IV, "Food Control," S. A. S. Leslie, Nigerian Secretariat, Lagos, April 22, 1941.
[89] Ibid.
[90] NAK, KANOPROF, 4494, "Food Control," Deputy Food Controller, Kano Province, Kano.
[91] Ibid.

of imported foodstuffs, such as rice and edible fats, which were almost certain to be restricted.[92] On April 22, 1941, S. A. S. Leslie, the colonial food controller, issued a circular that outlined the general scheme for food control in Nigeria. With the assistance of deputy food controllers at the local areas, Leslie was empowered by the government to direct the distribution of available supplies.

The Nigerian population quickly exploited the opportunities offered by the increased demand for local production. As the demand for local food products increased, Nigerian farmers sought to produce more to fill the vacuum created by import restrictions. A considerable number of men and women began to engage in the trade across different regions. The eastern and northern corridors were especially lucrative in the distribution of locally produced food items. Export of garri to northern Nigeria saw a phenomenal increase from 1,414 tons valued at £4,989 before the war to 6,804 tons valued at £57,661 in the first half of 1942.[93] By 1943, the transportation of food items from the Aba railway station to the north increased exponentially from the previous year. Foodstuffs, particularly cassava products and palm oil, were increasingly moved to northern Nigerian markets by traders, most of whom supplied these goods to retailers there. Shipping of other food items such as cocoyam, coconut, and maize made similar increases in the same period.[94]

Alarmed by the quantity of food items moving out of the region, district officials began to implement restrictions in order to stave off crises in their districts. Colonial officials extended these controls to rural areas in 1942 when they became concerned about the perceived exploitation of the war conditions and the scarcity of local food items in markets. J. V. Dewhurst, the district officer for Aba, was so concerned that he suggested prohibiting the movement of yams from the district. Writing to the colonial resident, he noted: "The increase in the export of yams is very great indeed and, in view of the fact that Aba normally imports yams, disquieting. So too is the increase in the export of maize and I am not certain that the export of this also ought not to be prohibited."[95] A. F. B. Bridges, resident of Owerri Province, invoked the Nigeria General Defence Regulation of 1941 (Food Control) in September 1944. Under the Garri Non-removal Revocation (Owerri Province) Order 1944, he prohibited the transportation of garri by

[92] "Recruiting in Nigeria," *The Times* (London), September 15, 1939, 7.
[93] NAE, ABADIST 14/1/872, File No. 1647, "Garri: Control of," Ikebundu Nzekwe to the District Officer, Aba, July 3, 1943.
[94] NAE, ABADIST 1/26/958. "Garri Control." The weight of a basket varied between 11/2 and 2 cwts.
[95] NAE, ABADIST 1/26/958, J. V. Dewhurst to the Resident, Owerri Province, Port Harcourt, August 12, 1943.

rail from Owerri Province to any station north of Enugu except with a permit signed by a competent authority or by a person authorized by the competent authority. Individuals were allowed a personal allowance not "exceeding eight pounds (8 lbs) of garri per person."[96]

Colonial regulations had deleterious effects. A significant volume of regional trade was in place before the war broke out in 1939, but these restrictions affected many local traders, some of whom had been involved in the business before the outbreak of the war. By 1942, more than 900 traders who were transporting garri to the north from Aba were affected by wartime trading restrictions.[97] Under the auspices of the Association of Garri Traders, Aba, a group of traders wrote several petitions to protest the restrictions imposed on their trade.[98] One such petition from F. U. Oha, a trader in the city of Aba, addressed to District Officer Dewhurst illustrates the effect of trade restrictions:

I feel it is but necessary for me to point out, Sir, that so far as the Garri Trade is concerned, I am a pioneer in that trade; and I have been earning for a considerable number of years my livelihood from it. I do not undertake this trade as a result arising out of the war nor with the intent of profiteering. I am following this trade because I have given a whole of my time to it and it has become my only means of earning a livelihood. In the circumstances, I sincerely trust the necessary permit will be issued to me accordingly so that I may continue with my trade unmolested and undisturbed.[99]

The food trade created opportunities for rural producers to generate more income while expanding prewar distributive trade within Nigeria. So many Nigerian traders saw colonial trade restrictions as disrupting their livelihood as "citizens" of the British Empire. When J. E. Akajiofo and fifteen other garri traders from Mbawsi, eastern Nigeria, who had been involved in the trade for a considerable period, wrote to the district officer in Aba on August 12, 1943, they described themselves as "British protected persons" seeking the "paternal clemency" of the district officer in matters affecting their "economic welfare."[100] They saw themselves as "eminent

---

[96] NAE, ABADIST 14/1/875. "Garri Control." "In Exercise of the Powers Vested in a Competent Authority by Regulation 140 of the Nigeria General Defence Regulations 1941 (No. 75 of 1941) As Amended by Regulations 4 of 1942 Made at Port Harcourt This 15th Day of September 1944."
[97] Ibid.    [98] Ibid.
[99] NAE, ABADIST 14/1/873, F. U. Oha to the District Officer, Aba, July 30, 1943.
[100] NAE, ABADIST 1/26/958. Letter written on behalf of the petitioner by The Nigerian Services and Commercial Bureau, 145 Jubilee Road Aba. They described their business as: "Letter Writer, Debts Collector, Business Adviser and Advertiser, General Contractor and so on." The traders were Mr. J. E. Akajiofo, Mr. M. N. Ojikwu, Mr. F. N. Anajemba, Mr. F. M. Orji, Mr. N. N. Atueji, Mr. Maduabuchukwu, Mr. J. C. Ike, Mr. P. J. Jiagbogu,

traders" who had been doing their best to "contribute monies and effort toward the Win-the-War Fund" as well as encouraging Nigerians to increase production badly needed commodities such as kernel. In relation to restrictions imposed on the garri trade, they wrote that their positions as produce buyers "are adversely affected." They pleaded:

We respectfully crave your indulgence with our hearts in our hands in praying that a reasonable quota of garri railment to the North be allocated us, taking into consideration our adverse position due to bad trade ... as a people under British protection and trusteeship, [we] have been experiencing severe hardship and are financially run-down as evident of bad trade. Our humble testimonies therefore demand your administrative assistance to help ameliorate the deteriorated situation by granting our humble request, thus helping us to have the means of meeting our needs and instruments towards the Empire's war effort.[101]

The restrictive trade regulations across different regions in Nigeria had been in place since 1942 but were often amended as circumstances changed in the country or in local provinces. In June 1945, the acting district officer for the Ikom Division began the restriction of yam and cocoyam exports from the division. The export of yams and cocoyam from the district was only allowed if one obtained a permit from the district officer.[102] The export of yams from Ogoja Province required a permit from the district Officer in Afikpo.[103] In Onitsha Province, the order restricted the movement of garri and yams from the Udi Division, "except under [a] permit signed by [a] 'Competent Authority.'"[104] Yet again, Dermot O'Connor, the colonial resident of the Awgu Division, issued an order restricting the movement of yams outside the division in May 1945.[105]

The root of the food crisis during the war lay in earlier policies. Toward the end of the 1930s, the food shortage in Nigeria was receiving attention in colonial circles. The Nigerian press criticized the colonial authority for its failure to curb inflation and for its pursuit of an unbalanced

---

Mr. Andrew Orizu, Mr. Joseph Oyekwere, Mr. N. U. Anazodo, Mr. G. I. Onwugaje, Mr. Paul Anene, Mr. Z. A. Okeke, and Mr. A. O. Okeafor.

[101] Ibid.

[102] NAE, AIDIST 2/1/433, File No. IK: 401/18, "Food Control," The Acting District Officer, Ikom to the District Officer Abakiliki, June 18, 1945.

[103] NAE, AIDIST 2/1/433, File No. OG: 2920/140, "Food Control," P. M. Riley, Resident Ogoja Province to District Officers.

[104] NAE, AIDIST 2/1/433, "Nigerian General Defence." For Cassava restrictions, see also NAE, AID 2/1/433, File No. OG: 2513/1265, "Nigeria General Defence Regulations: Order," P. M. Riley, Resident Ogoja Province to District Officers, June 26, 1945.

[105] NAE, AIDIST 2/1/433, "Nigerian General Defence Regulation Order: Garri and Yams," Resident, Onitsha Province to District Officer and Other Competent Authorities, May 16, 1945.

agricultural policy.[106] The colonial authority was already thinking of agricultural diversification to increase local food production and the income of rural farmers on the eve of the Second World War. This emphasis had much to do with the worldwide depression, which deepened in the 1930s. A 1938 report by the Department of Agriculture clearly stated that the production of export crops, important as this was to the wealth of the country and to the revenue of the government, "must not be subordinated to the production of foodstuff for local consumption, for those who are underfed cannot do the maximum amount of work."[107]

The drive to expand food and export production during the war marked a new phase in the process of agricultural planning and the transformation of the rural economy. The war created a crisis for the British at home, which the colonial authority sought to resolve by tapping into the human and material resources of the colonies. An examination of colonial agricultural policies during the war reveals the ambivalent nature of colonial policy and demonstrates how these policies generated crisis and threatened agricultural sustainability and peasant incomes. This economic crisis was directly related to the war measures adopted by the colonial governments as well as a decline in export prices.

However, while officials continued to emphasise export products many farmers were reluctant to invest in export products such as palm oil because of low prices.[108] Production from the Onitsha, Awka, and Agwu Divisions and the Nnewi District fell from 14,359 tons in 1939 to 10,100 tons in 1942.[109] Low prices forced many people to "abandon the harvest of oil palms."[110] An agent of the United African Company at Ogrugru in Onitsha Province reported in 1939 that "little produce was coming in."[111] After a meeting with middlemen and producers in 1939, the resident for Onitsha Province noted that there was "no doubt whatever that the people are holding up production – and if we are going to consider extended palm produce production the question of a guaranteed price must be answered."[112]

---

[106] Esse, "The Second World War and Resource Management in Eastern Nigeria," 148.
[107] Nigeria, *Annual Report of the Agricultural Department, 1939–1940* (Lagos: Government Printer, 1940), 1.
[108] L. Ugwuanya Nwosu (historian), in discussion with the author, Owerri, December 1999.
[109] NAE File No. 18038/70 Vol. II, CSE 1/85/8621, "Production, Onitsha Province," Kernels Production Officer to Deputy Controller of Kernels, Eastern Zone, June 14, 1943.
[110] Interview with Eleazer Ihediwa, aged circa seventy-one, at Owerrinta, July 24, 1999.
[111] NAE, OP, 130, ONDIST, 12.1/104, "Palm Oil Production," Resident, Onitsha Province to the Secretary, Eastern Provinces, Enugu, November 25, 1939.
[112] Ibid.

## Regulations, Control, and Restrictions

In addition to the battles fought on the front lines, the Allies faced an economic war. The Japanese in particular were fully conscious of the possibilities of economic warfare and essential supplies were likely to be "objectives for special attack."[113] The protection of essential supplies as well as access to them and the routes by which they moved became a matter of utmost importance and considerable urgency. The British colonial government implemented important economic measures during the war through the control of imports into Nigeria. The importation of goods into Nigeria was controlled through a system of import licenses. Whole arrays of goods ranging from cars, lorries, and motorcycle batteries to paper and stationery of all kinds came under import control.[114] Substitutes were found for many of these imported items, while the volume of such necessities was reduced to save shipping space and to economize the British labor system. The authorities monitored trade through the request of monthly returns of the major commodities from traders, which detailed sales and issues during the month, stock on the last day of the month, stock afloat on the last day of the month, and estimated sales and issues during the succeeding month.[115]

Authorities outside of Nigeria controlled the allocation of goods and materials deemed critical to the war effort. Through the Nigeria Supply Board, British authorities controlled the essential sectors of the Nigerian economy, including production and other activities that supported life in the communities.[116] The government seized control of the import of essential materials that were outside the scope of commercial companies. The government also played an increasing role in the distribution of imported goods. Individual importers were required to notify the government of the arrival of goods in the customs premises within twenty-four hours, giving full particulars of quantities and sizes of goods.[117] Such imports would not be released to the customs authorities without an authorization from a competent authority. The importer was required to transfer the articles to his premises, where they would be inspected before a release order permitting the importer to dispose of them could be conferred.[118]

Cotton products, which had become a major item of trade in the colonies by the beginning of the war, faced major restrictions. Cheap

---

[113] NA, CAB/66/23/6, "Memorandum by the Minister of Economic Warfare to the War Cabinet," March 1942, 4.

[114] See Appendix H in *Memorandum on the Organisation and Control of War Time Trade and Production*, 15.

[115] Ibid., 2.    [116] Ibid.    [117] Ibid.    [118] Ibid.

cotton from England was used in a variety of ways to make clothes and uniforms. African retailers usually bought their goods from major European trading firms and other foreign firms, mainly Lebanese-owned.[119] Duties on cotton piece goods increased by 50 percent and maintained the existing surcharge of 25 percent.[120] According to G. B. Ollivant, a representative of a major European trading company in West Africa, "Imports are only a fraction of the normal and depend entirely on shipping space."[121] Indeed the government acknowledged that "shortage of shipping tonnage remains probably the greatest single economic difficulty facing the Colonial Empire."[122]

There was a greater dependence on textile imports from Great Britain and items from India, especially shirting produced by Classes and Greys.[123] All stocks of dyed, printed, and woven goods, such as drills, prints, imitation native cloths, and domestics, as well as whites and grays, such as shirtings, bafts, and mosquito nettings, came from Britain. Due to the fact that nearly 100 percent of all cotton yarns, sewing threads, fishing twine, and yacht cord had been imported from Great Britain, it appeared "almost impossible to obtain these types of goods from any other country."[124] The Calabar Chamber of Commerce noted, however, that while whites, grays, and drills were imported increasingly from India, future imports from India were not likely to be diminished from previous years as India's production capacity was not large enough to "cope [with] the enquiries they are receiving."[125] The Calabar Chamber of Commerce remarked that "in a province like Calabar where there is an appreciable fishing industry, it is considered essential that these net cords and yacht cords should be imported in as large a quantity as possible."[126]

Stocks were in short supply during the war, warranting a considerable increase in the price of cotton prints. On September 22, 1941, Secretary of State for the Colonies Walter Guinness noted that the question of

[119] The main importing firms included: United African Company Ltd., Lagos; John Holt and Co. Ltd., Lagos; G. B. Ollivant Ltd., Lagos; Paterson Zochonis and Co. Ltd., Lagos; Compagnie Francaise de l' Afrique Occidentale, Lagos; Societe Commerciale de l'Quest Africain, Lagos; G. Gottschalck and Co., Lagos; London Africa and Overseas Ltd., Lagos; London and Kano Trading Co., Kano; J. F. Sick and Co., Lagos; Co-operative Wholesale Society, Lagos; Union Trading Company, Lagos; K. Chellaram and Sons, Lagos; and J. T. Chanrai and Co., Lagos.

[120] NAE, CALPROF, 3/1/2365, Home Chat, no. 5, September 1942, Lagos, September 16, 1942.

[121] NAE, CALPROF, 3/1/2335, G. B. Ollivant to the Resident, Calabar, Nigeria, October 8, 1941.

[122] NA, CAB/68/6/17, "War Cabinet Report for Month of April 1940," 12.

[123] NAE, CALPROF, 3/1/2335, G. B. Ollivant to the Resident, October 8, 1941.

[124] NAE, CALPROF, 3/1/2335, Calabar Chamber of Commerce to the Resident, Calabar, Nigeria, October 21, 1941.

[125] Ibid.    [126] Ibid.

supplies of piece cotton goods to colonial dependencies required urgent consideration.[127] To maintain essential supplies of cotton and textile goods in the colonial empire, the government considered several factors: the difficulty of producing supplies in the United Kingdom, the position of Japan in the conflict, uncertainty regarding supplies from India, and whether cotton goods could be obtained from the United States.[128] By 1946, European trading companies selectively sold available stock. Shirtings were in such short supply that some trading companies limited sales exclusively to old customers. They also sold to customers in payment for produce at the rate of one piece per ton of palm kernel or palm oil. Infact, there was a correlation between availability of imported trade goods and purchasing of produce. According to the manager of the French Compagnie Française de l'Afrique Occidentale (CFAO) at Calabar, this strategy would protect "our very low stocks in order to cover essential requirements as above stated until our next arrival" and "prevent the commodity, which is in very short supply, from finding its way into the Black market where it is resold at 25/- to 30/- per piece."[129] Such practices were not, however, supported by the government despite its attempt to encourage higher production. According to P. Pichon of the CFAO, it appeared that native producers were much more interested in goods "which they require for their own personal use than in cash payments against their produce."[130] Pichon continued: "We have found that amongst sundry other lines, white shirting, Grey Baft, prints, etc. were a powerful incentive for them and consequently we have let our produce dealers have a piece of each by ton of PK or palm oil."[131] The company purchased 300 tons of palm kernels and 100 tons of palm oil per month on average, and thus required a minimum of 400 pieces monthly on a normal basis only for produce trade.[132] With a stock of 286 pieces in October 1946, for example, the company could rationalize its business practice. In the view of the company, "it would have been sheer lack of foresight to sell it out indiscriminately and thus upset our whole produce organization already hampered by insufficient stocks."[133]

The regular supply of cotton goods in West Africa was linked to the provision of the goods essential to the war effort. The British Broadcasting Corporation (BBC) quoted the undersecretary of state for the colonies as saying in the House of Commons that people in

---

[127] NAE, CALPROF, 3/1/2335, "Imported Merchandise – Cotton Goods."    [128] Ibid.
[129] NAE, CALPROF, 3/1/2335, The Manager of CFAO Calabar to Sundry Produce Customers – John Edet-Asuquo, Calabar, November 19, 1946.
[130] NAE, CALPROF, 3/1/2335. P. Pichon, CFAO Calabar to Deputy Price Controller "Re: Alleged Refusal to Sell White Shirting," Calabar, November 22, 1946.
[131] Ibid.    [132] Ibid.    [133] Ibid.

England would have to go without new shirts so printed cotton goods could be made available for the natives of West Africa. He also pronounced that workers were being withdrawn from war industries to reopen Lancashire cotton mills in order to produce cotton piece goods. This policy was meant to encourage production and curb inflation:

In the ordinary way when prices for export produce are good the native producers spend their spare cash on imported consumer goods. It is the desire for cash to buy bicycles, hurricane lamps, pan, scent, cloth, morrow, umbrellas and so forth which inspires the peasantry to grow crops or to gather kernels in excesses of their own immediate needs. Imported goods are now very scarce and just when we are most anxious for the producer to get down to it the main incentive for him to do so is removed.[134]

In Britain, there was the desire to give the producer "something to spend his money on."[135] Cotton pieces were a popular line and, from the supply point of view, the most economical consumer goods that could be produced to meet the demands of the local population in the colony. Nonetheless, large quantities of these goods were not often available to meet demands. The average import of cotton piece goods for the years 1936–1938 was 231 square yards, of which 17.5 million (13.4 percent) came from now hostile countries or those occupied by the enemy. Nigeria's quota for 1942 was 95 million square yards, of which 35.5 million came from India.[136] The lack of imported goods increased inflation. As an official noted:

Money is pouring into Nigeria – as wages – the services are already spending 6 million pounds a year and with so much more – and the chief outlet for these funds at the moment is local foodstuffs, bride price, horses and the like. Unless an alternative outlet is made available the vicious spiral is bound to gain strength, and prices and wages [will] chase each other with increased speed.[137]

The currency situation was not ideal either. Normally currency returned to the Currency Board in the "slack season" (March–August) and again in the fall (September–October). Official reports indicate, however, that no money had returned to the Currency Board since May 1941, and more than £3 million had been issued since. The proposed payment of a separation allowance to the Nigerian troops by the army beginning in November would bring another £500,000 a year into Nigeria. Indeed, arrears from the Native Administration cost of living award, commonly known as "cola," which was introduced in July 1941 but paid retrospectively from October 1, 1941, and

---

[134] NAE, CALPROF, 3/1/2365, Home Chat, no. 5.    [135] Ibid.    [136] Ibid.    [137] Ibid.

increased Royal Air Force expenditures on landing grounds aggravated the situation.[138] The cost of living allowance that was paid to all government employees on salaries not exceeding £220 per annum increased government expenditures substantially and provided a substantial injection of cash into the economy.[139]

## Control of Foodstuffs and Crises of Everyday Living

Excessive profiteering remained a concern for colonial officials through-out the war. Officials monitored the retail prices of foodstuffs and intervened when there was significant price variation in the same area. The African Chamber of Commerce, Calabar, complained to the authorities in October 1942 about the prohibitive cost of goods in the town. The Chamber of Commerce had petitioned the chief secretary of the colonial government about what it regarded as profiteering in Calabar compared to Lagos.[140] Although the Chamber of Commerce may have exaggerated its claims, it seems that it was often difficult to implement uniform prices throughout the country. Effectively policing the local market would have been a daunting task as prices and invoices would have to be checked and freight and transport costs calculated before arriving at a final retail price.

Significant debate emerged among colonial officials about the best way to enforce restrictions and ameliorate their overall impact on the population. Consideration was given to the special needs of Europeans vis-à-vis their African counterparts. A colonial official in Kano, Dorothy Lindsay, suggested that all imports of food from England "should be prohibited and our requirements met locally or by South African products." However, even South African goods were to be "imported with discretion."[141] Lindsay also raised the crucial role of women during the war: "I think the extra work entailed by the use of permits could easily be overcome if women were called upon to run a local food control department under the supervision of a Government Official." Her assessment was that women in the country "could do a lot more work and while some may hesitate to embark on individual efforts I am sure that given an

---

[138] Ibid.
[139] On the cost of living allowance, see Nigeria, *Annual Report on Finance and Account of the Year 1941/43*, File No. 02226/S.4, prepared by Financial Secretary G. N. Farquhar, Lagos, January 20, 1944.
[140] NAE, CALPROF, 3/1/2329, "Control Prices," Agriculture Chief Marketing Officer A. H. Young to Food Controller, Nigerian Secretariat, Lagos, October 9, 1942.
[141] NAK, KANOPROF, 4494, Dorothy E. Lindsay, to J. R. Patterson, Resident, Kano, October 29, 1941.

objective, the success of which depends on their efforts, whole-hearted co-operation will be forthcoming."[142]

The comptroller of customs also regulated exports from Nigeria in order to control where such goods could be sold. Exceptions were made for the export of foodstuffs to the other West African colonies, which was dealt with by the food controller. Other West African governments were required to inform the Nigeria Supply Board of the quantities of foodstuff required, which then would be obtained by the food controller through public tender and shipped on government accounts.[143] Food control was an integral part of the Nigeria Supply Board's organization. Purchases were made from African producers at prices decided upon by the supply authorities in consultation with residents for each producing area. It was usual to prohibit exports from each area through normal commercial channels until the quota for government requirements had been met.[144] The food control policy sought to achieve a number of objectives, including drawing up the import quotas for foodstuffs still obtained from the United Kingdom or other countries and to ration available food appropriately. Rationing of individual consumption was carried out only in the case of Europeans and those Africans who had adopted European standards of life such as the urban educated class. In addition to individual rationing, the consumption of imported foodstuffs was restricted by controlling supplies to retailers. The policy also regulated the flow of native foodstuffs through the food controller to the main consumption centers. Most importantly, the policy ensured that requirements for the army, the Royal Air Force, and the American forces were met for locally produced foodstuffs.[145]

By October 1942, the acting chief marketing officer of the Department of Agriculture, A. H. Young, suggested that wholesale and retail prices be "determined in all areas according to the same formula."[146] In fact, Lagos had already adopted a system that Young regarded as an acceptable model. In Lagos, the retail price of an article was calculated by obtaining the price of the article at the producing center and adding all handling and transport charges to the local market plus "twenty per cent for profit."[147] The wholesale price was then obtained by adding 10 percent to the landed cost at Lagos. The formula did not apply to perishable goods, such as vegetables, where retailers required 25 percent of the profit to "cover any

---

[142] Ibid.   [143] NAE, CALPROF, 3/1/2365, Home Chat, no. 5, 4.
[144] *Memorandum on the Organisation and Control of War Time Trade and Production*, 4.
[145] Ibid.   [146] NAE, CALPROF, 3/1/2329, Young to Food Controller.   [147] Ibid.

losses."[148] It became a general practice for food controllers to fix the selling process for foodstuffs brought into their areas from other parts of Nigeria.[149]

Owing to the shortage of tinplate, only necessary foodstuffs were to be imported after May 1942. The staple commodities purchased under this scheme were corn, rice, and maize. The government encouraged the use of locally grown flour in order to eke out the limited supply of tinned white flour. As the importance of vegetable gardens became more pronounced every day, the food controller began circulating names of firms in South Africa that could supply suitable seeds.[150]

The production of wheat in Nigeria fell far short of the demand created by war conditions. On May 1, 1941, food controller S. A. S. Leslie wrote: "Agricultural Officers have been in the wheat market for some weeks and it has become clear that traders and middle-men have been cornering the wheat available in anticipation of soaring prices."[151] By May 1941, the government decided that all available wheat supplies would be purchased by the director of the Department of Agriculture. The Department of Agriculture allocated the stock to local mills, military authorities, and civilian consumers. To stimulate production, the director of agriculture paid the producers a price that averaged 1¾ d. per pound. According to the order, which came into effect on May 3, 1941, only sales to agricultural officers would be permitted. All dealers holding stocks in excess of 10 cwt. were required to declare them each month to the deputy food controller.[152] Offenders would be required to relinquish their stocks if they were found to be holding stocks in excess of the stipulated quantity.[153] The goal of this policy was to immobilize all stocks in the hands of dealers and make the director of agriculture the sole buyer in bulk.[154] The order applied to merchants, dealers, and traders and excluded producers, retailers, or private persons buying for their own use. However, the ability to effectively implement food control was often challenging. It was not always possible for dealers to accept the situation and abandon their hopes of big profits and sales to agricultural officers.

---

[148] Ibid.
[149] See *Memorandum on the Organisation and Control of War Time Trade and Production*. See also collection of letters and correspondence related to the war in Korieh, *"Life Not Worth Living."*
[150] NAE, CALPROF, 3/1/2365, Home Chat, no. 1, May 1942.
[151] NAE, CALPROF, 3/1/2326, "Wheat, Production and Sales Of," Food Controller S. A S. Leslie to Deputy Food Controller, Calabar Province, Calabar, May 1, 1941.
[152] Ibid.    [153] Ibid.    [154] Ibid.

## Control of Motor Transport and Allied Products

On September 4, 1939, R. M. Macdonald of the Church of Scotland Mission at Ikot Inyang, southeastern Nigeria, wrote to the district officer at Itu requesting a permit to use a Chevrolet Kit Car for the purpose of carrying on his work as district missionary. Macdonald's mission work extended a considerable distance from Itu to Odudu Ikpe in the Ikot Ekpene Division. He was also in charge of the Ikorofiong District extending into the Uyo Division at the time of his request. Macdonald noted in his request that control of the churches and schools in the two districts "would be very severely handicapped, without the use of a car."[155] Also, a superintendent of the Qua Iboe Mission wrote that "it is important in many ways that I have some liberty in the use of my motor, and while cutting down running to [the] lowest possible, I beg to apply for liberty to use it when circumstances require it. At the same time, I should be obliged if you would allow me to have the necessary permit to purchase a sufficient quantity of petrol."[156] The restrictions on the use of motor vehicles affected people from all walks of life. On September 6, 1939, Opara Nnadi wrote to the district officer in Itu, requesting a permit to use his lorry and a supply of about ten cases of petrol per month to cover approximately 1,150 miles. Nnadi, who appears to have been a commercial transporter, noted: "I use this lorry chiefly for the purpose of transportation of palm kernels and goods to and from outstations as business demands it and for the convenience and inducement to our distant customers."[157]

Indeed, the transport sector was at the intersection of many aspects of wartime planning and crucial in the war effort. The regulation confined the use of existing vehicles in Nigeria to "essential purposes only," including the evacuation of export produce and materials, the transport from areas of production of food supplies for the services, the maintenance of supplies for the native populations in the large centers, and the transport of imported supplies and petrol.[158] The general provisions governing the use of motor transport, whether private or commercial, were that except in cases of real emergency, of which the transport control officer was the final judge, road transport could not be used for the whole or part of any journey for which alternative transport – i.e., by rail or water – was available, and that where road transport was used, it must proceed by the shortest route to the nearest rail or rive transport.[159]

The controller of motor transport and the oil controller, assisted by four deputies representing the four transport zones into which Nigeria

[155] NAE, ITUDIST, 7/1/614-616, Rev. N. Ibok to the District Officer, Itu.     [156] Ibid.
[157] Ibid.     [158] Ibid., 5.     [159] Ibid.

had been divided, were responsible for the control of the movement of all civilian vehicles and the consumption of petrol and other petroleum fuels.[160] They also controlled the sale and distribution of motor vehicles, motor vehicle tires and tubes, and the retreading and recapping of tires. The controllers also exercised control of the distribution of bicycles throughout Nigeria.[161] In his study about Nigeria during the Second World War, O. U. Esse notes that the evacuation of "produce to the railways and seaports, carrying of coal for the use of seagoing vessels, transporting troops and military logistics, carrying foodstuffs from the production centers to the markets in the urban centers, and the transport of imported goods, including petrol and spare parts from the ports to the hinterland, relied on effective management of the transport sector."[162] In his view, the main objective of such control was to "ensure quick evacuation of produce to the railways and seaports, and to curb the activities of indigenous transport operators engaged in passenger traffic. It was this need that drew government attention to the industry more than in the previous years."[163]

Control also extended to the use of all civil motor transport. Privately owned cars and lorries were subjected to the same regulation. The quality of petrol allowed for use by private cars in a month was "strictly controlled and basic rations [were] issued in accordance with the essential needs of the owners."[164] The regulation governing the use of motor vehicles was implemented through a permit system and by limiting the quantity of petrol consumers could purchase. The regulation had an immediate impact on the society from the individual level to nongovernmental agencies working in the country. Permits to operate a vehicle restricted the holder to a certain area or route and for specific purposes. Compliance to the regulation was enforced by transport control police posted at strategic points on the highways and checkpoints at markets and other collection areas. Both the police and vehicle inspection clerks kept a census of all vehicles passing their posts, which were scrutinized by transport control officers and compared with issued permits.[165] These regulations

---

[160] The transport zones were divided into transport areas that were determined because "(a) they conform with the economic watersheds down which export produce and commodities of internal trade naturally flow towards a focal point, and (b) they ensure the shortest road haulage from place of production to the focal point, and thence to the nearest rail or river transport." See *Memorandum on the Organisation and Control of War Time Trade and Production*, 5.

[161] Ibid., 5.

[162] O. U. Esse, *Road Transport in Nigeria: The Development of Private Enterprise among the Igbo, 1920–1999* (Glassboro: Goldline and Jacobs, 2017), chapter 3.

[163] Ibid.     [164] Ibid., 6.     [165] Ibid.

that sought to control the use of civil vehicles contributed to the larger war effort.

Importers of motor vehicles were required to render stock and import returns to the controller of motor transport. Control of sales was effected by a permit system, which "authorize[d] the successful applicant to purchase a vehicle of the type required from a particular dealer." Applicants seeking to purchase motor vehicles submitted their request to the transport control officer of the area in which they resided, stating the purpose for which the vehicle was required. The controller issued permits to purchase in accordance with the stocks available and the needs of the applicant or the transport requirements of the particular area. The sale of secondhand vehicles was similarly regulated.[166] The sale of tires and inner tubes was controlled along the same lines as sales of motor vehicles. Buyers were required to surrender an equivalent number of used tires and tubes before new tires or tubes could be issued. Such surrendered tires were examined to select those deemed fit enough to be retreaded. The United Kingdom received the remainder as scrap rubber.[167] Control of the sale of vehicles, tires, and tubes was also extended to bicycles.

Closely linked to the vehicle permit was oil control. Access to petrol was strictly controlled through an import, export, distribution, and sale mechanism. Civil consumption of petrol and petroleum fuels was controlled by a coupon-and-permit system administered by the transport control officers. Owners of private vehicles received coupons entitling them to a basic ration of petrol that permitted a limited number of journeys between residence and place of business each month.[168] The sale of petrol to the public could only be permitted by the presentation of petrol coupons or a permit authorizing a vehicle owner to be in possession of a limited quantity of petrol.

The control of motor vehicles and petrol generated several petitions and supplications. These restrictions had been implemented as early as September 1938. B. J. Dike of Itu wrote to the district officer of Itu on September 5, 1939, seeking permission to continue to use his three lorries for commercial transport. Dike was involved in transporting palm kernels and palm oil between Umuahia and Itu for the United African Company and John Holt.[169] Both were European trading companies involved in the evacuation of essential war products. It is not clear how quickly these

[166] Ibid., 7.    [167] Ibid.

[168] *Memorandum on the Organisation and Control of War Time Trade and Production*, 6–7.

[169] NAE, ITUDIST, 7/1/614-616, B. J. Dike to District Officer, Itu, September 5, 1939.

appeals were resolved. But some petitions reveal what was perhaps a widespread frustration for petitioners. Invoking race, the proprietor of The Holy and Blessed Circle Home expressed these frustrations in two petitions reproduced here in full. The first was written on March 7, 1941. This petition is a recognition that "race" defined relations of power between the colonizer and the colonized.

> The Holy and Blessed Circle Home
> Ikot Aba, Itu, Nigeria, West Africa
> 7 March 1941

The District Officer,
Itu, Calabar Province.
Sir,

### Petrol Ration

You requested me to interview you in person on Friday the 14th instant at Nsaso Rest House at 10 a.m.

I was there at the appointed time and met you, you offered me no seat; you spoke to me in a way I did not expect of you, and I even have never and could never speak in the manner you did to me to my houseboy. The way and manner you spoke to me is still fresh in my memory and how, while trying to explain to you the inconveniences I often suffer from what you say is "a regular transport," you got up from your chair unceremoniously and with all force, saying, "Mr. Smartt you talk too much." Did you then insult me? You walked out of the Rest House leaving me alone in it and went straight to your car, was that not an insult also? While walking out I asked you whether you were going to increase the gallons of petrol you have already permitted; you answered forcefully, "no, not a drop." [W]hat next could I do[?] I was obliged to quit the place you left me standing, looking aghast as you were walking away majestically.

While I was passing, I bade you good morning but you did not answer me a word. Sum all this up and "my continued references to a colour bar" which, you wrote, "are not understood" will now be clear to you as broad day light. But for the Government you represent, believe me, I would have taught you a lesson – you would have missed your way to your car . . . by torrential forceful words that suited your action and the words then, you would have sworn that never in your life will you mete [sic] ill-treatment to a black man again. But for my King you represent I brooked all the insult but be very careful and learn how to deal as a gentleman to all and the sundry, irrespective of race. Please reduce your words into writing that you say I will not grant you permit to purchase petrol at all.

> I have the honour to be,
> Sir,
> Your obedient servant.
> [Signature][170]

---

[170] NAE, ITUDIST, 7/1/614-616, "Petrol Ration," Smartt to District Officer, Itu, March 7, 1941. The petitioner's full name was not included.

But the petitioner wrote an even more critical follow-up to his earlier petition on June 16, 1941.

The Holy and Blessed Circle Home
Ikot Aba, Itu, Nigeria, West Africa
16 June 1941

The District Officer,
District Officer,
Itu.
Sir,

You do not care whether my business close[s] down or not[,] being an African concern. You refuse to listen to reason and spoke harshly to me when you invited me to interview you at Nsaso in your Rest House and being not able to get the black-man to simply tremble and answer yes *sa massa*, you became infuriated and got up from [your] chair unceremoniously, walked out of the Rest House stepping majestically to your car and leaving the Nigger in the Rest House, whom you invited to see you. What can he do? But I leave you to your conscience. I wonder if you did not remember you are in the civil service and that I was a Private Gentleman. It is not the colour that counts mind you. Will you now understand that we Africans are now too good for half-baked measure? We want the best. It is our right.

I would have closed down the Home here but my good work must continue – must go on. For a short time though, since the caption of my work, my Home has contributed as [a] remarkably humanitarian Mission to the warfare against devastating forces of disease and to the alleviating of human suffering consequently, I have gone to Lagos and returned. I have affected [the] arrangement of one who [can] take up the management of my Home and I will shift to an open place, where I can deal with gentlem[e]n (Europeans) who see in their exalted positions a means of serving fellow creatures who appear not [to] be as well placed, gentlemen who believe that the best service of man to his fellow man is in being useful, gentlem[e]n who practice the doctrine of the brotherhood of man, not among his own people but among alien in race, language, culture etc.

Your attitude to me about my application for a permit to buy enough petrol to run my car[,] not [for] pleasure but for business[,] has moved me to take this step most reluctantly. For the future is still unknown and as Mr. Chapman is on his throne here, I have to flee to another place for [a] square deal. I know where I can appeal for a redress, but my time has not yet come. So I have chosen this alternative.

I will write you again [before] I depart. Soon we shall meet again, soon you will realize you've made a mistake.

Yours respectfully,
(Signature) Smartt

These sorts of petitions were rare in terms of the emotional outburst. Many petitioners framed their petitions as supplications. The confrontational attitude expressed in this petition may have informed the district officer's decision to ignore it. But Smartt's petitions reveal the constraints imposed by wartime policies and the degree to which few challenged colonial regulations through personal interactions with colonial personnel.

The formation of the West African Produce Control Board was one of the most important and significant changes during the Second World War. It marked the end of the old system of buying produce, in which buying firms acted independent of state control. With the new regulation, buying firms in Nigeria would, at least during the war, act merely as agents of the British government. All dealings in produce came under strict government control with the establishment of the board. The board also served as a means of stabilizing prices to producers' advantage. Cocoa, which was not in great demand during the war, was already subject to this control. The plan was to be extended to palm kernels and other products like palm oil, groundnuts, and ginger.[171] Like cocoa, the marketing of palm kernels came under the control of the West African Produce Control Board and prices were fixed by law. Under the new control scheme, exporters acted simply as agents of Her Majesty's Government for the purchase of palm kernels. The control of export produce provided the government the necessary power to control local production and marketing in Nigeria.[172]

The war consequently created the conditions for other kinds of illicit trade. It is obvious that in some parts of Nigeria emerged a thriving trade in illicit francs. These would be obtained in a Vichy territory at around 300 francs to the pound and taken into the French Cameroons and French Equatorial Africa (AEF), where they had a value of 177 francs to the pound. The potential profits were therefore considerable, particularly since the notes may even have been issued free to smugglers by Vichy authorities in order to swamp the AEF. A surprise raid on lorries returning to Kano from frontier markets produced some 276,000 francs. The carriers of the currency obviously knew they were committing a crime – notes were found buried in a tin of Fulani butter, others were located in a "bandage" round the leg of a gentleman who said he suffered from an ulcer, and yet others were abandoned in the lorries. Each arrested smuggler was convicted and imprisoned for three months. The French detected smugglers entering the Cameroons from the Maiduguri area in the northeastern part of Nigeria. They also caught a man who arrived at Duala by ship from Calabar with 10,000 francs in new notes. The trade was widespread and probably due as much to profit-seeking as to the machinations of the Vichy government. It was envisaged that the introduction of a new "Francs Libre" note issued in the AEF would help to

[171] NAE, CALPROF, 3/1/2365, Home Chat, no. 3, July 1942.    [172] Ibid.

stop the traffic, which the Free French naturally regarded with considerable alarm.[173]

Smuggling of goods increased across most colonial frontiers nonetheless. The British consul frequently reported on the condition of
life in the Spanish territory under Fernando Po, and, in 1943,
declared an acute shortage of food, labor, and gasoline on the island.
As a result, Spanish authorities on the island increasingly relied on
smuggled goods from Calabar to meet their food needs. In fact, the
president of the Board of Food Control in Fernando Po blamed
Nigeria, the British government, and the Allies for the critical state
of affairs in Spanish Guinea.[174] On November 11, 1943, Consul
General Harris reported that eighty-six cases of brandy were sent to
Nigeria by canoe in one day alone. Other commodities, such as palm
oil, were smuggled into Fernando Po from Nigeria by canoe.[175] At
the same time, Harris remarked that "legitimate petty traders come
across with goods for the Island on which they have to pay export
and import duties and for which they receive fixed prices far below
that paid to canoe-men."[176]

The Board of Food Control dedicated so much of its time to illicit
forms of trade that its normal work suffered in consequence. If
commercial relations with Nigeria were to be conducted properly,
officials argued, "it is essential that the canoe traffic be suppressed
and in order to do this is it necessary to get a whole-time launch
patrol service functioning along the coast."[177] The following
paragraph, which appeared in the *Ebano* newspaper, illustrates the
attitude of the authorities toward the illicit canoe traffic:

At the beginning of July there was a decrease in the number of canoes which
crossed from the shores of Calabar to our port. At present things are going back
to normal again and already there have been as many as 19 canoes arriving in
one day. They do not bring laborers but they do bring a variety of goods
especially palm oil. Lately they have tried bringing some bicycles. The profits
should not be inappreciable and now they have even brought two motor cycles.
Motor cycles and canoes: as through one might say skyscrapers and Nipa
huts.[178]

Evidently, the struggle to manage the scarce resources available during
the war taxed both the administration and the Nigerian population. The

---

[173] NAE, CALPROF, 3/1/2365, Home Chat, no. 1.
[174] PRO FO 371/34772, "Political Situation in Fernando Po," Consul General Harris,
    Duala, November 11, 1943.
[175] Ibid.    [176] Ibid.    [177] Ibid.    [178] Ibid.

control imposed on the local society remained a nagging problem for which people sought remedies through circumventing official polices.

At the heart of the wartime policy in the colony of Nigeria lay a basic objective that can be observed through the lens of economics. Nigeria was first and foremost a provider of important economic resources. Unlike the prewar policy that allowed local people latitude to produce goods in order to meet their basic needs, the wartime policy witnessed the direct intervention of the colonial state in local food production and the supply mechanism. Indeed, the war generated its own contradictions and crises, to which the imperial and colonial governments responded by imposing more control over distributive trade and the rural food supply in the colony. The need to meet the government's requirements for food and raw materials both significantly increased the commercialization of local produce and altered the nature of peasant–state relations.

The relative scarcity of basic needs during the war exposes the extent to which the local economy had become dependent on the importation of external goods, which could be produced cheaply and locally. Additionally, an examination of the political economy of the war shows that Nigeria, like its colonial counterparts in Africa, contributed much more than personnel and logistical support to imperial war efforts. Furthermore, colonial control and restrictions did not always work. Smuggling, hoarding, and fraud were rampant and made government control less effective.[179] Although incentives were lacking, farmers expanded production due to the more lucrative internal market system that existed in the country.

The British wartime policy and Nigerian participation are an indication of a new relationship between the empire and its colonial subjects based on the expansion of existing ones. The empire did not really care for the welfare of the Nigerian populations per se – especially not their right to engage in free economic activities and decision-making. The extensive regulation of life in the colonies often blurred the distinction between formal military forces and noncombatant civilians. Nigeria's civilian population, like that of other African colonies, also suffered the material shortages of the war. Nigerians frequently came under increased repression as the demand for war supplies tasked them often beyond their abilities. The war irrevocably changed the ability of different strata of society to control their lives from the early part of 1939. The rural and urban areas were asked to bear the hardship that was necessary to defeat Hitler. Their experiences and sacrifices have been inadvertently documented in colonial records.

---

[179] See also Falola, "Salt Is Gold," 431.

Because of the war, the colonial authority in Nigeria increased its control over the local population, including the implementation of labor policies that amounted to forced labor. Farmers, whose livelihood depended on the sale of palm produce, were discouraged by the intervention of the government and by low prices. Many were visibly discontented with the agricultural crisis and food insecurity. The emphasis on the production of cash crops disrupted how the rural population balanced production for the market and for subsistence. These conditions upset local safety nets.

Enforced restrictions on imports and exports became necessary due to grave shipping losses and the necessity for expediting the carriage of goods and commodities for the war, requisitioning of goods for the services, controlling prices, rationing, and profiteering. These factors all played their part in bringing to a head labor problems that were dormant at the beginning of the war and created fresh problems that would not otherwise have arisen.

Despite the enthusiasm that Africans expressed in their support for the Allies, many were unprepared for the consequences of the war. Nigeria gradually felt the impact of the war on its constituents' lives. To achieve the objectives of colonial control, Britain combined these regulations with aggressive media propaganda.

# 2 For King and Country
## Colonial Subjects and Wartime Intellectualism

"Eje kalo wa ekuro Kafi lu itila pa
Eje kalo wo ekuro ki ogun yi le pari."
"Let us go and search for palm kernel to beat Hitler to death
Let us go and search for palm kernel in order to end the war."[1]

Yoruba song

On September 16, 1939, two weeks after the British went to war with Germany, the pupils and staff of the Qua Iboe Mission Institute in eastern Nigeria's Uyo District wrote a letter addressed to the king and people of England. In their letter, they commented: "The attitude of Germany towards other whites has been a fearful shock to us, and our ardent wish is that the Germans be brought to their knees in the shortest possible time, so that some measure of peace may be obtained for the inhabitants of the world."[2] In a similar manner, the Okokuku of Okuku in Oshogbo District wrote a letter to support the British war effort. His letter assured the district officer of the readiness of council members "to produce starch of the required standard."[3]

These letters exemplify one of the most puzzling aspects of Africa's participation in the war – that colonial subjects could be the source of great support for colonial power. The sentiments expressed by groups and individuals throughout the Second World War also represent part of a larger narrative of Africa's encounter with colonialism as well as the discourse around empire and the world wars. These letters make us aware of the importance of African voices and how these voices speak in ways that have been profoundly shaped by the anxieties of the time. The letters expressing support for Britain during the war are also significant not only as expressions of African agency but as revelations of the impact of British propaganda on the attitude of Nigerians toward the war and the desire of different sections of the population to support the Allies. Moreover,

---

[1] Song from southwestern Nigeria that people sang in support of the war. Reproduced in Igbino, *Spidermen.*
[2] NAE, CALPROF, 3/1/2353, M. J. Essien and S. A. Ironde (Prefects on behalf of the entire school), Loyalty to the King and Government through His Honor, the Chief Commissioner, Uyo, September 16, 1939.
[3] National Archives, Ibadan (NAI), Oshana Division 1/1/504/8, Cassava Starch, October 21, 1939.

Nigerian reactions to wartime propaganda offer a fascinating contradiction between the civilizing mission of empire and imperial hegemony and an African population's desire to support an empire it had previously fought against. The fact that Africans embraced the Allied conviction that all nations and peoples deserve to live with freedom, liberty, and self-determination represents a significant step toward a redefinition of the empire–subject relationship during and after the war. The British attempt to appropriate notions of liberty and equality in order to elicit African support drew upon Germany's history of racism. It compelled Africans to view the Allied war effort as a cooperative partnership in which the African population became an important part of the defenders of civilization. This cultural and moral self-justification was expressed through propaganda on a scale never experienced before the Second World War. Significantly, wartime propaganda that drew upon the rhetoric of Germany as a common enemy helped wed colonial subjects to the British and Allied war effort.

All sides of the conflict in the Second World War generated incredible numbers of "visual" forms of propaganda such as posters, films, and exhibitions, as well as radio programs, as symbols for mobilization. Jo Fox has demonstrated how propaganda films were so crucial to winning the battle of hearts and minds for both Britain and Nazi Germany in World War II.[4] Both the radio and print media fed the local and foreign population details about the war. As musicologist W. Anthony Sheppard notes, propagandas clearly "encompass both the act of purveying certain beliefs or attitudes to a group of people in order to shape their opinions and ultimately direct their behavior toward a desired action, as well as the cultural products and texts appropriated or created to transmit those meanings and information and to incite the desired action."[5] In Nigeria, the media significantly shaped the opinions and views of each side of the war. It is hard not to marvel at the level of intellectual discourse generated by Nigerians during the war. On one hand, the media helped gauge public support for the Allies and anti-German sentiments. On the other, it provided evidence that the interest of local intellectuals and everyday people also shaped the framing of these discourses. Propaganda became a means of conducting war on an extensive scale.

[4] Jo Fox, *Film Propaganda in Britain and Nazi Germany: World War II Cinema* (Oxford: Berg, 2007). See also David Welch, *Persuading the People: British Propaganda in World War II* (London: British Library, 2016).

[5] W. Anthony Sheppard, "An Exotic Enemy: Anti-Japanese Musical Propaganda in World War II Hollywood," *Journal of the American Musicological Society* 54, no. 2 (Summer 2001): 303–357.

British officials recognized the significant role of propaganda in the battle to win the minds of colonial subjects. Coordinated by the Ministry of Information (MOI), propaganda messages ranged from motivational images demonstrating solidarity to bulletins that portrayed the power of the British over their enemies. As historian David Welch has argued in the context of British propaganda, both World Wars I and II "served to increase the level of popular interest and participation in the affairs of state."[6] The importance of winning "hearts and minds" throughout the British Empire during the Second World War bridged the gap between the soldier at the front and the civilian at home.[7] This view was projected at home and extended abroad in order to mobilize the entire resources of the state – military, economic, and psychological.[8] The projection of "the people's war," one of the principal concerns of the MOI, helped to boost the morale of the home front and to show allies and nations overseas "the unbreakable spirit of the British people."[9]

Propaganda, of course, was used by the government during the Second World War in its attempt to create a unified front between the empire and its subjects in a colonial setting fractured by racial, class, and political divisions. Britain was keen to keep the "support of the colonies in [its] Empire, including those in West Africa, and sent propaganda leaflets to try and help win their support."[10] Britain disseminated messages to its colonies through a variety of media propaganda aimed at discrediting Hitler and Nazism and extolling British virtues to harness economic and military support for the Allies. The war was painted as a struggle between good and evil, between liberal idealism and the horrors of extreme nationalism and racism. It portrayed Britain as a benevolent benefactor of the African population and drew attention to the way Nazi Germany tried to restructure a class society along racial and other discriminatory lines between 1933 and 1945. The German threat to Egypt, the North African campaign against Germany in Tobruk, and the East African campaign against Italy most certainly increased African interest in the globalizing war. There were of course economic and ideological

[6] Welch, *Persuading the People*, 22.    [7] Ibid., 7.    [8] Ibid., 22.
[9] Ibid., 81. For more on the British home front, see Calder, *The People's War*; R. J. Hammond, *Food* (London: Her Majesty's Stationery Office, 1951–1962); R. Mackay, *Half the Battle: Civilian Morale in Britain during the Second World War* (Manchester: Manchester University Press, 2002); Sonya A. Rose, *Which People's War? National Identity and Citizenship in Wartime Britain 1939–1945* (Oxford: Oxford University Press, 2003); I. Zweiniger-Bargielowska, *Austerity in Britain: Rationing, Controls, and Consumption, 1939–1955* (Oxford: Oxford University Press, 2000).
[10] "Convincing the Colonies: How Did Britain Try to Keep the Support of the People of West Africa?" London, National Archives, 2008, accessed January 9, 2019, www.nationalarchives.gov.uk/documents/education/ww2-propaganda.pdf.

implications of such a loss. British Secretary of State for Dominion Affairs Thomas Inskip made this clear: "There remains Africa not as a speculation but as a certainty."[11] If Germany were to be successful in dominating the continent, it would give Germany "a vast tropical empire, gold and minerals of southern Africa and a strategic position which will eventually mean World Empire."[12] Inskip further speculated that if both Egypt and South Africa were lost, India would also be lost, and Australia and New Zealand would fall within the American or Japanese sphere in the future. Essential supplies to Britain would be cut off.[13] Great Britain, although saving herself at home, would cease to be a world power and a beneficial force.

Wartime propaganda employed in the form of advertising, political campaigning, and community education generally shaped local perceptions of the war's morality. Such advertising portrayed the war as posing an eminent danger to the "liberties" enjoyed under British rule. As a British war bulletin bluntly put it: "Between totalitarianism and state worship on one side and national self-determination and democracy on the other, there can be no compromise, for the former cannot survive unless it is totally and universally applied."[14] By promoting particular views about the war – namely as a struggle between totalitarianism and self-determination in a universalist tone – the British colonial administration was able to draw the support of the Nigerian population. British propaganda brought the ideological import behind the war to colonial subjects and publicized a given doctrine or worldview through maintaining public morale and encouraging public support for the war effort. It further distinguished the liberalism of the Allied mission from the totalitarian and racist ideology of Germany and its Fascist cronies.

German and British propagandists took markedly different approaches in their public depictions of one another to win the hearts and minds of the African population. An elaborate system of media control and dissemination of information designed to promote particular views about the war was central to how each side portrayed the conflict. Such propaganda played a key role in garnering public support for the war in Africa. Additionally, Britain and France held an advantage over their common adversary, Germany. Both possessed significant African territories and

---

[11] NA, CAB/66/9/9, "The Strategical Outlook," Memorandum of Secretary of State for Dominion Affairs to War Cabinet, June 28, 1940, 3.
[12] Ibid.  [13] Ibid.
[14] NAE, CADIST, 3/3/177, "Summary Reports of War, Bulletin ETC," *Weekly Commentary*, no. 41, October 19, 1940, Resident Calabar, 1. On German propaganda in the Second World War, see Aristotle A. Kallis, *Nazi Propaganda and the Second World War* (New York: Palgrave Macmillan, 2005).

resources, which allowed them to mobilize considerable manpower and to facilitate a steady production of agricultural and mineral resources for the Allied war effort. These advantages were particularly employed by Britain in its successful mobilization of Nigerians, which ultimately led to the Allied victory. Germany, conversely, was not a significant player on the African colonial scene during the interwar years, having lost its colonies at the end of the First World War.

### German Propaganda

Censorship and state control of the media posed no problem in the already totalitarian Italy, Germany, Japan, and Soviet Union, but they were employed more aggressively during the war.[15] The importance of propaganda was not lost on the Nazis, who prided themselves on their effective use of demonization. Nazi propaganda was shaped by the ideology of "an aspiring totalitarian state" and the context of total war, as Aristotle Kallis excellently illustrates in his book *Nazi Propaganda and the Second World War*. Total war as he notes, had an all-encompassing effect on the state, state institutions, and subsequently on propaganda.[16] As George Orwell famously wrote, the language and propaganda of totalitarian dictatorships invariably employ "euphemism, question begging, and sheer cloudy vagueness."[17] He argued that, to "defend the indefensible" totalitarian regimes, one can substitute clinical abstractions for straightforward proper nouns and visceral verbs.[18] At the head of the German propaganda machine was Dr. Joseph Goebbels, who was appointed minister of propaganda and public enlightenment in March 1933. An important member of the National Socialist German Workers' Party and a talented politician, Goebbels would come to play a very important role in the future direction of German propaganda in what became a party-led takeover of the German state and in the context of total war. In 1933, the Propaganda Ministry seized control of radio broadcasting and attempted to censor what Germans could listen to. Listening to foreign radio broadcasts became an imprisonable offense in 1939, while tuning into news from foreign radio stations was punishable by death.[19] Indeed, the Nazis' prohibition of English-language radio broadcasts sought to undermine the British

---

[15] Welch, *Persuading the People*.    [16] Kallis, *Nazi Propaganda*, 12.

[17] Cited in Jeffrey Herf, "The 'Jewish War': Goebbels and the Anti-Semitic Campaigns of the Nazi Propaganda Ministry," *Holocaust and Genocide Studies* 19, no. 1 (2005): 51–80, at 54.

[18] Ibid.

[19] Imperial War Museum, "Media and War: The Battle for Hearts and Minds," accessed September 15, 2010, www.iwm.org.uk/upload/package/29/mediawar/technolww2.htm.

government, arouse class divisions in Britain, and weaken British resolve.
Yet these objectives were not successful in stopping the spread of British
propaganda.

The British War Cabinet produced a confidential analysis of German
propaganda fortnightly to keep abreast of German strategies in order to
counter them. The principal lines of German propaganda were outlined
in order of their importance in the following way: British Weakness,
British Brutality and Unscrupulousness, German Strength, and Military
Operations.[20] The predominant theme of German propaganda was an
insistence on the country's strength and the greatness of the Nazi Party.
This was given special prominence in radio broadcasts in Germany and
even greater importance in the German press. Germany devoted significant attention to its military operations in its propaganda. German propagandists used the devastating air attacks on merchant vessels over the
North Sea to promote the nation's superior military power. The publication of German figures of Allied and neutral shipping losses was as
important as an element of German propaganda for "home consumption
and to the neutrals as [it was] to Great Britain or to France."[21] These
figures also formed a considerable part of the broadcasts to enemy and
neutral countries.[22] German propagandists strategically juxtaposed
Great Britain as the enemy of neutral states and Germany as their friend
to elicit Axis support in the war. The promotion of the weak economic
and defense mechanisms of British and neutral countries also played an
important part in such demonizing propaganda.[23]

Furthermore, Germany exploited opposition and dissension to British
policies in its African colonies through anti-Allied propaganda. The
opposition of a large section of the South African population (especially
the Afrikaners) to joining in the war on the British side, the growing
opposition to British rule in India, and the difficulties faced by Britain
in the Middle East, Palestine, Iraq, and Egypt were exploited in German
propaganda. Germany did not forget to exaggerate the trouble in Ireland
and the lack of enthusiasm of the dominions to support Britain.[24] British
brutality and unscrupulousness received greater attention after the bombing of Munich and thus became a frequent theme in broadcasts to
Germany, neutral nations, and Great Britain itself.[25] Germany noted
Britain's chicanery, threats, and violence toward neutrals, which

[20] PRO, CAB/68/5/24, "Analysis of German Propaganda," February 1–15, 1940, Foreign
Office, February 23, 1940.
[21] Ibid.   [22] Ibid.   [23] Ibid.
[24] PRO, CAB/68/3/17, "Analysis of German Propaganda," Memorandum by the Secretary
of State for Foreign Affairs, December 4, 1939.
[25] Ibid.

effectively forced them onto the Axis side of the war as "only another proof for us of the infinite extent of British hypocrisy and despicability."[26]

The domestic problems confronting both Britain and France during the war were also used by Germany in wartime propaganda. From 1940, German propaganda focused special attention to dissensions within the British Empire in propaganda for home consumption and dispersal to neutral countries. This took place during a time of weakening economic conditions in Britain. The War Office acknowledged trouble in India due to the breakdown in negotiations between the viceroy of India and Gandhi, and the renewal of fighting on the North-West Frontier was utilized extensively by Germany to portray Britain's hegemonic and imperialist tendencies.[27] Germany painted the British as hypocritical, referencing the execution of two members of the Irish Republican Army as a "blood-tribute paid by the brave Irish people in its age-long struggle against the historic oppressor."[28]

Britain's class distinction was another underlying theme in German propaganda. For instance, Britain was incessantly portrayed as a society in which the "rich take the profits, while the poor bear the sacrifices" and "rationing affected only the poor."[29] In doing so, Germany painted the image of a society where the rich could take their meals in restaurants and educate their children at Eton while the poor lacked the basic necessities of life. Clearly, German propaganda devoted significant attention to Britain's imperialism, its exploitation of other nations, and the atrocities committed by its colonial agents. Both Germany and her allies sought to persuade the colonial peoples of the British Empire that the war was an opportunity to regain their independence.[30] The Germans strongly believed that the loss of these colonies would weaken Britain and its allies who also held colonies in Africa. German propaganda moreover drew upon Britain's past to achieve its aim, emphasizing that the same Britain that was responsible for the atrocious murder of 58,000 helpless Germans in Poland was also the "father of the slave trade, the opium traffic, and the concentration camp." In 1940, a British War Office memo reported, "England, the mask has fallen!" to accentuate its alleged bigotry.[31] Germany characterized Britain's hypocrisy as follows:

Just as the English plutocracy is trying to undermine the German people with lying slogans, it is daily pouring out lies to the neutral nations. Just as England has been personally commissioned by God to dominate the world, she has also been commissioned by Him to protect the peoples, and especially the little peoples.

---

[26] PRO, CAB/68/5/24, "Analysis of German Propaganda."    [27] Ibid.    [28] Ibid.
[29] Ibid.    [30] "Convincing the Colonies."
[31] PRO, CAB/68/5/24, "Analysis of German Propaganda."

This "Protectorship" of England is already very old. England has already taken Malta, Cyprus, Egypt, Aden, India and Burma, and, curiously enough, the "protected" always turned into an English colony. England did not take over German East Africa, Palestine, Transjordan and Iraq for strategical reasons, or German South-West Africa because of the diamonds, but only because "Germany was not capable of administering colonies," or because "the poor Jews" should be given a home, or because Transjordan and Iraq were to be educated for "independence." It was for the same sort of reason that England forced her guarantee upon Rumania and tried to do the same to the Baltic States.[32]

Although Goebbels claimed that German propaganda turned the British and its colonies and dominions against their government through these broadcasts, they were probably not that effective. The British public knew they were enemy broadcasts, and when the Germans started bombing the British mainland in 1940, public opinion turned very much against the German enemy. As historian Jeffrey Herf has argued, the Nazi leadership "translated radical anti-Semitism into a narrative of an innocent, besieged Germany striking back at an 'international Jewry'" and corroding the impact of communism.[33]

Germany's economic and colonial interests were an integral part of its propaganda and its larger ambitions. Having lost the First World War, Germany also lost its colonies in Southwest Africa (present-day Namibia), German East Africa (present-day mainland Tanzania, Rwanda, and Burundi), Togo, and Cameroon, where the Germans' brutality and racism were legendary. These German colonies became Trust Mandates under the Treaty of Versailles that ended the First World War and were consequently taken over by the League of Nations and other competing powers, particularly Britain and France. The loss of the West African territories to France and Britain, the partitioning of German East Africa between Britain and Belgium, and the allocation of Southwest Africa to the Union of South Africa was a painful pill to swallow for Germany. It illustrated the Allies' determination to make Germany pay for past atrocities, or what historian Peter B. Clarke describes as "two guilts fastened round [its] neck, the 'war guilt' and the 'colonial guilt.'"[34] The notion of colonial guilt in particular was pursued to protect "the interest of the 'native' population."[35] Through the Treaty of Versailles, Germany ceased to be a major player in the

---

[32] Ibid.

[33] Herf, "The 'Jewish War,'" 51. On anti-Jewish propaganda, see, for example, Jan Grabowski, "German Anti-Jewish Propaganda in the General Government, 1939–1945: Inciting Hate through Posters, Films, and Exhibitions," *Holocaust and Genocide Studies* 23, no. 3 (2009): 381–412.

[34] Clarke, *West Africans at War*, 23.     [35] Ibid.

European colonial enterprises in Africa. Consequently, the return of German colonies lost after World War I was one of the Nazi demands. The loss of the colonies not only signified Germany's diminished prestige and power on the global stage but also meant the loss of vital economic resources. Thus, the claim that Cameroon alone had nearly as much timber as all of Germany was depicted in posters as an integral part of Nazi economic propaganda.[36]

Germany's intent was to carve out a contiguous sub-Sahara African colonial empire "stretching in one uninterrupted sweep from the Atlantic Ocean to the Indian Ocean."[37] A German Ministry of Foreign Affairs document on November 6, 1940, illustrating this expansive area, listed most of the territories south of the Sahara, including western Nigeria, in what would constitute the German Colonial Reich in Africa.[38] The territories included Togo, Abomey, the Gold Coast, western Nigeria, southern Niger, and southern Chad as far as 150° N., Cameroon, French Equatorial Africa, the Belgian Congo, Tanganyika, Uganda, Kenya, Northern Rhodesia and Nyasaland, Southern Rhodesia, and Southwest Africa. Major ports within the area including Dakar, Conakry, Freetown, Duala, Pointe-Noire, Boma, Zanzibar, Dar es Salam, Mombasa-Kilindi, and Diego-Suarez, as well as islands off the coast of West Africa and the East African coast were to accommodate German military bases.[39] These African territories were to serve Germany's economic interest as part of the German resolve to create a Eurafrican territory and to reshape both Europe and the world. In the Gold Coast, the local press reminded the public of Germany's "intentions to reacquire the African territory which it had lost in the peace settlements ending the First World War."[40] At the ideological level, Africa would come under a colonial order that was radically different from British and French colonial ideology. German National Socialism and the German ideology of racial subordination would mean a more elaborate racial structure in which the white race would be the master race.

---

[36] See "Wood Resources of Cameroon." Courtesy of *Die wirtschaftspolitische Parole* 4 (1939), no. 16.

[37] Alexander Kum'a Ndumbe III, "Black Africa and Germany during the Second World War," in *Africa and the Second World War: Report and Papers of the Symposium Organized by UNESCO at Benghazi, Libyan Aram Jamahiriya, from 10 to 13 November 1980* (Paris: UNESCO, 1985), 57.

[38] Ibid.

[39] Bielfeld, "Die territorial Kolonialforderung an Frankeich im Rahmen der Gesamtforderung [The Claim on France for Colonial Territory Presented As Part of the General Claim]," Berlin, November 6, 1940. Cited in Kum'a Ndumbe III, "Black Africa and Germany."

[40] Wendell P. Holbrook, "British Propaganda and the Mobilization of the Gold Coast War Effort, 1939–1945," *Journal of African History* 26, no. 4 (1985): 347–361.

## British and Allied Counterpropaganda

The men who ran the war rooms in Europe on both sides of the conflict recognized the significant contributions African resources could make in the war. Thus, Britain channeled significant resources into wartime propaganda at home, in the colonies, and across its dominions in order to garner support for the war at home and to win the hearts and souls of its territories' inhabitants. In fact, mass media, like newspapers, radio, and film, which witnessed significant growth in the early twentieth century, were pivotal in World War II.[41] Their growth catered to both the upper-class, educated elite and to mass audiences.

British propaganda was organized by the MOI. Formed on September 4, 1939, the day after Britain's declaration of war, the MOI was the central government department responsible for publicity and propaganda in the Second World War.[42] The initial functions of the MOI were news and press censorship, home publicity, and overseas publicity in Allied and neutral countries.[43] For home publicity, the MOI dealt with the planning of general government or interdepartmental information and provided common services for public relations activities of other government departments. The Home Publicity Division undertook the campaigns requested by other government departments, specific regional campaigns, and those it initiated itself.[44] The General Production Division undertook technical work under Edwin Ableton, producing publicity materials to suit the changing events of the war. A substantial amount was spent on the production of posters, art, and exhibitions.[45] "Poster[s] proved a cheap and effective means of making short, powerful visual statements," and highlighted the specific or unique contributions individual countries were making to the war.[46]

A memorandum from the British minister of information, Sir John Reith, to the War Cabinet on July 26, 1940, addressed the significance of a consistent message that would sustain the morale of the people throughout the course of the war. While the morale of the people was high at the beginning of the war, the memo acknowledged, "the present mood might not endure indefinitely." It went on to add that "it would be important that we should be in a position to convey a clear and definite

---

[41] Chetty, "Imagining National Unity," 106.
[42] Rosaleen Smyth, "Britain's African Colonies and British Propaganda during the Second World War," *Journal of Imperial and Commonwealth History* 14, no. 1 (1985): 65–82.
[43] NA, Ministry of Information, INF Series and INF 3.
[44] Ibid. See also Ian McLaine, *Ministry of Morale: Home Front Morale and the Ministry of Information in World War II* (London: Allen & Uwin, 1979).
[45] NA, Ministry of Information, INF Series and INF 3.
[46] Welch, *Persuading the People*, 167.

picture of the cause which was at stake" should war weariness set in.[47] It was imperative, therefore, for Allied war propaganda to depict the war as a struggle between good and evil. Thus, mobilization embraced the ideological argument that the war was being fought for the interests of common men and women, including Africans. This view not only represented Britain's perspectives on the war but broadened its territorial scope to include other parts of the world. The campaigns that targeted the home audience also highlighted the contributions of other countries. Publications like *A Colony's Effort* in Nigeria or *Playing Their Part*, an annual publication of the MOI, highlighted the significant contribution of different parts of the British Empire.[48]

Throughout World War II, Nigerians were treated to a steady stream of war-related programming and publications. Anti-German propaganda in the form of radio broadcasts and news bulletins was directed to elicit support for the war at home and abroad. The widening of the European conflict was presented as "a world struggle between predatory totalitarianism on the one side and the forces which stand for individualism and national liberty on the other."[49] Britain promoted the virtues of Western democracy and the values of liberty, equality, and racial equity while presenting Germany and Hitler's fascist ideology as the antithesis of freedom. British propaganda emphasized that Hitler would turn Africans into slaves in German labor camps. So, while propaganda painted Hitler as evil on one hand, Britain, on the other hand, was presented as the protector of colonial peoples' liberties. This was an extension of the imperial ethos, including its civilizing mission. The use of such rhetoric as self-determination encouraged colonial subjects to fight a "just war" in support of both the British home front and their own local populations.[50]

Propaganda clearly contrasted two worlds of good versus evil. Using disease as a metaphor to describe Japanese, Italian, and German aggression, the British posited that their adversaries' influence could spread to other parts of the world. Acts of aggression such as the Japanese seizure of Manchuria and attempted engulfment of China, the Italian conquest of Abyssinia and seizure of Albania, and the German destruction of European freedom were said to represent "ulcers in the body politic of the world which tend to spread out from one growing patch of diseased

---

[47] PRO, CAB/65/8/25, "Memorandum," Minister of Information to the War Cabinet, July 26, 1940.

[48] Welch, *Persuading the People*, 161.

[49] CADIST, 3/3/177, Summary Reports of War, Bulletin ETC, *Weekly Commentary*, no. 42, October 27, 1940, Resident Calabar, 1.

[50] Richard Overy, *Why the Allies Won* (London: Random House, 2006).

tissue. The German invasion of Poland not merely precipitated the European conflict, but the world war, in which the future of every nation would be hazarded."[51] These assaults were also a call for a united effort by societies outside of Europe to deal with the Axis alliance, which was described as "a predatory syndicate which undertakes a wholesale trade in continents as a retail trade in nations."[52] These ideas formed the basis of Allied war propaganda both at home and abroad, and of the strategies adopted to sell the war to Africans.

The propaganda intended for the African population spread and promoted an eclectic set of goals. It emphasized the interdependency of the empire and sought to sell the war to Africans through the collective notion of "we are in this together." Recruiting propaganda stressed the unity of the British Commonwealth of Nations, even though this was not reflective of the previous relationship between metropole and colonial subjects. "For King and Country" was the rallying cry of British war propaganda throughout the empire. The message "the empire is at war" had an enduring impact.[53] Clearly, many were persuaded by the British propaganda in Nigeria. The Ututu Clan Executive Committee in southeastern Nigeria, for example, wrote in a letter of solidarity to King George VI:

Our British Government entered into this war just to secure peace, safety and freedom for the whole world in general. ... So far as it is sure to every good reasoning creature that right must win, we therefore fail to omit in our daily supplications that our British Government is on the right point, Victory must be their own. Our heartfelt sympathy goes to the bereaved families whose people had lost their lives and properties for the world peace.[54]

By portraying the war as a moral crusade and a battle between the free world and a tyrannical world dominated by Hitler's extremist ideology, British propaganda shaped Africans' perceptions of the war.

War propaganda was also linked to the production effort in Nigeria. Although about half a million Africans would eventually fight in Asia, the vast majority were called upon to support the war by increasing production of agricultural and mining products. British propaganda encouraged frugal consumption and sought to check social unrest associated with restrictions, new forms of colonial regulations, and recruitment. On all sides of the war, including the United States, propaganda played an

[51] CADIST, 3/3/177, "Summary Reports of War, Bulletin ETC," *Weekly Commentary*, no. 41, October 19, 1940, Resident Calabar, 1.
[52] Ibid.   [53] Welch, *Persuading the People*, 77.
[54] NAE, CALPROF, 3/1/2353, Loyalty to the King and Government, Letter to His Honour, the Resident, Calabar Province, Calabar.

important part in mobilizing the public.[55] The economic objective, specifically the charge for Africans to support the war effort through production, was foremost. The call for Africans to produce essential goods and to conserve resources during the war was seen as an extension of their patriotism toward the empire and for the common good. The outbreak of war gave new impetus to the British campaign for local production of agricultural products for export and foodstuffs. From 1939, the Department of Agriculture organized the production and exportation of produce and called on the African population to support the war effort through increased production of war necessities.

Moral support for the war and the associated anti-German crusade were systematically pursued in Britain. Member of Parliament Harold Nicolson predicted in October 1938 that Germany "would sooner or later demand colonies from Africa and under peremptory terms." He expressed the view that Germany may "demand Malay or Nigeria as compensation for its losses following the Treaty of Versailles at the end of World War I," and that the danger that such a proposition "would pose for Nigerians was not lost to the population."[56] Nicolson called on Britain to "work with the countries which feared Germany" and to strengthen British defenses.[57] The influential British newspaper *The Times* (London) wrote on November 16, 1938:

It is not unnatural, though it is really quite irrelevant, that recent events in Germany should have brought a spate of letters and speeches on the problem of the German claim to colonies. Certainly, this could hardly be regarded as a propitious moment by those, if there were any such, who had seriously considered its solution on the lines of merely "restoring" certain native territories in Africa. The savage outburst of the German Government against the Jews, their manifest indifference to the common prompting of humanity where a defenseless subject population is concerned, the wave of indignation and sympathy which has swept the civilized world – all these are convincing evidence that, where solution may eventually be found of the colonial problem, it will find no support nowadays if it lies in this direction. It is true enough the Jews are regarded in Germany with a positive hatred that would not extend to the African natives: true also that the German people, as distinguished from their rulers, may well be made ashamed and uneasy by these excesses of their party leaders. That does not affect the simple view of the case as it is held in this country – though it should prevent us from despairing of the future of Germany. What does matter is that no one at the

[55] On the United States' strategy, see Witkowski, "World War II Poster Campaigns"; Allan M. Winkler, *The Politics of Propaganda: The Office of War Information, 1942–1945* (New Haven, CT: Yale University Press, 1978); and Holly Cowan Shulman, *The Voice of America: Propaganda and Democracy, 1941–1945* (Madison: University of Wisconsin Press, 1990).
[56] "Mr Nicolson on Germany and Colonies," *The Times* (London), October 18, 1938, 16.
[57] Ibid.

moment feels disposed to risk the unconditional transfer of any backward race to the sort of subjection which finds favour in Germany today.[58]

While the ethnocentric attitude of *The Times* report is self-evident, it insisted that there were no plans to cede any African territory to Germany, emphasizing that there was no reason to "suppose that so crude a transaction [would be] contemplated by any responsible British Minister." The *Times* went on to affirm:

The agitation which has lately been exciting the settlers in Tanganyika, the rumour that Nigeria might be substituted as a peace-offering, the discussions which they have provoked, not only among West African traders but in the columns of serious American newspapers, have no solid substance behind them that anyone has been able to produce.[59]

Evidently, the position of *The Times* and British propaganda was generally counter to Germany's anticolonial stance. Britain's propaganda was a relentless attack against Germany and its prewar interest in colonial Africa and its extensive exploitation of the African population. Germany's long history of attacks on African peoples – namely, the massacre of between 60,000 and 100,000 indigenous Herero and Nama peoples of German South West Africa after they rose up against their German occupiers in 1904 – readily came to mind. These former German colonial subjects did not forget the genocide and famine Germany had brought upon them. Indeed, Hew Strachan's book on the First World War in Africa noted the ferocity with which the Germans "suppressed the wave of resistance that struck their colonies with simultaneous force between 1904 and 1906."[60] These genocidal acts foreshadow Hitler's Third Reich war crimes and "bear similarities to Nazi policies in Eastern Europe."[61] The inhabitants of the German colonies, in the opinion of Britain and the Allies, were "strongly opposed to being again under Germany's sway."[62]

Britain did not ignore previous Nazi policies in its propaganda. Indeed, hatred toward blacks was an integrated part of Nazi racist ideology. While Nazis primarily concentrated on Jews and antisemitism in framing their racist ideology in an intellectual, political, and cultural context, Germany's radical race ideology resonated with similar views rooted in previous perceptions of Africans. Figure 2.1, captioned "The result/

---

[58] "Germany and Africa," *The Times* (London), November 16, 1938, 15.    [59] Ibid.

[60] Hew Strachan, *The First World War in Africa* (Oxford: Oxford University Press, 2004), 3.

[61] Eric D. Weitz, "Review of *Nazi Empire: German Colonialism and Imperialism from Bismarck to Hitler*, by Shelley Baranowski," *Holocaust and Genocide Studies* 27, no. 1 (Spring 2013), 137.

[62] Cited in Clarke, *West Africans at War*, 23.

Figure 2.1 Propaganda slide depicting friendship between an Aryan woman and a black woman as a loss of racial pride. The caption reads: "The result/Racial pride fades." Germany, prewar.
(Source: US Holocaust Memorial Museum)

Racial pride fades," was a subtle critique of interracial mixing and relationship between the white and black races. Nazi race theories contributed to new forms of antiblack attitudes both prior to and during the war.

While there was no systematic Nazi program for the elimination of black people as there was for Jews and other groups, "the fate of black people from 1933 to 1945 in Nazi Germany and in German-occupied territories ranged from isolation to persecution, sterilization, medical experimentation, incarceration, brutality, and murder."[63] By contrasting the quality of life under British rule with Germany's oppressive regulations, Britain portrayed itself as the benevolent benefactor of the African people. This explication of good versus evil was portrayed in British propaganda posters (Figures 2.2–2.5).[64]

[63] US Holocaust Memorial Museum, "Blacks during the Holocaust," Holocaust Encyclopedia, accessed January 8, 2019, www.ushmm.org/wlc/en/article.php?ModuleId=10005479.
[64] The images are from a propaganda leaflet designed for distribution in West Africa, early 1940s, NA, INF 2/1 pt. 4. The images can be found as part of "Convincing the Colonies."

Figures 2.2–2.5 Propaganda leaflets designed for distribution in West Africa. National Archive, London (INF 2/1 pt. 4)

These propaganda posters were particularly engaging, bold, and witty, thanks to the emergence of graphic design as an important medium for communications. They were dramatic and also patronizing. Racial stereotypes of the benevolent empire helping to civilize the colonial subject were remarkably visible as part of British overall strategy. These images served a number of purposes. They offered the British an opportunity to shape popular opinion of the war by compelling Africans to visualize what life would be like if Germany won the war. These anti-German motifs, however, portrayed Germans as violent and aggressive, with Nazism being merely the latest manifestation of this national characteristic. While the posters were meant to generate anti-German sentiments while revealing the "cruelty" of the common enemy, they can be read to represent the contrast presented by the two ideological paradigms. They also reflect the basic premise upon which colonialism was established: the exploitation of African labor and resources for the European market and a veiled imperial war seeking to control these resources. British propaganda images adopt a form of liberalism that acknowledges the subordinate social and economic conditions of African colonial subjects. Evidently, these images further reflect a paternalistic liberal viewpoint toward Africans within a conscious effort to create a false sense of equality while unconsciously advocating the notion of European superiority.

British war propaganda clearly capitalized on emotions such as fear, anxiety, and, in some cases, pride. Nigerians who watched the propaganda pieces and read the newspapers and other print materials were indelibly persuaded by their messages. On why Africans should be concerned, a British war bulletin evoked these images of German attitude toward Africans. According to the report, the horrors of slavery were already resurrected in Germany. Polish prisoners had already been brought into Germany to work on German farms and were paraded in the markets so that the Germans "may take their choice of the fittest and strongest."[65] With specific consideration of its African audience, the bulletin made the point:

Germans will not be kinder to a race which they openly state they despise. In Nigeria now the farmer works on his own farm. Under German control he would work, probably unpaid on a plantation owned by a German. The whip would provide the incentive. Now, if an African is assaulted, the law protects him. There would be no such law under the Germans. Now the African can say openly what he thinks. The Germans deny that privilege even to their own people. Would they give it to Africans?[66]

[65] NAK, KANOPROF, 4494, "Go to It."
[66] NAK, KANOPROF, 4494, "The Solidarity of the British Empire."

Other British anti-German publicity materials proclaimed the benevolent attitude of the British toward colonial subjects and the fairness of British justice. In contrast to the British, the Nazis were portrayed as killing hundreds of men in occupied Europe and willing to do still worse things in Africa.

There were antecedents to Germany's attitude toward blacks during the Second World War. Like Jews, blacks were targets of the Nazi racial purification agenda. Many were forcibly sterilized, subjected to medical experimentation and eugenics, or killed. Africans in German society were marginalized and isolated socially and economically. But the stripping of Germany's African colonies by the Allies after World War I was both a political and an economic loss. The German personnel in Africa who returned to Germany after the First World War "took with them their racist attitudes."[67] Unlike other European colonizers in Africa, Germany implemented segregation policies that separated whites and blacks and banned mixed marriages in its colonies. The use of French colonial troops, which included Africans, in the occupation of the Rhineland in western Germany after the First World War "exacerbated anti-black racism in Germany."[68] Indeed, their presence was seen as a threat to racial purity, and racist propaganda against black soldiers "depicted them as rapists of German women and carriers of venereal and other diseases."[69] The offspring of black soldiers and German women were called "Rhineland Bastards."[70] Hitler's view on the African was clearly outlined in *Mein Kampf* (*My Struggle*). In *Mein Kampf*, Hitler charged that "the Jews had brought the Negroes into the Rhineland with the clear aim of ruining the hated white race by the necessarily-resulting bastardization."[71] One example, he wrote, would suffice to show how much the contemporary world was at fault in this matter:

From time to time our illustrated papers publish, for the edification of the German philistine, the news that in some quarter or other of the globe, and for the first time in that locality, a Negro has become a lawyer, a teacher, a pastor, even a grand opera tenor or something else of that kind. While the bourgeois blockhead stares with amazed admiration at the notice that tells him how marvelous are the achievements of our modern educational technique, the more cunning Jew sees in this fact a new proof to be utilized for the theory with which he wants to infect the public, namely that all men are equal. It does not dawn on the murky bourgeois mind that the fact which is published for him is a sin against reason itself, that it is an act of criminal insanity to train a being who is only an anthropoid by birth until the pretense can be made that he has been turned into a lawyer: while, on the other hand, millions who belong to the most civilized races have to

[67] US Holocaust Memorial Museum, "Blacks during the Holocaust."    [68] Ibid.
[69] Ibid.    [70] Ibid.    [71] Ibid.

remain in positions which are unworthy of their cultural level. The bourgeois mind does not realize that it is a sin against the will of the eternal Creator to allow hundreds of thousands of highly gifted people to remain floundering in the swamp of proletarian misery while Hottentots and Zulus are drilled to fill positions in the intellectual professions. For here we have the products only of . . . drilling technique, just as in the case of the performing dog. If the same amount of care and effort were applied among intelligent races each individual would become a thousand times more capable in such matters.[72]

Such characterisations of African peoples were effectively employed as well-designed instruments of propaganda against the Allies. Yet these racist sentiments could be levied against other colonial powers in Africa. Although the atrocities committed by the British and French pale in comparison to those committed by the Belgians in the Congo and the Germans in their African colonies, all thrived on the exploitation of the indigenous populations. While these preexisting attitudes toward Germany influenced perceptions of the country and formed an important moral and political premise that underlay anti-German propaganda during the Second World War, Britain and its allies espoused the notion of Germany's "colonial guilt" in "legitimizing their own colonial ambitions."[73]

Another key aspect of British propaganda was its unrelenting anti-Hitler character. The image of Hitler as a warmonger and anti-African was reflected in poster campaigns. Indeed, "Inside the News: A Weekly War Commentary," a column in the periodical *Varitas*, published on May 3, 1941, a time when Hitler had conquered most of continental Europe, noted that the world was on a threshold of a "World War." It continued that the nature of Nazi doctrine called upon every nation of the earth that believed in "freedom of spirit, in the right of every nation to fashion its own destiny, and in the system of multi-lateral exchange of goods which is designed (however imperfectly) to raise the standard and well-being of each participant."[74] Later events in the postwar period would show that these noble objectives did not apply to the African population and Britain's colonial subjects.

Britain extensively used print media to fuel its propaganda warfare. Posters were the most common method the nation employed to disseminate information. Leaflets were a cheap and effective way to sell the war to the public. Such advertisements usually highlighted what life would be like under German occupation. Anti-Fascist propaganda themes on the

---

[72] Adolf Hitler, *Mein Kampf*, 359. Cited in "The Solidarity of the British Empire."
[73] Clarke, *West Africans at War*, 24.
[74] "Inside the News: A Weekly War Commentary," *Varitas*, no. 69, May 3, 1941.

radio, in newspapers, and via poster campaigns with dramatic cartoons and drawings depicting such a future under Hitler's regime strongly compelled the African population to support the Allied war effort. Britain also used the radio, a medium that was available to 71 percent of British households in 1939, to promulgate propaganda messages. In contrast to German Fascism, British propaganda painted a picture of a society in which Africans and Europeans lived in harmony. Posters with graphic imagery served as agents of ideological distinction between warring factions and militant patriotism. The most prevalent images of this form of propaganda were depictions of Africans working as slaves under German rule, which illuminated Germany's unflattering colonial history in Africa.

As David Welch argues in his study of British propaganda, the MOI's strategy increasingly focused on reinforcing conviction in "the moral superiority of Britain's way of ordering the world."[75] In October 1940, under the leadership of H. V. Hodson as director of the Empire Division, the MOI "inaugurated a new initiative to inspire the British people and its Empire Crusade." Hodson's strategy was shifting the focus of propaganda from defeating Nazi Germany to the "more positive sentiment of preserving the Commonwealth."[76] The MOI portrayed the value of the British Empire through a strategic operation known as "to and about the British Empire."[77] As reflected in the posters that follow, British propaganda in Nigeria during the Second World War used cultural propaganda that sought to promote the image of a modern, dynamic nation and one of economic liberalism and trade, in contrast to Germany's depiction of Britain. As Figure 2.6 shows, Africans took a keen interest in the imageries and other forms of propaganda that portrayed a unified imperial Britain and the myth of commonwealth, where all races were united in a common course.

From 1940, news about the war was disseminated through news bulletins and reports. A bulletin called *Weekly Commentary* published by a colonial information officer, D. C. Fletcher, provided up-to-date reports of battles, victories, losses, and diplomatic maneuvers. Britain intensified its employment of news bulletins after the fall of France, when Britain remained the sole surviving bastion of freedom in Europe. The *Weekly War Bulletin* reported that "darkness would have fallen like a stroke upon the remnants of a free Europe, upon Africa and upon the

---

[75] Welch, *Persuading the People*, 83. See also Richard Overy, "Front Line II: Civilians at War," in *The Oxford Illustrated History of World War II*, ed. Richard Overy (Oxford: Oxford University Press, 2005), 293–321, at 293.
[76] Welch, *Persuading the People*, 160.    [77] Ibid., 161.

Figure 2.6 "Together." Young West Africans looking at a World War II advertisement for the armed forces of the British Commonwealth, ca. 1940 IWM: WA 14.[78]

Arab world of the Middle East" had the projected invasion of Britain's islands succeeded.[79]

The fall of France increased the perceived danger Germany could pose to Nigeria and other British colonies in West Africa. Accordingly, a 1939 Nigerian government publication emphasized the danger the country faced. At the beginning of the war, friendly French territory surrounded Nigeria. By the end of June 1940, however, that territory had changed overnight from a friendly area to one that was at least doubtful, if not hostile, in its intentions. Many came to believe that Germany "would use

[78] For similar posters, see NA, INF 3/318, Posters: Unity of Strength – Inter-Allied Posters: "Together" (British Empire Servicemen).
[79] CADIST, 3/3/177, "Summary Reports of War, Bulletin, etc.," *Weekly Commentary*, no. 42 27/10/1940, Resident Calabar, 1.

the French colonies as a base to mop up the four British West African Colonies."[80] This fear that Germany could take over the country helped to garner Nigerian support for Britain and the Allies.

The widely circulated *Weekly War Bulletin* was a choice tool for the dissemination of wartime propaganda. Its up-to-date reporting on the war appealed to many individuals, groups, and associations in Nigeria, who often requested a regular supply of the *Bulletin*. As the war continued in its first year, the African population followed developments with increasing interest, concern, and perhaps a level of apprehension. A case in point is when King E. E. E. Eyo II of Creek Town, Calabar, wrote to the Calabar district officer on October 1, 1940, requesting the "supply of war news" for his town. In his plea, he asked for the privilege of "hearing the news of the war" to be extended to his people as well as to other places in Calabar Province.[81] King Eyo was inspired by the government's regular supply of news bulletins and town hall–style meetings with Calabar residents through the Calabar Native Administration office and other groups. The extensive engagement with the local people in Calabar, a much larger urban area, must have played a part in King Eyo's request. King Eyo, a paramount ruler of Creek Town (western Calabar), may have been influenced by the old rivalry among the Efik city-states, especially Duke Town (Calabar). In appraising the situation, he wrote:

You have addressed us the other day in the Executive Committee about War Certificate units which we welcomes [*sic*] the idea and steps are being taken. I also understand that you have got meetings with different unions, schools even spoke with the women at that end to form this unit and I am also asking you to extend the same privilege to Creek Town and I am quite sure that our people here will welcome the idea just as at Calabar.[82]

Such requests were frequent and often devoid of latent rivalry between towns. As a matter of fact, they were expressions of the local people's commitment to help the British fight the war. For the Ijaw Tribal Union in Calabar, for example, a regular supply of the daily official war communiqué was important to "disseminate correct news of the war to the Ijaws ... and help to avoid their hearing and listening to wild rumours."[83] The bulletins were already being issued to the two largest settler communities in Calabar: the Igbo and Ibibio. *War in Pictures*, a magazine published by the MOI and issued in a Yoruba-language

[80] Nigeria, *A Colony's Effort*, 27.
[81] CADIST, 3/3/177, "Summary Reports of War, Bulletin etc.," King Eyo II to District Officer, Calabar, October 1, 1940.
[82] NAC, CADIST, 3/3/177, "Summary Reports of War, Bulletin etc.," King Eyo II to District Officer.
[83] NAC, CADIST, 3/3/177, Ijaw Tribal Union to District Officer, Calabar, June 16, 1941.

version, was very popular among attendants of the Ibadan and Ilesha reading rooms in western Nigeria. The British established the magazine as a means of influencing Nigerians with their Allied ideology.[84]

A plan was made to also distribute the bulletin in Arabic to the Hausa community in the eastern provinces. In fact, in July 1940, the resident of the Plateau provincial office, E. S. Pembleton, reported that Dr. Stirrett of the Church Missionary Society, Sudan Interior Mission, and Sudan United Mission had requested that additional copies of the edition be printed at no cost to the government and distributed among mission schools. The objective was to provide "authentic news" and to help "meet the need for reading matter in Hausa for pupils and ex-pupils of the schools."[85] In July 1941, the BBC planned a series of weekly newsletters specifically for West Africa to give those living in Africa "a background of information about World events."[86] The following year, a mobile propaganda unit began to travel to every corner of Nigeria to bring information closer to the general public through cinema shows.[87] Thus, British propaganda in this regard helped to secure the cooperation of Nigerians against Nazism and legitimized the British war mission.[88]

## Wartime Dissemination of Information and Nigerian Intellectualism

In his first broadcast as governor of Nigeria in March 1942, Sir Alan Burns appealed to Nigerians for "maximum effort in winning the war against aggression." In an opinion piece titled "Nigeria Replies," the *West African Pilot* agreed with the governor's optimism about Nigerian wartime support. "West Africans are ready to lay down their lives for survival, in order to make life worth living for our dear ones at home and abroad. . . . We feel it our duty, as an organ of public opinion, to assure His Excellency that Nigeria will not be found wanting either now or on the day of reckoning."[89] Ironically, significant levels of cooperation developed between the British colonial administration and the Nigerian intellectual

---

[84] Regan Buck Bardeen, "Propaganda in a Contested Space: British Efforts in Nigeria during the Last Decades of Colonial Rule," paper presented at the War and Propaganda in the Twentieth Century Conference, New University of Lisbon, Portugal, November 11–12, 2013. NAI, Oyo Prof 1/3140, vol. II, Information Officer, Lagos, Letter to Oyo Resident, April 22, 1943.

[85] NAK, KANOPROF, 4494, "New Bulletins for Mission Schools," Provincial Office, Jos, July 12, 1940.

[86] NAE, CADIST, 3/3/177, Information Office, Nigeria Secretariat, Lagos, July 2, 1941.

[87] NAE, CALPROF, 3/1/2365, Home Chat, no. 5.

[88] Clarke, *West Africans at War*, 38.    [89] *West African Pilot*, March 9, 1942.

elite, who had hitherto been agitating for political reforms. From the southern regions of the country to their northern counterparts, Nigerians of all persuasions saw the war as an event capable of destroying their way of life or as impending doom. Nigerians supported the British by writing comprehensive editorials and encouraging their countrymen and women to enroll in the army because they were equally afraid of German rule. A known enemy for them was better than an unknown angel.

The war led to the mobilization of Nigerian intellectuals who offered patriotic rationales for the participation of the Nigerian population. The war accelerated prior trends of intellectual production, but channeled them in a new direction. The leaders of Nigerian communities used the war to create space for a new political front within an empire in which they had been largely viewed as subordinate. In this matter, they were right; their contributions to the war effort and the British Empire's reliance on the colony redefined relations and in some cases created a more assertive claim to their membership in the empire. Excited by propaganda, people of various classes and statuses, ranging from traders, farmers, journalists, and the intellectual elite, were drawn into the war and offered good cooperation. *The Lagos Standard* newspaper confirmed the positive effect of Allied propaganda in influencing the minds of the Nigerian population. "We want to prove ourselves men, gentlemen, and loyal citizens of not only the empire that offers us protection but citizens of the World's Republic. ... *Civis Mundi Sum; Civis Mundi Sum!*"[90] Artists such as Ben Enwonwu, a premier African modernist and pioneer whose career opened the way for the postcolonial proliferation and increased visibility of African art, produced works to inspire support for the Allies. His depiction of seven African men extracting rubber from a dense forest of rubber trees was designed for reproduction and distribution to British West African colonies and sought to encourage the production of needed goods.[91]

The news of Hitler's early successes, the fall of France, and the possibility of even greater persecution under Germany greatly influenced African support for the war and produced striking demonstrations of African fidelity to the empire. In a speech aimed at generating support for the British among his subjects, the Oba of Benin declared that "the whole resources of Benin would be available for whatever service the British Government decided." He continued, "I want you to realize that it is good to maintain our military traditions and above all, I want you to

---

[90] *The Lagos Standard*, October 10, 1940, and November 2, 1940.
[91] See Imperial War Museum (hereafter IMW), PST 15391. Benedict Chukwukadibia Enwonwu, "Untitled," 1942.

be sure that Great Britain and the Empire are quite as strong as the Rock of Gibraltar."[92] The view of the majority of Nigerians was optimistic that good would prevail over evil. Frugality as a value system in the evolving war consumption ideology was reflected in such newspaper headline phrases as "local farm-bred mutton saves vital war shipping space," as propaganda campaigns called on Nigerians to make sacrifices. Similarly, an advertisement campaign, titled "Medicine for Dictators," for the Kingsway Chemist supermarket chain encouraged Africans to conserve the materials required to build planes.

"More bombers and more bombs" is the battle cry of the Empire. But please remember that many of the materials needed for aeroplanes and ammunition manufacture are materials which you have been accustomed to buying in different forms from Kingsway Chemists. The machinery that once turned out scissors now produces machine gun bullets. The men who once mixed cough cure now mix T.N.T. The whole of the Empire's resources are directed towards winning the war and consequently you, and incidentally the chemist who does his best to satisfy you, must necessarily go without much that you've been accustomed to buy from us in the past. So please bear with us and remind yourself that everything you want but can't get means something the enemy gets but certainly doesn't want.[93]

Similarly, in a message to the governor of Nigeria, Sir Bernard Bourdillon, the emir of Kano affirmed his people's willingness to make sacrifices to help the empire in its time of need: "I and my people are ready and with my Emirate's resources and my heart we shall make every endeavor loyally to help His Majesty in every way we can. I pray for the success of the British whose course I know so well."[94] In like manner, when the Oron Native Authority donated £200 to the British war effort, Secretary of the Authority E. E. Enyile called it "a small contribution to Britain's war expenditure of His Majesty's Government at home." Furthermore, in conveying their good wishes for Britain and the Allies in the war with Germany, "the aggressor," the Native Authority pledged its support as "one of the loyal groups under the One Throne and the peaceful and just flag of the British Empire," to do its utmost to lessen the empire's burden "in every possible way; and [to] be ever prepared, to render all possible assistance in the war ... When need shall arise, their people will endeavor in every way possible to contribute to the feeding of the local army which His Majesty's Nigerian Government is raising in

---

[92] "Native Attitude in Nigeria," *Nigerian Eastern Mail*, December 9, 1939, 7.
[93] *Nigeria Civil Servant* (Official Organ of the Civil Servant Union) 2, no. 1 (January 1944), 17.
[94] Ibid., 13.

support of the Empire's defence programme."[95] Groups and associations also pledged loyalty to the king and support for war resources. The Ibibio Farmers' Association, representing farmers from six districts of Ibibio land, eastern Nigeria, expressed their commitment in a letter to the British Crown as follows:

Having learned of the unceasing effort of His Majesty's Government in the interest of peace, and having been informed by our leaders that the German Government was not anxious for peace but had decided to plunge the world into misery and untold suffering, [we] do hereby resolve to place our resources and energy at the disposal of His Majesty's Government, and do hereby renew our already unshaken loyalty to His Majesty.[96]

Moreover, Chief Udo Akpabio, the Okuku of Tucana from the Kit Ekpene District, pledged his loyalty to the king and to the British government: "Owing to the international situation and crisis now in Europe, your most humble subject, on behalf of myself and my people send you my heartfelt sympathy as a token of loyalty and appreciation of your Government under whose realm we enjoy inexpressible liberty and innumerable amenities. I also wish you success through God's help."[97]

Nigerians' perception of the conflict as a moral war elicited an unprecedented level of cooperation between Britain and Nigeria. Government and native administration personnel pledged loyalty to the king and the government of Britain. In a telegram directed to the king and the British government, the Ibibio Clan Council pledged loyalty to the sovereign throughout the war with Germany.[98] The Ututu Clan Executive Committee wrote: "It goes without saying that our British Government's chief policy is that everyone should be at liberty as the Almighty God created us."[99] Noting that the news of war did not take it by surprise, the committee asked to be

[95] NAE, CALPROF, 3/1/2353, Loyalty to the King and Government. Oron Native Authority to the Resident, Calabar Province, Calabar.

[96] Ibid. This letter requested that copies of this resolution be forwarded to His Honour the Resident Calabar Province for transmission to His Excellency the Governor in Lagos through His Honour the Chief Commissioner Eastern Province. Chief Benjamin Umo of Ikot Ekpene, Gen. President; Chief Ntuen Ibok of Egwanga Opobo, Deputy Gen. President; Chief Jacobs Udom Akpan of Ikono, Vice President Ikot Ekpene; Udo Ekong of Abak, President Abak District; Akpan Ukuku of Ibiono, President Itu District; Oduono Nkana of Ibisipo, President Uyo District; Mr. G. Uffort of Ikpa Nung Asan, President, Egwuanga Division.

[97] NAE, CALPROF, 3/1/2353, Udo Akpabio (Okuku of Tucana, Ikot Ekpene District) Message of Condolence to His Majesty the King and Emperor, through the Secretary of State for the Colonies.

[98] NAE, CALPROF, 3/1/2353, Loyalty to the King and Government. Ibibio Clan Council to the Resident, Calabar Province, Calabar.

[99] NAE, CALPROF, 3/1/2353, Loyalty to the King and Government, Letter to His Honour, the Resident, Calabar Province, Calabar.

advised on the way it could help and proceeded to say: "Many of our chiefs and old people are already full of panic by the unfounded rumours flying through the bush. We are endeavoring to re-assure them and to show them that we see with His Excellency that 'to be quiet' and to do our own business, and to pay taxes promptly will be a very real help to the Government in the present difficulty."[100]

The Nigerian population was heavily involved in the production and dissemination of anti-German information and propaganda. There was an unprecedented level of collaboration between the local press and the colonial government in the fight against Nazism.[101] The colonies, according to Bonny Ibhawoh, "were also sites for the production of imperial war propaganda and Africans were central to colonial propaganda machinery."[102] The mass media coined a number of idiomatic phrases such as "nail Hitler" that shaped the way Nigerian villages and towns perceived the war. Nigerian-controlled media outlets were as eager as their European counterparts to promote Nigerian support for the war. For the first time, Nigerian newspapers played a crucial role as the British wisely cultivated a working relationship with the local press that had hitherto been very antagonistic toward imperial Britain. Such cooperation was critical to the British propaganda effort in Nigeria. The local press helped to spread to the public the British manipulation of specific ideological differences and graphic images of German brutality. Indeed, Nigerian journalists and intellectuals found themselves cast into a world in which they defended British colonial policy and minimized their anticolonial stance. Scholar Peter Clarke notes that this paradox resulted from the fact that most Nigerian journalists preferred the British to the German system of colonial rule. Thus, their engagement against Germany was "to prevent a German takeover of the British colonial possessions."[103]

Newspaper editorials and coverage of the war were featured prominently in major newspapers such as the influential *West African Pilot*. Founded in 1937 by Nnamdi Azikiwe, a leading Nigerian nationalist, the *Pilot* played a crucial role in selling the war and raising anxiety by devoting part of its layout to reports on the imminent conflict before the war even started. The paper played a vital role in sensitizing the Nigerian population, especially the Igbos, to the arrogance of colonialism and its civilizing mission. However, its anticolonial stance changed during the war. Throughout the war, the *Pilot* appealed for support of the Allies:

---

[100] NAE, CALPROF, 3/1/2353. Loyalty to the King and Government through His Honour the Chief Commissioner, Uyo.
[101] Mordi, "The Nigeria Win the War Fund," 89.
[102] Ibhawoh, "Second World War Propaganda," 221.
[103] Cited in Clarke, *West Africans at War*, 27.

Now that the war is becoming intensified on the economic as well as on the military front, far from being lackeys of Imperialism, as some ill-disposed leftists abroad might think, this newspaper urges support, morally and materially, towards the cause of the Allies. Much as we would criticize British Colonial Administration, it is plain that, with all its faults, it promises a safe and secure future to all of us, only, at times, it is felt that the promise is vague and indefinite. Howbeit, we are at war. Let us put our shoulders to the wheel and let the cylinder work on all fours in order to destroy Hitlerism. Our Empire is in need. Let us render to it all the aid we could.[104]

*The Comet*, a Nigerian weekly journal, wrote an article along the same lines:

Both Great Britain and France are fighting for an ideal, and representing as it does whole-hearted assistance to a struggling nation which has taken up arms to preserve the independence, it is the duty of every freedom loving individual to strengthen the arms of those who whole-heartedly rustle for human freedom – Let Loyalty and Duty be our watch word in this hour of trial.[105]

The role of indigenous media outlets, especially newspapers, before and after the war, provides evidence of the influential role of propaganda but also shows local initiatives from the indigenous elite to present the war from an African perspective. Like other local newspapers, the *West African Pilot* changed its anticolonial stance for most of the war. As historian Godfrey Uzoigwe observes, "It was through Zik's chain of newspapers, particularly, the *West African Pilot*, that some educated Igbo along with other Nigerians became politically aware. The paper's motto, 'Show the Light and the People will find the Way,' had a compelling appeal."[106]

It does not appear that local newspapers were directly told what to publish or how to present the news of the war, but the *West African Pilot's* anticolonial stance, for example, was mitigated by what was considered the greater danger posed by Hitler. Many members of the Nigerian elite were aware of the discourse on race and the genocide that was being carried out on the basis of racialized ideology. Like other war propaganda, the paper consistently presented Hitler as an oppressor who chose to "bully the conscience of men believing that force would win him all that his soul desired."[107] The *West African Pilot's* relentless attack on the German dictator portrayed him as "one who closed his heart to the rights

---

[104] Cited in Mordi, "The Nigeria Win the War Fund," 89.
[105] "Native Attitude in Nigeria," *Nigerian Eastern Mail*, 13.
[106] Zik's other newspapers were the *Sentinel* (Enugu), the *Nigerian Spokesman* (Onitsha), the *Express* (Port Harcourt), the *Eastern Nigeria Guardian* (Port Harcourt), the *Southern Nigeria* (Ibadan), and the *Comet* (Kano) (northern Nigeria's first daily newspaper).
[107] *West African Pilot*, September 4, 1939, 2.

and liberties of other[s]."[108] The news of Hitler's invasion of Poland and the devastation of Polish towns and villages by German soldiers was evidence that Hitler was out to conquer the rest of world and proof of Hitler's determination to end civilization and the liberty of all non-Aryans.

Like many Africans, Nigerians came to despise Hitler, viewing him as a growing threat to the world, including Africans. Hitler's invasion of Poland and his actions against other Europeans nations led Nigerians to embrace the British policy of "all hands on deck." Nigerians perceived the war as something that had been thrust on the British Empire by Hitler and German aggression. Local newspapers captured the sentiment of the Nigerian population. In one of its many editorials and commentaries on the war, the *West African Pilot* called on Nigerians to "Snap out of It!" as part of the newspaper's effort to encourage support for the war. "Nigeria is a vital link in the British Empire defence system," the paper wrote. It continued, "Nigeria must play a no mean part in those things that will eventually contribute to the downfall of the Axis powers."[109] A June 1940 *Daily Service* editorial declared that there were many who could not escape the feeling that Nigeria was not pulling her full weight as far as Africa's war effort was concerned. "We are not in a position to vote millions out of the public treasury towards the Imperial Government's war expenditure, which must now be running to several million pounds daily."[110] However, Nigerians believed there were many ways in which they could help. The people were prepared, "if only government would indicate in what way they could be useful."[111]

There was a historical reason for Germany's animosity toward the major colonial powers in Africa. Although a comparatively late colonial power, Germany's chancellor, Otto von Bismarck, viewed German colonial possessions as a stabilizing influence at home and the expression of the country's greatness abroad. While European powers dreamed of imperial ambitions, colonial territories in Africa and elsewhere offered economic potential in the emerging imperial world order and a global trading system. However, the First World War was a turning point in Germany's imperial ambition with the loss of its African colonies after the war. Germany's imperial ambition in the era was therefore largely an attempt to liberate Germany's sons in those colonies.[112] Thus Germany's colonial history found its way into public discourse on both sides of the ideological divide. Prior to the Second World War, German officials persistently demanded the return of Germany's former African

---

[108] Ibid.    [109] *West African Pilot*, March 12, 1942, 2.
[110] Mordi, "The Nigeria Win the War Fund," 89.    [111] Ibid.    [112] Ibid.

colonies that had been "stolen" from it. In a speech before the Reichstag on April 28, 1939, Hitler claimed:

Now there is no doubt that the Anglo-Saxon people have accomplished immeasurable colonising work in the world. For this work I have a sincere admiration. The thought of destroying this labour appeared and still appears to me, seen from a higher human point of view, as nothing but the effluence of human wanton point of view, as nothing but the effluence of human wanton destructiveness. However, this sincere respect of mine for this achievement does not mean foregoing the securing of the life of my own people.[113]

He further demanded:

The only claim I have ever made, and shall continue to make, on England is that for a return of our Colonies. But I always made it very clear that this would never become the cause of a military conflict. I have always held that the English, to whom those Colonies are of no value, would one day understand the German situation and would then value German friendship higher than the possession of territories which, while yielding no real profit whatever to them, are of vital importance to Germany.[114]

The insistence on the return of German African colonies, however, was also stated a few months earlier. In declaring the opening of a new German colonial training school near Berlin on December 3, 1938, General Ritter von Epp, the governor of Bavaria and the president of the Reich Colonial League, noted that the school would give instruction on the "fundamental principles of colonization and colonial policy," including racial questions and "the dangers of colonial Bolshevism." Epp used the occasion to demand the return of German colonies, which he contended were taken "on slanderous pretexts and under false pretenses."[115]

The Nigerian population was acutely aware of the ideological struggle between the Fascist regimes in Germany and Italy and the rest of Western Europe. Though they had expressed anticolonial sentiments in the past, their support for the war was also a manifestation of their dislike for the hegemonic nature of Germany's colonial and racial ideology. Speeches by German officials were an important tool of propaganda against Germany and helped to garner African support in those parts of the continent where the brutality of Germany's colonial policy was still fresh in the minds of many Africans. The graphic images of Africans as slaves depicted in

---

[113] See R. N. Lyne, "Germany's Claim to Colonies: The African Mandates," *Journal of the Royal African Society* 38, no. 151 (April 1939): 273–280, at 280.
[114] Ibid.
[115] "Germany Persists in Demand for Return of Her Colonies," *West African Pilot*, December 3, 1938, 1.

posters would have sent chills up the spine of any African. Many could not imagine life under German rule. But it was the events of 1938 emerging from the possible transfer of Nigeria to Germany to appease Hitler that caused a high degree of apprehension among Nigerians all over the world.

In 1938 came rumors of British Prime Minister Neville Chamberlain's intention to transfer Nigeria to Germany. A publication in the *News Review* on November 7, 1938, revealed Chamberlain's alleged intentions and relayed that he would make a trip to Paris on November 23 to discuss the details of the transfer.[116] While there was no official pronouncement by the British to dismiss this claim, there was none to refute it. The general reaction from Nigerians at home and abroad was one of shock and disbelief. The thought that Nigeria would be ceded to Germany by Britain as compensation for its lost colonial territories in Africa "caused considerable anxiety and immeasurable panic throughout Nigeria ... and elicited from Nigerians profuse professions of unalloyed loyalty to Britain and their readiness to pay the supreme price in defense of the Empire."[117] In Dublin, African students passed a resolution calling on His Majesty's Government to respect the rights of Africans in Nigeria to choose the authority under which they live. In their resolution, they explained:

The African people, who inhabit this region of the world, appreciate our British connection and we have learned to love British traditions and political ideology. We have had the opportunity to observe the principles and practices of the ideology of the totalitarian States and we appreciate what they think of Black Peoples, as members of the human race. Those of us who are British Protected Persons feel that if Great Britain would consider it morally justified to handover its Colonies to any foreign power for purposes of the appeasement of Europe, it cannot do the same in the case of Colonial Protectorates without becoming guilty of a gross betrayal of trust.[118]

In Harlem, New York, African and African American residents, under the auspices of the Ethiopian World Federation, began to agitate against what they described as an "unusual policy." Nigerians in New York could not bear to envision life under Nazis who regarded African colonial peoples as "beasts of burden."[119] They explained their reasoning for such apprehension:

If Jews, who are members of the Caucasoid race as the Germans, are not good enough to be "Aryans" and are expelled from Germany, then there is no telling to what extent the Nazis will go towards humiliating the Africans. ... It is the opinion

[116] *West African Pilot*, November 8, 1938.
[117] This question was already being raised in several editorials by the *West African Pilot* by 1938. See ibid.
[118] Ibid.    [119] Ibid.

of the officers and members of the Ethiopian World Federation and the peoples of African descent here, American, West Indians, Africans, etc., that Nigerians should act now by protesting against the alleged transfer.[120]

Nigerians' view of life under Nazi Germany was reinforced by anti-Fascist propaganda when the war broke out in 1939. With a great conviction that life would be better under a British colonial system than under German rule, it is hardly surprising that the Nigerian population joined the counterpropaganda war to ensure the defeat of the Nazis. For many Africans, the prospect of Britain losing the war would not mean the end of colonial domination and imperial hegemony, but rather the emergence of a new and unknown world in the hands of aggressive imperial powers "with far less benign colonial intentions and method than Britain."[121]

### "We Are Fighting under the Same Flag": Effects of Propaganda

Allied counterpropaganda was effective for several reasons. Chiefly, the condition of Germany's former colonial territories in Africa before the end of the First World War was generally more repressive than other imperial powers. Additionally, the global condemnation of Germany's racist policies significantly swayed public opinion against Nazism. Its racist doctrines in particular did not win any African allegiance to Germany. Indeed, Africans were not oblivious to what Fascism would mean for them. John Henry Smythe of Sierra Leone recalled the impact Hitler's *Mein Kampf* had on him in an interview with Martin Plaut of the BBC: "We read what this man was going to do to the blacks if he gets into power. And he attacked the British and Americans for encouraging the blacks to become doctors and lawyers."[122] These perceptions were powerful in driving African opinions and support for the war. Nnamdi Azikiwe, Nigeria's most visible anticolonial crusader, called on his fellow Africans: "Read them and weep my fellow Africans, but don't keep weeping because we must resist this challenge by concerted action in partnership with the Mother Country."[123] This was a moment of unparalleled collaboration between the metropole and the colony.

The experience and practice of violence in German colonial rule in Africa came back to haunt Germany and influenced perceptions that made Nigerians more readily inclined to support Britain's Second

---

[120] Ibid.     [121] Jackson, *Distant Drums*, 4.
[122] Quoted in Plaut, "The Africans Who Fought in WWII."
[123] *West African Pilot*, cited in Opata and Apeh, "In Search of Honour," 115. See also Olusanya, *The Second World War and Politics in Nigeria*, 42.

World War propaganda. Although neglected until recent times, German colonial war and mass extermination of the Herero and Nama peoples of present-day Namibia "would qualify from today's perspective as genocide."[124] Referencing the German colonial past, Birthe Kundrus draws parallels between the earlier atrocities in German South West Africa (Deutsch-Sudwestafrika) to National Socialism.[125] The simple mention of the name of Germany as a colonizing power in West Africa conjured up a state of affairs in the minds of Nigerians that may be "fittingly described as 'pandemonium in Mundo' and which invariably stirs from the depths of their souls the most repulsive feelings of horror, of intense disgust and acute bitterness against the fiendish orgies of German tropical rule."[126] Such sentiments found expression during the debates in the Nigerian Legislative Council shortly after the outbreak of the Second World War. The Nigerian elite's support of the British war effort was reflected in the contributions of members of the council during a debate on the extra tax burden to be imposed on the people of Nigeria as a means of sustaining the British war effort. B. D. E. Amobi, who represented the Igbo division in the council, urged the people of Nigeria to support the British.[127] According to him, "it is only in this Government that our freedom lies."[128] H. S. A. Thomas expressed the sentiments of many in the council when he noted that the period of the war was not a time for controversies. In his view, this was a period when "we [Nigerians] have to work and co-operate for a common end."[129] The common end as understood by the entire population was to defeat Hitler.

As the war encroached, developments in Europe and Africa received significant attention and furthered anti-German ideology. Previous experiences from the First World War and colonialism had shown Africans that their fate was inextricably linked to the wills of more powerful colonizing powers. The colonies, which consisted of huge reserves of men, food, and raw materials vital to the success of the British war effort, made them "potential German military targets, and, therefore, psychologically conditioned them to fight on the side of Britain."[130] The

---

[124] Henning Melber, "How to Come to Terms with the Past: Re-visiting the German Colonial Genocide in Namibia," *Africa Spectrum* 40, no. 1 (2005): 139–148, at 144.

[125] Birthe Kundrus, "From the Herero to the Holocaust? Some Remarks on the Current Debate," *Africa Spectrum* 40, no. 2 (2005): 299–308, at 300.

[126] F. Omu, "The Nigerian Press and the Great War," *Nigeria Magazine*, March/May 1968, 44–49. Cited in Clarke, *West Africans at War*, 27–28.

[127] Esse, "The Second World War and Resource Management in Eastern Nigeria," 29.

[128] Legislative Council Debates, December 4, 1939 (Lagos: Government Printer, 1940), 81. Cited in Esse, "The Second World War and Resource Management in Eastern Nigeria," 29.

[129] Ibid.    [130] Mordi, "The Nigeria Win the War Fund," 88.

psychological conditioning of Africans "had been facilitated by pre-war British propaganda, which emphasized Hitler's equation of Africans with apes in his *Mein Kampf* and their possible enslavement in the event of German victory."[131] Nigeria's many years of close economic ties with Great Britain helped draw the country into war with Germany. By the onset of the war, the entire fabric of Nigeria's economy was deeply interwoven with that of Great Britain. The defeat of Britain in the war would likely spell doom to the Nigerian economy. It was the realization of this prospect more than any other that urged the business community in Nigeria to declare support for the British war effort.[132]

Allied propaganda and its demonic portrayal of Hitler stirred a deep fear of white supremacism among Africans, prompting Lagos's *Weekly Record* to describe the German mind as diseased and distorted by "false doctrines as regards the effectiveness of brute force and unspeakable terrorism."[133] *The Comet* went further to compare Germans as psychologically manipulated by Nazi leadership. In the view of the newspaper, the German

is not the unsophisticated man that God made and endowed with a free mind and will. He is a living puppet deleteriously manipulated by an arbitrary despot, Hitler by name. If the fuehrer has any regret at his incapability to create man in his own image, he certainly has the consolation of being able to fashion him into the shape that satisfied his lunatic fancy.[134]

Africans viewed the war from many perspectives, which helped to permeate fear. For many, the prospect of falling under German control was deeply disturbing, and they were thus eager to support the war as active participants. Even though they did not see themselves as having a stake in the outcome, their commitment was unreserved. The Nigerian elite, who were steeped in English literature, history, and mannerisms, as well as admirers of British political systems and institutions, "found it easier to grasp the British point of view than the German's in the war."[135] Their support and sympathy were, from the beginning, partial to Great Britain. Nigerians' suspicion of German intentions and their friendliness and sympathy toward the British made support for the British inevitable.[136] As one elite, N. D. Oyeinde, declared during a Legislative Council debate, "When England is fighting Germany she

[131] Ibid.
[132] Esse, "The Second World War and Resource Management in Eastern Nigeria," 19.
[133] Ibid.
[134] Ernest A. Edyang, "The Man That Hitler Made," *Nigerian Eastern Mail*, October 28, 1939, 7.
[135] Esse, "The Second World War and Resource Management in Eastern Nigeria," 19.
[136] Ibid.

is defending Nigeria, she is defending our side, the peace and prosperity which we enjoy, our existence and the existence of our people as human beings and the future destiny of our dependents."[137] While the ideological framing of imperial propaganda originated in the metropole, its consumption and reframing was shaped by perceptions of colonial subjects and their interests in the discourses around liberty and self-determination.

Judged from the point of view of imperial officials, British propaganda was a remarkable success in Africa. Africans responded by volunteering their resources to the war effort and by making contributions to the war fund. Northern Nigerian emirs were making regular monthly contributions to the war fund from the beginning of the war. By the first quarter of 1942, their contributions had totaled around £245, which amounted to about 5 percent of their monthly salary.[138] Many public officials in every part of the country made similar contributions. Indeed, the *West African Pilot* emphasized that the enthusiasm to contribute "our services towards the overthrow of tyranny from the world must not be allowed to dampen our enthusiasm to contribute our money also to the great cause."[139] The paper warned:

Whether you are a man or a woman, you must have your part to play and everyone must realize that fact. You may have your worries; you may not have things as you would have them be. But remember that these little inconveniences which you suffer compare very insignificantly with the major issue that confront us here and the rest of the freedom-loving mankind.[140]

Nigerians, like other members of African colonies, were hungry for news about the war. This was largely due to the impact of the propaganda war as well as outright rumors, which were rife as the news of an imminent war spread throughout the colony. At an Empire Press Union Conference held in London at the end of June 1939, it was suggested that official and semi-official information should be conveyed to the colonies: "It is the colonies more than the self-governing Dominions who need informing."[141] Nigeria, therefore, instituted a Publicity Advisory Board to disseminate information about conditions in Europe. Its leaders also hoped that the board would disseminate news from the colony to the British public in order to prove its loyalty to the British Crown.[142]

---

[137] N. D. Oyeinde, Legislative Council Debates, December 4, 1939 (Lagos: Government Printer, 1940), 81. Cited in Esse, "The Second World War and Resource Management in Eastern Nigeria," 29.
[138] *West African Pilot*, April 27, 1942.   [139] Ibid.
[140] *West African Pilot*, March 12, 1942.   [141] *West African Pilot*, September 11, 1939.
[142] Ibid.

But Nigerians were often interested in news that directly concerned their own world, including news about Nigerian soldiers. One frustrated colonial official noted that "the mass of the people in [the] 'bush' are not greatly interested in the war except as it affects them personally in terms of increased produce prices and the creased cost of imported goods."[143] They were rather more interested in "those recounting the individual adventures and experiences of solders than those describing the course of the campaigns."[144] Another colonial official expressed the same sentiments:

Knowledge that Britain will win the war is now general. Not understanding much about the size of the world, and the scale of the war, individual victories do not mean much to the average African of Oyo Division. It seems a long war to them, and after each victory announced they are somewhat surprised that victories can be so big without a final decision being reached. All that the people definitely know is that Britain will win, and when informed of fresh victories, they courteously pray God that Britain will win soon.[145]

Propaganda had an enduring impact on the local population, judging by the expression of moral and financial support that poured in as soon as the war began. Such support came from private, public, business, and civic organizations, and from voluntary groups. Yet the Nigerian population drew upon discourses on race and identity in their response to imperial demands, placing transnational cooperation at the center of Second World War relations and discourses. Nigerians looked beyond their immediate conditions and the shortcomings of British colonial policy to advance a transnational ethos. The Aro Executive Committee in the Eastern Region of Nigeria remarked: "We are prepared to render assistance of any nature whenever called upon to do so, to keep the Flag of the British Empire flying."[146] Similar views were expressed in various parts of the empire and its dominions. British policy in this period contrasted with earlier ones in which the attendant men had wide-ranging latitude to define the contours of local administrations. What emerges when one looks at the role of British colonies in Africa, Asia, and the dominions is a global perspective that aimed to pull the empire's resources together to most effectively wage the war threatening Europe.

British propaganda made a tremendous impact on the local population and was effective in winning the support of several classes in Nigeria. By extending propaganda to colonial subjects, Britain drew African support

---

[143] NAI, OYO, Prof 2/3 C. 227, Vol V, Letter, Ibadan Northern District, Oshogbo to the Senior Resident, Oyo Division, July 3, 1944.
[144] Ibid.   [145] Ibid.
[146] NAE, CALPROF, 3/1/2353, Loyalty to the King and Government, Aro Executive Committee.

and dramatically increased the dimensions of its economic extraction of local resources and labor. British propaganda brought an aura of African importance to the war at a time when European domestic production and moral support was low. In Nigeria, officials appealed to the sentiments of the local people, while each warring side portrayed itself as savior of the African people. Colonial officials used propaganda to garner political support from Africans while lending legitimacy to a colonial system that had faced abundant challenges due to the economic crisis arising from the Great Depression.

Both sides of the conflict broadcasted what they perceived to be an ideal world to the African population. The discourse surrounding the war presented around the universalist ideals of freedom shaped African responses. For Africans, who had seen nearly half a century of colonial domination, the war rhetoric was something that appealed to them and their perception of the ideals upon which their effort was requested. The propaganda intended for the colonial audience to recognize the contributions of African colonial subjects in the war effort, sought to encourage participation and mobilize local resources and production of agricultural goods, and stressed the unity and interdependency of the empire.

Different elements of the colonial society, including Nigerians, promoted war propaganda and implored the Nigerian population to support the war. But they also developed new ideas and thoughts and questioned colonial authority. Due to the persuasive influence of such propaganda, Nigerians responded enthusiastically to its call to action. The enthusiastic involvement of so many Nigerians in the propaganda war had much to do with the internal interests of colonial subjects. The intellectual dimensions can be gleaned from the way the Nigerian nationalists positioned themselves during the war. They were motivated to join in the war against Hitler and rally on behalf of an empire they had fought against in the past because there was popular consent for intervention against tyranny. Furthermore, there was a level of willingness on the part of the Nigerian population to participate in the interest of their societies. The rumor that Britain was attempting to appease Germany by ceding Nigeria to satisfy Germany's imperial ambitions in Africa was unsettling. It was enough reason to rally support against Germany in Nigeria. This view was continuously highlighted as Germany challenged the rest of Europe at home and abroad.

Despite the preexisting tensions between Africans and the colonial authorities before the war, propaganda encouraged Africans to join the war effort on the side of the Allies because doing so presented, in their view, a lesser evil to Hitler's nationalist and racist ideology. Thus, propaganda proved an excellent method to test the fluidity of the changing relationship between the empire and its subjects. The propaganda intended for African audiences reasserted the idea of the "interdependency" of the empire. Recruiting propaganda stressed the unity of the British Commonwealth of Nations. The call on Africans to produce goods and conserve resources during the war was seen by the colonial government as an extension of their patriotism toward the empire. The local media, especially the *West African Pilot*, pushed these same themes, emphasizing that a victory for Germany would be the end of freedom, liberty, and equality and concluding that African support of the Allied Powers was the best option.

Nigerians were indeed responding to an elaborate system of media control and the dissemination of ideas designed to promote particular views about the war in the British colonies. The rhetoric of "empire" was a major source of legitimacy and social control used for organizing the war effort – particularly the propaganda developed by Britain and the local African intellectuals that portrayed the war venture as inclusive of African interests. Discourses around the legitimacy of the war against Nazi Germany helped to break down previous divisions between "empire" and "subject" peoples, forcing each side to organize around the common goal of defeating totalitarianism, arguing that a threat to Europe was a threat to the world, including African societies.

While this notion of constructing a new identity as citizens of the empire differed for Europeans who settled permanently within colonies and who initially reinvented themselves as "various kinds of colonial Britons," colonial subjects constructed these new identities as circumstances changed and depending on class. This was the case in the two global wars of the twentieth century in which subject peoples across the British Empire became willing and unwilling participants. As was the case during the Second World War, the distance between the British Empire and its colonial subjects narrowed metaphorically and literally. Most of these emerging connections were largely influenced by economic and political motivations. Their intersection with colonial ideology and imperial understanding of the place of colonial societies within the larger frame of long-standing imperial discourses is significant in understanding how they drew from the imperial core and the culture of the "official mind." Obviously how the colonies responded was shaped by how the colonial population negotiated its own interest, which, in some cases, resulted in undercutting metropolitan interests.

These attitudes and ideologies of imperial citizenship, which colonial subjects sometimes ascribed to themselves, helped in forging a new cohesion and relationship that had the practical effect of drawing support for the war from the local population. As this relationship developed during the Second World War, the British drew heavily from what Daniel Gorman describes as the perennial paradigm of empire that was "*imperium et liberates* – how to maintain both structure and unity while also preserving the cherished ideal of freedom." This paradigm was especially clear in how the British articulated the war against Germany.[147]

---

[147] Daniel Gorman, "Wider and Wider Still? Racial Politics, Intra-imperial Immigration and the Absence of an Imperial Citizenship in the British Empire," *Journal of Colonialism and Colonial History* 3, no. 3 (2002): 1–24.

# 3    The Home Front
## Colonial Subjects and the Burden of Empire

All of the Empire of the King of England has determined to help England in this terrible war – Australia, Canada, New Zealand, South Africa, India, and all the people of Africa who are loyal subjects of our King, are gathering all their strength and are sending soldiers and money and all they have to help in this great struggle, because they believe in freedom and prosperity, and hate oppression and destruction.

"Governor Addresses Northern Nigeria Chiefs in Conference," *West African Pilot*, May 14, 1941, 1

Raymond Ejiogu, a native of Mbaise in Owerri Province, enlisted in the Nigeria Regiment in the Signal Corps on February 2, 1941. Before joining the army, he had been a primary schoolteacher. Ejiogu was one of many young men who joined the army because it provided employment opportunities. Inspired by British propaganda, Nigerian men like Ejiogu contributed to the Allied cause as soldiers or laborers. In a detailed diary that he kept most of his life, Ejiogu wrote: "When I had no luck for civil employment, I went and joined [the Army]."[1] Ejiogu's obituary noted that "the Army was a veritable safety net, which provided provincial youths such as Mr. Ejiogu and his comrades with the opportunity to improve their human capital and for adventure."[2] Many young men were also eager to prove their manhood as citizens of the empire. When Austin N. Ilione wrote to the army commandant in Lagos, Nigeria, he said that he was eagerly wishing to be "initiated early in how to defend [the empire] and offend with arms." He continued: "Should my paper receive immediate attention let me come now to avoid rawness, browness, and untold inconveniences that may ensue from ignorance in the use and avoidance of arms."[3] His letter, though comical and bombastic in its language, reflects the zeal and enthusiasm of many young men in Nigeria at the time. Ejiogu's and Ilione's accounts, like those of many

---

[1] "Obituary: Raymond Chilaka Ejiogu, E. C. Ejiogu's Father, Is Dead at 97," *Sahara Reporters*, June 21, 2011, accessed July 1, 2016, http://saharareporters.com/report/obitu ary-ramond-chilaka-ejiogu-e-c-ejiogu%E2%80%99s-father-dead-97.
[2] Ibid.
[3] R. A. Wright, "A Letter from Oka," *The Times* (London), December 7, 1939, 9.

African war veterans, represent a significant but neglected aspect of the African experience in the Second World War. Such perspectives gleaned from memoirs and letters highlight the role of African soldiers in the war and shift the narrative away from the narrow focus on European experiences.

A few months after the war began, distress calls and appeals for help were ringing out in the colonies from official quarters. Nigerian men and women responded extraordinarily to wartime mobilization. Colonial officials advocated for maximum colonial contributions to the immediate war effort in the form of supplies and a reduction of the demands on men, material, and money, which might be released to the empire either at home or overseas. From 1939 to 1945, Nigerian men and women gave numerous contributions to the war effort through the production of foodstuffs and other agricultural commodities, human investment, and material craftsmanship. Agriculture and mining remained the biggest industries in the country at the time, while the production and manufacturing of goods, especially food crops, began to expand significantly because of the war. Nigerians from all walks of life assisted the imperial government by producing export crops (such as palm produce), foodstuffs, and minerals to support the war effort. On the average, a significant percentage of the population was engaged in one form of production or other related to the war.

Nigerians, like other colonial subjects, forged an alliance with the empire that drew upon the commitment of the colonies to support Britain at a time of great need. Support from different layers of the colonial administrative structure, whose own security was threatened by Hitler, was visible. So, when members of the Okobo Native Authority in eastern Nigeria wrote to the king on October 7, 1939, they were clearly not looking beyond their own immediate circumstances to support the empire. In their letter forwarded through the British governor of Nigeria, they expressed their heartfelt sympathy to the British monarch regarding the war with Germany and pledged their loyalty to him. They expressed their desire to support the war effort. "[W]e have passed this day unanimously, from the bottom of our hearts, that a donation of fifty pounds (50) from our Reserved Fund, is to be taken and sent ... to the Imperial Government at Home; to be used in the war which has been forced upon the British nation."[4] Similarly, other native authorities like the Aro Executive Committee offered prayers and pledged support to the empire "over which the Sun never sets." With full confidence that Great Britain, France, and their allies "will and must win the Nazi Government in the

---

[4] NAE, CALPROF, 3/1/2353, "Loyalty to the King and Government."

war," the committee pledged to "render assistance of any nature whenever called upon to do so, to keep the Flag of the British Empire flying."[5]

The local press became a bastion of support for a system that it had despised in the past. A *West African Pilot* editorial reflected this sentiment, popular among Africans: "We are in the midst of the most destructive war the world has yet seen and it is the duty of every citizen of this country, as it is of every liberty-loving soul in every part of the world, to bear the greatest sacrifice ungrudgingly and contribute his maximum in every way possible, little or great to bring the success of the Allied forces nearer."[6] Yet some individuals and groups found their support for the war effort tempered by a profound attention to their own need for survival. The Farmers Protection Society from Shasha village in Lagos, which was founded on February 3, 1941, perhaps in response to colonial wartime policies and measures, pledged its "unfeigned loyalty and devotion to the throne and person of His Majesty the King Emperor," and prayed for the success of British arms against Hitler, who they called the "Enemy of Civilization and Democracy."[7] But the society expressed its loyalty while seeking clarifications relating to price control of agricultural commodities. The association saw government intervention as contrary to the ideals and ideology of colonialism that claimed to protect native peoples. In their view, the attempt to control the price of local agricultural products ran contrary to the practice that allowed the native population "free enjoyment of their possessions, and by all lawful means to prevent and restrain all violence and injustice which may in any manner be practiced or attempted against them."[8] Thus, there were differences in the way Europeans and Africans perceived the war despite the common belief that Hitler must be defeated.

The financial cost of the war was met by taxes and contributions from the general population of the empire. Estimated at £23.3 million in gifts and £10.7 million in interest-free loans, as well as £14 million in low-interest loans, these funds supported the British war effort to the detriment of colonial subjects.[9] Native administrative authorities and civil and public servants also contributed funds. F. B. Carr, who served as the Owerri Province resident and later as chief commissioner in charge of the eastern provinces in 1943, recalled the local population's desire to

---

[5] Ibid.    [6] *West African Pilot*, February 12, 1942.
[7] NAI, Comcol 1, 197, vol. III, Petition, Farmers' Protection Society to Commissioner of the Colony, February 11, 1941.
[8] Ibid.
[9] Marika Sherwood, "Colonies, Colonials and World War Two," BBC, March 30, 2011, accessed January 15, 2019, www.bbc.co.uk/history/worldwars/wwtwo/colonies_colonials_01.shtml.

support the war effort at the outset. In his memoir, he wrote that raising money for war purposes "became a dominant feature of daily life and the response was quite astonishing."[10] He further recorded:

[The] "Win the War Fund" and "Spitfire Funds" were fully supported and even the poorest – and none was particularly well off in those days – gave their bit. The salaried classes, clerks and the like with a meagre average of, say, £50 a year volunteered a monthly deduction from their pay. ... Indeed, a wave of loyalty seemed to sweep through the country and even in the remote villages all seemed to want to help.[11]

Nigerians accepted the challenge, and the local press articulated the need to contribute "towards warding off the German menace."[12] Writing on January 20, 1939, in relation to Germans' perception of Africa, Nigerian nationalist Nnamdi Azikiwe surmised as follows: "Read them and weep my fellow Africans, but don't keep weeping because we must resist this challenge by concerted action in collaboration with the Mother Country."[13] This attitude was the prevailing view of most Nigerians during the war.

### Supporting the Mother Country: The Colony of Nigeria and Its Home Front

Colonial extraction of African resources and labor was not new. What was new was the intensity of these extractions during the Second World War. The basic factors that informed the Allied economic war strategy underwent significant changes as the resources of the Far East passed under the control of Japan and Germany in 1942. This shift had the potential to strengthen Germany and Japan and posed challenges to the Allies.[14] The major strategic objectives of Allied economic warfare in 1942 included preventing Germany and Japan from establishing economic exchanges by blockade running and opening regular communications by land or sea. Britain was alarmed by the threat such initiatives posed to its war efforts. As one colonial report noted, Japanese successes "have already denied to the Allies important supplies of rubber, tin, wolfram, chrome, oil and food, and, if they continue, may leave the Americas and Africa as the Allies' only trans-oceanic sources of supply."[15]

---

[10] RH, Mss Afr. s. 546, F. B. Carr Papers.    [11] Ibid.
[12] Mordi, "The Nigeria Win the War Fund," 88.
[13] West African Pilot, cited in Olusanya, The Second World War and Politics in Nigeria, 42.
[14] NA, CAB/66/23/6, Memorandum by the Minister of Economic Warfare to the War Cabinet, March 1942, 2.
[15] Ibid.

Indeed, the British War Office acknowledged in a March 1942 report that the Allies faced an "economic war of the same kind and scale as that which they have waged against Germany hitherto."[16] The enemy, in particular the Japanese, the report continued, "are known to be fully conscious of the possibilities of economic war and essential supplies are likely to be objectives for special attack."[17] The Allies sought to increase economic pressure on the neutral border states adjacent to German-controlled Europe and the Vichy French colonies to the "fullest extent which the military situation permits, with a view both to obtaining supplies and to denying to the enemy resources which are becoming more than ever essential to him."[18] The encouragement of all forms of passive and active resistance to economic exploitation within the occupied countries both in German-occupied Europe and in the Far East became an important part of the proposed strategy. Minister of Economic Warfare Roundell Palmer noted metropolitan France and Vichy colonial possessions (French North and West Africa and Madagascar), "acquired greater significance as a link between two enemy worlds."[19] These conditions increased the strategic importance of the West African colonies as sources of badly needed produce.

The replacement of goods hitherto sourced elsewhere became so crucial for Britain and its allies that they turned to the colonies. This strategy was especially crucial after access to tropical goods from the east drastically declined. A memorandum by the secretary of state for dominion affairs detailing telegraphic communications between General Jan Smuts and Winston Churchill revealed the strategic importance of the colonies to the British war effort. "To save Empire and Commonwealth," Smuts noted, "it is therefore necessary to hold Africa south of the equator at all costs in this war. It is very rich in tropical and mineral resources apart from its strategical position."[20] The economic developments in Nigeria during World War II led to an economic boom in the agricultural sector and in minerals, but it also unleashed hardship on the general population.[21]

Although part of a sprawling British imperial possession, Nigeria proved an important source of support for Britain. Local agricultural and forest products and minerals from Nigeria provided crucial supplies

---

[16] Ibid., 4.    [17] Ibid.    [18] Ibid., 2.    [19] Ibid., 4.

[20] NA, CAB/66/9/9, Memorandum by the Secretary of State for Dominion Affairs, June 28, 1940, 2.

[21] The economic developments in Nigeria during World War II had intended and unintended consequences. The economic crisis faced by Britain forced it to exert more control over the economy of Nigeria through a series of regulations and controlled price mechanisms. See Amadi, "Political Integration in Nigeria, 1939–1945."

to Britain and the Allies. The colonial government mobilized the local population for production of exports and produce meant for local consumption. Military authorities devoted significant effort to the salvage of materials that could be processed to support the war effort. Steel scraps were largely used by the Nigerian railways, though a certain quantity was exported to South Africa. Mild steel was distributed by the government to Nigerian blacksmiths for the production of agricultural tools. The government increasingly recognized the obstacles it faced. For one, the general gross volume of colonial export worsened as the war continued. The whole of the European market, formally of considerable importance for most colonial exports, had virtually been lost. The report by the secretary of state for the colonies noted that in addition to the loss of major European markets, large quantities of primary goods from the Netherlands, Belgium, and the French Empire were cut off from their normal markets. The report emphasized that the "problem of disposing of excess supplies of export commodities from the Allied Empires has therefore arisen in a very acute form."[22]

The commodities most affected were oilseeds, nuts, vegetable oils, cocoa, coffee, bananas, sisal, hide, and skin. But even trade in commodities that had hitherto been unaffected by the war, such as tea, began to experience difficulties as a result of the rapidly moving events of the war.[23] The secretary of state for dominion affairs noted in a memorandum that:

When we have to add to this loss of European markets the prospect that imports into the United Kingdom may at any moment have to be very severely curtailed as a result of further attacks on shipping or ports, it becomes clear that producers in British Colonies may be faced with destitution, owing to the impossibility of marketing their produce, unless some means is found of giving them relief.[24]

The governor of Nigeria created the Nigeria Supply Board to coordinate production and transport and to deal with other wartime economic services, such as import, food, and price controls.[25] The board was instituted to deal with the increased demand on the British government as a result of the disruption of access to resources in the Far East. The board now drew its resources from existing government functionaries, including the general manager of the Nigerian Railway, the director of agriculture, the food controller, and two commercial representatives from the West African Supply Centre. The board was delegated to draw up a

[22] NA, CAB/68/7/1, Memorandum, Report by the Secretary of State for Dominion Affairs, July 19, 1940.
[23] Ibid.    [24] Ibid.
[25] NAE, CADIST, 3/3/179, "Circular" No. 6, 6/1942, Nigeria Supply Board, T. Hoskyns-Abrahall, Agriculture Chief Secretary to the Government, Nigerian Secretariat, Lagos, February 6, 1942.

program indicating quantities of export and to "set out in detail the action necessary in order to secure maximum production."[26]

The appointment of Lord Swinton as resident minister for West Africa in June 1942 was an important attempt by the colonial government to pull the resources of the region together. Swinton, former secretary of state for the colonies from 1931 to 1933, was the chairman of the United Kingdom Commercial Corporation. The government noted that "it has been felt for some time past that the situation in West Africa demanded the establishment of a high representative of His Majesty's Government to ensure effective co-operation in the prosecution of the war of all services civil and military in West Africa."[27] Swinton's past position as secretary of state for the colonies and the combination of his experience in that office and other cabinet offices were vital to his new post as "an interpreter of H.M. Government to West Africa and of West Africa to H.M. Government."[28] The creation of the new office was a government initiative to meet wartime necessities. It had no long-range political significance and entailed no constitutional changes in the four British colonies of Nigeria, the Gold Coast, Sierra Leone, and Gambia. These colonies remained under their own governors who, on all regular questions of colonial administration, would continue to function under the authority of the secretary of state for the colonies.[29]

In keeping with pulling the resources of the West African colonies together, Swinton was charged with the task of coordinating the new and varied functions of the imperial government. He was empowered to promptly settle matters within the government's general policy rather than to refer such matters to the colonial office. Swinton's role also gave him the power to give directions to the four civil governors on all matters relating to the war and to provide broad political guidance to the local authorities, both civil and military. The establishment of a war council consisting of the governors of the West African colonies and senior representatives of the army, navy, and air force was an essential step in cementing his authority in the region.[30] Swinton felt that the changes in organization would continue into the era of peace for the benefit of the population as a whole. In the achievement of the Anglo-African wartime partnership, he found the best answer to critics of British colonial administration.[31] Nigerians were there-fore now called upon by Britain to make sacrifices in the war against Nazism.

A new economic situation developed after the fall of France. Germany's victories in 1940 resulted in what Martin Alexander describes as the "undoing of an entire alliance of the western democracies of

[26] Ibid.    [27] NAE, CALPROF, 3/1/2365, Home Chat, no. 2, June 1942.
[28] NA, CAB/68/7/1, Memorandum, Report by the Secretary of State for Dominion Affairs, July 1940.
[29] Ibid.    [30] NAE, CALPROF, 3/1/2365, Home Chat, no. 4, August 1942.    [31] Ibid.

Europe, not simply the fall of France."[32] In his view, the fall of France was "shorthand for the political and military crisis for the Allies" in May to June 1940.[33] The Netherlands and Belgium followed in short order. In military terms, it was a huge upset accompanied by massive economic consequences. Britain appeared to be about to face the same fate. As historian Paul Mulvey observes, Britain "seemed destined to be the Third Reich's next victim."[34] Winston Churchill's admonition of Germany in his "Finest Hour" speech to the House of Commons on June 18, 1940, was a call on Britons to save themselves and to create a better world. That world included the colonies, dominions, and all who believed in the very existence of Western civilization.

The necessary military measures and other activities undertaken to find new sources of goods transformed West Africa into an important field of action for many departments in Britain as much as it changed the life of the people in Britain's dependencies. In a global comparative framework, there were remarkable parallels between the Nigerian experiences and those of other British and French colonial possessions. Eric Jennings has shown Free French Africa relied extensively on African resources and labor from 1943 by "funneling natural resources to the [A]llies, redirecting the colony's economy into an Anglo-American sphere, and imposing hash colonial practices that they justified by involving the war effort."[35] An extraordinary paradox of this relationship is a recognition by Britain that it would have to depend on the colonies, whose population occupied a subordinate position in the whole mantra of colonialism as a civilizing mission.

Nigeria, in particular, was strategic for other reasons, as Figure 3.1 reveals. Nigeria suddenly became important as a strategic link in the Allied defense system and a staging post for troops and supplies. Its significance increased after the fall of Malaya and was enhanced from the time the United States entered the war. Nigeria's abundant resources, size, and population transformed it into a provider of indispensable troops for the campaign in the Indian subcontinent and the main producer of essential goods for the conduct of the war on all fronts.[36] Nigeria was transformed into what Lord Swinton described as a "great strategic highway for air

[32] Martin S. Alexander, "The Fall of France, 1940," in *The World War Two Reader*, ed. Gordon Martel (New York: Routledge, 2004), 7–39, at 7.
[33] Ibid.    [34] Mulvey, "The British Empire in World War Two (Lecture)."
[35] Eric T. Jennings, "Extraction and Labor in Equatorial Africa and Cameroon under Free French Rule," in *Africa and World War II*, ed. Judith A. Byfield, Carolyn A. Brown, Timothy Parsons, and Ahmad Alawad Sikaing (New York: Cambridge University Press, 2015), 200–219, at 201.
[36] "World War II and Post-War Trends," Online Nigeria, October 12, 2005, accessed November 5, 2017, www.onlinenigeria.com/independence/?blurb=635.

Figure 3.1 Nigerian laborers working on a runway at Ikeja, near Lagos, an airfield on the West African Air Reinforcement Route from the Gold Coast to Egypt, May 27, 1942 (IWM CM 3015)

communications, a naval base for convoying shipping bound to and from the Cape, and a source of vital raw materials, particularly tin and rubber."[37] The country's economic production was enormously important, especially in the production of raw materials like palm produce. Nigeria's contributions was clearly outlined in the publication, A Colony's Effort. But the country contributed much more than badly needed resources.[38]

## Recruitment of Nigerian Soldiers

The possibility that war could break out in Africa and the Far East led to a more systematic planning of the contribution that the colonial dependencies could make to the empire's military effort. On October 16, 1939, the War Cabinet requested that the Colonial Office prepare a report about how the manpower and resources of the colonial empire could best be

[37] "Lord Swinton on West Africa's War Effort," *West African World*, August 21, 1943.
[38] Nigeria, *A Colony's Effort*, 5.

utilized. How to draw upon the resources of the colonies and dependencies had been the subject of lengthy examination and discussion between the War Office, the Colonial Office, and the colonial governments. The problem was further complicated by the vast region involved and the diversity of these colonies. The considerable number of colonial dependencies differed widely in their geographical situations, racial compositions, economic structures, and forms of government. Indeed, the military forces raised in the colonial dependencies, for instance, were more numerous and better equipped in September 1939 than in August 1914, when Britain declared war on Germany.

Colonial powers actively enlisted African soldiers in the Great War. Britain was no exception as it also conscripted colonial subjects on a massive scale to fight its wars. According to Ashley Jackson, "the use of colonial troops represented an outstandingly successful mobilization of the empire in support of the British war effort."[39] In fact, Africans from the British Gold Coast fired the first shots in the successful French and British invasion of what was then German Togoland on August 28, 1914, during the First World War.[40] Local military forces increased in strength, and a number of smaller colonies' local defense forces were established where none had existed. The increased call for military preparedness heightened colonial demands on local manpower in East Africa, where the numbers of men in the local forces in September 1939 were approximately 11,100 as compared with 4,700 in August 1914. Other colonial dependencies witnessed massive recruitment of military manpower and the Nigerian population certainly made a greater sacrifice in the name of the empire than it did in the First World War. Beyond Africa, colonial dependencies like Trinidad saw a recruitment of 1,490 men as compared with 260 in the First World War. In Hong Kong, 1,450 were enrolled as compared with 520, and, in Malaya, the figure stood at 10,220 as compared with 3,400.[41]

The enlistment of Africans and other people of color within the British Empire was a dilemma for Britain. An amendment to the Army Act

---

[39] Ashley Jackson, "Supplying War: The High Commission Territories' Military–Logistical Contribution in the Second World War," *Journal of Military History* 66, no. 3 (2002): 719–760, at 719. The British Empire also relied on its Asian territories from India to Singapore for huge quantities of soldiers and raw materials. On support from Asia, see Christopher Alan Bayly and Tim Harper, *Forgotten Armies: Britain's Asian Empire and the War with Japan* (London: Penguin, 2005).

[40] E. J. Grove, "The First Shots of the Great War: The Anglo-French Conquest of Togo, 1914," *Army Quarterly and Defence Journal* 106 (1976): 308–323. See also David Killingray, "African Voices from Two World Wars," *Historical Research* 74, no. 186 (November 2001): 425–443.

[41] NA, CAB/67/4/15, War Cabinet, "Utilization of the Man-Power Resources of the Colonial Empire," January 1940.

passed in 1938 by the Army Council restricted entry to "men of pure European descent."[42] The navy and the air force had policies that limited enlistment to men of pure European descent and reserved the officer cadre to British subjects of pure European descent when "aliens" were accepted.[43] West Indian and black students from Cambridge, Oxford, and Newcastle universities who sought to enlist in the Officers Training Corps "complained that they had been barred on racial grounds." When Dr. Leo March, a Jamaican-born dentist, applied to join the Royal Air Force (RAF) he was turned down because "he was not of pure European descent."[44] This policy put Britain in a very awkward position: how could it explain racial discrimination against its colonial subjects of color that flew in the face of its fight against Nazism? The official British policy of encouraging potential volunteers from the empire to stay in their own countries, where they "could render better service by continuing, for the time being, to represent Imperial interests," began to change as Britain prosecuted the war beyond Europe.[45]

African participation as soldiers and laborers for both France and Britain during the Second World War was enormous. About 140,000 Nigerians would eventually enlist in the Second World War as soldiers.[46] As historian David Killingray notes, three divisions of Africans troops "helped guard France's western frontier" in September 1939, and the African army in colonial Chad provided a lifeline for De Gaulle's army when France fell in 1940.[47] The role that Africans played in assisting the British Empire would extend to other theaters of war where they fought and provided essential labor for the empire. Confronted with an acute shortage of manpower, the Allied war effort required Africans to play a central role in supplying men like Sylvester Okafor Ogbechie, a noncommissioned officer of the British Army's Nigerian Army Auxiliaries of the Middle East Forces Command, pictured in Figure 3.2 with fellow soldiers, who was one of many soldiers who saw action in Burma and was killed on his way back home after the end of World War II in September 1945.

A surge of popular enthusiasm in rural villages and towns in Nigeria fueled enlistment in the army on an unprecedented scale. Many Nigerians, like their counterparts from West and East Africa, had joined the Allied forces as soldiers, porters, drivers, artillerymen, engineers,

---

[42] Ashley Jackson, "New Research on the British Empire and the Second World War: Part I," *Global War Studies* 7, no. 1 (2010): 30–57, at 47.
[43] Ibid.    [44] Ibid.    [45] Ibid., 48.
[46] Saheed Aderinto, "Isaac Fadoyebo at the Battle of Nyron: African Voices of the First and Second World War, ca. 1914–1945," in *African Voices of the Global Past: 1500 to the Present*, ed. Trevor R. Getz (Boulder, CO: Westview Press, 2014), 107–138.
[47] Killingray, "African Voices from Two World Wars," 425.

Figure 3.2 Nigerian soldier Sylvester Okafor Ogbechie and his fellow African military servicemen in the Middle East, April 8, 1945[48]

medics, clerks, infantrymen, and carriers as well as in other capacities.[49] The vast majority of those who joined were volunteers recruited into hastily created military units, which consisted mostly of individuals from the lower classes who saw the army as a way out of rural poverty. However, there were other motivations for these individuals as well. Among the Igbo in particular, their enthusiasm was rooted in the opportunities offered by the war. Most came from poor backgrounds and regions that faced systemic economic problems. For them, the war became a source of survival. The records of manpower needs from West and East African colonies reveal the proportionately high demand made on Nigeria in 1942. A provisional arrangement by the West and East African Governors' Conferences decided that the raising of additional African recruits for noncombatant service in the Middle East Command should be apportioned among the various territories. The British requisitioned 50,000 men from Nigeria, 10,000 from Ghana, and 40,000 from

[48] S. Okwunodu Ogbechie, "Remembering African Servicemen of WWII," May 31, 2010, accessed April 30, 2019, http://aachronym.blogspot.com/2010/05/remembering-african-servicemen-of-wwii.html.
[49] "Africa's Forgotten Wartime Heroes."

various East African colonies, for an estimated total of 100,000 men from all British colonies.[50]

When Private Isaac Fadoyebo joined the Nigerian regiment of the Royal West African Frontier Force (RWAFF) to fight for Britain, he represented what would become a large contingent of thousands of men from West Africa who became central to the Allied campaign in Burma. For Fadoyebo, military service offered an opportunity to escape the unemployment and poverty of his village in 1942.[51] Fadoyebo "simply saw military service as a good job" and recalled in his memoir: "Without consulting my parents and other relations and caring less about the consequences I took a plunge into the unknown by getting myself enlisted in the army at Abeokuta in January 1942 at the age of sixteen."[52] Motivation for mobilization varied across class and political conditions. Gilbert Uzor, another volunteer, was forced by poverty in his rural village of Umunomo in southeastern Nigeria to join the army. Gilbert was encouraged by the "financial benefits that the army offered."[53] Another solder, Umaru Wamba, recalled: "I was so jealous when my friend joined the army. To wear the khaki was a thing of pride and when the girls saw me they would always call me over."[54] Like Fadoyebo and Uzor, many other young men saw joining the army as an opportunity to escape poverty and to affirm their masculinity, among other incentives.

Because of the opportunities the military offered, Nigerians embraced the opportunity to join with great interest and excitement. A *Times* (London) correspondent in Lagos reported on September 14, 1939, that "Africans, who have enrolled in the Territorial Army in large numbers, are training with enthusiasm."[55] Such eagerness was also remembered by Major J. J. Cherns, who wrote in his memoir: "To the African army life is a ritual. To the British troops drill is boredom, to be endured. To Africans it is part of an initiation to being a soldier, to be practiced and perfected."[56] Similarly, Lord Swinton noted, "At the beginning of the

---

[50] NA, CAB/68/9/3322, July 1942. From East Africa, the numbers were distributed in the following way: Kenya 5,000, Uganda 10,000, Tanganyika 15,000, Nyasaland and Northern Rhodesia, 10,000.

[51] Isaac Fadoyebo and David Killingray, *A Stroke of Unbelievable Luck*, edited with an introduction by David Killingray (Madison: University of Wisconsin, 1999), 17.

[52] Ibid.

[53] Interview with Gilbert Uzor, World War II veteran, Ununomo, Ahiazu Mbaise, December 24, 2000. See also Jackson, "Motivation and Mobilization for War."

[54] "WWII's Forgotten Army: West Africa's Soldiers in Burma," *The Guardian*, August 14, 2015, accessed December 1, 2017, www.theguardian.com/world/video/2015/aug/10/forgotten-army-world-war-two-west-african-soldiers-burma-video.

[55] Our Correspondent, "Recruiting in Nigeria," *Times* (London), September 15, 1939, 7.

[56] IWM, 03/23/1, Private Papers of Major J. J. Cherns, "Walk through the Valley": With 6 (West African) Brigade in Arakan, 1943–1945.

war there were few West African regiments, but an enormous army, with the necessary transports, as well as schools of training, had since been organized and equipped. A number of these troops served in the Middle East, including Abyssinia, and had done good work there."[57]

However, participating in the war was not without its costs, and many risked all they had to join the army. I. A. Ade-Olatunde, an employee of the Nigerian Railway, offered his service soon after the war broke out. Ade-Olatunde was a tally clerk in Kano on a salary of £54 per annum. Although railway employees were deemed to be performing essential services and not permitted to join the forces at the time, he was willing to leave what was a relatively comfortable job for the higher honor of answering His Majesty's call for service in the war.[58]

Nigerians viewed enlistment into the army during the Second World War as proof of their loyalty to the empire, their intellectual capability, and self-actualization. For them, it was also a demonstration of their masculinity and personhood within a colonial setting in which realization of equal rights was not possible. But African enlistment occurred because of many changes during the period, including the large number of soldiers required as the war expanded beyond Europe. The dependency on the colonies for much needed human and material resources also allowed for more tolerance and acceptance.[59]

Many African men were forced to fight in the name of the empire. Although European sources spoke of them as volunteers, forced recruitment was widely practiced during the wars in which colonial subjects participated. The chairman of the Veterans' Union in Kinshasa, Democratic Republic of Congo, ninety-three-year-old Albert Kuniuku, recalled forced recruitments: "I was working in a textile company when they came to take us away. Then they went to other companies. All the young workers were recruited. No one was younger than 30."[60] In Nigeria, chiefs and local leaders mobilized their men in what was seen as a fight between good and evil. A BBC report noted: "Mohammed was just 16 when he was pressed into British military service in northern Nigeria against his will."[61] Known as Private African Banana, Mohammed "went on to travel 6,300 miles (10,100

---

[57] "Lord Swinton on West Africa's War Effort."

[58] NAI, CSO 26/36229/S.I., Letter, General Manager, Nigerian Railways to Chief Secretary to Government, November 1, 1939, No. S.R. 504.

[59] For an impressive survey of African soldiers in the British colonial army, see Killingray and Plaut, *Fighting for Britain*.

[60] Theresa Krinniger with Saleh Mwanamilongo, "Africa in World War II: The Forgotten Veterans," DW, May 7, 2015, accessed August 15, 2017, www.dw.com/en/africa-in-world-war-ii-the-forgotten-veterans/a-18437531.

[61] "Africa's Forgotten Wartime Heroes."

km) to the jungles of Burma in the Royal West African Frontier
Force."[62] In the same vein, Nigerians from other ethnic groups were
forced to join the colonial forces as well. For instance, the Tiv, in
addition to playing an important role in the local labor recruitments
for the Jos mines, were "forcefully conscripted and enlisted to fight in
the Second World War."[63] Once they joined the army, many Nigerians
faced discrimination and harsh conditions. As BBC Africa analyst
Martin Plaut recalls about the African soldiers, "many found that once
they enlisted they were badly treated. The reality of military life for
African soldiers like Nigerian Marshall Kebby was very different from
the propaganda."[64] Indeed, Marshall Kebby recollects: "As a colonial
soldier I had very rough treatment. At that time we hadn't even a single
Nigerian officer, all were British. And many of us revolted against
injustice, what I might call man's inhumanity to man."[65]

The RWAFF served as a cadre for the formation of two West African
divisions and fought with the Allied forces in Italian Somaliland,
Abyssinia (modern Ethiopia), and Burma. Made up of men from the
British colonies of Nigeria, Ghana, Gambia, and Sierra Leone, the orga-
nization developed over the years into a fighting force, beginning with the
Ashanti War at the very beginning of the twentieth century. The colonial
military had drawn men from the Northern and Middle Belt Regions of
Nigeria from the inception of the RWAFF. Its members participated in
the First World War in Togoland, the German Cameroons, and German
East Africa, as well as Abyssinia, early in the Second World War. The
RWAFF earned many military honors in its history.

Its use in Burma was the first time the RWAFF, with supporting arms
and in considerable strength, was employed outside of Africa. Nigerians
made up more than half of the total force of 90,000 West African soldiers
deployed to Southeast Asia after 1943, as part of the British Army's 81st
and 82nd (West Africa) Divisions.[66] These troops played a prominent
part in the liberation of Burma. Lieutenant John A. L. Hamilton, a British
officer who worked with the West African regiment, gave a detailed
account of Africans' involvement in the war outside of the African continent. "It may surprise many that West African troops were engaged in
the war in Burma."[67] Most of the 100,000 recruits in the Burma

---

[62] Ibid.     [63] NAK, MAKPROF, File No. 315, "Benue Province Annual Report."
[64] "Africa's Forgotten Wartime Heroes."
[65] Quoted in Plaut, "The Africans Who Fought in WWII."
[66] "African Soldiers in World War II Asia: Battlefront for the Defense of the
Commonwealth: Apology, Recognition and Reparation Do Matter," Africa and
Science.com, accessed November 14, 2016, http://africa-and-science.com/?p=2546.
[67] IWM, 62/193/1, Lieutenant John A. L. Hamilton's account (twenty pages and five maps)
of his time as an officer with the 1st Battalion, Gambia Regiment (6th [West African]

campaign were from the Nigeria and Ghana divisions of the RWAFF. At the time of the Japanese surrender, more than 100,000 West and East African troops were serving in Burma, India, and Ceylon. The West Africans were by no means at home in the jungles of Asia. Indeed, most did not come from similar geographical environments. Yet African soldiers learned to live and move in the jungle. The West African formations, noted Major J. J. Cherns, a British army officer who served alongside Nigerian soldiers, were peculiarly adept at moving through difficult terrain, which would have been considered impassable by more conventionally organized formations.[68] Cherns acknowledged that the 81st Division (West Africa), which included the Nigerians, was "hastily raised early in 1943, was sent overseas insufficiently trained, with many officers, like myself, who had only very recently joined and knew nothing of its men or their language except what they could pick up very quickly."[69] The formation training of the Nigerian regiment was done in India before the division was quickly dispatched to Arakan, Burma. The successful advances of the 11th East African Division down the Kabaw Valley in the 1944 monsoon and those of the 81st and 82nd West African Divisions in the Arakan were the most valuable achievements, drawing high praise from campaign commanders.[70] Cherns praised the men for their bravery and quick adjustment to the adverse conditions they confronted.

At once, with barely time to look at the maps, and even before it was completely assembled and supplied, it was assigned to make its way across immensely difficult country, to operate in an isolated role far out on the flank of the main Arakan forces, totally dependent, once in the Kaladan, on air supply and evacuation. It sustained this role continuously for a year and a quarter, never out of contact with the enemy, never withdrawn for rest and replenishment, increasingly short of European strength particularly, operating through the monsoon in conditions to which mere description can give little meaning to those who did not experience them.[71]

Cherns's account reveals the rapidity with which these ill-trained men were deployed in the battlefield.

Africans were used for a variety of tasks and odd jobs that did not fall strictly into the category of soldiering. The divisions relied heavily on the

Brigade); the operations of the 81st (West African) Division in the Arakan, Burma, January–April 1944, including the formation and training of the division in India, March–November 1943; operations in the Kaladan Valley, November 1943–January 1944; and the First Kaladan Campaign and the subsequent withdrawal from Kyauktaw, January–April 1944.

[68] Cherns, "Walk through the Valley."    [69] Ibid.

[70] NA, CAB/129/2, Report for the Month of August 1945 for the Dominions, India, Burma and the Colonies and Mandated Territories, October 2, 1945, 10.

[71] Ibid.

African soldiers who were first-line transporters on carriers, loading supplies and carrying equipment on their heads. The batteries had African
carriers for their guns and ready-service ammunition. The 1st and 2nd
Battalions in the east were made up of "carriers" who did "the donkey
work such as carrying the mountain guns, mortars, and ammunitions for
the armed forces."[72] The carriers were trained men who could take the
place of casualties as fighting men, thus their official designation was
"unarmed soldier" (UAS).[73] An infantry platoon of thirty-four fighting
men had fourteen carriers escorted by two armed men. Three mortars in a
platoon were also head-loaded.[74]

Each European officer kept an African personal servant who was paid
by the government. These Africans, who came mostly from the Southern
Region of Nigeria, later enlisted as noncombatants. In the words of
Arthur C. Boreham, who served in the Nigerian regiment of the West
African Frontier Forces, these "boys . . . did all the cleaning, washing and
ironing, made the bed, and tidied up the room, [and] prepared a hot bath
each evening."[75] Although the Hausa shunned most of these jobs as
women's work, Boreham observed, they required a fair ability to speak
the English language, which most northerners did not have.[76] Certainly
twisted logic about the superiority of one ethnic group over another in
Africa and of Europeans over Africans generally was a characteristic of the
global conflagration upon which Europeans had built their mission to
civilize and their view of Africa from the nineteenth century. Boreham's
comments on the role of Africans confirm the long-standing prejudice of
the British toward southern Nigerians, especially the Igbo, and reveal the
British attempt to hurriedly raise an indigenous labor corps to support the
regular army. Despite the fact that the northern and southern recruits
were distinguished by their physical attributes and preconceived notions
of the Nigerian northerner as the martial race, there is no evidence that
the northerners performed better than their southern counterparts on the
war front. The war changed European ideas about the so-called martial
race and broadened the ethnic composition of African combatants. Prior
to the war, the British had drawn largely from the northern ethnic groups,
most of whom constituted the core of the West African Frontier Force at
the period of the British conquest of Nigeria. As Oliver Coates has shown,
the experiences of such soldiers as the Ijebu of western Nigeria, as with the
Igbo, "were typical of all colonial African soldiers." The experiences of

[72] Arthur C. Boreham, *Saga of a Suffolk Soldier* (Worcester: Square One Publications,
1990), 148.
[73] IWM, 62/193/1, Hamilton's account, and the papers of Brigadier P. J. Jeffreys (93/29/1),
Major M. S. Clarke (94/1/1), and Major E. S. Stafford. See also Hamilton, *War Bush*.
[74] IWM, 62/193/1, Hamilton's account.    [75] Ibid., 145.    [76] Ibid., 146.

southerners such as the Ijebu and the Igbo were indicative of the rapid changes in military service during the war, the rapid expansion in recruitment "away from supposedly martial races and career soldiers," and the increasing mobilization of African soldiers "who had no especial bond to military service, nor any tradition of serving the British Army."[77]

Despite the important roles Africans would play in the war and the accolades they received from high-profile figures like Prince Philip, the Duke of Edinburgh, the preconceived notion of Africans as uncivilized savages persisted. The Eurocentric views portrayed by European writers such as Joseph Conrad and Joyce Cary, as well as earlier European administrators in Nigeria, appear in the memoirs of the British soldiers who served in the Nigerian regiment. John William Moore, who volunteered to go to Nigeria to train the Nigerian regiment in September 1943, recalled the menial jobs performed by Africans: "All N.C.O.'s [noncommissioned officers] and officers had a personal servant whose duty it was to do our washing, ironing and other general duties." In spite of the central role that African troops played in the war, Moore, like many Europeans, looked down upon his African counterparts: "Most of them had never had clothes before and when they were issued with boots they did not know what was the right or left foot. Being ignorant they often sold their clothes to the local villagers and we often had the trouble of going to the village to get the clothes back."[78] With an air of superiority, he wrote: "I got on well with the African troops, they seemed to respect us because we had more intelligence than they did and they were better looked after by the army than in their own villages."[79] Such racially motivated perceptions were widespread. John H. Morrow has argued in his study of black Africans during World War II that racist preconceptions about the "inferior" abilities and intelligence of Africans "paralleled white Americans' prejudices against African-Americans" and led to British and French attempts to systematically omit, diminish, or discredit the achievements of African soldiers.[80]

The idea that their Nigerian counterparts were uncivilized was by all accounts an extension of the stereotypes and prejudices that the British maintained about Nigerians, especially those from the east. H. P. Palmer,

---

[77] Coates, "The War, Like the Wicked Wand of a Wizard, Strikes Me and Carry Away All That I Have Loved," 4.

[78] Julie Salmon, "War Experiences in Nigeria and Burma," WW2 People's Year, BBC, November 9, 2004, accessed January 2019, www.bbc.co.uk/history/ww2peopleswar/stor ies/47/a3249047.shtml.

[79] Ibid.    [80] Morrow, "Black Africans in World War II," 12.

a British revenue commissioner, remarked on a visit to southern Nigeria in 1913:

The Eastern Provinces is some centuries behind the countries west of the Niger in natural development. Consequently, the social organization of its peoples is less easy for a European administration to deal with than the National organization of peoples like the Yorubas and Hausa. "Native" ideas, Native laws, and Native administrative machinery are so far remote from their European counterparts, that the destructive force of any European administration at all is proportionately greater than when applied to countries whose conceptions are more advanced and obvious.[81]

This view had not changed much by the start of the Second World War. Even during the war, the British authorities created boundaries of racial and ethnic difference. As Arthur C. Boreham recalled, those selected to serve in the four British colonies in Royal West Africa were advised "to learn the Hausa language as quickly as [they could]."[82] This was necessary because most of the British expeditionary force in Nigeria was composed of Hausa or northerners as well as peoples from the Middle Belt area. The Igbo who joined the army during the Second World War in various capacities, for example, were really being introduced to the colonial armed forces for the first time. They were joining for other reasons than merely the pacification of the colony, but their work was no less important to the war effort. From April 1941, when southerners enlisted into the army, efforts were made to keep them away from their Hausa counterparts. Southerners, who Boreham often referred to as "bushmen" to distinguish them from the supposedly enlightened soldier – the worthy northerner – were enlisted as tradesmen such as painters, carpenters, bricklayers, copper and tinsmiths, or medical orderlies.[83] Boreham described the Igbo in particular as a trustworthy people who made good house boys, cooks, or medical orderlies. Yet these were also men who sacrificed their lives to support the Allied war effort. Nigerian troops, like their European counterparts, made the arduous journey to the jungles of Burma to fight for the empire.

These firsthand accounts reveal the changing relationship between black African soldiers and imperial rulers over the course of the war. In some situations, racist preconceptions about the "inferior" abilities and intelligence of Africans led to attempts to discredit the accomplishments of African soldiers.[84] Still, a few were not blinded by racism and prejudice, as Hamilton recorded in his memoir:

[81] RH, Mss Afr. S. 1873, Robert Bernard Broocks Papers, Report Compiled by Mr. H. P. Palmer, Revenue Commissioner, on Visit to Southern Nigeria (ca. 1914).
[82] Boreham, *Saga of a Suffolk Soldier*, 136.     [83] Ibid., 148–149.
[84] Morrow, "Black Africans in World War II."

It was certainly not the fault of the African soldiers if 81 Division disappointed its masters at Corps HQ and Army HQ. Though at home in West Africa they did not normally live in the jungle (or up trees), they adapted well to the arduous and trying conditions of Arakan with patience, endurance and seldom-failing good humour. They marched a very long way ... mostly over atrocious going, seldom on the level, and almost always in full marching order. With hand tools only (picks, shovels and machetes), they constructed some 150 miles of Jeep track, built four Dakota strips and twice that number of Moth strips (the last requiring the clearance of over 3,000 trees in four and a half days).[85]

Hamilton further remarked that his Nigerian counterparts "followed their leaders in attack and stayed with them in defence; they were more ready than most to engage in hand-to-hand combat, often resorting to their machetes."[86] He had special praise for the carriers or unarmed soldiers, about whom he commented:

[They v]ery seldom panicked, though when under attack by a determined enemy with a 40 lb load on one's head and only a machete and perhaps a grenade for defence, it takes a good man not to do so; their stamina was amazing, and some of their feats of strength and balance under awkward loads over difficult going were almost beyond belief.[87]

Other British officers testified to the bravery of the Nigerian soldiers as well as their endurance under very difficult conditions. Cherns's initial apprehension about the employment of West African soldiers evaporated as soon as he began to interact with them. He revealed in his memoir that his "initial misgivings, on arrival in Nigeria, about the capacity of the troops for modern warfare were quickly dispelled in action, the West Africans may not have been the world's crack infantry but they were unsurpassed as jungle fighters, as their Japanese opponents, who should know best, later acknowledge."[88] Cherns further remarked that African soldiers "behaved well and steadily showed astonishing physical endurance and unfailing cheerfulness under extremely trying conditions."[89] Cherns recalled that these colonial soldiers "rapidly adapted themselves and generally proved their worth as soldiers over a year's varied and intensive campaigning without a real rest – some with virtually no rest at all."[90]

Remarkably, many within British society knew very little about the African members of the empire at the outbreak of the war. The conflict

---

[85] IWM, 62/193/1, Hamilton's account, and the papers of Brigadier P. J. Jeffreys (93/29/1), Major M. S. Clarke (94/1/1), and Major E. S. Stafford. See also Hamilton, *War Bush.* General Woolner's estimate for the first campaign is 1,500 miles for the average infantryman.

[86] IWM, 62/193/1, Hamilton's account.     [87] Ibid.

[88] Cherns, "Walk through the Valley," 125.     [89] Ibid.     [90] Ibid.

brought Africans and a portion of the British population into close contact with each other for the first time. Many African soldiers and non-commissioned officers distinguished themselves and gained awards for showing leadership, tactical understanding, and courage in battle.[91] Cherns wrote the following praise for Nigerian troops in his memoir: "For my part I learned to value them – Munchis, Ibos, Yorubas, and Hausas and others – as human beings, with human qualities, at close quarters and in trying circumstances."[92] Accordingly, Prince Philip later described the 81st Division as "unique in the story of the British Empire." As the largest concentration of African troops during the Second World War, these men played "a very significant part in the victory of the 14th Army over the Japanese in Burma."[93] Their counterparts from the French African colony of Senegal, the Tirailleurs Sénégalais, and the King's African Rifles of British East Africa "fought valiantly in both the First and the Second World Wars."[94]

Despite African successes, the relationship between African soldiers and their European counterparts was not devoid of racial prejudice. While the film *Africa's Fighting Men*, produced by Britain and intended for African audiences, explicitly revealed the efforts and support of Africans in the war effort and depicted them as brave, loyal men willing to make any sacrifice for the empire, it simultaneously portrayed them as different from and inferior to their white comrades. The commentary prejudicially described Africans as people whose great strength and endurance was "an invaluable asset," but who were "at their best when fighting in the bush."[95]

Boastful language of superiority was not uncommon in the colonial context and other cultural encounters generally. Military and colonial officials used language that most clearly spoke to the perceived superiority of the Europeans. A significant image reinforced in colonial messages about African soldiers was their presentation as "a collective body, repeatedly shown training ... most notable for its lack of action footage."[96] In protest, an African teacher from Chalimbaba asserted: "Show us films of actual fighting face to face ... bombing towns, sinking ships, so that we may understand war: not manufacturing airplanes, repairing guns, inspecting troops etc., which are mostly unintelligible and quite

[91] Ibid.   [92] Ibid.
[93] His Royal Highness the Prince Philip, Duke of Edinburgh, "Foreword," in Hamilton, *War Bush*.
[94] Morrow, "Black Africans in World War II," 12.
[95] Ministry of Information (Great Britain), *Africa's Fighting Men*, 1943, Colonial Film, accessed January 14, 2019, www.colonialfilm.org.uk/node/180.
[96] Ibid.

uninteresting to us Africans."[97] Such images of Africans as carriers, it was perceived, belittled the efforts and sacrifices of African soldiers. The image of African soldiers fighting without proper uniforms and shoes was an extension of European attitudes toward Africans as whole – as less human than Europeans. Indeed, Timothy Parsons has explored why East Africans in the King's African Rifles "served a foreign power, which denied them the rights of full citizenship and was at best paternalistic and at worst openly oppressive."[98] The sense of the white man's superiority was omnipresent, even in the jungles of Burma.

The negative attitude toward black soldiers was not limited to the British. In the United States, black soldiers were stereotyped. Julius Becton Jr., an African American veteran of the Second World War, recalled: "They thought black soldiers couldn't fight – that they were not trustworthy and had no leadership skills."[99] Even after President Truman signed Executive Order 9981 on July 26, 1948, following several lynchings of black veterans in the South, there was still resistance against a full integration of the army. Black troops had fought with valor in World War II, but, Becton remembered, they were "treated unfairly by U.S. forces and even their prisoners of war."[100]

Unfortunately, few memoirs by Africans who engaged in the Second World War exist today, which inhibits historians from knowing more about the experiences of Africans who helped defeat Germany, Italy, and Japan. The few that do exist paint a remarkable portrait of the courage and tenacity of African soldiers and their struggle with race and racism.[101] One exception was Pilot Officer Peter Thomas of the British RAF. Robert Kakembo, a Ugandan veteran of the Second World War, documented Thomas's wartime experiences in his memoir, *An African Soldier Speaks*, in which he praised this

[97] Rosaleen Smyth, "The British Colonial Film Unit and Sub-Saharan Africa, 1939–1945," *Historical Journal of Film, Radio and Television* 8, no. 3 (1988): 290. Cited in Ministry of Information, "Africa's Fighting Men."
[98] Timothy H. Parsons, *The African Rank-and-File: Social Implications of Colonial Military Service in the King's African Rifles, 1902–1964*. Social History of Africa (Portsmouth, NH: Heinemann, 1999).
[99] DeNeen L. Brown, "'They Thought Black Soldiers Couldn't Fight': The Tragic Stories Behind the Executive Order That Eventually Desegregated the U.S. Armed Forces," *Washington Post*, July 24, 2018, accessed January 15, 2019, www.washingtonpost.com/news/local/wp/2018/07/24/feature/they-thought-black-soldiers-couldnt-fight/?noredirect=on&utm_term=.eca7a8b2f86b. On black integration in the US Naval Academy, see, for example, Robert J. Schneller Jr., *Breaking the Color Barrier: The U.S. Naval Academy's First Black Midshipmen and the Struggle for Racial Equality* (New York: New York University Press, 2005); Phillip McGuire, ed., *Taps for a Jim Crow Army: Letters from Black Soldiers in World War II* (Lexington: University Press of Kentucky, 1993).
[100] Brown, "They Thought Black Soldiers Couldn't Fight."
[101] Robert Kakembo, *An African Soldier Speaks* (Edinburgh: Edinburgh House Press, 1946).

extraordinary African soldier from Nigeria. Thomas was the first African to be granted a commission into the RAF, no small feat in a period when Africans were not allowed to enlist. Thomas had drawn attention to the color bar when he requested to join the RAF in 1940. Born in 1914 in Lagos, Thomas recounted his fascination with war from reading stories of the Great War and how he longed for a similar opportunity to come his way. Although Thomas was told by a Mr. Wilkinson, who was leaving to join the RAF, that he did not think Africans would be considered for the RAF, Thomas was not deterred, noting that now the color bar was being removed and he should "trust that he shall be given the opportunity of serving the Empire at this time of dire need."[102] In a letter to the chief secretary to the government in Lagos, Thomas presented his case:

I am resolved that nothing but death will deter me from taking an active part in the struggle against the evil forces now threatening to deprive the world of civilization, freedom of thought and speech and all that one holds dear and I pray that I will not be put off with stock reply that the Government considers that in my present employment I am best serving the State. I stoutly refuse to accept that view at a time like this when youths of my age are sacrificing their lives for privileges which I will eventually enjoy.[103]

Although Thomas was intelligent and from a very influential Nigerian family, it took the persuasion of Charles Wooley, chief secretary to the government of Nigeria, to make a case for him. His personal letter supporting Thomas's application stated that Thomas was the son of "one of the leading lights from the African community in Lagos" and was "very anxious to enlist in the RAF."[104] Thomas received a favorable response to his tenacious request. He traveled from Nigeria to enlist in the RAF and arrived in Britain in February 1941. On September 17, 1942, he became the first African to qualify as a pilot in the RAF and the first to be commissioned as an officer.[105]

Thomas became a role model for West Africans. Robert Kakembo has suggested that Thomas, along with other prominent African war figures, help generate pan-African, rather than specifically ethnic, pride among Africans. Thomas's case does differ, however, from the cases of the majority of other Africans who fought for the British. He is presented as an anomaly and such focus on his exceptionalism is framed to present an individual who has excelled and who is an equal to his British

---

[102] NAI, CSO 26/36229/S.I., Letter, Emmanuel Peter Thomas to Chief Secretary to the Government, Lagos, June 3, 1940, 1.

[103] Ibid., 2.

[104] Cited in Stephen Bourne, *The Motherland Calls: Britain's Black Servicemen and Women, 1939–45* (Gloucestershire: History Press, 2012), 97.

[105] Ibid.

counterparts. His image and presentation appear in contrast to the "repeated scenes of Africans training and transporting materials" to inspire other African soldiers.[106] In support of this, Kakembo wrote in his memoir:

We have begun to think together as a race. We are all concerned when we hear of some unfortunate happening to Africans in some part of Africa or outside it. We are all happy and clap our hands when we see on the pictures in a cinema, Pilot Officer Peter Thomas of Lagos, Nigeria, the first African to be granted His Majesty's Commission in the RAF. We are proud of him. He is one of us. He is an African.[107]

Although the number of black pilots remained modest, a memorandum for the Air Ministry in early 1945 estimated "that 422 'coloured' (West Indian, West African, and South Asian) flyers had served as aircrew during the war, with a further 3,900 serving as ground crew." The Colonial Office widely publicized their efforts.[108] Trinidadian flying officer Ulrich Cross spoke on BBC Radio's *Calling the West Indies* and featured prominently in the film *West Indies Calling*. The Colonial Film Unit also produced an extended film, *Pilot Officer Peter Thomas, RAF* (No. 40), which portrayed Thomas "during his leisure time, when he takes part in the social and religious life at the Station." Toward the end of the war, Thomas earned admission to Middle Temple Law School, but he died in January 1945 after hitting high ground while flying out of RAF Madley in Herefordshire.[109] Yet Thomas was just but one of the thousands of Nigerians who provided the military support that aided the Allied victory.

## Nigerian Labor and Wartime Production

Although the Second World War did not have battlefields in many parts of Africa, the continent nevertheless had its own home front. Nigerians at home prepared for the possibility of any attack on the homeland. In 1942, Nigerians called for the establishment of an African Volunteer Force comparable to the European model. They regarded the volunteer force as essential to equipping them with knowledge of military science and tactics in order to withstand any enemy attack. A Civil and Military Reserve (Home Guard) was proposed in Nigeria by the government

[106] Cited in ibid., 97.    [107] Cited in ibid.
[108] Martin Francis, *The Flyer: British Culture and the Royal Air Force 1939–1945* (Oxford: Oxford University Press, 2008), 59. See also Martin Francis, "Men of the Royal Air Force, the Cultural Memory of the Second World War and the Twilight of the British Empire," in *Gender, Labour, War and Empire: Essays on Modern Britain*, ed. Philippa Levin and Susan R. Grayzel (New York: Palgrave Macmillan, 2009), 197–218, at 186.
[109] Roger Lambo, "Achtung! The Black Prince: West Africans in the Royal Air Force, 1939–46," in *Africans in Britain*, ed. David Killingray (London: Routledge, 1994), 179–196, at 156.

and its provisions discussed with military authorities in 1942.[110] Colonel Mabb was appointed the commanding officer of the reserve. Under the program, Europeans and Africans could be called for service with the Home Guard on passive defense or military service.[111] In the event of hostilities breaking out, the members of the Home Guard could be called upon to join the nearest military unit and fight.[112]

Colonial natural resources were essential in sustaining the army and the population of imperial powers, and they supported the essential logistical systems essential for executing the war.[113] When German and Italian domination prevented supplies coming through the Mediterranean, an alternative route was established through West Africa. From the port of Takoradi in Ghana, a string of air bases led across Nigeria, Chad, and Sudan to Cairo. Kano, in northern Nigeria, was part of the "Takoradi Route" for aircraft carrying supplies and reinforcements to British and American forces in Egypt.[114] The West African region was the only channel through which Allied aircraft could be sent to the Middle East, Russia, India, and China. This led to the construction of aerodromes in West and Central Africa. Nigeria alone had thirty large airfields, fully equipped with control rooms, hangars, buildings, and camps, while others were laid out in the Gold Coast, Sierra Leone, and Gambia.[115] A newly constructed runway at Ikeja, north of Lagos, Nigeria, was one of the vital staging posts on the West African Air Reinforcement Route to Egypt. West African airfields were to become a vital part of the Allied war effort. Thousands of aircraft flew over West African routes, including those that came from the United States in the first few months of the North African campaign. The route from West Africa to Khartoum and Cairo offered a rapid service to carry essential items required by RAF squadrons into the Middle East and beyond.[116] Emphasizing the importance of the region to the Allies, an American who visited West African airfields stated that if such airfields had not been available in the first two

---

[110] NAE, CALPROF, 3/1/2365, Home Chat, no. 1. This meant a delay in bringing the scheme into operation.
[111] Only those who were actually required would be called up for training on a part-time basis of two afternoons a week. The British resident, in consultation with the senior military officer in an area, would be the competent authority to call men up and allocate them to duties. Ibid.
[112] Ibid.
[113] See, for example, Simo Laakkonen and Richard Tucker, "War and Natural Resources in History: Introduction," *Global Environment* 5, no. 10 (2012): 8–15.
[114] IWM, ART LD 2178, Julian Trevelyan, "An Air Raid Warden at Kano, Northern Nigeria," 1942, www.iwm.org.uk/collections/item/object/26544.
[115] NAE, CALPROF, 3/1/2365, Home Chat, no. 4.
[116] NA, CAB/67/8/90, Memorandum by the Secretary of State for Air, November 5, 1940, 2.

months of the campaign, "the big bombers could not have arrived on the battle front in time to take an effective part in it."[117] Apart from building aerodromes, the American noted, there had been an "immense amount of constructional work in port developments, extension of railways and laying of new lines, improvements to existing roads and the building of new ones, the laying out of camp sites and oil installations."[118]

In addition to the disruptive effects of the building of this infrastructure, Britain initiated the systematic extraction of natural resources that affected the lives of most Nigerians. The demands made during the war multiplied both qualitatively and quantitatively the extraction of strategic raw materials and Nigerian manpower. This process provided the key to much of the distress felt by ordinary people and their response during the war. The British, like their counterparts in other areas of Africa, relied on African labor to achieve their goal of imperial extraction. The exploitation of African labor in the colonial period occurred as a result of "the creation of a monetarized commodity surplus." In the case of West Africa, "commodity production and class relations were already much more developed than in most parts of the continent, which had important consequences for twentieth-century capital accumulation."[119]

There was an unprecedented demand for various categories of both skilled and semiskilled manual labor. In fact, colonial reports detected a shortage of labor in certain categories in which there was previously unemployment. Laws were rapidly adjusted "to adapt them to the changed conditions."[120] Labor conditions were particularly affected by the various changes "in the process of placing the economy of the country on a war basis."[121] Semiskilled laborers were rapidly trained by the government to "take the place of skilled labor, and unskilled labor to replace the semi-skilled."[122] The high standard of skill previously insisted upon in certain kinds of work was to some extent lowered. The increased demand for labor led to an offer of increased pay and better working conditions.

New labor legislation brought Nigerian law more closely into conformity with UK law. For instance, the Trade Union Ordinance of 1938 became more pronounced in 1939. The most important measures introduced after the outbreak of the war were the Trade Disputes (Arbitration and Inquiry) Ordinance, the Workmen's Compensation Ordinance, and

---

[117] Ibid.    [118] Ibid.
[119] William M. Freund, "Labour Migration to the Northern Nigerian Tin Mines, 1903–1945," *Journal of African History* 22, no. 1 (1981): 73–84, at 74–75.
[120] NAE, CALPROF, 3/1/2365, Home Chat, no. 4.    [121] Ibid.    [122] Ibid.

consequential amendments to the Criminal Code, the Forced Labour Ordinance, and the Minerals Ordinance.[123] The new labor legislation introduced during the war gave legal sanction to organized unions of workmen and employers on lines similar to those in the United Kingdom. A few labor unions that were already in existence before the war were given official recognition by the British government. It was the view of the government that organized labor could no longer have been postponed, even if war had not broken out. The new legislation, therefore, only hastened the natural sequence of events.[124] Following the recommendation of Major Orde Browne in his "Report on Labour Conditions in West Africa," the government formed the Department of Labour to supersede the existing arrangement by which individual officers had been appointed to undertake labor duties. The department assisted in the labor organization of the country and remedied trade disputes and other labor difficulties that were bound to follow industrial development in Nigeria.[125]

Nigerian labor proved even more crucial at home as expansion in the production of agricultural and mineral goods in the country required the recruitment of additional labor. Besides the role Africans played in the theaters of war, a considerable number of West Africans worked in munitions and other war factories in England. In one particular factory, records show that there were "nearly 150 of them: some of them are skilled workers and have risen to posts of responsibility, storekeepers, chargemen and the like."[126] These workers were mainly drafted as home guards for internal security in the colony.

Forced labor had been used in the construction of infrastructure, including roads and railways. Africans were frequently employed as porters and workers in other sundry services. This labor was mostly free and often conscripted. Between 1923 and 1926, for example, the British colonial administration in Nigeria conscripted more than 24,000 laborers in addition to more than 35,660 casual laborers for the construction of the Nigerian railway that linked Port Harcourt to Kaduna.[127] In particular,

---

[123] In similar circumstances in 1917, the government found it necessary to pass the Master and Servants Ordinance, which governed all important labor questions until it was replaced by the Labour Code of 1929.

[124] NAE, CALPROF, 3/1/2365, Home Chat, no. 4.     [125] Ibid.

[126] NAE, CALPROF, 3/1/2365, Home Chat, no. 5.

[127] See C. C. Jacobs, "Forced Labor in Colonial Nigeria," in *A History of Labor in Nigeria*, ed. M. Y. Mangvwat (Jos: University Press, 1998), 47. Cited in Philip Akpen, "Forced Labor in Jos Tin Mines: The Psychological and Emotional Implications for Women in Tiv Society, Central Nigeria 1902–1945," paper presented at the Second International Conference of the Transatlantic Group on "Gendering Global Transformations," Owerri, July 2006.

the Tiv of Central Nigeria paid a high price, as Nigerian historian Philip Akpen notes. In 1923, about 4,000 Tiv youths were forcefully conscripted for the construction of the railway.[128] They played similar roles later in the construction of the Makurdi Bridge from 1928 to 1932.[129]

In January 1942, plans were made by the government to set up a West African Military Labor Corps in Nigeria. Africans were to be enlisted for the duration of the war as noncombatant soldiers for service anywhere within the continent. With an estimated 1,040 laborers, each group would consist of forty gangs with a headman capable of speaking English, a cook, and twenty-four laborers. As much as possible, each gang was to consist of people from the same community or district.[130]

Labor recruitment for the army, construction projects, and export production and food supply created a huge demand for the Nigerian labor force. The mines, docks, and construction sector continued to demand skilled craftsmen and technicians, which were in short supply before the war. According to the 1942 *Annual Report of the Department of Labour*, "the surplus of casual unskilled workmen, who in normal times found it difficult to secure regular employment, has been almost entirely absorbed."[131] The mines, docks, and construction sector continued to demand skilled craftsmen and technicians, which were in short supply before the war. With an inadequate supply of training facilities in Nigeria before the war, Nigerians could not immediately meet the enormous and abrupt demand on their resources.[132] In order to ensure an ample supply of labor for the production of essential products and to ensure that labor was available where it was needed most, the government introduced various economic stimulus measures, including the Employment in Essential Works Regulations, the Overtime Regulations, and the Compulsory National Services (Essential Mines) Regulations. Although such measures restricted the free mobility of local labor in 1942, they were designed to "keep the right man in the right place, and to direct additional men to the industries which need them."[133]

---

[128] NAK, MAKPROF, File No. 1848, "Railway Labor Camps." Cited in Akpen, "Forced Labor in Jos Tin Mines."

[129] NAK, MAKPROF, File No. K3401; NAK, MAKPRO, File No. RDS/2, "Benue Bridge Construction"; W. A. Perkins and H. S. Jasper, *Nigeria: A Descriptive Geography*, 3rd edn. (Ibadan: University Press, 1980), 139. Cited in Akpen, "Forced Labor in Jos Tin Mines."

[130] NAE, CADIST, 3/3/269, File No. CAD 285, Formation of West African Military Labour Corps, January 29, 1942, Memo, Lt. Col. A. A. and QMG.

[131] Nigeria, *Annual Report of the Department of Labour, Nigeria, for the Year 1942*, vol. 1 (Lagos: Government Press, 1943).

[132] Ibid.    [133] Ibid., 2.

## Export and Domestic Production

From the outset of the war, it was clear that enormous quantities of agricultural products, food, and minerals would be produced at home in Nigeria to make up for the shortfall resulting from German aggression and the disruption of British trade. In Nigeria, the government made reasonable arrangements to prepare for war in which the Department of Agriculture was expected to play a significant role. Perhaps it was the experiences of the First World War that lay at the root of the strategy of economic mobilization in both Britain and its colonial possessions. The policy of economic self-sufficiency within the empire was evident in how the Department of Agriculture envisaged its role. Colonial officials like J. R. Mackie, the director of agriculture, came to the conclusion that a substantially greater demand would be expected from his department than prior to the war. Due to its peacetime role as the backbone of the colonial economy, the Department of Agriculture became the main focus of the reorganization in the country to meet the demands imposed by the war. The dual phenomenon of cash production and the war, therefore, transformed rural life in the late 1930s and 1940s.

The war expanded the economic link and production chain between the colony and the empire and the colonial state's relationship with local producers. The need for agricultural goods, minerals, and other resources created new demands and brought the expansion of the production of existing products such as palm oil. However, the most important demand for local support centered on the agricultural sector. As the United Africa Company noted during the war: "The rich products of West Africa, and the indomitable 'will to win' among her peoples ... both combine as a most vital contribution towards certain victory. As the Allied striking power increases, so demands increase on all our energies and resources, to build up that power to overwhelming strength."[134]

Early in 1938, the government began to make plans that included the control of food as part of its overall defense strategy. Using existing colonial institutions, the British used every structure of authority to encourage local support for the war. The local administrative authorities in the region threw their weight behind British preparation for war. The Food Defence Plans Department of the Board of Trade issued a report that broadly outlined the preparations made for feeding the nation in time of war.[135] The plans included buying the food required in major emergencies and anticipating every problem that would arise during the

[134] *Nigeria Civil Servant* (the official organ of the Civil Servant Union), no. 1 (January 1944), 49.
[135] *Nigerian Daily Times*, April 30, 1938, 1.

first six months of war. Furthermore, the control of available food would be imposed immediately after the outbreak of hostilities.[136]

Mackie was well aware of the enormous task that would be imposed on the Department of Agriculture. He strongly believed that he and the department had a great responsibility to support the war effort, and he sought an early reorganization of the department in order to meet the demands of war. The first step was to prepare a list of "precedence" during the war and for the future work of the department in Nigeria.[137] This list was necessary to avoid confusion and to prevent wasting time in converting the department's peacetime role to meet wartime goals.[138] Part of the organization Mackie proposed included a restructuring of personnel and the agricultural stations throughout the country and grouping the country into crop zones to maximize production and the use of manpower, and to guarantee prices for farmers.[139] Most of the northern provinces concentrated on the production of groundnuts, while the eastern and western provinces focused on the production of palm oil and kernels, respectively. A significant effort was also to be made in developing new areas for groundnut production in Niger, Ilorin, and Kabba Provinces and the Oyo Division. Mackie recommended that Adamawa, Bauchi, Plateau, southern Zaria, and northeastern Niger, or what he described as "pagan districts," should be part of all wartime agriculture production drives. According to him, these areas "should have important possibilities, if not for export crops, then for food crops" to meet Nigeria's needs.[140] With their abundant population and high standard of farming, Mackie wanted to tap their productive capacity, despite the considerable risk involved in trying to persuade farmers to grow crops for export.

The Nigerian staff was expected to play a crucial role, and plans were made to provide more training, especially because the department lacked adequately trained indigenous personnel.[141] In addition, the government viewed a guaranteed buying price and higher prices for agricultural goods as an incentive for increased production. Mackie noted that the government should be prepared to subsidize various export crops in times of necessity.[142]

It is understood that steps are being taken by the British Government to prevent profiteering in the U.K., it is therefore most unlikely that prices in Nigeria will soar to the heights reached during the last war; but on this account guaranteed prices

[136] Ibid.
[137] RH, Mss Afr. s. 823(1), Captain J. R. Mackie, Papers on Nigerian Agriculture, 1938–1945.
[138] Ibid.   [139] Ibid.   [140] Ibid.   [141] Ibid.   [142] Ibid.

**Your Groundnuts help to FEED Fighting Forces**

*Thank you Nigeria!*

Figure 3.3  Poster encouraging export production in Nigeria
(IWM PST 15390)

become all the more necessary if production is to be increased and maintained in excess of the highest point yet reached and in the event of price levels not exceeding those paid during record years.[143]

This subsidy considered the closure of German and Italian markets to Nigeria exports.[144]

The drive for West African colonies to produce essential goods increased after 1942, when Japan overran the Far East. Nigeria played an essential role in meeting demands for palm oil, palm kernels, groundnuts, and rubber.[145] While traditional Nigerian exports such as palm oil, palm kernels, and rubber continued to figure importantly in the war, Nigeria was encouraged to develop other foodstuffs, minerals, and products, including timber. Perhaps the most important items of export during the war were vegetable oil products, consisting

---

[143] Ibid.

[144] The department's proposal was based on the expected demands for Nigerian export by the United Kingdom, its allies, the neighboring British colonies, and French colonies.

[145] Nigeria, *Annual Report of the Agricultural Department, 1939–1940.*

Map 3.1  Products of Nigeria
(Source: Nigeria, *A Colony's Effort*, 1939)

of palm oil from the south and groundnut oil from the more arid
northern region.[146] Besides its traditional prewar use as a lubricant,
palm oil became essential for the production of munitions and explosives. A considerable part of palm oil was used in the production of
glycerin, which was used in making explosives. Palm kernel oil was also
in great demand for the production of animal feed. In sum, the military
demands for Nigerian palm produce, colonial officials reported, "are
heavy and likely to increase."[147] However, production in these goods
also came from plantations in Cameroon.[148] The twenty-one plantations
located in Cameroon, totaling 239,814 acres and employing 14,975
laborers, drew most of their labor from eastern Nigeria. Overall, the
export value of principal agricultural products from Nigeria, especially
palm produce, increased. For example, the export value of palm kernels
increased from £1,500,000 in 1940 to £3,117,000 in 1943, while the

---

[146] NAE, CALPROF, 3/1/2365, Home Chat, no. 1.    [147] Ibid.

[148] Cameroon had become a League of Nations mandate after Germany lost the First
World War. The Cameroon plantations were under the management of the Custodian
of Enemy Property. See Nigeria, *Annual Report of the Department of Labour, Nigeria, for
the Year 1942*, 3.

export value of palm oil increased from £1,009 in 1940 to £1,587 in 1943.[149]

Forestry officers stationed throughout the country campaigned for an increase in the production of rubber. Rubber, like other export crops, was bought by purchasing firms at fixed prices and on an agreed commission.[150] The production drive for groundnuts and beniseed was also intensified. Individuals used groundnut oil in many guises, such as salad oil, sardine oil, lubricant, illuminant, and margarine. Its residue was also used in the production of animal feed. The large quantity of groundnut that Germany stocked before the war also demonstrates its importance during wartime.[151] Production accelerated with significant resources in land and labor devoted to its cultivation during the war.

Despite considerable effort by the colonial government and Nigerian farmers to boost export production, not all previous export crops were needed in large quantities during the war. One such crop was cocoa. Yet the government encouraged its production.[152] However, a proportion of what was produced was destroyed by the Nigeria Supply Board to sustain the interest of local farmers. Government officials argued that offering an entirely inadequate price to the farmer would force him to "neglect his trees and so encourage disease" or "cut them down so as to grow annual crops in their place."[153] This would ruin cocoa farmers and cocoa production in Nigeria at the end of the war. The failure of the cocoa industry would have had unpalatable political implications, hence the government's desire to keep cocoa production alive.[154]

On the other hand, rubber had special strategic importance to the Allies, and the government made every possible effort to stimulate its production.[155] Although rubber had been produced from the beginning of the twentieth century, particularly in western Nigeria, its production and export remained insignificant and sporadic. In fact, Africa accounted for about 1 percent of the world's rubber in 1939.[156] The breakout of the Second World War and the fall of the Far Eastern territories of Malaya and the East Indies increased the importance of African rubber. The

---

[149] Helleiner, *Peasant Agriculture*, 500–501.
[150] *Memorandum on the Organisation and Control of War Time Trade and Production*, 9.
[151] Nigeria, *A Colony's Effort*, 7.
[152] Cocoa is a very valuable crop even in peace times and grown over a large area in the western provinces.
[153] NAE, CALPROF, 3/1/2365, Home Chat, no. 5.      [154] Ibid.
[155] NAE, CALPROF, 3/1/2365, Home Chat, no. 1.
[156] William G. Clarence-Smith, "Africa's 'Battle for Rubber' in the Second World War," in *Africa and World War II*, ed. Judith A. Byfield, Carolyn A. Brown, Timothy Parsons, and Ahmad Alawad Sikaing (New York: Cambridge University Press, 2015), 166–182, at 166. On the Nigerian rubber industry during the war, see E. O. Egboh, "The Nigerian Rubber Industry, 1939–1945," *Nigerian Field* 44 (1979): 2–13.

demand for motor tires and tubes significantly increased the strategic importance of Nigerian rubber. The search for wild rubber in the Yoruba country now extended to the delta regions of Nigeria as well as Cameroon, where there were some organized rubber plantations. The supply of these items was very low by 1942. Colonial sources noted that the supply position by May 1942, especially for commercial vehicles, was "extremely unsatisfactory and more and more lorries are becoming immobilized."[157] This situation was further complicated by the fact that many new vehicles being imported into this country in this period were arriving without tires. Transportation was limited to essential services in order to conserve the dwindling stock of tires.[158] This made it imperative to increase rubber production and the recycling of used tires and tubes. Lord Swinton wrote in 1943 that the search for more rubber became a "sort of treasure hunt by natives and their families over the thousands of miles for the wild rubber trees, but with the willing assistance of the chief, bigger yields were secured."[159] Although the quantities produced could not compare with production in the Far Eastern territories, Nigeria's rubber nonetheless became vital to the British war effort. With the support of chiefs, rubber production improved, with about 6,000 tons of rubber produced in Nigeria in 1943.

Scavenging for rubber also provided additional materials for recycling. The United African Company collected all scrap rubber in return for "out-of-pocket expenses only" before shipment to the Rubber Control in the United Kingdom.[160] The rubber controller in the United Kingdom proclaimed that "every scrap of rubber is wanted."[161] An official circular asking everyone to take part in the campaign for collection in Nigeria was issued in June 1942. All tires fit for retreading were to be purchased by the government and sold under permit to the public after retreading. This was necessary in order to conserve all material possible under the prevailing circumstances.[162]

Timber was another resource required in large quantities during the war. Nigeria's forest belt, which was parallel to the sea, acted as a timber reservoir to fuel construction demands during the war. Considerable and varied building programs undertaken during the war relied on supplies from Nigeria.[163] Commenting on the centrality of Nigerian timber to the war effort, a Nigerian government report noted that it "is difficult to know

---

[157] NAE, CALPROF, 3/1/2365, Home Chat, no. 4.
[158] NAE, CALPROF, 3/1/2365, Home Chat, no. 5.
[159] "Lord Swinton on West Africa's War Effort."
[160] *Memorandum on the Organisation and Control of War Time Trade and Production*, 10.
[161] Ibid.    [162] NAE, CALPROF, 3/1/2365, Home Chat, no. 2.
[163] NAE, CALPROF, 3/1/2365, Home Chat, no. 1.

what the country would have done, also what the fighting Services would have done, without this supply and without the means available for turning the raw timber into finished products."[164] Dwelling houses, offices, stores, and hospitals in Britain were built from Nigerian timber. In addition, a large export of timber and frame houses ready for erection grew from Nigeria to other West African colonies. In *A Colony's Effort*, the Nigerian government claimed:

A great quantity of timber was also used in the construction of furniture and fittings for these buildings, not to mention bridge-building and the timber required for shuttering concrete and for railway sleepers. There were also many minor but useful things made from timber: for example, 75,000 tent pegs were made and shipped within four days of an order being received; and many thousands of sets of draughtsman and boards were made for the Services.[165]

A pilot sawmill was set up at Aponum in Ondo Province to utilize timber that would otherwise be wasted. The products were mainly used for a variety of local purposes, including the production of shingles for roofing in place of corrugated iron and "boards for making boxes and simple furniture."[166] The number of Nigerian laborers employed in the existing sawmills in Lagos and Sapele increased to meet the new demand. Over the period, research was conducted by the government in the northern parts of Nigeria and even in comparatively arid areas for trees that could be used for building purposes and for rougher kinds of furniture.[167]

In tandem with the reorganization of agriculture and trade, the government introduced measures expected to have long-term financial implications for both the local population and Britain. For example, a proposal was made by the Department of Agriculture for the production of vegetables. The goal was to obtain bean, cabbage, cauliflower, tomato, lettuce, cucumber, radish, carrot, turnip, and beetroot seeds from Europe to support local production. G. Bryce, director of agriculture in Ibadan, argued that the increased production of vegetables and the expansion of market gardening "will be of permanent and lasting benefit" to Africans.[168] Growing perishable vegetables at or near railway stations or near ports not only made quick delivery of fresh goods to consuming areas possible, but also made vegetables available to parts of the country unable to grow them successfully.[169] To boost the local supply of meat, the government proposed the expansion of production at Moor Plantation,

---

[164] Nigeria, *A Colony's Effort*, 11.      [165] Ibid.      [166] Ibid., 12.      [167] Ibid., 11.
[168] G. Bryce, Director of Agriculture, Ibadan, to Assistant Director of Agriculture, Northern Provinces, Zaria, September 13, 1939, Notes on the Organization of Vegetable Production.
[169] Ibid.

Ibadan, and Ilorin Stock Farm. Other proposals included a cattle multiplication farm project, the purchase of 1,000 heads of N'dama cattle, and the establishment of a poultry farm in Nigeria's Western Province.[170]

## Wartime Food Production Pressures, Policies, and Responses

The challenge confronting Britain in relation to wartime food production was enormous. Once again, Nigeria and its farmers were expected to prepare to meet Britain's foodstuff needs. The war generated interest among every class in Nigeria. A *West African Pilot* editorial of February 12, 1942, reflected the popular sentiment among Africans at the time: "We are in the midst of the most destructive war the world has yet seen and it is the duty of every citizen of this country, as it is of every liberty-loving soul in every part of the world, to bear the greatest sacrifice ungrudgingly and contribute his maximum in every way possible, little or great to bring the success of the Allied forces nearer."[171] By July 1942, the newspaper noted that Nigerian farmers and producers had made splendid responses to such requests, despite what the paper projected to be the impending "menace of food difficulties looming in the horizon."[172]

Preparations to increase food production started even before the war began in 1939. The critical importance of local food production was reflected in the shift in the policy of the Department of Agriculture after 1939.[173] The restructuring included the establishment of a marketing department in November 1939 and the appointment of Mr. E. McL. Watson as marketing officer. The marketing department studied the internal trade patterns of Nigeria and developed strategies to reduce dependency on the importation of food items by increasing internal production. Nigeria, as a self-sustaining region, was expected to be an important source of foodstuff for West African colonies.[174] Understanding the food requirements of other West African colonies became an essential part of planning for war. In a dispatch to Nigeria's colonial administration, the secretary of state for the colonies urged it to "exert every possible effort to obtain maximum production of export crops."[175] The emphasis on foodstuffs was essential because the war condition allowed for the potential to market "the surplus in other West

---

[170] RH, Mss Afr. s. 823(1), Captain J. R. Mackie, Papers on Nigerian Agriculture, 1938–1945.
[171] *West African Pilot*, February 12, 1942.    [172] *West African Pilot*, July 29, 1942.
[173] NAE, 499, EKETDIST, 1/2/50, "Food Production in Nigeria, 1935–1951," 7.
[174] Nigeria, *Annual Report of the Agricultural Department, 1939–1940*, 3–4.
[175] NAE, 499, EKETDIST, 1/2/50, "Food Production in Nigeria, 1935–1951," 7.

Table 3.1 *Rice imports into Nigeria, 1936–1940*

| Year | Imports (Tons) |
|------|----------------|
| 1936 | 14,942 |
| 1937 | 13,627 |
| 1938 | 9,327 |
| 1939 | 7,264 |
| 1940 | 2,715 |
| 1941 | – |

*Source:* NAK: Minagric I/I 3700, vol. II, Food Production Reports, 1941

African colonies ... making the mining industry of the Gold Coast and Sierra Leone a source of wealth to the Nigerian peasant farmer."[176] Essentially, the wartime food production policy was driven by a desire to compensate for shortfalls in imports and its potential to generate income for the Nigerian farmer.

From 1940, the Department of Agriculture began to concentrate on the production of food staples.[177] Funds previously allocated for the development of export products such as palm produce were diverted to the food production project and propaganda.[178] The production of rice, which was increasingly imported from abroad before the war, received significant attention under this scheme. As Table 3.1 reveals, rice importation had virtually ceased by 1941, after reaching a peak of 14,900 tons per year in 1936.[179] Rice production received a boost in Azumini in the Eastern Region, where swamp rice was grown.[180] However, rice production was not successful in all areas. In Onitsha Province, a combination of drought and poor management reduced yields to only 2,000 for the 500 tons of rice planted in 1943.[181] The attempt to produce other food crops such as potatoes and certain vegetables arose due to the disruption of imports during the war.[182] These types of foodstuff catered to the needs of European residents and the army.

---

[176] Nigeria, *Annual Report of the Agricultural Department, 1939–1940.*
[177] NAE, EKETDIST, 1/2/50, File No. 499, "Food Production" Memo: Agricultural Officer Abak to D. O. Calabar, July 12, 1940.
[178] Ibid.    [179] Ibid.
[180] Esse, "The Second World War and Resource Management in Eastern Nigeria," 157–158.
[181] NAE, OP, 1865, vol. VI, ONDIST, 42/1/1264, "Annual Report, Onitsha Province, 1943," 65.
[182] These imports included French beans, cabbage, cauliflower, tomatoes, lettuce, cucumbers, carrots, and beetroots.

The attempt to produce more food locally did not achieve the goal of stabilizing production and prices for some essential foodstuffs and commodities. In 1940, for example, the United Africa Company (UAC) purchased a consignment of chili peppers in Niger Province to export. Its competition with local users caused such a steep rise in prices that farmers began abandoning cotton cultivation in favor of chili peppers. The price of chili peppers before the UAC commenced buying the item was six shillings and four pennies per cwt in January 1940, but the price rapidly rose to fourteen shillings and six pennies per cwt after the company began to make purchases.[183] The price of other staples such as garri also increased rapidly. The price of a ninety-pound bag of garri rose from four shillings at the beginning of July 1943 to seven shillings by the end of the month.[184] This increased demand for foodstuffs drew many farmers away from the production of export crops. British ethnographer J. S. Harris, who studies aspects of the economic life of the Igbo in eastern Nigeria, reports that Ozuitem men who were primarily yam growers and only occasionally palm oil and palm kernel producers, laborers, or traders are influenced by the changing nature of cash crops, particularly palm produce, in making decisions about what economic activity to engage in.[185]

When the European controlled "factories" pay a high market price, more men in Ozuitem and surrounding areas are attracted to the manufacture of palm produce, and their partial or complete withdrawal from the sphere of farming makes them dependent upon the yam growers, to whom they pay high prices for yams. With the fall in price of palm produce which, when it goes low enough, practically prohibits native production of palm-oil for sale, these men retire to their own farms, so that the yam yield is greatly increased and in the face of a decreasing demand the price of yams decline.[186]

This claim reveals how closely individuals made rational economic decisions based on market forces. These trends continued during the war as the demand for foodstuffs pushed prices higher.

Colonial food policies were shaped by local conditions and capabilities. In the Northern Regions, significant effort was channeled toward the production of several food items, but with a substantial focus on grains. The program in the north commenced in 1940, following the directives of the secretary of state for the colonies that all colonial administrations

---

[183] Nigeria, *Annual Report of the Agricultural Department, 1939–1940*, 44–45.
[184] NAE, ABADIST, 14/1/873, File No. 1646, "Garri Control," District Officer, Aba to Secretary, Northern Provinces, July 29, 1943.
[185] J. S. Harris, "Some Aspects of the Economics of Sixteen Ibo Individuals," *Africa* 14, no. 6 (April 1944): 302–355, at 302.
[186] Ibid., 303.

"Study the Storage of Foodstuffs in the Colonial Empire," in order to "adopt some measures of food storage in the various states."[187] Yet there were two contradictory developments on the agrarian scene in northern Nigeria during the Second World War: food requisitioning by the colonial state and the deprivation faced by food producers as well as the implementation of "import-substitution agriculture" programs during the war years, whose success exposed the neglect of food production in prewar agricultural policies. Zuwaqhu Kalli-Abungwon Bonat has noted the conflicting views expressed by colonial officials, who imposed hegemony on the peasantry and of the peasants themselves in the northern provinces. These views reveal the class and social divisions that characterized northern Nigeria societies and were reinforced by colonial policies. The responses by the emirs were different from those of the agricultural officers regarding food reserves and food deficits. While officials characterized some areas in the regions as food-reserve deficient regions, some local leaders drew from existing stereotypes and divisions to explain the availability or otherwise of food reserves. According to the emir of Zaria, "Hausa areas preserved grains, while the non-Muslim areas were said to squander their grains in beer and did not keep reserves."[188] This implied that the "reserves" in the Hausa areas could be taken to meet war requisitions, while the grains "'squandered' by the beer-drinking 'pagans' could also be taken away." Both the emirs of Katsina and Daura claimed that "peasants held stocks of food which lasted them four to five months after harvest, which the same peasants then off-loaded on to the market when there was no danger to the new crops."[189] Interestingly, while the British agricultural officers reported no surplus grains, provincial emirs reported surpluses, including that squandered on frivolous pursuits.[190]

This set the stage for massive food requisitioning by the colonial government, despite the destitute conditions of the farmers and their inability to support their own subsistence.[191] Government officials sought to meet the need for grains and other products by monitoring production and imposing production quotas and artificially low prices and requisitions. The northern provinces were divided into "requisition areas" to satisfy specific targeted

[187] NAK, Minagric I/I 3700, vol. II, Food Production General, Secretary of State's circular dated January 4, 1940. Cited in Zuwaqhu Kalli-Abungwon Bonat, "The Colonial Phase of the Underdevelopment of Zaria Province, 1902–1945" (Unpublished MA thesis, Ahmadu Bello University, Zaria, Nigeria, July 1985), 775.

[188] Cited in Bonat, "The Colonial Phase of the Underdevelopment," 775.

[189] NAK, Minagric I/I 31657/S.3, Economic Organization of Grain Production in War Time. For more on the subject, see Bonat, "The Colonial Phase of the Underdevelopment," 775.

[190] Bonat, "The Colonial Phase of the Underdevelopment," 777–778. [191] Ibid., 775.

areas of need.[192] Significant quantities of local food production were directed toward feeding the army, to the detriment of the local population. Food supply quotas were allocated to various provinces in the Northern and Middle Belt Regions to meet colonial demands. Food supply for the mines came from Plateau Province, western Bauchi Province, northeastern Zaria Province, southeastern Kano Province, Benue Province, and eastern Niger Province. Military food supplies came from Zaria Province (west of Dutsen Wai and Southern Districts), southern Katsina Province, southeastern Sokoto, southwestern Kano Province, western Niger Province, and Adamawa Province.[193] Due to persistent shortages of corn, northwest Sokoto, northern Katsina, Daura Emirate, northern Kano Province, Gumel and Hadejia Emirates, and north and northeast Borno Province were exempt from the supply of guinea corn for the army and mines.

It is hard not to be overcome with disbelief at the rate by which local producers were deprived. The grain requisitions from northern Nigeria between May and September 1942 were 4,295 tons, of which 2,269 tons were for the military.[194] From 1943 to 1944, the Middle Belt area was asked to collect 6,800 tons of guinea corn and millet.[195] An agricultural officer observed that in the Northern Region, "most of the milk, cream, meat, pork and potatoes produced in the area went to feed troops stationed in Zaria."[196] Local producers received 90 to 100 shillings per ton of grain delivered for the military, and approved commercial firms, the UAC, and John Holt, who then delivered the same at the cost of £4 per ton to the military authorities.[197] Government takeover of foodstuffs was successful. Grain delivery in the northern provinces increased dramatically, from 130 tons in the last three months of 1941 to 843 tons in the first three months of 1942.[198] Such dramatic increase in the quantity of grain requisitioned by the authorities could only but generate food crisis for the local population.[199] A total of 843 tons was delivered in the period between January and March 1942, compared to 130 tons in October to December 1941.

[192] NAK, Minagric I/I 4500, vol. II, Guinea Corn, General, circular dated February 6, 1942.
[193] Bonat, "The Colonial Phase of the Underdevelopment," 784.
[194] The figure does not include Kano and Ilorin Provinces. NAK: Minagric I/I 4500, vol. II, Guinea Corn General. Bonat, "The Colonial Phase of the Underdevelopment," 785.
[195] The areas comprised Oyo, Ilorin, Kabba, Benue, and Nigeria.
[196] NAK, Minagric I/I 3700, vol. III: Food Production Report, NPs, November 1, 1941. Cited in Bonat, "The Colonial Phase of the Underdevelopment."
[197] NAK, Minagric I/I 3701, vol. II, Report for January–March Quarter, 1942.
[198] Data are based on food production estimates in Bauchi, Borno, Katsina, Sokoto, and Zaria Provinces for 1941. Bonat, "The Colonial Phase of the Underdevelopment," 782.
[199] Ibid., 782.

Nevertheless, the war had some positive effects on the internal market for food crops. The market for food items created an incentive for farmers to increase production. Between June 1943 and May 1944, for example, a total of 5,825 tons of garri was exported from the Eastern Region to northern Nigeria towns.[200] The increase in the quantity of food items exported to the north created opportunities for farmers in the east to increase production, and consequently their incomes. But at the same time, exports led to inflation in the exporting regions of eastern Nigeria. As is illustrated in Chapter 4, the government was forced to regulate the internal trade of foodstuff by limiting the quantity that traders could export and by implementing controlled prices for garri and other food items.[201]

Wartime policies acutely frustrated consumer spending. A significant reduction in imports occurred in 1942 due to the War Production Board's policy of stopping or limiting the production of civilian goods. As a result, the sale of durable goods at retail dropped 33 percent from 1941 to 1942 and an additional 50 percent from 1942 to 1943.[202] Much of this course of action was due to the need to save shipping space. This policy resulted in the development of a whole range of secondary industries locally as well as in Britain. More food had to be produced locally, and new industries arose for the production of materials that were previously imported.

The demands for agricultural and forest products during the war represented a new phase in the British extraction of resources. The scale increased more than ever before. The demand for resources moreover had implications for the local environment. More than any other period in African history, the European demand for agricultural products led to massive deforestation and greater intensification of land use. Little attention, however, was given to the environmental implications of the demand for African timber and other resources. The excessive demands of agricultural and other forest products during the war only exacerbated a process that was rapidly transforming the environment at the beginning of the twentieth century.

## Production of Minerals

Nigeria's mineral resources such as tin, manganese, chrome, and iron ore became tremendously important to the war effort. The loss of Britain's

---

[200] See NAE, File No. 1646, vol. IV, ABADIST 14/1/875, "Garri Control" District Traffic Superintendent, Port Harcourt to the Local Authority, Aba, July 15, 1944. About 3,677 tons was railed from the Aba station. The other stations were Ogwe (988 tons), Omoba (280 tons), Nbawsi (222 tons), Umuahia (492 tons), and Uzuakoli (166 tons).

[201] See Allister E. Hinds, "Government Policy and the Nigerian Palm Oil Export Industry, 1939–49," *Journal of African History* 38 (1997): 459–478.

[202] "Lord Swinton on West Africa's War Effort."

Southeast Asian market put more pressure on Nigeria for mineral resources. Indeed, the loss of Malaysia early in 1942 "brought Nigeria into prominence as an alternative source of essential mineral especially of tin."[203] While the demand for tin, in particular, had been previously inconsistent, this geopolitical shift made a tremendous demand on the mining community.

The development of the tin mining industry in Nigeria dates back to the first decade of the twentieth century in the Jos area of central Nigeria. By 1929, the mines around Jos were producing one-tenth of the world's supply of tin. Machinery was extremely difficult to obtain and had to be supplemented by manual labor on an "unprecedented scale."[204] The mines relied on the combined effort of the government, chiefs, and head-men of the districts in the northern provinces to provide the requisite new labor force. Native authorities were required to supply the mines monthly labor quotas, especially during the peak period between 1920 and 1944.[205]

Demand for mine laborers increased dramatically at the outbreak of the Second World War. At the beginning of the war, a colonial report noted that many miners enlisted in the field companies of Royal Engineers, which formed as part of the Nigerian regiment.[206] Normal mining labor consisted of about 30,000 Africans, some from the habitual laborer class who came and went as they wished, others from local villages who wanted "money for taxes and household purposes."[207] A supplementary 3,000 laborers were demanded from all over the country.[208] The additional labor demanded in the mines meant significant reorganization of the arrangements to deal with the needs in transportation, camps, and food to feed laborers from different parts of the country with different dietary habits. The increased demand for food meant special calls on areas far afield that were already supplying generous quantities of food for the armed forces.[209]

The expansion of the tin mining operation in Nigeria required an additional labor force of about 45,000 men.[210] Army recruitment and a push for production of other essential goods had already depleted the available labor force around the mining communities. In February 1942, the government attempted to import 10,000 conscripts under the Nigeria Defence (Compulsory National Service) (Essential Mines Northern Provinces) Regulation No. 23 of 1942 from other provinces in northern

---

[203] Nigeria, *Annual Report of the Department of Labour, Nigeria, for the Year 1942*, 2.
[204] Nigeria, *A Colony's Effort*, 9.
[205] Akpen, "Forced Labor in Jos Tin Mines." See Bonat, "The Colonial Phase of the Underdevelopment."
[206] Nigeria, *A Colony's Effort*, 8.    [207] Ibid., 9.    [208] Ibid., 5.    [209] Ibid., 9.
[210] Ibid., 5.

Table 3.2 *Distribution of laborers by province*[213]

| Province | 1941 (Year) | 1942 (Year) | Total (Men) | Percentage increase |
|----------|-------------|-------------|-------------|---------------------|
| Bauchi   | 2,500       | 3,500       | 6,000       | 14%                 |
| Benue    | 7,000       | 8,000       | 15,000      | 14%                 |
| Borno    | 1,500       | 3,000       | 4,500       | 100%                |
| Kano     | 2,000       | 2,500       | 4,500       | 25%                 |
| Katsina  | 1,650       | 2,000       | 3,650       | 21%                 |
| Niger    | 1,000       | 1,500       | 2,500       | 50%                 |
| Plateau  | 2,500       | 3,000       | 5,500       | 20%                 |
| Sokoto   | 2,250       | 3,500       | 5,750       | 55%                 |
| Zaria    | 2,250       | 4,000       | 6,250       | 77%                 |
| Total    | 22,650      | 31,000      | 53,650      | 36%                 |

*Source:* K. S. Agber, "European Commercial Enterprise and Underdevelopment in Tivland" (Unpublished PhD dissertation, University of Jos, 1994), 169

Nigeria. A government memo on the labor question impressed the need for some 70,000 casual laborers in the mines.[211] Wartime labor needs forced the British to implement a more coercive system that generated a significant increase in local labor for the mines, as Table 3.2 reveals. Quotas were allocated to the nine provinces in the Northern Region, with Benue Province providing the highest quota of 7,000 men in 1941 and 8,000 men in 1942.[212]

By the end of 1942, the labor force in the mines had reached 70,800 men, 14,000 of whom were compulsorily recruited from other provinces. About 15,000 volunteer laborers came from within Plateau Province, where the mines were located, to supplement 42,000 permanent employees from mining companies.[214]

Production increased significantly to meet wartime needs as new laborers settled down to work. However, the government was still not meeting its need in terms of tin production in 1942. The revised estimate of 16,000 to 17,000 tons in tin production for 1942 was less than the desired figure of 20,000 tons.[215] This was blamed largely on the lack of labor, which correlated to an inadequate food supply.[216] It was one thing to recruit laborers, but another to keep them in the mines. Many of the enlisted men would not stay in the mines for a variety of reasons. The location of the mines on a plateau varying in height from 3,500 to 4,500

[211] K. S. Agber, "European Commercial Enterprise and Underdevelopment in Tivland" (Unpublished PhD dissertation, University of Jos, 1994), 68.
[212] Ibid., 169.   [213] Adopted from ibid., 169.
[214] Nigeria, *Annual Report of the Department of Labour, Nigeria, for the Year 1942*, 1.
[215] NAE, CALPROF, 3/1/2365, Home Chat, no. 4.   [216] Ibid.

feet above sea level posed additional problems. The laborers could not engage in any food production due to the elevation. Most of the food for the mines had to be imported from elsewhere. Furthermore, many men fell sick due to the grueling nature of mine work. Lacking sufficient trained medical staff and equipment as well as the capacity to take on the additional burden of the large number of new recruits, the mines fell short in both attracting and retaining laborers.[217] Labor conditions were also poor. According to the 1942 labor report, by the end of July, only 515 of these men were still at work due to the authorities' poor "organization for their welfare."[218] Even though laborers were expected to work for four months with the possibility of renewing their contracts for up to two years, they were not allowed to bring their families to the mines. The obvious psychological impacts from the policy of separating families made the mines a less attractive condition for many workers. Indeed, many male heads of household only embarked on labor migration as a result of the outbreak of the war. In the Middle Belt of Nigeria, particularly among the Tiv, Philip Akpen has argued, the process of labor recruitment had an emotional and psychological impact on women because of the "aggression to which their men were exposed." Oral accounts collected among the Tiv describe the brutality of the Native Authority Police who served under the British and who were described as instruments of torture and violence during the recruitment process.[219] Sometimes a father was recruited along with his sons, forcing women to assume new roles in their respective families. These numerous adverse conditions limited the prospects of mining.

Labor demands and forced recruitment revealed a dark side of British wartime policies. An estimated workforce of 1,800 "unwilling laborers were conscripted into the tin mines of Jos under appalling conditions and at low wages."[220] Labor recruits endured even more hardship, trekking "like slaves to . . . Makurdi because of hunger and other brutalities on the way as well as snake bites and attacks by the crocodiles."[221] Others died crossing rivers when canoes capsized. Conditions at the tin mines in Jos were described as unbearable because those who finally arrived were severely affected by cold weather conditions. Most of the recruits had come from warmer climates. In July 1942, for example, thirty-two

[217] Nigeria, *Annual Report of the Department of Labour, Nigeria, for the Year 1942*, 2.
[218] Ibid.
[219] Akpen, "Forced Labor in Jos Tin Mines." Akpen conducted a group interview with some elderly women in Gboko Town, Benue State, on June 17, 2006.
[220] Njoku, "Nigeria: World War II."
[221] William M. Freund, *Capital and Labor in the Nigerian Tin Mines* (London: Longman, 1981), 138.

laborers, mostly Tiv, died of pneumonia.[222] Diseases such as dysentery, diarrhea, jaundice, smallpox, and bronchitis, along with accidents, caused many deaths. Overcrowding, poor diet, and inadequate medical facilities contributed to the deplorable conditions these miners faced. Between October 1942 and December 1943, about 714 of these forced laborers died in the tin mines. About 26 percent of these were Tiv in the Middle Belt.[223] The difficulty of obtaining imported food items had forced the government to abandon the policy of providing rations to the laborers. Norwegian stock fish, which had formed an important staple and a source of protein, was also no longer obtainable.

The failure of this early experiment in labor recruitment led to the appointment of J. J. Emberton, a senior resident, as administrative director of minerals production. Emberton received wide powers to recruit the necessary labor, fix wage rates, and provide for the welfare of laborers during the four-month period when their services were required at the mines. Mr. A. D. Storke, the general manager of the Rhodesian Consolidated Selected Trust, was called upon to visit Jos Plateau and inspect the operations of all mining companies to recommend how tin production could be improved.[224] The government's desire to reorganize the mining sector led to the appointment of two administrative officers, R. M. Frost and C. W. Miehie, as welfare agents.[225] These appointees were further charged with launching propaganda work in Plateau Province to "stimulate the flow of voluntary labour."[226]

The Colliery at Enugu in eastern Nigeria played a central role in Nigeria's war effort due to the huge increase in railway traffic to the region. The discovery of coal in 1909 near Enugu spurred important economic and social development in the region, and Nigeria at large, before the war began. The development of Enugu as a city and the headquarters of the Eastern Region owes much to the discovery of coal in the area. Although the coal found was not of a very high quality, it adequately supported local industrial development in the railway and the maritime sectors. Average output was about 300,000 tons per year.[227] Like other mining towns, Enugu experienced a wartime boom due to the demand for coal and also witnessed an increase in labor migration from outside the surrounding areas as a direct result of this. A greater tonnage of coal was produced in Enugu than any other metal in this period. The Enugu Colliery supplied coal for the railway and all public undertakings, in addition to meeting the needs of surrounding territories. By 1942, the

---

[222] Ibid.    [223] Ibid., 147.    [224] NAE, CALPROF, 3/1/2365, Home Chat, no. 4.
[225] Nigeria, *Annual Report of the Department of Labour, Nigeria, for the Year 1942*, 2.
[226] Ibid., 1.    [227] Nigeria, *A Colony's Effort*, 11.

daily paid labor force at the Enugu mines averaged 3,350 men, 1,566 of whom were engaged in the peak of the war in 1942. Output was about 34,000 tons a month.[228] The revenue from coal for 1941–1942 surpassed government estimates by 33,000 pounds and 39,819 pounds, respectively.[229]

The colonial solution to the demands of the war led to some reforms in the mines. The rate of pay increased in July 1942, when the government awarded the "cost of living allowance" to all of its employees.[230] For daily paid workers, the allowance was calculated on the basis of the twenty-six working days in a month. There was also a plan to introduce a housing scheme for the workers from money provided under the Colonial Development and Welfare Fund. By the end of 1942, about a third of the 415 model houses planned under the scheme had been constructed. New welfare officers were also appointed at the Colliery and at the Nigerian Railway in Lagos. The latter focused on the problem of juvenile unemployment and delinquency in Lagos.[231]

Other minerals mined at Jos, in central Nigeria, such as columbite and wolfram, became essential in steel manufacture. Columbite was sent to the United States to make high-grade steel, and the United Kingdom and the United States required wolfram at the outbreak of the war chiefly for the production of high-speed steels and tipping armor-piercing shells. This became more urgent after the Allies lost supplies from China and Burma. Therefore, a Wolfram Production Board was set up in Nigeria to stimulate production. British officer Lieutenant Colonel John Dent-Young was seconded from the army and sent to South Africa to secure supplies of machinery and engage the necessary staff.[232] Dent-Young began his mining career as a surveyor with Northern Nigeria (Bauchi) Tin Mines Ltd. in April 1912 and later fought in the Cameroons (East Africa with the 1st Battalion, Queen's Own Nigeria Regiment) during the First World War. The board was responsible for prospecting, mining, and directing existing producers.[233] Mica, which was used in the production of electrical and other industrial components, was also badly needed, so several known sources of mica in Nigeria were investigated in 1942. In fact, to highlight the urgency, the government

---

[228] Nigeria, *Annual Report of the Department of Labour, for the Year 1942*, 3.
[229] Nigeria, *Annual Report on Finance and Account for the Year 1942/43* (Lagos: Government Printer, 1944), 3.
[230] Ibid.    [231] Ibid., 4.
[232] NAE, CALPROF, 3/1/2365, Home Chat, no. 2. See also Nigeria, *The Nigerian War Relief Fund: Its Aims and Achievements* (Lagos: Government Printer, 1943).
[233] NAE, CALPROF, 3/1/2365, Home Chat, no. 2.

requested anyone with knowledge of alternative mica deposits to inform the Nigeria Supply Board of its whereabouts for extraction.[234]

## Financial Contribution

On September 16, the governor of Nigeria, Sir Bernard Bourdillon, invited seventy influential figures in Nigeria to a meeting in the Government House in Lagos. The invitees represented a cross-section of communities and organizations throughout the country. The meeting was called to explore the ways the Nigerian population would assist British and other Allied victims of the war.[235] The collective devotion of Nigerians of all classes is reflected in the enthusiasm with which they embraced the governor's appeal and the huge sums of money they raised that supported the British population. On June 15, 1940, the *Nigerian Daily Times* inaugurated the Nigeria War Relief Fund.[236] The fund operated until January 28, 1946. Its objective was to raise money for the purchase of a tank or an airplane to donate to the British Army. Nigerians were encouraged to raise £50,000 by the end of the first year. With its joint secretariat located in the Department of Labour in Lagos, the Nigerian War Relief Fund embarked on an aggressive fundraising campaign throughout the colony. It targeted every group that had the potential to contribute or raise cash to support the British war effort, from the civil service to schools and community associations to women's groups.

Through the Nigerian War Relief Fund, Nigeria played a significant role in supporting the British war effort financially. Throughout the country, the Nigerian War Relief Fund periodically held fundraising events such as Poppy Day collections, where poppies and flags were sold to raise funds. Native authorities and other government departments were required to raise funds. By the beginning of October 1940, the *Nigerian Daily Times*'s Win the War Fund had raised £32,000, with a singular donation of £7,000 from Sokoto Province.[237] Fundraising efforts in the city of Calabar included a jumbo sale and fun fair at the Roman Catholic Mission Convent, an open-air, nondenominational service collection for war relief funds, and tattoos and a concert sponsored by the RWAFF. Other fundraising activities included a baby show, a school community concert, a wrestling tournament, dances at European and

---

[234] Ibid.

[235] For more on the activities of the Nigerian War Relief Fund, see Njoku, "The Burden of Imperialism."

[236] Mordi, "The Nigeria Win the War Fund," 88.

[237] *Nigerian Daily Times*, October 3, 1940, 1.

African clubs, and an exhibition of "native" plays, cinema shows, and athletic contests. The amount of money raised at these events totaled £1,240 19s.[238] Marika Sherwood has estimated that the people of Nigeria "sent a quarter of a million pounds to the war charities," even though local wages were only 2s. (10p) per day during the period.[239] The West African colonies alone sent a "total of one and a half million pounds to the charities, and their governments granted Britain £1 million in interest-free loans."[240] Nigerian aid to the British government was "generous and extensive."[241] The emir of Katsina gave a personal donation of £5,000 for a tank, which was named after him. The colonial government in Nigeria sent £100,000 to the United Kingdom for the prosecution of the war.[242] By the end of September 1942, Nigerian monetary support for the purchase of aircraft was £124,331.[243] As tables 3.3 to 3.5 reveal, support for the war was widespread throughout the various regions of Nigeria.

Nigerian women's contribution to the fundraising effort and the war was essential. They actively raised funds under the Nigeria War Relief Fund. Violet Bourdillon, wife of the British colonial governor, became the patroness of the Ladies' Progressive Club, an organization established during the governorship of Sir Graeme Thomson to promote contact between women of all races in Nigeria. Lady Bourdillon's involvement began when she was asked for advice on how to give a dinner party, how to decorate a room, and how to "send the husband off to work in the

Table 3.3 *Contributions by the people of eastern Nigeria as of April 1941*[244]

| Province | Nigeria War Relief Fund (£sd) | Troops Comfort Fund (£sd) | Win-the-War Fund (£sd) | Total (£sd) |
|---|---|---|---|---|
| Calabar | 1,612.5.9 | 305.0.3 | 705.10.1 | 4,625.18.1 |
| Ogoja | 172.7.5 | 9.19.8 | 386.12.3 | 568.19.4 |
| Onitsha | 1,396.5.10 | 26.11.10 | 1,395.19.10 | 3,509.5.9 |
| Owerri | 1,398.0.0 | – | 4,917.0.0 | 6,315.0.0 |
| Total | 4,578.19.0 | 341.11.9 | 7,405.2.0 | 15,019.3.2 |

*Source:* Esse, "The Second World War and Resource Management in Eastern Nigeria," 123

[238] NAE, CADIST, 3/3/179, "The Nigerian War Relief Fund: Calabar Division," Savingram from District Officer, Calabar to the Resident, Calabar Province, Calabar, June 1, 1945.
[239] Sherwood, "Colonies, Colonials and World War Two."    [240] Ibid.
[241] Opata and Apeh, "In Search of Honour," 115–116.    [242] Ibid.    [243] Ibid.
[244] NAE: 18834, CSE. 1/85/9295, History of the War, 1939. Cited in Esse, "The Second World War and Resource Management in Eastern Nigeria," 123.

Table 3.4 *Monthly contributions to the war fund by emirs of the northern provinces, 1942*

| Identity of contributor (emir) | Amount contributed (normal monthly contribution) (£sd) |
|---|---|
| Abuja | 250 |
| Adamawa | 868 |
| Agaie | 100 |
| Bauchi | 868 |
| Bida | 868 |
| Biu | 300 |
| Borno | 2,500 |
| Bussa | 100 |
| Dubai | 150 |
| Fika | 550 |
| Gombe | 500 |
| Gorgoram | 350 |
| Gumel | 1,000 |
| Gwandu | 500 |
| Hadeija | 200 |
| Igbira | 9,100 |
| Ilorin | 176 |
| Jamaare | 1,100 |
| Kaiama | 100 |
| Kano | 3,500 |
| Katagum | 500 |
| Katsina | 1,934 |
| Kazaure | 434 |
| Keffi | 166 |
| Kontagora | 3,150 |
| Lafiagi | 1,134 |
| Lapai | 1,100 |
| Misau | 3,000 |
| Muri | 8,100 |
| Nassarawa | 1,100 |
| Pategi | 1,000 |
| Shendam | 1,100 |
| Sokoto | 3,000 |
| Wamba | 1,260 |
| Yauri | 276 |
| Zaria | 1,000 |

*Source:* Nigerian Daily Times, April 24, 1942, 6

Table 3.5 *List of initial contributors to the Nigeria Win-the-War Fund*[245]

| Identity of contributor | Amount contributed (£sp) |
| --- | --- |
| His Excellency | 100, 0 0 |
| J. N. Zarpas and Company | 25,10 0 |
| Administrative staff of the colony | 50, 0, 0 |
| Irvin and Bonnar | 25, 0, 0 |
| The Hon. A. Alakija and Mrs. Alakija | 21, 0, 0 |
| E. F. A. Tomlinson, Esq. | 20, 0, 0 |
| Dr. and Mrs. Ellis | 5, 0, 0 |
| A. Le Mare, Esq. | 5, 0, 0 |
| B. Papadopulos, Esq. | 1, 10, 0 |
| Total | 252, 20, 0 |

*Source:* Nigerian Daily Times, June 17, 1940, 1.

Table 3.6 *Contributions to the Nigeria Win-the-War Fund, August 1940*

| Contributor | Amount contributed (£sp) |
| --- | --- |
| Abeokuta Committee Win-the-War Fund (2nd Contribution) | 102, 3, 4 |
| Ilesha NA and People (1st Contribution) | 178, 9, 4 |
| Benue Province Europeans | 63, 19, 6 |
| Benin European Club | 50, 19, 6 |
| Port-Harcourt Club proceeds of Mrs. W. Mac Donald's Nightly Raffle | 36, 4, 0 |
| Benue Province Africans | 25, 7, 0 |
| African Staff British West African Timber Company | 18, 0, 0 |
| Nigerian Union of Teachers | 6, 5, 0 |
| Royal Hotel Dances (4th Contribution) | 8, 0, 0 |
| Alhaji Lagos | 1, 17, 6 |
| Sokoto Emirate | 5, 216, 11, 1 |
| Gwandu Emirate | 885, 7, 1 |
| Illo District | 33, 8, 1 |
| Sokoto Province | 9, 610, 3, 7 |
| Emir, Chiefs and Peoples of Zaria Province | 1, 674, 3, 7 |
| Buea, Proceeds of dance at Residency | 140, 1, 5 |
| Benue Province (including £100 from Anonymous Benue No. 2) | 125, 0, 0 |
| The Club Hitler Club (1st installment) | 100, 0, 0 |
| **Total Subscriptions to the Fund** | **18, 279, 0** |

*Source:* Nigerian Daily Times, October 31, 1940, 1; Nigerian Daily Times, September 18, 1941, 1; Nigerian Daily Times, August 27, 1940, 5.

[245] *Nigerian Daily Times*, June 17, 1940, 1.

morning to be good."[246] Henceforth she used the club's platform to raise funds for the war. From 1939 onward, the club worked to raise money for the War Relief Fund and for the education of several children.[247] The financial contributions from the northern provinces was significant, As Table 3.4 reveals, the emirs of the northern provinces provided a steady of source of fund for Britain.

Nigerians contributed to the war effort both directly from provincial budgets, and through individual subscriptions and contributions by businesses. By 1940, substantial amounts of money was being collected from these sources (see Table 3.6). It is not surprising that European women in Nigeria and their Nigerian counterparts cooperated in the humanitarian sector. The notion of imperial citizenship was reflected in their work as daughters of the empire. In November 1939, a Women's Emergency Committee consisting of European and African women was formed in Port Harcourt of Owerri Province as part of the Nigerian War Relief Fund. The committee's primary aims were to undertake work of national unity and raise money for the fund. The committee played an important role in coordinating and accepting subscriptions from all con-tributors to be added to the Nigerian War Relief Fund.[248] Particularly interesting is the intellectual consciousness of schoolchildren, whose roles in the war have yet to be seriously studied. These children contributed to the Win-the-War Funds in multiple ways. Some children gave shows to raise money for the war. Other schoolchildren proudly sang anti-German war songs and believed their headmaster's order that every palm kernel they collected would be used to buy a nail for Hitler's coffin.[249]

The strength of the colonial population in supporting Britain during the Second World War was reflected in the monetary contributions secured from nearly every class of society in Nigeria. In a letter on February 25, 1946, Julius Elias or Lord Southwood, chairman of the Hospital for Sick Children in London, appealed to the Nigeria War Relief Fund for donations to assist Britain's ailing youth. Thanking the fund for a previous donation of one pound and ten shillings, he wrote:

This letter has come many, many miles to reach you. And, now that it is at last at rest before you – will you read it carefully? Will you please? Its message is so very important. It is about little children who are sick and who need your help. Far across the seas, in the bomb-scarred city of London, where this much-travelled

[246] R. D. Pearce, "Violet Bourdillon: Colonial Governor's Wife," *African Affairs* 82, no. 327 (April 1983): 267–277.

[247] NA, CO, 657/47, Colony: Annual Report for the Year 1939. See also Crown Colonist, November 1939. Cited in Pearce "Violet Bourdillon."

[248] "Nigerian War Relief Fund Owerri Province," *Nigerian Eastern Mail*, November 11, 1939, 3.

[249] Achebe, *The Education of a British-Protected Child*, 18.

letter was posted, there is a certain Hospital . . . a children's Hospital . . . our needs are still great, still as urgent . . . Will you, then, help us again? Will you, please?[250]

Such letters reveal a high degree of cooperation across the British Empire and the extent to which the Nigerian War Relief Fund provided actual relief to the British population and government. To the Nigerian subjects of the empire, it was an expression of their loyalty and support to the British government in its fight against the aggression of Nazi Germany.[251]

### Conclusion

The Second World War represented the greatest burden the British Empire placed upon its former African colonies. Until this time, the military history of the war has often overlooked the enormous burden placed upon the African population. The war marked a new phase in the structure of the colonial economy and provided the "emergency situation needed to mobilize the human and material resources" of colonial Nigeria and other British colonial possessions in order to "ameliorate the people's suffering which resulted from scarcity of essential commodities during the war."[252] It led to increased extraction of local resources, an expansion in infrastructure, and the development of mineral extraction.

The colonial government employed several strategies to bring about the acceleration of local production and trade as well as the consolidation of economic and distributive activities during the war. Besides the extensive use of persuasion and propaganda, colonial authorities employed coercive methods to police local production and distribution. In many cases, local chiefs heeded the advice of colonial officials and persuaded their subjects to produce needed goods. In other cases, colonial officers employed regulations where ordinary appeals had little effect. Administrative officers used these methods extensively to control trade and distribution and impose price controls. The relationship previously defined by British economic interest was reformed into a collaborative alliance between Britain and its colonial subjects. This new relationship shared the collaborative goal of winning the war against Hitler's evil intents.

Britain expressed a highly paradoxical attitude toward Nigerian peoples, consistent on one hand with the goal of imperialism as an economic venture, and on the other hand, paralleling specific colonial polices with the Allies' commitment to the preservation of liberty and

---

[250] NAE, CADIST, 3/3/179, "The Nigerian War Relief Fund," February 25, 1946. Emphasis in the original.
[251] Ibid.
[252] Esse, "The Second World War and Resource Management in Eastern Nigeria," 17.

self-determination. Nigerians supported the war with enthusiasm, but they bore the burden of war production at home. They felt the impact of this increase in production on their lives in many ways: enduring food shortages, compulsory labor, and the gradual effects of higher prices. Still, their roles in these wars were intricately connected to the colonial experience. What emerged was a complex but ambivalent relationship between the British Empire and its colonial subjects in Nigeria during the war.

# 4  Voices of Protest
## Austerity, Regulations, and Social Protest

Consider the lives of a family which may perish as a result of the measures which have been taken to restrict the gari trade.

> Mr. A. Damola to District Officer, Aba District, July 21, 1943

We are also British protected persons and are entitled to [our] share of British Justice and fair play.

> Omoba Garri Traders Union, August 25, 1944

On Friday, December 18, 1942, three women, Moriamo Aduni, Ribiatu Adukunle, and Rabitu Balogun, made a brief appearance before His Worship Mr. J. N. Scot at the Saint Anna Police Court in Lagos. The three accused persons pleaded guilty to profiteering by selling food items above the stipulated market price. Moriamo Aduni's crime was selling one bottle of groundnut oil to a certain woman for 7 pence instead of the 6.5 pence fixed by the government. For her crime, Moriamo was fined 10 shillings. The second accused, Ribiatu Adukunle, was charged for selling 12 ounces of meat to one boy for 6 pence instead of 4.5 pence on November 19 at Faji Market. The third accused, Rabitu Balogun, had sold five bottles of groundnut oil to one woman for 2 shillings and 11 pence instead of the fixed price of 2 shillings and 8.5 pence. For their offenses, they were fined 20 and 30 shillings, respectively.[1] In another case, a magistrate, Stella Thomas, sentenced Alice Ewo to a fine of 5 pounds 10 shillings or one-month imprisonment with hard labor for selling six sticks of cigarettes for 6 pence instead of the fixed price of five cigarette sticks for 4 pence.[2] Female trader Abigail Odukogbe was sentenced to a fine of 5 pounds or one month in prison by a court in Lagos for selling sugar above the controlled price. Likewise, Asunmowu Musa was sentenced to one month in prison or 2 pounds and 10 shillings for selling half of an *olodo* measure of native-produced rice above the controlled price of 2.5 shillings.[3] Even children did not escape the harsh hammers of colonial

---

[1] "Three Women Who Profiteered Are Fined 10/-, 20/-, and 30/- Respectively," *Daily Service*, December 29, 1942.

[2] "Woman Who Profiteered in Pirate Cigarettes Is Fined £5.10," *Daily Service*, December 29, 1942.

[3] Broadcast by the Inspector of Prices, November 5, 1942, Lagos (Printed and Published by the Service Press Limited).

courts during the war. A juvenile, Onwuamana Emeribe of Suru Lere in Lagos, was sentenced to ten strokes of the cane for selling two tins of Gloria Milk at 1 shilling instead of two tins at the controlled price of 10 pence and 5 ounces of sugar for 3.5 pence instead of 8 ounces for 3.5 pence.[4]

As these various cases illustrate, the war was fought in the spaces of everyday life, where children and the most economically vulnerable women, like petty traders, worked to support the war abroad, while bearing its burden at home. Over the course of the war, the issue of surviving the economic crisis and dealing with colonial regulations and control became personal for many Nigerians, especially the poor. These cases reveal that despite the desire on the part of many Nigerians to support the war, their families faced the difficult task of surviving the depression that the war left in its wake.[5] While mobilization and the difficulties of managing the war economy placed considerable strains on imperial systems, officials addressed these through wartime reforms and an extensive array of new regulations.[6] Fundamentally, wartime policies and regulations were made possible within the frameworks of colonialism and its hegemonic structures. Section 140 of the Nigeria General Defence Regulation of 1941, which among other things regulated available food, gave enormous powers to "relevant" and "competent" authorities, including the courts. The law empowered colonial authorities to regulate or prohibit the production, treatment, keeping, storage, movement, transportation, distribution, sale, purchase, and use or consumption of "articles of food in any description and in particular for controlling prices at which such articles may be sold."[7] The law provided that anyone convicted of any offense under this regulation was liable to imprisonment of a term not exceeding one year or to a fine not exceeding £500 or to both. While the law may have targeted major traders and distributors, every trader, including small-scale market vendors, were not spared the full weight of this law. Such harsh treatments and the

---

[4] Ibid.

[5] For the impact of the depression in other African contexts, see John Lonsdale, "The Depression and the Second World War in the Transformation of Kenya," in *Africa and the Second World War*, ed. David Killingray and Richard Rathbone (New York: St. Martin's Press, 1986), 97–142.

[6] These include controlled prices of food items and other materials regarded as essential to the war effort. See, for example, the Nigeria General Defence Regulation, 1941, Control of Supplies (Food and Merchandise-Stock Returns) Order, 1942; Nigeria, *Memorandum on the Organisation and Control of War Time Trade and Production*.

[7] NAE, File No. MISF 121, "Defence Regulations Including the Nigerian General Defence Regulation, 1941 and Other Miscellaneous Regulations," 2. See also Sydney Emezue, "Managing Wartime Shortages: The Salt Palaver in the Okigwe Division of Eastern Nigeria, 1939–1945," *Nsukka Journal of History* 2 (1990): 1–26, at 6.

imposition of fines and imprisonment on the most vulnerable in society carried a clear message: British colonial officials were willing to apply severe penalties for even the smallest infraction.

From the start of the war, there was no doubt in the minds of colonial officials that new and often inconvenient measures had to be enacted to mobilize colonial resources to meet wartime needs. At home, the war forced common Englishmen and women to unite in what Jose Harris describes as a "metaphysical entity: an entity which transcended the divisions of class, sect, self-interest and libertarian individualism that normally constitute the highly pluralistic and fragmented structure of British society."[8] Britain moved away from an economic ethos fixated on "market economics and administrative muddling-through into an era of planning, rationing and economic management."[9] This shift did not just affect British citizens at home, for British subjects in the colonies were also subjected to a greater degree of state regulation and compulsory mobilization of physical resources.

In fact, a food crisis was imminent in Nigeria toward the end of the 1930s. Up until the eve of the war, the colonial Department of Agriculture had concentrated much of its agricultural development program on export crops, especially palm oil, cocoa, cotton, and peanuts.[10] Significant attention was also paid to the development of new crops with potential for export. Progress was made in the expansion of the export crop sector due to the potential for capital accumulation. Conversely, the food production sector received very little attention from colonial officials, and Nigeria increasingly relied on food imports to feed a rapidly growing population.[11] The Nigerian press criticized colonial policies for their failure to curb inflation and their emphasis on export agricultural policy.[12] The war exposed the structural weakness of colonial agricultural planning and the lack of direct incentives for peasants in the area of food production. However, colonial officials were already aware of the food crisis and its inherent problems for agriculture on the eve of the Second World War. The report of the Department of Agriculture for 1938 clearly recognized the difficulty. "The production of export crops, important as

---

[8] Jose Harris, "War and Social History: Britain and the Home Front during the Second World War," *Contemporary European History* 1, no. 1 (1992): 17–35, at 17.

[9] Ibid.     [10] Nigeria, *Annual Report of the Agricultural Department, 1939–1940*, 1.

[11] On some historical perspectives on the food crisis in Africa, see, for example, Food and Agriculture Organization, *Perspectives Study on Agricultural Development in the Sahelian Countries, 1975–1990*, 3 vols. (Rome: Food and Agriculture Organization, 1976); Richard A. Easterlin, *Population and Economic Change in Developing Countries* (Chicago: University of Chicago Press, 1980); C. K. Eicher, "Facing Up to Africa's Food Crisis," *Foreign Affairs* 61, no. 1 (1982): 151–174.

[12] Esse, "The Second World War and Resource Management in Eastern Nigeria," 148.

this is to the wealth of the country and to the revenue of the government, must not be subordinated to the production of foodstuff for local consumption, for those who are underfed cannot do the maximum amount of work."[13] These general economic conditions had much to do with the worldwide depression of the late 1920s. From 1929, the export value of Nigeria's principal agricultural products (cocoa, palm kernels, palm oil, and groundnuts) fell significantly and continued to fall except in 1937. By 1938, there was a drastic decline in the value of exports.[14] Colonial restructuring of the agricultural policy was shaped by the changing fortunes of peasant agriculture, low export earning, and rising costs of import of foodstuffs.

I have observed elsewhere that the critical elements in British colonial agricultural policy before the war were British economic interests and demands by the metropole. Consequently, Nigeria's agricultural policy created a lopsided project that lacked a balance between export production and food production. So, while the export quantities and values increased, the output in the food sector declined progressively.[15] For historian John Iliffe, British colonial motives in this period "combined self-interest and altruism because the depression had shown that impoverished colonies were politically dangerous and could not buy British exports."[16]

Administratively, a major restructuring of the Nigeria economy by the colonial authorities took place as soon as the war began with attention paid to the production of items. Sir Frank Stockdale, the agricultural adviser to the colonial secretary, advised J. R. Mackie, the director of the Department of Agriculture, that Nigeria, like other colonial territories, should endeavor to be self-sufficient in food supplies.[17] In a memo to agricultural officers, the government requested that the Department of Agriculture assist the imperial government by "producing such crops as it may ask." The memo further required Nigeria to be self-supporting in foodstuffs, including those normally imported from elsewhere.[18] The

---

[13] Nigeria, *Annual Report of the Agricultural Department, 1939–1940*, 1.

[14] Helleiner, *Peasant Agriculture*, 500–501.

[15] Korieh, *The Land Has Changed*. See also E. T. O. Oyatoye, "The Administration of Agricultural Development in Nigeria: An Assessment of Past and Present Agricultural Policies," *Agricultural Administration* 14, no. 2 (1984): 101–113.

[16] John Iliffe, *A Modern History of Tanganyika* (Cambridge: Cambridge University Press, 1979), 437.

[17] NAE, RIVPROF 8/5/430, "Policy of the Agricultural Department," Circular Memo D. A 14/252, J. C. Mackie to the Chief Secretary to the Government, October 26, 1939.

[18] Nigeria, *Annual Report of the Agricultural Department, 1939–1940*. See also Nigeria, *An Address by His Excellency the Governor, Sir Bernard Bourdillon to the Legislative Council, 4 December 1939*, 4–13; Nigeria, *Legislative Council Debates, March 17, 1941* (Lagos, 1941), 11.

overall strategy of the Department of Agriculture was to ensure self-sufficiency in food production, reduce imports, and conserve valuable resources that could be channeled into the war effort. Indeed, there was a perception that Nigeria could produce enough food to feed the country's population and meet Britain's import needs for other colonies in West Africa. This new drive contrasted with the laissez-faire pace of prewar agricultural planning.[19] The drive to expand food and export production during the war marked a new phase in colonial agricultural policy.

In September 1939, the new agricultural policy was put in place. The Department of Agriculture focused its attention on local food production in addition to the export crops that would support the war effort.[20] Colonial officials pursued these goals with great zeal. J. A. G. McCall, an agricultural officer, summed up the prevailing ideology: "The production business is our particular war effort, and surely that should come first, even if other duties of administration have to suffer thereby."[21] To deal with the shortage of supplies, the Department of Agriculture concentrated its efforts on improving production for crops such as rice, which had increasingly been imported into the country before the war. In 1936, for example, Nigeria imported 14,900 tons of rice.[22] Effort was made to grow local rice as a substitute for the imported brands. In Onitsha Province, about 500 tons of rice were planted in 1943.[23] However, success was limited. Drought, poor management, and lack of enthusiasm reduced yields to only 2,000 tons. However, rice production was more successful in other parts of the Eastern Region such as Azumini, where the environmental conditions favored the planting of swamp rice.[24] The

[19] For the state intervention in and directing of peasant production and marketing, see Chima J. Korieh, "The State & the Peasantry, Agricultural Policy, Agricultural Crisis and Sustainability in Southeastern Nigeria, 1900–1995" (Unpublished PhD thesis, University of Toronto, 2013). For British economic policy in Africa during the war, see, for example, David Killingray and Richard Rathbone, eds., *Africa and the Second World War* (New York: St. Martin's Press, 1986); and Deborah Bryceson, "Household, Hoe and Nation: Development Policies of the Nyerere Era," in *Tanzania after Nyerere*, ed. Michael Hodd (London: Pinter Publishers, 1989), 39.
[20] NAE, EKETDIST 1/2/50, File No. 499, "Food Production" Memo: Agricultural Officer Abak to D. O. Calabar, July 12, 1940.
[21] NAE, File No. 1642, Aba District, 1/26/ 907, "Palm Produce Production," J. A. G. McCall, Controller of Oil Palm Production, Owerri Province to District Officers, Owerri Province, 3/2/44; NAE, Ogoja Province, Annual Report, 1943, 8.
[22] NAE, Ogoja Province, Annual Report, 1943.
[23] NAE, OP, 1865, vol. VI, ONDIST. 42/1/1264, Onitsha Province, Annual Report, 1943, 65.
[24] Esse, "The Second World War and Resource Management in Eastern Nigeria," 157–158.

failure of local production did not improve the food conditions in Nigeria following the drastic reduction in importation of rice by 1941.

The supply of food items in this period was not seriously threatened by the war. While a few items such as milk and flour were already rationed in Lagos, the government anticipated a severe shortfall of other essential food items. As stated earlier, the role of the colonial food controller was to devise the mechanism for rationing essential food item should the need arise. The role of the food controller was complemented by the appointment of E. McL. Watson as marketing officer. As part of the reform introduced by the British to effectively control the local economy, the marketing officer became an important part of the economic planning as it related to agricultural production, distribution, and marketing of farm products. The anticipated role of Nigeria in meeting domestic needs as well as supporting the economy of other West African territories brought contradictory experiences of "modernization" policy within a colonially imposed program that limited the ability of local farmers and traders to operate within a free market system.

A supplies department was created in 1942 to achieve the outlined objectives. The agency was empowered to organize food supplies for both the army and mine workers and to ensure that the government had ample reserves of food. The work of the marketing department was complemented by the supplies department and by the creation of the post of chief supply officer. By the end of March 1943, the organization purchased 10,300 tons of millet, 2,700 tons of rice, 7,000 tons of yams, 3,400 tons of maize, and 18,200 tons of guinea corn.[25] However, the anticipated increase in local food production did not materialize for many reasons. For example, the local production of rice was not significant enough to meet prewar demand levels. Furthermore, imported rice was preferred over locally produced rice because of its perceived higher quality. The production of vegetables was encouraged in order to meet the needs of the army, European residents, and a heightened potential for an export market. In 1940, the United Africa Company (UAC) purchased for export a consignment of chilies in Niger Province. Competition with local users caused such a steep rise in prices that farmers began abandoning cotton cultivation in favor of chilies. In January, before the UAC commenced buying chilies, the price was 6 shillings and 4 pence per cwt, but it rapidly rose to 14 shillings and 6 pence per cwt because of UAC purchases.[26] Other local staples, especially garri and yams, had become expensive beyond the ability of many to purchase them, forcing

[25] Ibid.    [26] Nigeria, *Annual Report of the Agricultural Department, 1939–1940*, 44–45.

the government to introduce a series of schemes and measures to regulate the price of food items.[27]

Wartime policies had significant consequences for the Nigerian people on an economic, social, and personal level. The war narrowed individual freedom and reinforced the hegemonic conservative tendencies of colonial control. Cruelty and political pandering are not mutually exclusive; they went hand in hand during the war. In fact, Britain was acting rationally in order to solve two related problems: self-preservation in a competitive international environment and propping up its legitimacy with the rally-around-the-flag nationalism that portrayed Germany as a common enemy of the empire and its far-flung peoples. Indeed, the Nigeria Defence Regulation of 1939 (amended in 1941), conferred extra powers on different colonial departments and created new ones to deal with the war crisis. The regulations introduced to curb rising costs, manage the scarcity of resources, and facilitate the management of the war economy disrupted the economic life of many Nigerians, including farmers and traders. The demand for local food imposed a heavy burden on the local population. The low levels of food production in some parts of the country created scarcity, while the soaring prices for foodstuffs sparked severe inflation in Nigeria. Local populations were most affected by the rising cost of basic food items. For example, the price of a ninety-pound bag of garri increased from 4 shillings in the beginning of July 1943 to 7 shillings by the end of the month.[28] Garri, among other foodstuffs like yams, was key to feeding the army during the war.

By 1942, the demands for local foodstuffs in the northern region and elsewhere increasingly drew many rural farmers and traders into the local food trade. Demands for yams, garri, and cocoyams, among other items, increased significantly due to wartime needs and reduced imports from abroad. Interregional trade between the Eastern Region and the north was at its peak by the second year of hostilities. Arthur Boreham, who fought with the Nigerian regiment, reported in his memoir that a "shortage of salt in the colony nearly caused riots in the south of the country, at Lagos, Ibadan, Onitsha and Port Harcourt. At one time it was serious, as we thought we might have to go out to quell it, but the police managed to quieten things down."[29] Alarmed by the deteriorating conditions in the local economy and the quantity of food items moving between the regions, officials began to impose strict restrictions on the movement of food items, such as yams, cocoyams, and garri, between the

---

[27] See Hinds, "Government Policy and the Nigerian Palm Oil Export Industry."

[28] NAE, ABADIST, 14/1/873, File No. 1646, "Gari Control," District Officer, Aba to Secretary, Northern Provinces, July 29, 1943.

[29] Boreham, *Saga of a Suffolk Soldier*, 153.

regions to ensure controlled distribution of these items. Growing concern over the threat of urban and rural food insecurity in Nigeria prompted the colonial authorities to regulate the distribution of both imported and locally produced foodstuffs. The government's control of the local food supply was achieved through the imposition of price controls on locally produced goods along with restrictions on where local producers and traders could sell their products. In a broadcast on November 5, 1942, the inspector of prices drew the public's attention to the Food Control Order enacted in 1942 (Public Notice 208 of 1942). The order stipulated that "no person shall in connection with a sale or proposed sale of any article of food: buy or sell or agree or offer or invite any offer to buy or sell any article of food at a price higher than the controlled price." The order further stated that "any purchaser of food who knows or has good reason to believe that any other person has sold food to him in contravention of any of these provisions of the Order shall inform the nearest police Officer."[30]

From 1943, the colonial authorities imposed a series of regulations to deal with the skyrocketing price of food items.[31] Known as the Pullen Marketing Scheme, the controlled price measure enabled the government to cap prices of food items in Lagos and other designated markets. The "Pullen Price," named after Captain Pullen, the food controller, had a significant impact on small traders, especially women retail traders, who traditionally controlled the production and sale of foodstuffs.[32] Selling price-controlled items above the stipulated price amounted to an offense referred to as "profiteering." Convicted offenders were forced to pay fines or went to prison. The stiff and often disproportionate punishments imposed by the courts to punish even young children speak to the economic, physical, and psychological impact of the war on the local population. They also reveal the willingness of the British to treat colonial subjects with little sympathy while demanding loyalty, compliance, and obedience even when these measures threatened the very survival of the local population. The cases that opened this chapter reveal that colonial authorities took several steps to enforce compliance and that contributed

---

[30] Broadcast by the Inspector of Prices.

[31] *Memorandum on the Organisation and Control of War Time Trade and Production*, 13.

[32] Petitions and protests against controlled prices came from across most of southern Nigeria. Urban areas such as Aba and Lagos were important sites of these social movements. See Wale Oyemakinde, "The Pullen Marketing Scheme: A Trial in Food Price Control in Nigeria, 1941–1947," *Journal of the Historical Society of Nigeria* 6, no. 4 (1973): 413–423; Emily Kamm, "Price Control, Profiteering, and Public Cooperation: The Lagos Market Women's Association and the Limits of Colonial Control" (Unpublished BA honors thesis, Paper 309, Portland State University, 2016); Korieh, "Urban Food Supply."

Table 4.1 *Control of local foodstuffs in Abakaliki Division*[33]

| Articles | Quantity | Prewar price | Quantity | Present price | Quantity | Controlled price |
|---|---|---|---|---|---|---|
| Yams: September–March | 12 large | 1/– | 6 large | 1/– | 9 large | 1/– |
| | 15 medium | 1/– | 10 medium | 1/– | 12 medium | 1/– |
| | 30 small | 1/– | 20 small | 1/– | 17 small | 1/– |
| April–August | 6 large | 1/– | 3–4 large | 1/– | 5 large | 1/– |
| | 15 medium | 1/– | 8–9 medium | 1/– | 9 medium | 1/– |
| Rice (local) | 24 | 1/– | 8 cups | 1/– | 10 cups | 1/– |
| Garri | 12 | 1 d | 6 cups | 1 d | 8 cups | 1 d |
| Egg (hen) | 4 | 1 d | 2 | 1 d | 4 | 1 d |
| Egg (duck) | 2 | 1 d | 2 | 1 d | 2 | 1 d |
| Pepper | 2 cigarette cups | 1 d | 1 cigarette cup | 1 d | 2 cigarette cups | 1 d |
| Plantain | 10 | 1/2 d | 6 | 1/2 d | 8 | 1/2 d |
| Banana (ripe) | 12 | 1/2 d | 8 | 1/2 d | 12 | 1/2 d |
| Oranges | 10 | 1/2 d | 5 | 1/2 d | 6 | 1/2 d |
| Okro | 40 capsules | 1/2 d | 15 | 1/2 d | 20 | 1/2 d |
| Cassava | Large basket | 3 d | large basket | 6 d | Large basket | 5 d |
| Coco yam | 8 | 1 d | 8 | 1 d | 8 | 1 d |
| Groundnuts | 24 cups | 1 d | 4 cups | 1 d | 6 cups | 1 d |
| Palm oil | 1 bottle | 6 d | 1 bottle | 9 d | 1 bottle | 8 d |
| Palm wine | Calabash | 2 d | Calabash | 3 d–4 d | Calabash | 2 d |
| Ideal milk | 6 oz. tin | 4 d | 6 oz. tin | 8 d | 6 oz. tin | 6 d |

[33] *Source*: NAE, CALPROF, 3/1/2329, District Officer, Abakiliki, November 9, 1942.

enormously to the suffering and, in some cases, the humiliation of the victims of imperial control. The punishments allowed by emergency regulations, including acts of physical violence such as flocking, were employed to exert economic and psychological control on Nigerians. Table 4.1 illustrates the limits on what people could charge for most local food items. However, the price ceiling on both local and imported basic items did not improved the general economic condition.

The passion to support the war against Germany notwithstanding, World War II created numerous victims among colonial subjects, with stiff sentences imposed for even the smallest infraction. To control rising inflation, colonial authorities instituted price-controlling measures by the second year of the war. High prices for both imported merchandise and locally produced food items were creating major concerns for the authorities. Consequently, as Ashley Jackson has noted, the British acted "more imperialistically than ever before,"[34] and imperial control became more hegemonic.[35] The laws and regulations enacted to reduce profiteering by traders was a technique for dealing with food scarcity.

Newspaper editorials paid close attention to the implementation of price control regulations and the effect they were having on women marketers. It was immoral, in the view of many, to send women to jail for minor offenses such as selling items for one penny above the stipulated price. A *Daily Service* editorial from December 4, 1942, expressed the sentiments of many:

If these discriminatory punishments are allowed to continue, the Natives of this country who form the majority and uneducated class of this community will soon begin to think that there is one law for the rich and one for the poor which is certainly not British Justice. In some instances, Magistrates do not even allow [the] option of [a] fine for profiteering to the value of a penny.[36]

---

[34] Ashley Jackson, "African Soldiers and Imperial Authorities: Tensions and Unrest during the Service of High Commission Territories Soldiers in the British Army, 1941–46," *Journal of Southern African Studies* 25, no. 4 (1999): 646–665, at 646.

[35] Iliffe, *A Modern History of Tanganyika*, 436. For British economic policy in Africa during the war, see, for example, Killingray and Rathbone, *Africa and the Second World War*. In the case of Nigeria, most of the early literature focused on the impact of the war on nationalism, as well as local contributions of personnel to the war effort. See, for example, Clarke, "The Development of the West African Forces in the Second World War"; Crowder, "The Second World War"; Kerslake, *Time and the Hour*; and Gabriel Olakunle Lucania, *The Second World War and Politics in Nigeria, 1939–1953* (London: Evans Brothers, 1973). See also Basil Davidson, *Modern Africa: A Social and Political History*, 3rd edn. (London: Routledge, 1994), 63; and David Anderson and David Throup, "Africans and Agricultural Production in Colonial Kenya: The Myth of the War as a Watershed," *Journal of African History* 26 (1985): 327–345, at 327. I have addressed aspects of the impact of the war on the Nigerian urban population. See Korieh, "Urban Food Supply."

[36] "Penalties Inflicted for Profiteering," *Daily Service*, December 1, 1942.

By denying Nigerians food security and a living, the colonial government denied its own subjects basic human rights – the same rights for which the colonial government was enlisting Nigerians to fight against Germany.

Other critics saw these colonial regulations and their disproportionate forms of justice as part of a larger assault on indigenous culture and an insensitivity to the economic conditions faced by the local population, especially the poor. Indeed, historian Judith Byfield has argued that the critical roles played by women in the economy in Abeokuta and other Yoruba provinces as producers and retailers "meant that very few economic decisions failed to impact their livelihood."[37] As the *Daily Service* editorial commented, to sentence a woman "to three months in prison for selling a tin of milk a penny over the controlled price when the very firm from which she purchased the milk might be allowed by a change in control price to raise its price the following day above the price at which the woman sold, seems to us rather hard lines."[38] There was a determined effort to encourage the colonial authorities to consider the local conditions of the people, specifically the women and petty traders.[39]

Groups like the Nigerian Youth Movement were particularly concerned about the effect on women. On November 6, 1942, Dr. Aiknola Maja of the Nigerian Youth Movement appealed to the governor of Nigeria to use his influence to prevent this form of punishment for women for offenses related to profiteering. "In African society," he noted, "the idea of women being sent to prison is highly obnoxious."[40] Drawing on traditional ethical ideology, he explained that "women and men are not usually subjected to the same form of punishment and however strongly families might feel the disgrace of male members being sent to prison for any offence, the disgrace and slur for any female member being similarly punished is a thousand fold greater."[41] For the local populations, the aggressive policy of the government and the imposition of stiff punishment were unacceptable for people simply trying to survive. Such punishment in African eyes was "only reserved for cases of the worst type."[42]

The Nigerian Youth Movement raised concerns about the prejudicial application of the price restrictions, pointing out that price controls favored European trading firms that raised prices arbitrarily but did not face the same harsh treatment as petty traders. Although some European firms were fined for glaring profiteering, a fine of £200 to £500 was a "fleabite in the face of exorbitant profits."[43] The implementation of these regulations and

---

[37] Byfield, "Women, Rice, and War," 155.    [38] "Penalties Inflicted for Profiteering."
[39] Ibid.    [40] Ibid.
[41] "Imprisonment of Women for Profiteering," *Daily Service*, November 18, 1942.
[42] Ibid.    [43] Ibid.

the perceived discriminatory punishments led to moral and ideological tensions. Colonial subjects used British notions of justice in their petitions to the government. For instance, the *Daily Service* editorial reflected that British justice "is always tempered with mercy as it is not adulterated with the propensities of the Laws of the Medes and Persians."[44] Drawing upon Enlightenment ideas was important in how local people appropriated the British rule of law and its purpose to protect colonial subjects.

Such protests often fell on deaf ears. In September 1944, H. L. M. Butcher, who had become the district officer for Aba, introduced even more radical measures. In a memo to the native councils and court clerks, he directed that all garri permits granted to middlemen and traders be cancelled on September 1. Butcher was unhappy that traders had not adhered to the conditions of the garri permits. Some traders engaged in illegal practices and had induced the railway staff to send up far more than they were allowed.[45] He blamed African agents of Aba traders for "grossly excessive prices" in the north and scarcity in the Aba Division. In its place, he proposed that Mr. Bleasby, a European manager of Gibbons Transport Aba, act as the government's agent for buying garri at designated centers in the district and arrange for its distribution to native administrations in the northern provinces. He further proposed to set up a committee of middlemen and producers who would have the power to fix the price of garri to ensure that it would be "plentiful and cheap" locally.[46] Similar actions had been taken in Calabar, where African traders were forced to supply garri to Mr. Nicholas, another European. The power of the native food controller to fix the prices of food items in the market limited the freedom of farmers and traders, a program they resented.[47]

Other districts implemented similar restrictive measures and controls. In June 1945, the acting district officer for the Ikom Division prohibited the export of certain food items from the district, specifying that "no person shall export yams and coco-yams from the Ikom Division except under permit from the District Officer."[48] The resident for Ogoja Province also prohibited the export of yams from that province in June 1945. Buyers were required to obtain a permit from the district

[44] Ibid.

[45] NAE, ABADIST 14/1/875, File No 1646, vol. IV, "Gari Control," H. L. M. Butcher to the Councils and Court Clerks, Aba Division, September 2, 1944.

[46] Ibid.

[47] Esse, "The Second World War and Resource Management in Eastern Nigeria," 170.

[48] NAE, AIDIST 2/1/433, File No. IK: 401/18, "Food Control," Acting District Officer, Ikom, to District Officer, Abakaliki, June 18, 1945.

officer in Afikpo.[49] Similarly, Dermot O'Connor, the resident for the Awgu Division, restricted the transportation of yams outside of his division.[50] The restriction affected some farmers in the Abakaliki Division, who could not buy seed yams in the market because of the restrictions. The resident for Onitsha Province issued an order restricting the export of garri and yams from the Udi Division "except under a permit signed by a competent authority."[51] Perhaps the most important consequence of these restrictions was the disruption of the prewar food security arrangements that supported the urban population and several rural communities.

### The Local Response: Protest Petitions and Supplications

Personal accounts of the Second World War in Nigeria are rare. Even rarer are accounts from Nigerian civilians who lived during the war. While the war provided an opportunity for British imperial authorities to extend control by centralizing and establishing hegemony over the economic activities of ordinary Nigerians, these attempts did not go uncontested. Resistance, however, did not always fall into the binary classification of "fixed power versus organized opposition." Resistance, especially in relation to colonial subjects, was also subtle and more ambiguous than is often portrayed.[52] This oversimplification of the nature of resistance has been criticized by scholars such as Michael Foucault and James Scott, who claim that binary conceptualizations of resistance fail to account for less institutionalized and passive forms of protest.[53] Steven Feierman's *Peasant Intellectual* is important in explaining the forms of resistance and the intellectual discourses that shaped the response of Nigerian farmers, traders, and ordinary people to the hardship generated by the war and the wartime colonial regulations.[54] Feierman points to the importance of peasants in creating and achieving political objectives by employing

---

[49] NAE, AIDIST 2/1/433, File No. OG: 2920/140, "Food Control," P. M. Riley, Resident, Ogoja Province, to District Officers, January 15, 1945.

[50] Ibid.

[51] NAE, AIDIST 2/1/433, "Nigerian General Defense Regulation Order: Gari and Yams," Resident, Onitsha Province, to District Officers and Other Competent Authorities, May 16, 1945. For cassava restrictions, see also NAE, AID 2/1/433 OG: 2513/1265, "Nigeria General Defense Regulations Order," P. M. Riley, Resident, Ogoja Province, to District Officers, June 26, 1945.

[52] Serry B. Ortner, "Resistance and the Problem of Ethnographic Refusal," *Comparative Studies in Society and History* 37, no. 1 (1995): 173–193, at 174.

[53] See, for example, Michel Foucault, *The History of Sexuality*, trans. Robert Hurley (New York: Vintage Books, 1978); Scott, *Weapons of the Weak*.

[54] Steven Feierman, *Peasant Intellectuals: Anthropology and History in Tanzania* (Madison: University of Wisconsin Press, 1990), 4.

cultural norms that often "draw upon a rich variety of past forms of political language."[55] Looking critically at the framing of protests in non-Western societies, such an inclusive framework highlights a diverse range of issues or identities relevant to group and community interests, including gender, sexuality, subsistence, subcultures, and countercultures. Such a framework contextually informs how the men and women who experienced the war and its effects in Nigeria responded to colonial wartime policies and economic depression. Even under war conditions, the colonial government was confronted with competing interests and with ordinary Nigerians whose support for the war was crucial and yet must be balanced with everyday struggles for survival. Colonial overreach was employed to force compliance by Nigerians, but metropolitan and colonial interests were not always compatible. By engaging the politics of colonial control, Nigerians brought matters of everyday survival to bear on colonial policies.[56]

Nigerians responded to colonial regulations by employing a unique form of protest – petitions that addressed the impact of wartime regulations on their lives. Petitions had already been extensively employed to address grievances before the war. This unique mode of communication between colonial officials and subjects was employed more frequently from the 1920s. Most addressed concerns with judicial decisions in the colonial courts, and by the 1930s, petitions against tax rates had become common. As historian Saheed Aderinto argues in his analysis of juvenile petitioners in 1940s Lagos, petitions are "useful data for mapping out everyday encounters with colonialism."[57] Petitions became an ideal vehicle for channeling the counterhegemonic discourse of colonial subjects, because colonial authorities accepted petitions as a legitimate means of addressing individual and group concerns. Petitions were widely used

---

[55] Ibid., 3.

[56] Indeed, the basic factors identified in an illuminating commentary on social movements by Irving M. Zeitlin were present, especially the *discontent*, which involves the existence of widespread dissatisfaction with existing conditions. The second factor identified by Zeitlin is the existence of an *ideology*, which appeals to the discontent and through which they articulate conceived change and the process of action. The third factor is the existence of *leaders* who can articulate the issues, inspire the masses, spread the ideology, and create an organization capable of managing the day-to-day activities of the movement. The fourth factor is the availability of enough *power resources*, both human and material, to challenge the prevailing social order. Zeitlin's analytical framework provides a valuable insight on how we might apply it to specific historical examples and moments. See Irving M. Zeitlin with Robert J. Bryn, *The Social Condition of Humanity*. Canadian edn. (Toronto: Oxford University Press, 1991).

[57] Saheed Aderinto, "'O! Sir I Do Not Know Either to Kill Myself or to Stay': Childhood Emotion, Poverty, and Literary Culture in Nigeria, 1900–1960," *Journal of the History of Childhood and Youth* 8, no. 1 (2015): 273–294, at 274.

during the war by many individuals to address the impacts of colonial regulations.

By the end of the war, hundreds of petitions had been written by traders, groups, or associations. The petitions and supplications that appeared during the war, however, differed in their focus from prewar petitions. Wartime petitions overwhelmingly concerned food control and the restrictions placed on local trade.[58] They addressed a specific historical episode that created conditions beyond the control of local colonial authorities. Furthermore, most of the petitions were written by the lower class, specifically farmers and traders, who employed the strategy of sending petitions more frequently but in a language that was quite ambivalent. While many used petitions to appeal to colonial authorities regarding their condition, they objected to several regulations and restrictions imposed by the British as part of the war measures. Although we do not know how many of these petitioners made it through to the colonial authorities over the course of the war, their petitions offer a lens through which we can understand the broader attempt by colonial administrators to control the Nigerian population through the restriction of movements, surveillance, and the extraction of resources.

Petitions ranged from basic pleas written in simple language to epistles more sophisticated in style and expression often embodying the language of human rights and European notions of liberty. Sophisticated petitions were written by well-educated professional petition writers who often used technical language and bombastic rhetoric meant to impress upon the European officials that they understood their rights and those of their clients, as protected under British law, even though they were not technically British citizens themselves. Most of these petitions, however, are associated with what has been called a "rhetoric of humility and disavowal," which positioned colonial officials as benefactors indebted to the protection and well-being of their subjects.[59] The petitions reveal the shifting language used by the local populations to address their needs during a period of food scarcity and exorbitant prices.

Government control of the local food supply was achieved through the imposition of price controls on locally produced goods. The native food controller was given the authority to fix the prices of food items in the market. Beginning in 1943, several local government authorities invoked

---

[58] Korieh, *"Life Not Worth Living."*

[59] See Susan Ziska, *Signatures of Citizenship: Petitioning, Antislavery, and Women's Political Identity.* Gender and American Culture Series (Chapel Hill: University of North Carolina Press, 2003), 7. Cited in Shelly Rosenblum, "Review of *Signatures of Citizenship: Petitioning, Antislavery, and Women's Political Identity,* by Susan Ziska," *Canadian Review of American Studies* 36, no. 1 (2006): 117–121, at 119.

the Nigeria General Defence Regulations (Law No. 75 of 1941), which came into effect during the war in order to regulate local trade in food items and imposed controlled pricing of basic items. The price controls and food regulations affected the trade in garri in most of the eastern part of the country and impacted the trade of grains in the north.[60] The scarcity of food items created an incentive for farmers to increase production and the increased demand for garri and palm oil in northern Nigeria worked against external exports. The demand for garri and other food items also created opportunity for traders, some of whom entered the foodstuff retaining trade because of the profit that could be made quickly, especially in northern Nigerian towns. From the export of a mere 1.414 tons of garri from eastern Nigeria to the northern provinces in 1937, the figures increased rapidly when the war began, reaching 6,907.12 tons in the first half of 1941.[61] Rural farmers were abandoning cash crops in favor of food crops because of higher profits. J. S. Harris, who studied the economic lives of sixteen Igbo individuals on the eve of the war, notes that farmers in the Ozuitem area moved between yam production and palm produce depending on the product that provided the higher price.[62] Farmers were making similar economic decisions during the war in response to higher prices for foodstuffs. The increase in the quantity of food items required in the north created the opportunity for peasants to increase production, and consequently the incentive for new traders to take advantage of the opportunities offered for accumulation of capital. In requesting the permit to rail garri to the north, a group of traders in Aba requested permits to engage in the foodstuff trade because of the poor price of produce (palm oil and kernels). They asked for a reasonable quota of garri, which they would transport to the

---

[60] Garri is made from tubes and roots of the cassava plant and was the main source of carbohydrates for most people in sub-Saharan Africa. It was and still is the most important food item for easterners in Nigeria. On the application of the regulations, see, for example, NAE, AIDIST 2/1/433, "Nigerian General Defence Regulation Order: Garri and Yams," Resident, Onitsha Province, to District Officers and Other Competent Authorities, May 16, 1945. For cassava restrictions, see also NAE, AID 2/1/433 OG:2513/1265, "Nigeria General Defence Regulations Order," P. M. Riley, Resident, Ogoja Province, to District Officers, June 26, 1945. NAE, File No. 1646, vol. IV, ABADIST 14/1/875, "Gari Control," Omuna Native Court to District Officer, Aba, November 1944. NAE File No. 1646, vol. IV, ABADIST 14/1/875, "Export of Garri to the North by Garri Traders Will Stop on 1st September," *Nigerian Eastern Mail* Press Representative to District Officer, Aba, August 29, 1944. On related petitions, see Korieh, *"Life Not Worth Living."*
[61] NAE, File No. 1646, vol. IV, ABADIST 14/1/875, "Gari Control," District Officer, Aba, to Senior Resident, Port Harcourt, July 20, 1942.
[62] This study was carried out with the Social Science Research Council for 1938–1939. See Harris, "Some Aspects of the Economics of Sixteen Ibo Individuals," 303.

north to help "offset the impact of the depression in the produce market."[63]

The imposition of price controls generated resentment from peasants because of the general economic decline and the excessive cost of living, which also created problems for farmers. Some farmers refused to produce at government-fixed prices, since imported items (on which they spent their income) were not on the control list.[64] Letters of petition came from a variety of individuals, including traders, farmers, and lorry drivers, all of whom had cause to complain.[65] Those who were denied permits or access to rail garri to northern Nigerian towns following the imposition of restrictions by the colonial government sought remedy through petitions. Although most district officers ignored many of these petitions, several Nigerians, particularly from the Eastern Region, extensively used petitions and supplications to address their concerns.

The vast majority of Nigerians understood the war from the perspective of its impact on their personal lives rather than through the ideological lens as "just war" in defeating Hitler and totalitarianism. Amos Okafor, who was trading in garri between Aba and the northern cities of Kano, Bukuru, Ngoro, and Jos before the war, was one of those who struggled because of the wartime restrictions imposed on Nigerian traders. Okafor, who had traded garri for twelve years prior to the war, was not happy with the allocation of four bags of garri per month by the district officer. He was quite distressed, because prior to the restriction, he had railed between 50 and 100 bags of garri per month. To run his business, he had retained a private post office letter box for which he paid 10 shillings yearly as well as a property and water rate of 2 pounds 12 shillings annually. His income tax to the state, moreover, was based on his prewar volume of trade. The monthly allocation of four bags, he wrote, "would very much cripple [his] business" and jeopardize the livelihood of his family.[66]

Amos Okafor was not alone. Several other traders also suffered under the rigid regulations. The introduction of trade restrictions disrupted trading networks that citizens had established long before the war and that they had freely used with little intervention from the government. In A. Damola's petition, he asked the district officer to "consider the lives of

---

[63] Petitioners: Mr. J. E. Akajiofo, Mr. M. N. Ojikwu, Mr. F. N. Anajemba, Mr. F. M. Orji, Mr. N. N. Atueji, Mr. Maduabuchukwu, Mr. J. C. Ike, Mr. P. J. Jiagbogu, Mr. Andrew Orizu, Mr. Joseph Oyekwere, Mr. N. U. Anazodo, Mr. G. I. Onwugaje, Mr. Paul Anene, Mr. Z. A. Okeke, and Mr. A. O. Okeafor.

[64] Esse, "The Second World War and Resource Management in Eastern Nigeria," 170.

[65] Byfield, "Women, Rice, and War," 162.

[66] NAE, ABADIST 14/1/872, Amos Okafor to J. V. Dewhurst, District Officer, Aba, July 8, 1943.

a family which may perish as a result of the measures which have been taken to restrict the gari trade."[67] Prior to his engagement in the garri trade, Damola was a ticket collector for one of the motor transport owners in Aba. He was thrown out of work following the implementation of transport control, which resulted in the removal of many commercial lorries from the road. Drawing attention to the impacts the restrictions were having on the lives of his family, Damola's requisition reveals that the war was fought in the spaces of everyday life where many ordinary people, like the petitioner, worked to achieve the goals of the empire abroad while engaging with and fighting the politics of colonial control, particularly in matters of everyday survival.

When another trader, J. E. Akajiofo, and fifteen other garri traders wrote their petition to a district officer on August 12, 1943, they under-scored their status as people under British "protection and trusteeship."[68] Their petition further emphasized the "severe hardship" and financial difficulty they were experiencing due to trade restrictions imposed on garri.[69] For these petitioners, the British had a duty to live up to their "paternalistic" obligation to protect their colonial subjects. As Oliver Coates argues, these petitions were written in a "context informed by competing forms of colonial and military authority, complicated further by the language of loyalty and patriotism specific to wartime."[70] Embedded in the petitions is a hope that they would be read by colonial administrators. It did not often happen. Thus, beneath the enthusiasm of the Nigerian population in supporting the empire's war effort lay deep anger resulting from the demand made on their meager resources. As these petitions demonstrate, the local population addressed the issues of survival even as they sought to support the war. Their pleas strategically employed moral appeals in seeking redress, but these petitions were "written with the specific purpose of engaging officialdom."[71]

For many petitioners, the policies of the government were morally wrong and unjust, and their petitions highlight these sentiments. For instance, when V. N. Nwabufo contacted the British district officer in Aba, eastern Nigeria, on July 8, 1943, he wrote that he was petitioning to "seek justice." His name was omitted from the list of approved garri

---

[67] NAE, ABADIST 1/26/958, A. Damola to J. V. Dewhurst, District Officer, July 21, 1943.
[68] NAE, ABADIST 1/26/958, Letter written on behalf of the petitioner by the Nigerian Services and Commercial Bureau, 145 Jubilee Road, Aba, August 12, 1943. The petition described their business as: Letter Writer, Debts Collector, Business Adviser and Advertiser, General Contractor, etc.
[69] Ibid.
[70] Coates, "The War, Like the Wicked Wand of a Wizard, Strikes Me and Carry Away All That I Have Loved," 7.
[71] Ibid., 4.

traders even though he had traded the commodity before the war. Frustrated by the omission, he expressed his bewilderment:

I cannot imagine the reason why names of old traders in garri railing to the North as myself [were] listed on the roll of traders to continue and my name was deleted – the memory of your obedient servant jumped into a cog; and suspected an intrigue on the whole situation to parties that your worship set at the affairs of recommending they would continue garri traders. . . . Your servant is duty bound, as a protected person.[72]

Like many others, Nwabufo was caught in the attempt to manage the deteriorating economic conditions that confronted the empire and its colonial subjects. Nwabufo's petition leaves little doubt about the growing dissatisfaction and distress among Nigerians. His petitions reflect the seemingly paradoxical connection between British colonial policies and the crisis faced by traders and farmers, and the daily anguish of civilians as they attempted to deal with the disruption brought by the war on their lives.

Other traders faced the same dilemma. Some of the most moving expressions that emerged from the petitions during the war came from traders who felt the threat to their family's survival. On July 11, 1943, a trader, Mr. O. O. Muoma, wrote to the British district officer for Aba. In his petition, titled "Injustice: Garri Railing to the North," he told the district officer that his name was deleted from the list of traders permitted by the government to export garri to northern Nigeria towns. Like Nwabufo, Muoma considered this development "abnormal" and an "injustice."[73] He wrote in his petition that cutting him out of the garri trade deprived him of his livelihood and threatened the lives and subsistence of his two sons, who lived in the northern city of Kano.[74] Another trader, J. O. Okorocha of Mbawsi, protested his allocation of a "meager quota of 10 bags of garri." Okorocha, who had exported 209 bags of garri to northern Nigeria in 1942, stated that the quota allocated to him "is too poor considering my intensive trade last year . . . I beg of you to remedy the situation and award me what is due."[75]

The restrictions also caught some people completely by surprise. J. E. Akajiofo of Mbawsi wrote to the Aba district officer on September 1, 1943, requesting a permit to rail his yams to northern Nigeria for sale. Akajiofo had purchased sixteen tons of yams in July 1943, which would have been railed to the north that month, but unfortunately one of his sons died. Akajiofo was forced to leave the yams

[72] NAE, ABADIST 14/1/872, File No. 1646, "Gari Control," O. O. Muoma to District Officer, Aba, July 1, 1943.
[73] Ibid.    [74] Ibid.    [75] Ibid.

at the railway station while he traveled home for his son's funeral. After he returned on August 11, he was issued a consignment by the station master on August 14. The next morning when he wanted to transport the yams, he was informed that he could not rail the yams because the district officer in Aba had restricted the export of yams to the north.[76]

Another trader, Eze, who had been a long-time yam trader, was caught in the same dilemma. He had yams ready to be transported to Kano and Jos in northern Nigeria, but was unaware of the new permit requirement. He pleaded to the district officer:

I humbly beg to state that on absence of the previous knowledge, that yams shall be under permit, I t[a]ke the liberty to ask your worship to grant me a special permit to rail out those baskets I have already got at the Station. ... Therefore I humbly crave for your mercy consideration and [please] attend to this matter immediately by granting me the permit as requested otherwise my said food stuff will rot due to [its] long stay in the shed.[77]

The district officer wrote back to Eze, but regretted that he could not "accede to [his] request," a familiar response to such petitions.[78] Petitions requesting less government intervention were rejected by officials who saw them as representing personal interests that worked against wartime goals.

Petitions rarely resolved matters in favor of petitioners. The sources do not indicate that petitioners were successful in persuading officials to change policy based on individual appeals. Repeat petitions reveal that officials often ignored these petitions. Denied a response to previous petitions, G. I. Udeh, who had applied to the district officer for the Abakiliki Division several times for permission to transport seed yams to Awka for planting, wrote again on May 19, 1945. Udeh had lived in Abakiliki for twenty-five years and had no seed yams to plant in his hometown. Drawing attention to his previous requests, which were ignored, he begged for permission to carry seed yams to Nawfia in Awka for planting. With the farming season coming to an end, Udeh further wrote the district officer. He had become desperate, lamenting that the planting season "remains not more than 20 days now," and begged the district officer to reconsider.[79] While the outcome of Udeh's application is not known, his letter was not an isolated case. It represented a typical problem faced by many farmers. These emotional petitions are

[76] NAE, ABADIST, 1/26/958, File No. 668, J. E. Akajiofo to District Officer, Aba, September 1, 1943.

[77] NAE, ABADIST 1/26/958, File No. 668, "Application for Grant Export of Yams under Permit," E. M. Eze, Trader to District Officer, Aba, August 13, 1943.

[78] Ibid.

[79] NAE, AIDIST 2/1/433, 450, G. I. Udeh to District Officer, Abakiliki, May 19, 1945.

striking evidence of the increasingly negative impact the war had on the rural population. Such emotion was expressed by David H. Kubiri when he sought a permit to sell garri in the north:

I with all civility prostrate to ask earnestly, in the name of your families and home, in the name of British justice, which makes an Englishman superior to other races, in the name of all [unclear word], and in the name of your past honour and trust, which has designated his worship as a capable and able rule[r]. [T]hat the permit of gari might be rendered to your humble servant so that the families may not die away for starvation.[80]

The personal – and often intimate – petitions of Nigerians as in the case of Kubiri paint a unique portrait of a rough-and-tumble time and enable us to hear their voices and reaction to wartime policies. Most importantly, these petitions paint a vivid picture of daily life and the practical realities of living under wartime conditions for colonized subjects of the Allied Powers. As Andrew Verner has argued in his examination of peasant petitions during the Russian Revolution, "instead of simply looking at the petitions as another, if unusual, set of documents, by which peasant thoughts and desires are transparently revealed," they should be treated as an "integral part of the complex negotiations among, as well as between, the peasants and the outside," and their content regarded as the "results of strategic choices made by their authors in the context of their surroundings."[81] The emotions expressed in these petitions and many others show the level of societal dissatisfaction felt by many Nigerians, yet the humble phrases employed remind one of the paternalistic structures of colonial society. In the experiences of these petitioners, one sees a persistent marginalization of peasant interests in this period of intensified insecurity created by the colonial economy.

Petitions reveal the thoughts and emotions of ordinary people toward the restrictions imposed on them as well as a deep understanding of Britain's dependency on their resources. Petitioners linked their trade to their ability to pay income taxes and support the government financially. As such, some petitioners linked their request by citing their contributions they made as taxpayers to the colonial government. The petition from Augustine Ebirim on May 25, 1944, reveals that he had been a garri trader since 1934. Once the war disrupted his normal trade to the north, he applied for a permit from a district officer. His petition reveals that he had paid 15 shillings as income tax on account of thirteen bags allocated

---

[80] NAE, ABADIST 14/1/872, File No. 1646, "Gari Control," David H. Kubiri to District Officer, Aba, July 5, 1943.
[81] Verner, "Discursive Strategies in the 1905 Revolution."

to him since the permit scheme came into effect.[82] J. C. Ikedionwu of Aba, who had been instructed to pay an income tax of £4, wrote: "I am one of those among gari traders whom you have highly taxed in the income tax of this year. . . . Some of us whom their income tax is lesser than mine are included in buying the gari and sending it to Fernando-Po, but your poor servant was missed saying that I was late on the very specified date of approval."[83] The requests made by B. M. Anarado, Aron Okoye, J. Muojeje, and Anene Nath to trade in garri were denied by the district officer. Although they had formally sent between forty and forty-six bags of garri to the north, their new request to send garri to Calabar and Cameroon helped them to offset the income tax levied upon them in the 1943/1944 tax year.[84] The logic in these claims is that they would be unable to pay taxes with less money since income taxes had previously been based on volume of trade.

An intersection of many forces between the empire and its subject peoples was at play in Nigeria. These included individual survival under war conditions, patriotism toward the empire in the face of many economic challenges at home, and the global attempt toward defeating Hitlerism. The Association of Garri Traders in Aba noted on August 25, 1944, for example, that its members, through their trade, were contributing their quota toward the defeat of Hitlerism in order that democracy would rule the world and all forms of man's inhumanity to man be wiped off the face of the earth.[85] They resolved:

That this British Government which does not permit any discrimination against any peoples of the Empire will protect us from the discrimination in trade which Mr. H.L.M. Butcher, District Officer, Aba, is introducing into this town, as it appears that the garri trade will be taken away from us and given to the Europeans who are fighting to win Hitler as we are doing . . . it is the most discouraging, the most scandalous act any Representative of His Majesty the King can show to the King's peoples at this critical moment of world history.[86]

Some petitioners regarded engagement in trade as a contribution toward the empire's war effort. Petitioner George Ikulugan of the Ahada Division in the Eastern Region saw his involvement in trade as a "common cause, to win the war."[87] Yet these petitions were expressions of several elements

---

[82] By 1942, an Anglo-Spanish labor agreement induced the large-scale movement of contract laborers from eastern Nigeria to Spanish Fernando Po. This obviously increased the demand for garri and other foodstuffs from Nigeria to feed the plantation laborers. See NAE, ABADIST 14/1/878, Augustine Ebirim to District Officer, Aba, May 25, 1944.
[83] Ibid.     [84] Ibid.
[85] NAE, ABADIST, 14/1/875, A Resolution by the Association of Garri Traders, Aba, August 25, 1944.
[86] Ibid.
[87] NAE, ABADIST 14/1/875, George Ikulugan to District Officer, Aba, ca. July 1943.

of local interaction with the empire at a time of war, to express support for the empire during the war, to highlight the contributions of Nigerians to the war effort, and to support the overall discourse against Nazism and totalitarianism. Despite the sense of common goals engendered among the empire and the Nigerian population, the widespread and unprecedented ethic of self-sacrifice was tempered often by protest against government regulations and restrictions.

There are several cases of request for personal use. The restrictions on trade across regional lines affected household survival strategies and subsistence. When a public servant, D. H. McArthur Slessor of the Geological Survey Department, Kaduna, wrote on August 23, 1943, to the food control officer in Aba District in the Eastern Region, he requested permission to buy food for members of his household. Slessor had previously applied to the colonial resident in Port Harcourt in July for an individual permit for one bag of garri to be railed from Aba for personal consumption. The application was refused on the grounds that individual permits could not be issued. On August 6, he addressed a further communication to the resident in Owerri outlining his request. His second petition was rejected under the claim that garri was controlled in the northern provinces. McArthur Slessor described his situation:

I have a family of 12 souls: 6 children, 4 relatives staying; self and wife, and in view of the quantity of commodities requires: 1 only bag of gari, 2 only bag of yams, and the number of persons involved you will agree that the need is indeed genuine and personal, and there can be no room for any portion of it being used for sale or barter.[88]

Nneka Ikwuazom, a civil servant at the headquarters of the Sleeping Sickness Service in the northern province of Kaduna, wrote on July 27, 1943, to the Aba district officer requesting permission to buy garri from Aba in the eastern province for personal use. Ikwuazom, who had a family of six, requested permission to bring in one ninety-pound bag of garri every two months. Her petition stated that the price of garri "has soared very high here and the supplies are so scarce that I thought I should appeal to you for your assistance in the matter. We have just arrived from the Southern Provinces (Calabar) and find things very hard with us with regard to foodstuff supply." A group of Igbo migrants in Kaduna under the aegis of the "Ego-Bu-Dike Society" ("Money Is Power") made a similar request for a permit to buy and rail garri from Mbawsi in the Aba District. In their petition to the district officer, the twelve petitioners

---

[88] NAE, ABADIST 14/1/875, File No. 1646, vol. IV, D. H. McArthur Slessor to Food Control Officer, Aba District, August 23, 1943.

noted a monthly requirement of about forty-four bags mainly for the use of themselves and their dependents.[89]

Ikwuazom and other migrants to the north are examples of an increasing population of Igbo people and other southerners that made northern Nigeria their home as colonialism created opportunities for them in other parts of the country. Whether they worked in the public service or as traders, these emigrants depended on the Eastern Region as an important source of food items, especially garri and palm oil. Restrictions affected the traders who had been making a living moving these items from the east to northern towns, where a large number of Igbo migrants were residing for work and business. Ikwuazom and other emigrants suddenly faced increasing shortages and unaffordable prices due to the restrictions and scarcities caused by the war.

Colonial regulations did not necessarily distinguish between requests for commercial transactions and requests for household sustenance. Both cases were often treated the same under the regulations. Several petitions throughout the war capture the frustration of individuals whose basic food requirements were caught in the bureaucratic hurdles of official regulations and restrictions. Even basic household requirements were not distinguished from allotments assigned to commercial traders. If the intent was, as one colonial official argued, to prevent numerous persons from embarking "on the export gari trade with the hope of making vast profits at the expense of their own people," then all were caught in the web of colonial oppression and control.[90]

Women's role as producers, traders, and heads of households during the war created what Mia Nagawiecki calls "alternative and unorthodox sites for political engagement."[91] Such engagement in the politics of everyday survival drew from the framework popularized by political anthropologist James Scott, who shows how disfranchised groups like the women and men in Nigeria resorted to everyday acts of resistance as expressions of their informal political culture, or "infrapolitics."[92] Controlled pricing threatened the income of women, who directly

[89] J. D. Ogbolu, patron; J. A. Ashibogwu, President; J. C. Uwechua, Vice President; R. C. Nwaboku, Secretary; C. C. Mordi, Treasurer; R. C. Nwuga, Auditor; J. O. Ofordu, Finance Secretary; J. I. Ashibogwu, member; W. O. Ikediashi, member; T. O. Miwah, member; W. O. Nobei, member; S. E. Akwe, member. NAE, ABADIST 14/1/875, Ego-Bu-Dike Society to District Officer, Aba, Kaduna, August 16, 1943.
[90] NAE, ABADIST 14/1/874, E. N. Inglius, Resident, Owerri Province to Gari Traders Association, Aba, September 18, 1943.
[91] Mia Nagawiecki, "American Women at War," National Endowment for the Humanities, February 2016, accessed January 17, 2019, www.neh.gov/sites/default/files/inline-files/american_women_at_war.pdf.
[92] Ibid.

controlled the production and sale of produce foodstuffs such as garri.[93] General uncertainty in the local economy, coupled with price control measures, generated protests among market women. Rice and bean traders in the city of Onitsha petitioned the resident for Onitsha Province on July 1, 1942, regarding the implementation of government-imposed prices in the market, which took effect on June 16, 1942. In a carefully detailed calculation, the traders estimated the losses they incurred due to the price control.[94] An Onitsha garri trader and twenty others petitioned the district officer for Onitsha on July 17, 1942, requesting that the authorities reconsider the market price imposed on garri. In their petition, the traders noted that the recommended price of 10 shillings per bag of garri was below the estimated delivery price of 12 shillings per bag from Aba, where Onitsha traders bought their goods.[95] One article in the *Daily Service*, published on April 3, 1943, and titled "Those Trade Restrictions (3)," wrote that "whilst strict and oppressive control is exercised over the prices of local foodstuffs, European firms which import foodstuffs from overseas are permitted to make uncontrolled profits."[96]

Engagement in protests enabled market women on the home front to bring their concerns to local administrations. Nigerian women played a vital role in drawing attention to and articulating the realities surrounding colonial intervention in the local economy. Through the selective use of language, rhetoric, symbols, and framing mechanisms, women challenged the colonial authority's articulation of the role of the local population in the war. While women did not challenge the ways in which the war was popularly understood, they separated everyday needs for survival and the broader rhetoric of war and empire.

Nigerian petitions were used to address other familial situations. Oliver Coates has captured the impact of family separation during the war on traditional familial support mechanisms and communal obligations.[97] The experiences of Ijebu soldiers who served in South Asia and the Middle East typify how soldiers and their families "strove desperately to maintain customary obligations during the men's military service."[98] Petitions from Ijebu soldiers as well as those from their families reveal

[93] Mba, *Nigerian Women Mobilized*, 103.
[94] NAE, EP OPC 122, vol. vii, ONDIST 13/1/2, "Food Control," Onitsha Rice and Garri Traders to Resident, Onitsha Province, July 1, 1942.
[95] NAE, EP OPC 122, vol. vii, ONDIST 13/1/2, Dominic Ezenwa and 20 Others Representing Garri Market Traders to Resident, Onitsha Province, July 17, 1942.
[96] "The Food Controller Makes a Statement," *Daily Service*, April 8, 1945.
[97] Coates, "The War, Like the Wicked Wand of a Wizard, Strikes Me and Carry Away All That I Have Loved."
[98] Ibid., 1.

that soldiers were bound by a powerful sense of obligation to their extended family not only in terms of financial support, but also in relation to labor, security, administration, and redistribution."[99] Throughout the war, countless appeals were made to colonial officials that reveal how the war changed individual circumstances. When Joseph Fowokan wrote to request the return of his son, who had been in service for four years, he hinged his request on the deprivation he had endured and the general crisis his son's absence had brought to his life.[100]

Fowokan was one of many who had been deprived of the prewar support system that relied on family and communal ties. This support was essential for the elderly such as Fowokan. Although he had no objection to his son's enlistment, his son's absence had affected his welfare, marriage, and social standing in the village. He articulated: "I am now stricken in age and lonely in this house," and continued, "the villagers are now taking advantage of this to ride me in matters relating to personal affairs."[101] Indeed, with many young men joining the army and leaving their homes for very long periods, the elderly suffered the loss of care and labor that young men provided. Fowokan went on to describe the essence of his petition and request:

As necessity compels me to petition both the Imperial and Colonial authorities to please kindly arrange for the release of my son, to return home to look after my health for the few days, if God willing to spend on the earth, until the end comes. I feel daily that I am deteriorating in strength and health. I am afraid therefore that if this continue, I may eventually die, and in consequences of this, the record of my things will perish.[102]

Most of the population supported the war against the enemy and many petitioners were not outraged at the enlistment into the army, for they understood the importance of such service to the empire. But the demands made on their often limited resources did not overshadow the personal obligation that individuals owed to their families. When Joseph Fowokan petitioned again on July 31, 1945, he drew attention to how sons in particular were intimately involved with the welfare of parents and their kin group. His carefully drafted petition spoke to deeply rooted social obligations and expectations. When he wrote, "I am the only one living in my house," he was drawing attention to the loneliness and lack of care his son's absence had caused.[103]

---

[99] Ibid.
[100] NAI, IJEBU PROF 2758, vol. II, African Forces Overseas: Welfare, Joseph Fowokan to District Officer, Ijebu Province, unknown date.
[101] Ibid.    [102] Ibid.    [103] Ibid.

Colonial officials were indifferent to the culture from which their African soldiers came. Absent in the often emotionally detached responses from colonial officials is any understanding of the petitioner's perspective. As Coates succulently outlined, "in blithe ignorance of soldiers' complex social obligations and the degree to which they preoccupied enlisted men, the D.O. [district officer] opined as to how 'there is usually some relative . . . who can help.'"[104] By contrast, petitioners like Fowokan understood

> military service not as a job excluding other forms of labor and social identities, still less does he recognize that the military was fundamentally at a remove from civilian society. Instead he regards his son's occupation as being one among several competing obligations and stresses that it is not military discipline, or the war itself, that keeps his son away, but instead "the Imperial and Colonial authorities" who can be personally engaged to grant Fowokan the favor of releasing his son.[105]

Significant too was the absence of appeal to the government for support or any other forms of charity. The articulation of "poverty" in these petitions indicated that petitioners sought no material goods or money as an exercise of mercy or compassion from the colonial authorities. Rather the importance of human labor, companionship, and social and familial relationships is articulated through these petitions that sought the return of sons, husbands, or relatives. Here then is a corpus of life-writing that offers insight into what Will Jackson characterizes in another context as "the micro-politics of intimacy and empire."[106] Here people relied on family networks and kin-based obligations that had become disrupted by the war.

Wartime policies had important gender implications. Although the mobilization rate of men was quite high in the army and construction-related services, the participation of women in the production of much-needed goods on the home front was enormous. Women's petitions reveal the changing roles they played during the war. Many participated in the wartime economy and trade in foodstuffs. Women's petitions indicate that most of them had husbands or the main breadwinners in their families enlisted in the war. Their petitions further reveal the increased roles women played in the family as heads of households and the main providers of family subsistence. The war had a psychological and economic impact on women. In parallel fashion to Anni P. Baker's study of

---

[104] Coates, "The War, Like the Wicked Wand of a Wizard, Strikes Me and Carry Away All That I Have Loved," 22.

[105] Ibid.

[106] Will Jackson, "The Shame of Not Belonging: Navigating Failure in the Colonial Petition, South Africa 1910–1961," *Itinerario* 42, no. 1 (2018): 85–101, at 87.

army wives' experiences on the American frontier, army wives in Nigeria faced peculiar circumstances related to domestic concerns and everyday survival and childrearing.[107] Some women used their family conditions and temporary separation from their spouses to participate in the expanding regional and local foodstuff trade during the war. Most stepped out of the home, and the petitions they wrote during the war frequently blurred the boundaries between public and private spheres. The intimate, informal details they sometimes contain are important to understanding the complexities of the circumstances faced by colonial officials and Nigerians in the context of the war.

Life for a military spouse was not easy. Those whose spouses had gone to war confronted the same problems faced by soldiers' wives elsewhere. Petitions by women such as Agnes Garuba touch on both patriotism and the everyday challenges faced by women on a personal level and in the area of familial relations. Ordinary Nigerians like Garuba balanced their personal needs with the larger objective of supporting the British war effort. She made clear this ambivalent collaboration between the metropole and colonial subjects when she wrote requesting permission to trade in garri: "We all are in the same flag. That's why we don't care to send our husbands, brothers and young fathers to fight for the same flag."[108] It is clear from her petition that the war reordered society and household dynamics in significant ways. For Garuba, who had depended on her husband for subsistence, the war was the beginning of a new reality and a bleak future for her and her four children. Garuba told the Aba district officer in her petition that she had to resort to trading garri because she could no longer rely on her husband, who had joined the war, to provide for their family. She metaphorically described herself as a widow who virtually had to fend for herself and her children. She therefore called on the government to issue her a permit to trade in garri so she could support her family. Garuba's public expression to colonial officials offers insight into the precarious nature of life during the war and the extraordinary steps taken by ordinary people to confront the crisis and the restrictions during the war. Her letter reveals the way women sought to negotiate the varied policies and wartime measures designed to control the Nigerian population. Petitions by women thus provide an opportunity to explore the changing gender dynamics of the colonial society and the war. They

---

[107] Anni P. Baker, "Daughters of Mars: Army Officers' Wives and Military Culture on the American Frontier," *Historian* 67, no. 1 (2005): 20–42.

[108] NAE, ABADIST 1/26/958, "Gari Control," Mrs. Agnes Garuba to District Officer, Aba, July 22, 1943. The reference to the flag (the Union Jack) is to draw attention to the common objective of defeating Hitler and the necessary sacrifices Nigerians were making by sending their men to fight.

express the changing structure of the home, and, by extension, how the cycling of men into war created a new world in which women took on a greater responsibility for the subsistence of the family and decision-making.

## Wartime Control and Protest Movements

Other forms of social protest were employed, particularly by market women. The regulation of local trade forced women in Owerri Province and the Aba and Bende Divisions to protest the government's regulation of the price of garri in 1944.[109] In October of the same year, women in the Ikot Ekpene market protested government agents who purchased garri in the market at the government-imposed price. The women perceived these interventions as an attempt to take over their cassava farms. Mass demonstrations by women armed with cassava sticks and leaves broke out in other parts of Ibibioland, including Nto Edino, Ikot Abia, Odoro Ikot, and Mbuso.[110]

Market women, under the aegis of the Lagos Market Women's Association, protested the Pullen scheme after its director, Captain A. P. Pullen, sought to impose a price control plan on essential goods and trading items dominated by women. Led by Madam Pelewure, the president of the Market Women's Guild, the women presented their petition against the Pullen scheme to the commissioner on November 24, 1943. Their twenty-six-point item for protest had about 1,201 signatories, who signed on behalf of 8,000 market women. They emphasized the impact of the economic crisis and government intervention on their lives: "We the 8,000 Lagos Market Women humbly and respectfully beseech your Excellency not to approve the Pullen Scheme which is about to deprive us all of our hitherto exclusive trading rights through which we earn our honest livelihood, support our families, educate our children and pay our lawful township and water rates."[111] As in past social movements, women employed protests and petitions to address their concerns and to frustrate the smooth implementation of regulation policies. In time, editorials in Nigerian newspapers such as the *West African Pilot* lent support to the women's voices along with political elites, incorporating these widespread grievances into the political agitation of the period.

---

[109] NAE, File No. 1646, vol. IV, ABADIST 14/1/875, "Gari Control," Omuna Native Court to District Officer, Aba, November 1944.
[110] Ibid.    [111] *West African Pilot*, November 27, 1943.

The similarities with previous responses to issues of livelihood are striking. The government wartime policies, including produce inspection and new trade practices, fostered disillusionment that manifested in various protests that increased in frequency from 1929. Just as women in colonial eastern Nigeria responded to the introduction of colonial taxation and the effects of the Great Depression, women also attempted to make sense of the world around them following the economic crisis brought by the Second World War.[112] In urban Lagos and other parts of Yorubaland such as Abeokuta, scholars have documented how women sought to draw upon indigenous ideology as well as rational economic discourses to address colonial regulations and control.[113] In all, the protests underscore the discontent rooted in the economic conditions of the war.

In much the same way that individuals were affected by wartime policies and expressed their disillusionment through petitions, the urban areas also expressed their collective disaffection about the war's impact on their lives. By the 1930s, Nigeria had witnessed significant urban development and expansion. The urban population in Nigerian cities had grown at an astronomical rate of more than 15 percent annually in the first decades of the colonial period. Lagos Township, for example, had a population of 126,000 in 1931. Enugu and Onitsha had a combined population of a little over 1.1 million in 1931, and the population of Ibadan was 990,000 that same year.[114] These urban towns were not spared the agony and hardship of the war. A major consequence of wartime restrictions was the disruption of prewar food security arrangements that supported the urban population. Urban areas faced a real food crisis during the war because the majority of urban food supplies came from rural farmers. This is seen in the letters and opinions expressed by groups, associations, and the local press to the authorities in the affected cities.

The Aba Community League, an association representing unions, ethnic groups, and communities in Aba Township, wrote petitions on

[112] The most important protest related to the introduction of taxation and the economic crisis of the late 1920s and early 1930s was the "Women's War of 1929," popularly known as "Ogu Umunwanyi." On the 1929 women's revolt, see Toyin Falola and Adam Paddock, *The Women's War of 1929: A History of Anti-colonial Resistance in Eastern Nigeria* (Durham, NC: Carolina Academic Press, 2011); and Matera, Bastian, and Kent, *The Women's War of 1929*.

[113] See, for example, Kamm, "Price Control, Profiteering, and Public Cooperation"; Oyemakinde, "The Pullen Marketing Scheme." For the food crisis in Lagos and Abeokuta, see Byfield, "Women, Rice, and War," 160.

[114] Nigeria, *Annual Abstract of Statistics, 1960* (Lagos: Federal Government Printer, 1960), 4. See also H. I. Ajaegbu, *Urban and Rural Development in Nigeria* (London: Heinemann, 1976), 32.

behalf of its members who were concerned with the garri control policy. They requested that J. V. Dewhurst, the district officer, furnish them with justifications for introducing the garri control:

It is presumed that by this measure Your Worship is endeavouring to ameliorate the plight of local gari consumers in connection with price; but so that there may be no undue hardships and unnecessary confusion, I am directed to solicit your clemency, for an extension of the time limit to, the earliest, end of July, in order not only to allow traders to recover any cash or other advances they might have launched out to producers against deliveries, but also to afford both you and us the opportunity of meeting all interested sections in the gari business – cassava farmers, gari producers, local consumers and the various grades of traders – to discuss and stabilize price and to devise ways and means whereby any possible problem that may arise when the permit or quota system actually comes into operation, may be neutralized.[115]

The league also drew attention to the food crisis facing the city in another petition to the district officer on August 2, 1941. Following the restrictions on the movement of foodstuffs, the petitioners noted that the town was faced with an inadequate supply of food, which exposed the inhabitants to "very grave danger of famine."[116] Indeed, the Aba Garri Traders Association had expressed dissatisfaction with the quota system imposed by the district officer, arguing that the method "will annihilate the garri trade, and undoubtedly impoverish the average trader involved and render life not worth living."[117] As free citizens of the empire, the association argued, "we have a right to live, and this right we pray for an amendment to the method or system of control."[118]

The voices in these petitions are indispensable in contextualizing different aspects of colonial engagement with Nigeria during the war, including the state of individual and communal experiences and well-being. They reveal the intersection between the big political questions at stake in the war and specific local conditions and concerns. The moral rhetorical characteristic embedded in local petitions created a distinction between the people's perceptions and the dominant colonial order; this moral distinction characterized the colonial regulations and policies as unethical and wicked.

[115] NAE, ABADIST 14/1/875, Aba Community League to J. V. Dewhurst, District Officer, Aba, June 28, 1943.
[116] The league represented most of the unions, ethnic groups, and communities in Aba Township. See NAE, ABADIST 1/26/958. File No. 668, "Foodstuffs: Yams, Plantains, Cocoyam, etc. Requested Prohibition of Railment or Exportation of in Future," Honorary Secretary, Aba Community League to District Officer, Aba, August 2, 1943.
[117] NAE, ABADIST, 14/1/873, File No. 1646, "A Resolution," Garri Traders Association, Aba to Resident, Owerri Province, July 29, 1943.
[118] Ibid.

## Transport Control

Life was disrupted in other ways by the war, as illustrated by the petitions of Nigerians related to use of motor vehicles. Indeed, the movement of all civilian vehicles and the consumption of petrol and other petroleum fuels were strictly restricted and regulated.[119] Restrictions and regulations on the use of motor vehicles and the rationing of petrol created a heavy burden on individuals, businesses, and voluntary agencies. Except in cases of real emergency, the general provision governing the use of private or commercial motor transport empowered the transport control officer to make the final judgment on when road transportation could be used for the whole or part of any journey for which alternative transport was available.[120] Restrictions on the use of private cars, lorries, petrol, and purchase of bicycle accessories were meant to conserve available stocks for war purposes.[121] The quantity of petrol allowed for use by private cars was strictly controlled. Basic rations were issued in accordance with the essential needs of the owners.[122] The policy that required importers of motor vehicles and accessories to render returns of stock and imports to government officials presented a burden for businesses.[123] Like for food-stuffs, the sale of motor vehicles, motor types and tubes, and bicycles was controlled through a permit system, which authorized the successful applicant to purchase a specific vehicle from a designated dealer. The transport control officers were empowered to approve such applications after determining the purpose for which the vehicle was required.

Restrictions extended to the sale of secondhand vehicles and parts.[124] Recycling used items, including motor tires, was encouraged, and the surrender of used tires that were of good quality was required from applicants for purchase of a vehicle.[125] Wartime regulation ensured that the use of existing vehicles in Nigeria was confined to "essential purposes only," including the evacuation of export produce and materials, the transport

---

[119] See ibid., 5.

[120] Alternative means of transportation were by rail or water. Where road transport was used, it had to proceed by the shortest route to the nearest rail or river transport. See *Memorandum on the Organisation and Control of War Time Trade and Production*, 5.

[121] See Control of Bicycle Spare Parts and Accessories (Eastern Provinces) Order, 1943. See also *Memorandum on the Organisation and Control of War Time Trade and Production*, appendix.

[122] *Memorandum on the Organisation and Control of War Time Trade and Production*, 6.

[123] See "Control of Sale of Motor Vehicles, Motor Types and Tubes and Bicycles," *Memorandum on the Organisation and Control of War Time Trade and Production*, 7.

[124] The control of tires and inner tubes was on the same line as that of motor vehicles. In addition, buyers of new tires or tubes were required to "surrender an equivalent number of used tyres and tubes." *Memorandum on the Organisation and Control of War Time Trade and Production*, 7.

[125] Ibid.

from areas of production of food supplies for the services, the maintenance of supplies for the native populations in the large centers, and the transport of imported supplies and petrol.[126] The transport zones were divided into areas determined by whether: "(a) they conform with the economic watersheds down which export produce and commodities of internal trade naturally flow towards a focal point; and (b) they ensure the shortest road haulage from place of production to the focal point, and thence to the nearest rail or river transport."[127]

The regulation had an immediate impact on the society, from individuals to nongovernmental agencies working in the country. Agricultural officer Norman Herington noted that the scarcity of petrol and the restrictions on transportation prevented agricultural officers from giving much attention to some of the activities of the department, including visiting the school farms, an essential part of the department's work before the war. According to Herington, "it was becoming difficult to reach all the schools because of petrol rationing and the growing scarcity of tyres and spare parts. I had to make use of passenger lorries and bicycles when at times my Kit Car became unsafe for long distance journeys."[128] B. J. Dike, owner of three motor lorries, asked for permission to continue to use his lorries. All three lorries were used in moving palm kernel and palm oil from Umuahia to Ikot Ekpene and Itu. In his appeals to the Itu district officer, he wrote, "My reason for desiring to continue with my lorries is because my capital is invested in them, and I depend solely on returns from these services for my living."[129]

A permit to operate was restricted to certain areas or routes and for specific purposes. Opara Nadi, whose vehicle was stranded on the Owerri–Onitsha road, could not bring his lorry to Itu, where he was stationed, without a permit to continue the trip. He asked for a permit to drive his lorry back to his station. How long he had to wait for such a permit is not clear. Compliance was achieved by using transport control police posted at strategic points on the highways, by mobile police checkpoints at markets, and by other collection areas and freight checkpoints at which authorities inspected permits. Police and vehicle inspection clerks kept a census of all vehicles passing their posts, which were to be scrutinized by transport control officers and compared with past permits issued.[130]

The sale of petrol or petroleum fuel to the public was only effected "by surrender of petrol coupons, or under a permit authorizing the owners of

---

[126] Ibid.    [127] Ibid.
[128] RH, Mss Afr. S. 1779, Norman Herington, Papers, Photos, Agricultural Education Officer, 1944.
[129] NAE ITUDIST 7/1/614–616, B. J. Dike to District Officer, Itu, September 5, 1939.
[130] *Memorandum on the Organisation and Control of War Time Trade and Production*, 6.

the vehicle to be in possession of a limited quality of petrol." As Uwakwe Esse notes in his study of colonial control during the war, the restrictions on transportation created a heavy burden on African transporters, who in some cases petitioned officials in order to express their views on such restrictions.[131] Owners of private vehicles were issued coupons entitling them to a basic ration of petrol based on a previously approved and "limited number of journeys between residence and place of business each month."[132] The permit system administered by transport control officers disrupted life as well as business. The Motor Transport Union at Onitsha protested what it called "favoritism and business monopoly" when the chief commissioner of the Eastern Province gave one Mr. Melikian a monopoly of the lorry transport business in the area during the war.[133] They argued: "We deeply regret that such a treatment should be meted to us, lorry owners, at this critical moment of the war, when it is our mind to do the best we can in support of the war effort."[134] The sentiments expressed in these petitions, of course, were mediated by local socio-cultural and economic contexts that the authorities who developed and implemented these policies did not often consider. In articulating these feelings, William Rosenberg remarks that historians face the problem of "access to the historical actualities of feeling itself through sources in which emotional expression may be mediated by social and cultural values quite different from their own."[135] Hidden, as well as glaring, in these letters and petitions are the visible ideas of racial difference and the inscribed privilege of the colonial institution and personnel. The language and conceptual ideas they express also reflect the subjugated and subordinate position of the Nigerian population. Restrictions in the transportation sector, however, also affected some European personnel, most of whom were in the region as missionaries, and employees of European trading firms and medical facilities that catered to the African population. Their requests for allocations of petrol and other needs reveal a widespread crisis in this period and

---

[131] O. Uwakwe Esse, "Road Transportation in Nigeria As a Private Enterprise among the Igbo, 1920–1999" (Unpublished PhD thesis, University of Nigeria, Nsukka, 2003).

[132] *Memorandum on the Organisation and Control of War Time Trade and Production*, 6–7.

[133] NAE, CSE 1/85/8614, vol. III, Association of African Importers and Traders of Cycle Spare Parts, Aba, October 15, 1943. Mr. Melikian is probably a Lebanese, most of whom dominated the distribution of imported goods in Nigeria in the period along with European trading companies.

[134] Ibid.

[135] William G. Rosenberg, "Reading Soldiers' Moods: Russian Military Censorship and the Configuration of Feeling in World War I," *American Historical Review* 119, no. 3 (June 2014): 714–740, at 715.

the difficulties encountered in carrying out essential services related to missionary work and and other social services.[136]

## Failure of Colonial Control

Colonial restrictions and regulations were not always successful. Regulations were mostly enforced on the railways and in large urban markets and retail outlets because they could be more easily policed. Archival records describe an informal market system, which began to emerge because of government regulations. In August 1943, the secretary of the Aba Community League wrote to the Aba district officer regarding what he described as "unauthorized markets outside the township."[137] It seems that large-scale traders suffered most from the restrictions. Small-scale traders, in contrast, may have survived on the available opportunities offered by the informal market.

Some local traders could circumvent the officially approved channels. In July 1944, for example, the government estimated that about 200 tons more than the permitted quota of garri were exported to the north under illegal conditions.[138] Some traders moved between different buying stations to maximize their profits and increase the quota allocated to them. Such smuggling activities prompted the resident for Owerri Province, A. F. B. Bridges, to invoke the Nigeria General Defence (Food Control) Regulation of 1941, which prohibited the export of garri by rail from Owerri Province to any station north of Enugu without a permit. Although travelers were permitted to export only a personal allowance not exceeding £8 per person,[139] people found creative ways to get around these restrictions that sought to achieve the goals of "controlling prices and standardizing and regulating a market sector that Pullen described as 'uneconomical,' 'unbusinesslike,' and 'irregular.'"[140] In reality, the attempt to regulate the market, Emily Kamm argues, was not solely about prices but was an extension of "colonial notions of rationality, standardization, efficiency, and even docility into market spheres dominated by women that operated by their own norms and customs, outside of the colonial framework

---

[136] See several petitions from Church of Scotland Mission at Ikot Inyang, Qua Iboe Mission, Mission Hospital, Itu, and from European trading companies such as John Holt & Co. Ltd. and United Africa Company.

[137] NAE, ABADIST 1/26/958, File No. 668, "Unauthorized Markets Outside the Township," Secretary Aba Community League to District Officer, Aba, August 2, 1943.

[138] NAE, ABADIST 14/1/875, File No. 1646, vol. IV, "Export of Garri to the North by Garri Traders Will Stop on 1st September."

[139] Ibid.    [140] Kamm, "Price Control, Profiteering, and Public Cooperation," 3.

dominated by men."[141] The failure of the Pullen scheme, for example, was blamed on the abnormal context in which the policies were implemented. In the view of officials, "Nigeria [was] not a normal country."[142] Such comments, however, were an extension of colonial views of the backwardness of African societies and the paternalistic attitude of European colonial officials.

The dwindling food supplies and the rising cost of living in the cities was not a crisis of production but a crisis of distribution.[143] The food situation in Nigeria up to 1942 was generally good. Nigeria could meet its requirements for a variety of goods such as butter, ham, bacon, rice, and wheat flour that were imported in prewar times. The Department of Agriculture and the Veterinary Department had put considerable effort in this direction. Domestic needs were generally met, and some spare goods were exported to neighboring countries. Government policies created artificial scarcity, disrupted the local distributive system, and affected the incomes of many local traders at a period when the market for food crops would have led to increased income for farmers and less reliance on income from cash crops.

Things changed rapidly by the following year in terms of higher prices and scarcity. A black market in local foodstuffs had developed by 1943, causing a degree of scarcity in cities such as Lagos and in other large urban areas. Among the most notable of these food items was garri, palm oil, and groundnut oil, and the hold-up of these items was responsible for the shortages. The *Daily Service* reported on January 6, 1943, that a flourishing black market for these commodities existed and those who were willing to pay above the official control prices could be trusted by dealers. But the withholding of supplies was due to the fact that the prices at which dealers obtained their goods "would not permit them to sell at the control prices except at considerable loss."[144] Nigerians voiced their condemnation of profiteering, and such sentiment was reflected in the *Daily Service* report: "We are uncompromisingly against all profiteering, hoarding and the setting up of 'Black Markets,' and those who indulge in such practices at the expense of the community will receive no sympathy from us."[145] There were other reasons for the scarcity of foodstuffs. The lack of transport to bring food from producing areas was evident. There were reports of traders buying goods in places like Oyo, Ilesha, and Ijebu in the western provinces and reselling them in the same area or incurring huge losses due to the lack of transport.[146]

---

[141] Ibid.    [142] Ibid.    [143] Korieh, "Urban Food Supply."
[144] "'Black Market' in Local Foodstuffs," *Daily Service*, January 6, 1943.    [145] Ibid.
[146] "Inefficient Price Control in Local Foodstuffs," *Daily Service*, January 7, 1943.

Controlled pricing of local and imported products had economic consequences too. While it protected the interest of the consumer, it did not always
safeguard profit to the trader who employed his/her capital and energy and
who was equally entitled to a livelihood.[147] Additionally, there were people
who made quick money and profited from illegal activities. These "congeni-
tal racketeers," as the *Daily Service* described them, were "allies of Hitler" and
"our enemies" who should be fought to the death.[148] Many petitioners tied
their demands to the basic ideology for which Europeans were fighting the
war. They used the new demands made by the colonial government to point
out the contradictions inherent in the colonial system vis-à-vis the notion of
protecting liberty and freedom. Some petitions exposed the way that colonial
regulations enforced a distinction between Africans and Europeans, arguing
that the new regulations implemented by the colonial government had
become part of waging of war on them.

A group of sixteen traders in Aba tried to persuade the authorities that
their participation in trade was important for their livelihood and an
essential war activity. In a petition titled "Exportation of Garri from
Mbawsi to North," the petitioners cast their letters as a threat to the
livelihood of British-protected subjects. Part of their petition is worth
quoting in detail:

As a people under British protection and trusteeship, [we] have been experiencing
severe hardship and are financially run-down as evident of bad trade. Our humble
testimonies therefore demand Your Administrative assistance to help ameliorate the
deteriorated situation by granting our humble request, thus helping us to have the
means of meeting our needs and instruments towards the Empire's war effort.[149]

## Understanding Petitions in the Colonial Context

As reflected in these petitions, an important feature of the dialogue
between colonial officials and colonial subjects during the war is how
colonial subjects employed European rhetoric about rights and democratic ideals to demand fairness in a period when war had disrupted social
and economic life. Despite the rhetoric of freedom, equality, and human
rights that was central to Allied propaganda against Germany and its
allies, the British colonial authority maintained its stronghold on colonial
societies. Indeed, the colonial system in all its manifestations – political
domination as well as economic exploitation – expanded during the war.
Yet these letters place the colonized Nigerian population at the center and

---

[147] Ibid.    [148] Ibid.
[149] NAE, ABADIST 1/26/958, Letter Written on Behalf of the Petitioner by the Nigerian
Services and Commercial Bureau, 145 Jubilee Road, Aba.

present them as historical actors with pliable cultures and communities. Moreover, they provide a more accurate and powerful understanding of the processes of colonization, its impact on particular groups and communities, its role in social and economic change, and how local societies fit into our understanding of the larger twentieth-century global political economy.

Petitions and protests as outlined earlier are indicative of many issues that dominated the colonial period. Many were prudent in their use of language and clearly written to elicit sympathy. Yet others were intent on drawing the attention of British officials to the larger philosophical ideals of democracy, equity, and fair play – concepts upon which the colonial project was imposed in the first place. Such expressions of a deep understanding of the contradictions inherent in colonialism cogently highlight the fact that Nigerians were aware of these paradoxes. Many found colonial control and restrictions a major contradiction: although colonial officials were attempting to stabilize an economy disrupted by a European war, Nigerians could not understand why officials were disrupting the attempt by local people to engage in activities they thought were contributing to the war effort, as well as providing them with avenues to survive the economic crisis that came with the war. Documentation of the kind that emerged during the war is necessary for understanding the determination and endurance of the people in the face of the enduring impacts of colonialism and the efforts of the colonial authorities to intervene in the local economy by imposing rules and regulations for war purposes. The genre is important for understanding coloniality, the development of infra-politics, self-determination, and the intellectual background of decolonization. The keen interest that colonial officials developed in their content and context reflects how the letters of petition operated as political activity.[150]

Who drafted the petitions? They were apparently written by a broad range of people with some Western education and literacy: schoolchildren, village teachers, and government employees, especially court clerks, who subverted their employers. Nigerians with some level of education wrote their own petitions, often in their own hands. Others were written by professional petition writers on behalf of clients. In this way, they conveyed the expressions, viewpoints, and perspectives of those who wrote them. Professional petition writers, many of whom had some

---

[150] James Daybell sees letters as playing an important role in "political" activity or the expression of interest in politics by women in early modern England. See *Women Letter-Writers in Tudor England* (Oxford: Oxford University Press, 2006), 4.

specialized training, used the petitions of their clients to challenge the ideological underpinnings of colonialism. These indirect attacks on the colonial state regarding the contradictions of colonialism were often beyond the scope mandated by clients. Some of these court clerks earned extra income through moonlighting as petition writers. This led to the emergence of a cadre of professional letter writers. Due to the rivalry within the profession, they developed and honed an art form. Some may consider their vocabulary bombastic, tending to exaggerate, and indeed developing a stylized vocabulary of protest. The question about whether they expressed the voices and feelings of the victims or used the occasion to parade their own literary genius is difficult to answer.

Overall, the ability of Africans to write or to hire professional letter writers gave local people the capability to speak out about power. It not only gave civilians the opportunity to write about their concerns but established a dialogue with colonial powers – a dialogue that received some level of respect because it fit into the familiar structure of European habits of expression. These letters and petitions of an often lowly class of farmers and traders defied the perceived social and political order of the colonial era. Yet a critical distinguishing character of these petitions lies in who wrote them in terms of class and gender. Most were written by men from the lower classes. Although support for the war cut across class lines, most of the upper class or African elite were less concerned with the issues of daily survival that lay at the root of these petitions and supplications. Although some were written to attract sympathy, many were intimate expressions of individual conditions, which vividly displayed a clear understanding of the larger context that gave rise to such conditions.

Nigerian letters display emotional reactions to the Great Depression – despair, cynicism, anger – and attitudes toward colonial intervention in the production and marketing of produce. With the failure of other forms of resistance, letters and petition writing became a powerful weapon in the African struggle against the colonial state. But these petitions did not always lead to the desired result. Most colonial officials valued the letters, perceiving them as a way to gauge public opinion and sentiment. Colonial officials listened and replied to some petitions, but ignored many others. Critically, however, petitioning was an instrument extensively employed by colonial subjects to challenge colonial policies, regulations, and institutions, in attempts to shape outcomes and present local perspectives. Thus, wartime petitions open a window into an African society's encounter with imperialism in the context of a global conflict and provide the opportunity to read these individual actions by petitioners as part of a local encounter with colonialism rather than simply as African acceptance of imperialism.

These petitions were not meant as propaganda. They offer several perspectives into African lives and put the reader in direct contact with the victims of colonial control, evoking a feeling of what it was like to live through the era. Yet we can read beyond African voices in these letters and petitions. They offer a lens through which we can understand the broader attempt by colonial administrators to control the colonized through the restriction of movements and surveillance, extraction of resources, and other means. The overall effect of these letters and petitions is that they put people in the colonial context and provide individuals with diverse life stories and points of view from the perspectives of Africans. World War II–related petitions in particular reveal the distinctively diverse ways groups of Nigerians – urban and rural – were affected by colonial regulation and general wartime conditions. Colonial restriction disrupted the economic life of the African populations and threatened their survival. Despite the exigencies of war, Nigerian petitioners saw themselves as paying the ultimate price – becoming the sacrificial lamb as colonial subjects. By creating a space to address their own personal issues, petitioners were also creating space to participate in the larger discourse that went beyond their immediate need for survival. They, by extension, moved into the realm of public discourse on war and economic policy. The content and context in which these petitions were written suggest that the impact of the war was felt within both urban and rural contexts. These petitions reveal the local economic conditions and production systems that linked a broad range of people, classes, and spatial categories – a system that became even more interconnected through war.

The Second World War generated conflicting notions of imperial citizenship. The Nigerian population carried asymmetrical identities spurred by the condition generated by the war itself and the demand made upon them by the colonial state. Though not fixed, historical documents, they indicate the lower classes such as traders, farmers, and the rural and urban poor were more concerned with daily survival than the ideological rhetoric of imperial citizens. These unique conditions presented peculiar challenges to the Nigerian population as well as colonial authorities during the war. However, they also provide an opportunity to assess how local historical contexts informed the unique path taken by local farmers and traders.[151] While the Nigerian population supported the war against Germany, its people prudently opposed the radical

---

[151] I have dealt with these issues in detail in Korieh, *The Land Has Changed.*

economic policies introduced by authorities. In a sense, they accepted the ideological reasons that dragged the empire and its far-flung colonial subjects into the war but contested some of the steps taken in its prosecution. The petitions Nigerian traders wrote to colonial officials provide unexpected insight into the changing nature of local and indigenous responses to wartime policies and programs in addition to the forms of African agency that addressed issues of everyday concern.[152]

Indeed, the economic inadequacies during the war and the frequent changes in colonial policies to address wartime problems only led to great dissatisfaction among Nigerians.[153] The demands of the war forced the British to restructure the local economy, in order to ensure that Africans produced the necessary commodities to support the British war effort, and to compel the local population to see the value of their sacrifice. The vigorous propaganda campaign emphasized the importance of producing more food and export produce to support the war effort. The unprecedented level of mobilization and new regulations and control peasant production eventually became a burden for the local population in Nigeria.

The relative scarcity of basic needs during the war reveals the extent to which the local economy had become dependent on the importation of goods, which could have otherwise been cheaply produced locally. That is part of the contradiction of colonialism. Additionally, the examination of the political economy of the war shows that the colony of Nigeria, like its counterparts in Africa, contributed much more than personnel and logistical support toward imperial war efforts. Furthermore, colonial control and restrictions did not always work. The local traders used their ingenuity to cope with the circumstances created by government intervention. Smuggling, hoarding, and fraud were rampant and made government control less effective.[154] Although the incentives were lacking, farmers expanded production due to the more lucrative internal market system that existed in the country. Overall, sections of the Nigerian population responded to wartime policies in several ways. The petitions, which were employed increasingly during the war, served a double function: expression and protest. This latter function was especially important during the war in that it was often the only form of public expression allowed by colonial officials. The often intricate intertwining of colonial policies with the daily lives of the local population suggests that outcomes were also

---

[152] For a greater exploration of this topic, see Korieh, "May It Please Your Honor," and Korieh, *"Life Not Worth Living."*
[153] Emezue, "Managing Wartime Shortages," 1.    [154] See Falola, "Salt Is Gold," 431.

shaped by the actions and responses of the African population. These local reactions and responses demonstrate the variety of ways Nigerians of all classes, genders, and ages attempted to deal with the shortages that characterized the period of the war within the free capitalist market economy that had become their economic system.

> So, despite all the adversity and disaster, we conquered over evil and were
> triumphant in the end and finally the glorious day came when the war was
> declared over. The incredible release from fear and pain had at last
> encompassed us and can only be described fully by those who experienced
> it. There was just sheer unadulterated jubilation with no order whatsoever
> despite the conspicuous absence of many alcoholic drinks. The masses
> were more intoxicated with Victory than with alcohol!
>
> Joan Styan, London

Germany's unconditional surrender was received all over the British
colonies and overseas dominions with thanksgiving and deep relief, as
recalled by Joan Styan of London.[1] On behalf of all ranks in the West
African Command, Lieutenant General Brocas Burrows, general officer and commander in chief, congratulated the West African troops
on the magnificent part they played in defeating the Japanese. Paying
tribute to the role of West African soldiers, he declared: "By your
bravery, your devotion to duty and your cheerful bearing in the face
of hardship, you have built up a tradition of which everyone in West
Africa is proud."[2] Fifteen thousand of these African soldiers died
fighting for Britain in the Second World War.[3] Nigerian veterans of
the Second World War made up more than half of the total force of
the 90,000 West African soldiers deployed to Southeast Asia after
1943.[4] By war's end, as many as 100,000 Nigerians had fought in
Asia and the Middle East.[5]

Although some senior British officers were often dismissive of the contributions of African soldiers and made condescending remarks about

---

[1] "VE Day Remembered," BBC, May 6, 2005, accessed January 18, 2019, www.bbc.co.uk
/history/ww2peopleswar/categories/c54817; NA, CAB/66/65/35, "Report for the Month
of April 1945 for the Dominions, India, Burma and the Colonies and Mandated
Territories," May 22, 1945.

[2] NA, CAB/66/65/35, "Report for the Month of April 1945 for the Dominions, India,
Burma and the Colonies and Mandated Territories."

[3] "WWII's Forgotten Army."    [4] Ibid.

[5] Njoku, "Nigeria: World War II." For Nigerian contributions to the British war effort, see
also Njoku, "Burden of Imperialism," and Njoku, "Export Production Drive in Nigeria
during World War II."

those Africans who fought with them, the Colonial Office in London acknowledged that African soldiers helped beat the Italians out of Somalia and Abyssinia, defeating the best Blackshirt battalions and African conscripts the Italians sent against them.[6] West African soldiers, of which Nigeria contributed two regiments, defended British West African colonies from attack from French colonial territories. They helped take Madagascar, went on to the Middle East to defend British interests, and deployed to the Far East to fight Japan.[7] World War II historian David Killingray noted the strength and resolve of West African soldiers during their deployment in Burma, where they fought among steep, wooded valley slopes.[8] Elvet D. Price's recollections of his service during the Second World War with the Royal West African Frontier Force is full of praise for his Nigerian counterparts. Price wrote that the West Africans "did a marvelous job in Burma and outfought some of Japan's crack troops in the Arakan."[9] Remarkably, however, the celebration that followed the end of hostilities was betrayed by the struggles to deal with the war's aftermath.

Significant sociocultural and political changes occurred at the end of the war across various fronts. How did the wartime experiences of Nigerian soldiers help in transforming the social and political landscape? How did the end of the war become the impetus for the restricting of colonial relations and a redefinition of the relationship between the metropole and the colony? Nigerians experienced changes at home, in their local villages and communities, as veterans, and in politics as they attempted to redefine their relationship with the colonial state. While remembrance and commemoration and educating the postwar generation were rare on the African side, new manifestations of masculinity, changing attitudes around power and authority, and expressions of modernity became visible legacies of the war in rural communities.

## End-of-War Repatriation and Social Changes

In April 1945, a leave and repatriation scheme was approved for African troops in the India and Southeast Asia Command. Under this policy,

---

[6] NA, CAB/66/65/35, "Report for the Month of April 1945 for the Dominions, India, Burma and the Colonies and Mandated Territories."

[7] Jackson, *The British Empire and the Second World War*, 171.

[8] Al Jazeera Correspondent, "The Burma Boy: Barnaby Phillips Follows the Life of One of the Forgotten Heroes of World War II," Al Jazeera, July 22, 2012, accessed January 18, 2019, www.aljazeera.com/programmes/aljazeeracorrespondent/2011/08/201182813522 8487172.html.

[9] IWM, 84/23/1, Elvet D. Price Papers, "Some Wartime Memories of Nigeria and the West African Soldiers."

African troops would return to West and East Africa after approximately three years of overseas service, subject to available space on ships.[10] The general demobilization of the African troops serving overseas began in late 1945, although ship space prevented the whole brigade from returning as one party.[11] So "to the rollicking strains of Home Again and the regimental marches of the Royal West African Frontier Force," the *Nigerian Eastern Mail* wrote, the first contingent of the West African Expeditionary Force – 1,500 men of the 14th W. A. Ack-Ack Brigade from Nigeria and Sierra Leone – embarked from Bombay on September 28, 1945.[12] They were among the first men to leave West Africa for India in May and June 1943. The arrival of Nigerian soldiers in a transit camp in Ikeja, just outside Lagos, was followed by welcoming ceremonies and a victory march through Lagos past the governor-general at the saluting base.[13] The local press was full of the news and pictures of the Nigerian troops' return, along with accounts of their role in the Burma campaigns.[14]

The mobilization exercise all fell on Major J. J. Cherns, who had vast experience working with the Nigerian soldiers. He had served as an officer with the Royal West African Frontier Force (RWAFF) in Nigeria, India, and Burma from May 1943 to February 1946. His service with the 4th Battalion Nigeria Regiment, the 6th (West African) Brigade, and the 81st (West African) Division in Nigeria, India, and the Arakan between May 1943 and February 1944 was valuable in overseeing the postwar demobilization.[15] After the festivities, the serious business of demobilization was under way, and it was no simple matter. It involved sorting out the troops, arranging for their pay and gratuities, resolving various other matters and disputes, and arranging their passage home from Lagos. The diverse regional origins of the Nigerians created major challenges to the demobilization. After they had been paid, the demobilized soldiers traveled in escorted parties in special trains to their home areas, where district officers arranged transport to their villages.[16] Cherns commanded a demobilization train, which carried some 400 demobilized soldiers, first traveling north to Kano, and then westward and southward, finishing up at Enugu, and stopping at specified points en route to hand soldiers over to the local district officer at their final destinations.[17]

While it was generally desired that the West African divisions in India should be sent home as soon as possible, the task faced logistical

[10] NA, CAB/66/65/35, "Report for the Month of April 1945 for the Dominions, India, Burma and the Colonies and Mandated Territories."
[11] *Nigerian Eastern Mail*, October 27, 1945, 6.   [12] Ibid.
[13] IWM, 03/23/1, Cherns, "Walk through the Valley."   [14] Ibid.   [15] Ibid.   [16] Ibid.
[17] Ibid.

challenges. The enormous difficulties in doing so were expressed by key military and civilian officials. On a visit to the West African divisions in India in October 1945, Major H. P. James, a senior resident, noted that the desire to send off 5,000 troops during December 1945 and another 8,000 a month from January was going to be hampered by shipping difficulties.[18] Hardships in troop movements were anticipated, as the colonial government worked to balance priorities between needed troop movements and the shipping of goods and foodstuffs across the empire. From January 1946, approximately 3,000 to 4,000 soldiers were transported per month from India. An additional 3,000 per month were expected to return from the Middle East starting in April 1946. The return of about 7,000 ex-servicemen per month was expected from both the Far East and the Middle East. A considerable number of these solders were to be returned home, beginning with those who enlisted before 1941.

There were many motivations for such a speedy return to West Africa. Officials expressed the fear that it was undesirable to keep the West African troops in India for longer than necessary, because such a prolonged stay after the war "can only have a very bad effect on them."[19] Foremost in the minds of British officers was the impact the interactions with Indians could have on the political consciousness of African soldiers. In Major H. P. James's view, life in the army "has been a tremendous education to the men. They have become in general much more confident in themselves." Their experiences in India had already shown that the soldiers had begun to regard themselves as superior to the Indian civilians, "who they look on with good natured tolerance mixed with contempt."[20] James expressed the view that "indeed physically and often mentally they seem to be much superior and I have heard that in some places the Indians have referred to them as 'Black Sahibs,'" or ones with an unfair bias toward English or Western culture.[21] There were concerns that this disposition toward the British might be corrupted if these soldiers were allowed prolonged interaction with Indians.[22] Such an attitude was expected to be carried over to their home countries and expressed in ways that could threaten the sociopolitical order in the

---

[18] NAE, CADIST 1/3/21, "West African Troops Abroad: Visit by Major H. P. James," Senior Resident, Report on a Visit to 81st Division in India, 1.
[19] Ibid.    [20] Ibid., 1.
[21] Ibid., 5. The term "Black Sahib" derived from the original derogatory term "Brown Sahib," a term used to refer to native South Asians who imitate Western – typically English – lifestyles and have been heavily influenced by Western culture and thinking. The term was also used as a mark of respect in India to address or to refer to a man in a position of authority, especially white government officials in the period of British rule.
[22] Ibid.

colonies. This new consciousness would pose a challenge for the colonial state should African soldiers begin to exercise their agency and confidence in relation to colonial authorities.

Indeed, mounting challenges faced by the British during the war and African participation in the war transformed imperial discourses and the nature of African perceptions of themselves in relation to the empire. James did point out that nervous colonial officials sought to deal with real and imaginary rebellions:

It is very difficult to say what attitude these men will take up when they return to civil life. I should think that the Nigerian Hausa and the men from the northern territories of the Gold Coast will give little trouble. There may be many malcontents among the Southerners, but I should say that the majority will want to settle down to useful life, with reasonable opportunities for employment. ... The change to civil life as soon as the novelty of getting home has worn off, will be very great. If they feel that their services in the Army are really appreciated and as much as is reasonable is being done for them, I should say they will settle down without serious trouble but with the reservations that the reaction of the West Africans are always unpredictable.[23]

He added that it "is important that they should be treated with as much consideration as is possible" in the ways they have "become used to it in the Army."[24]

Major James was not alone in expressing such sentiments and reservations. Colonial officials had anticipated other problems. On February 14, 1941, Deputy Chairman of the West African Governors' Conference W. J. A. Jones wrote to the colonial secretary's office in the eastern provinces seeking comments and suggestions regarding any problems that would likely arise at the end of the war. Foremost on the minds of colonial officials was the anticipated effects of the demobilization of thousands of African men who had been employed as soldiers and in auxiliary services, such as drivers and hospital orderlies, and who had enjoyed a higher pay. Their relatively secure source of income and standard of living changed after the war. The postwar environment lacked systematic demobilization policies. The demobilization of African orderlies like motor drivers, signalers, and laborers in the Royal West African Auxiliary Corps units gave way to discontent among many who descended from highly paid jobs into the ranks of the unemployed. In Kenya, for example, colonial authorities debated the reabsorption of former servicemen. Legislative Council officials "worried that disgruntled askaris would refuse to return to the 'tribal' reserves, fall prey to nationalist agitators, demand entry into trades to which their military service had

---

[23] Ibid., 5.    [24] Ibid.

introduced them or engage in the violent crime that some had committed while on leave."[25] These conditions posed important challenges to colonial authorities as they sought to recognize the special role played by African soldiers while accommodating their specific interests in the post-war economic planning.

While the Allied victory evoked great satisfaction among colonial subjects, the dismantling of the elaborate system of controls and regulations that managed many aspects of life and the economy during the war was expected to raise several other problems. Recruiting and mobilizing a large army from the African colonies for war was a process spread over several years.[26] The demobilization and repatriation of more than 300,000 soldiers who had served in southern Europe, North Africa, the Middle East, and Asia into the civilian life of the colonies was a huge task.[27] Indeed the Conference of Governors of British East African Territories had noted that postwar problems were likely to be one of greater chaos and confusion than the war itself."[28] The First World War experience was still fresh in the minds of many of these officials. Indeed, the *Nigerian Eastern Mail* expressed these concerns in an editorial on October 6, 1945. While the paper praised the African heroes of the Burma and Middle East campaigns, it pointed out:

In the next three or four months, some eighty thousand military crusaders will return to their homes throughout West Africa. While we welcome the return of our valiant sons we must expect to find them different from the men who left our shores as soldiers not so very long ago. It is hoped that ample provisions are being made for them so as to spare them the disastrous effects of disappointment. They have earned the praise of their commanders for their noble contribution to victory. By their valour and heroism West Africa has scored a higher place in the world of nations.[29]

Despite the violent brutality that characterized British colonialism, there was nonetheless a sense that both the empire and its colonial subjects shared a common goal in their desire to stop German aggression. The war, however, transformed African attitudes toward the empire. Nigerian soldiers returning from war, like their counterparts in other African countries, had a reference point for comparison about their identity and

[25] Hal Brands, "Wartime Recruiting Practices, Martial Identity and Post–World War II Demobilization in Colonial Kenya," *Journal of African History* 46, no. 1 (2005): 103–125.

[26] David Killingray and Martin Plaut, "Going Home and Demobilisation," in their edited volume, *Fighting for Britain: African Soldiers in the Second World War* (Woodbridge: James Currey, 2010), 179–202.

[27] Ibid.

[28] NA, CADIST 3/3/242, "'Post War Problems,' Notes by the Deputy Chairman, the Examination of the Problems Which May Arise after the War."

[29] "The Home-Coming of W.A. Troops," *Nigerian Eastern Mail*, October 6, 1945, 4.

their claim for rights as part of the British Empire. Their experiences imbued in them new notions of citizenship and freedom. The transnational context in which these arguments were presented provided a larger scope for political discourse that questioned the legitimacy of the empire's domination in the colonies. At one level, views about their racial identity became pan-African in orientation. Robert Kakembo, a Ugandan veteran who had risen to the rank of a regimental sergeant-major by 1944, was one of the few Africans to document his experience as a soldier. In his memoir, he recalled that Africans began "to think together as a race."[30] Kakembo went on to say:

We are all concerned when we hear of some unfortunate happening to Africans in some part of Africa or outside it. We are all happy and clap our hands when we see in the pictures in a cinema Pilot Officer Peter Thomas of Lagos, Nigeria, the first African to be granted His Majesty's Commission in the R.A.F. We are proud of him. He is one of us. He is an African.[31]

At the end of the war, Nigerian soldiers, like their fellow Africans, came home with novel ideas, fresh perspectives, and new expectations. The idea of the white man's invincibility and racial superiority was destroyed by the war. In his memoir, *A Stroke of Unbelievable Luck*, Isaac Fadoyebo, a Nigerian veteran of World War II who fought against the Japanese in Asia on behalf of the empire, recalls the harrowing experiences of the African soldiers in the jungles of Burma. The depiction of Isaac Fadoyebo's experiences in the film *The Burma Boy*, by filmmaker Barnaby Phillips, captures what Stephen Bourne calls the irony in the story of African soldiers like Isaac who traveled the world and fought in the jungles of Burma. Such men he said, "saw that white and black were not so different after all."[32] Both were "capable of courage, cowardice, intelligence, stupidity."[33] The common humanity, which these men came to realize and understand, increasingly undermined Britain's imperial authority.

Perhaps this idea of a universal humanity also influenced African interpretations of the war. German journalist Karl Rössel, who spent ten years researching the topic in West Africa, observes that "during the war the African soldiers saw their so-called rulers from Europe lying in mud and filth, they saw them suffering and dying … as a result, they realised that there are no differences between people."[34] Robert Kakembo recalled in his memoir:

[30] Kakembo, *An African Soldier Speaks*, 19–20.    [31] Ibid.
[32] Bourne, *The Motherland Calls*, 110.    [33] Ibid.
[34] Krinniger, "Africa in World War II."

It is clear that the majority of African soldiers came into the Army not to fight for King George VI or to defend the Empire. No. The King and the Empire mean and still mean nothing to them. The men you see in the forces came to help a certain kindly lady missionary or a good District Commissioner whose wife plays with their children.[35]

Men such as Kakembo viewed the war through a wider lens inspired by relations built within the colonial system rather than the desire to save the British Empire.

Another kind of African joined the army because he was ideologically opposed to Nazism. Robert Kakembo drew attention to how Hitler's *Mein Kampf* and what he wrote regarding Africans influenced those who joined the war on the side of the British. He claimed that those men bore Hitler a grudge for writing the following words: "From time to time our illustrated papers publish the news that in some quarters of the globe a Negro has become a lawyer, a teacher, a pastor, or even a grand opera singer. ... This is sin against reason itself; it is an act of criminal insanity."[36] According to Kakembo, the Africans who knew these words "came not only to fight for the preservation of the Empire but to frustrate the accursed man's ideals and save themselves and their children from cruelty and permanent bondage."[37]

Certainly Nigerians, like their fellow Africans, were fighting for self-preservation, a battle that continued at the end of the war. By recruiting all those African men to defend their empire, however, the British in the end may have undermined it.[38] The result of the Second World War was another major setback for European countries that had colonies in Africa and a catalyst to the development of African nationalism. As Suryakanthie Chetty argues in the case of South Africa, a British dominion where white minority rule had put Africans in a subordinate position, black South Africans responded by making greater demands for equal treatment in the military. The racial politics in South Africa prevented Africans from bearing arms. Such a demand was itself associated with masculinity and citizenship in a war ostensibly fought for the principles of democracy.[39] The war proved the most important source of challenging colonial hegemony and hastened the rise of an African voice.[40] The British emerged out of the war victorious but severely weakened, and other European

---

[35] Kakembo, *An African Soldier Speaks*, 8–9.    [36] Ibid.    [37] Ibid.
[38] Bourne, *The Motherland Calls*, 110. On Britain and discourse on decolonization, see John Darwin, *Britain and Decolonization: The Retreat from Empire in the Post-War World* (London: Macmillan Education, 1988).
[39] Chetty, "Imagining National Unity," 106.
[40] Rosaleen Smyth, "War Propaganda during the Second World War in Northern Rhodesia," *African Affairs* 83, no. 332 (1984): 345–358.

powers had been defeated, an outcome that starkly undercut the myth of European invincibility.

## Ex-soldiers and the Crisis of Resettlement

The world that Nigerian soldiers returned to in 1945 was a changed one. They came home to a changing political, economic, and social landscape that posed many challenges to the ex-servicemen and the general population. The societies to which African soldiers returned faced great economic hardship. Ex-servicemen demanded reparations from the colonial state for their service, which were not often fulfilled. In his study on demobilization in Kenya, Hal Brands has shown that African veterans sought to "maintain the socioeconomic gains they had accrued through African Rifles (KAR)." Like their counterparts elsewhere, they sought middle-class employment and challenged existing relationships within the colonial state.[41]

In 1945, the task of resettlement of ex-servicemen was carried out by a newly created special branch in the Department of Labour known as the Lagos Employment Exchange. Headed by Commissioner of Labor E. A. Miller and a large number of area resettlement officers and clerks, the branch was devoted to the repatriation of ex-servicemen. The location of the office in Lagos attracted a large number of men who came to the city in search of employment.[42] By December 31, 1945, about 32,784 troops had been demobilized and 16,122 of them had registered for employment. However, only about 4,738 had been placed in employment. This was a significantly low number considering that about 35,840 troops served in India and Burma alone. More than 43,000 troops served in the Middle East and West Africa, according to the labor report.[43] To discourage the migration of large numbers of ex-servicemen to Lagos, plans were made to establish regional offices and facilities where ex-servicemen could obtain employment in the vicinity of their homes. By December 31, 1946, about 96,227 troops had been demobilized and 61,566 registered for employment. But only 19,500, a small fraction, had been placed in employment. By the end of 1947, the general demobilization of troops was completed with the arrival of the last contingent of 2,500 garrison troops from the Middle East, and about 113,027 troops

---

[41] Brands, "Wartime Recruiting Practices, Martial Identity and Post–World War II Demobilization in Colonial Kenya."

[42] Nigeria, *Annual Report of the Department of Labour and on the Resettlement of Ex-servicemen, 1945* (Lagos: Government Printer, 1946), 17.

[43] Nigeria, *Annual Report of the Department of Labour and on the Resettlement of Ex-servicemen, 1945*, 17.

had been demobilized. The employment outlook remained unsatisfactory. According to the labor report for 1947, 75,934 ex-servicemen had registered for employment and 30,228 had been placed in employment.[44]

The resettlement plan was given the force of law with the enactment of the Employment of Ex-servicemen Ordinance No. 48 of 1945, which came into effect on June 1, 1945.[45] The law authorized the government to plan for the return to civil life of demobilized ex-servicemen who voluntarily joined the force or were conscripted. The suitable civil employments included jobs as caretakers, cleaners, gatekeepers, and watchmen. Registration centers for employment, headed by an area resettlement officer, were established in Lagos, Kaduna, Ibadan, Enugu, and Victoria. In addition, registration centers were established in every administrative division in the country with a few exceptions in the northern provinces. Employers were compelled to engage ex-servicemen when vacancies arose "up to a certain number known as the employer's quota."[46] This quota was initially set at 5 percent and by 1946 it was raised to 10 percent, and a special percentage of 50 percent was introduced for motor drivers from October 1, 1946.[47] A registered employer could not engage a civilian driver until 50 percent of his drivers were ex-servicemen. The majority of ex-servicemen did not gain paid employment in the public or civilian sectors. For many, navigating the bureaucracy and the employment registration exercise must have been daunting. Many still had roots in rural villages that urban migration would have disrupted.

The government established other programs that aimed to help ex-servicemen to support themselves or be self-employed. In 1947, the government established the Trade Training School for ex-servicemen at Enugu. This school provided a refresher course over a six-month period to give further training to ex-servicemen who already had army experience in their particular trade in order to place them on an equal footing with their civilian counterparts. The scheme was popular among ex-service tradesmen, including carpenters, general fitters, vehicle mechanics, and bricklayers. By February 1947, about 129 ex-servicemen had taken

---

[44] Nigeria, *Annual Report of the Department of Labour and on the Resettlement of Ex-servicemen, 1947* (Lagos: Government Printer, 1948), 37.

[45] See Employment of Ex-servicemen Ordinance No. 48 of 1945. See also related supplemental regulations: Employment of Ex-servicemen (Amendment) Regulation, Public Notice No. 16 of 1945; Ex-servicemen Registration Centre and Designated Classes Order, Public Notice No. 149 of 1945; Employment of Ex-servicemen (Standard Percentage) Order, Public Notice No. 19 of 1945, Employment of Ex-servicemen (Employers Registration Centre) Order, Public Notice No. 170 of 1945.

[46] Nigeria, *Annual Report of the Department of Labour and on the Resettlement of Ex-servicemen, 1945*, 19.

[47] Nigeria, *Annual Report of the Department of Labour and on the Resettlement of Ex-servicemen, 1946* (Lagos: Government Printer, 1947), 23.

advantage of the scheme. Other schemes focusing on agricultural training were established by the government in order to address the resettlement problem. In Oyo Province, a number of ex-servicemen were taken into the Oyo Native Administration Farm School in 1947. These ex-servicemen and their families were provided with accommodation and a subsistence allowance. The trainees received instruction in three types of farming: hand cultivation, plough cultivation, and cultivation assisted by smaller livestock. Pig breeding was taught and cattle were kept for milk and for ploughing the farm. The men were expected to go back to their villages at the end of the two-year course to put into practice the improved farming methods that they learned. In addition to the training offered to ex-servicemen, their wives were to be trained in weaving.[48] This was in line with the long-held colonial perception of the male farmer, which in reality was contrary to the mode of production in Nigerian farming systems. A sum of £1,000 was provided in the 1947–1948 estimates in respect of agricultural courses for ex-servicemen in the northern provinces. During the 1947 resettlement program, the Kafouoli Training Farm in Katsina Province offered a course on improved farming methods to fourteen ex-servicemen. The limited area available for training farms at this center limited the number of people accepted in the scheme.

The government was not under any illusion that all ex-servicemen would be offered employment or return to their villages as farmers. A scheme to recruit independent artisans and craftsmen was planned. The objective was for the government to sell artisans' tools at the cheapest possible rates to ex-servicemen from stocks acquired from the army. This was not very successful because the scheme did not meet with a wide response, prompting the government to modify its order for sets of tools from the United Kingdom. However, about 288 tool sets were purchased by individual ex-servicemen under this scheme while some tools were purchased by the Department of Education to equip the Trade Training School at Enugu. About 225 ex-servicemen benefited from the program, whereby 10 percent of all sewing machine imports were reserved for ex-servicemen who wished to set up shop as tailors. Despite these steps, the resettlement of ex-soldiers remained a general source of concern to officials. According to a government report, "the general reluctance on the part of many ex-servicemen to accept unskilled labouring work, even where they are 'illiterate' and have no qualifications for other types of work, has allowed one of the greatest potential sources of employment – the Cameroons Corporation – to remain virtually untapped."[49] So there

---

[48] Ibid., 38.    [49] Ibid., 39.

was dissatisfaction at many levels and things were allowed to develop pragmatically as the initial demobilization effort was concluded.

The most critical issue for the ex-servicemen remained employment. Many ex-servicemen did not find new employment that fit their changed lifestyles. The petitions of several ex-servicemen reveal unsuccessful attempts to gain new employment and the challenges they faced in accessing funds to establish businesses. On July 26, 1944, for example, Ekpenyong A. Ekpenyong of Calabar in the Eastern Region wrote to the British resident in Calabar, H. P. James, seeking employment. Following time in the Nigerian Volunteer Defence Force in Calabar, Ekpenyong joined the army in 1940 and served until he was wounded during the East African campaign. In his letter to the resident, he stated that he had pledged to help the British Empire for the duration of the war but could no longer do so because of his injury. Having recovered, although physically incapable of rejoining the army, he pleaded for employment in the civil service so that he would no longer have to rely on his family.[50] The contributions of the hundreds of thousands of Nigerians like Ekpenyong who served with the British forces helped in the Allied victory. Yet they came home to unemployment and apathetic colonial officials.

Petitions written in the postwar period by ex-servicemen reveal that Britain did not treat them with any sense of indeterminateness. Yet they remarkably portray both entitlement and a sense that the state had an obligation to provide support. In a letter to the government in 1949, Godfrey Nwaikiwu, who served in the Second World War, described the conditions faced by ex-servicemen in this way:

I should like to bring to your notice the sufferings of us ... ex-servicemen ... some were discharged as far back as 1943–45 ... and now not considered for employment at all. It is [not] obvious how a man can remain an applicant for so long [without] think[ing] of bad things. I shall be very grateful if any assistance of any kind can come from you regards helping the ex-servicemen. How can a human being live [as an] applicant for many years when he received no assistance ... and will not be compelled to steal?[51]

Men like Nwaikiwu faced the challenge of finding suitable employment on their return, and most who had sought new opportunities in the urban areas became a social problem for the government and other members of society. As many of the demobilized men marched in procession to the district and labor offices seeking employment, one commentator noted that Nigeria will be "literally flooded with restless and discontented men

[50] NAE, CALPROF, 17/1/154, "Application from Soldiers for Embayment."
[51] Cited in G. O. Olusanya, "The Role of Ex-servicemen in Nigerian Politics," *Journal of Modern African Studies* 6, no. 2 (1968): 221–232, at 227.

who would hardly go back to settle in their former occupations."[52] The *West African Pilot* echoed the frustrations of Nigerians regarding the conditions of ex-servicemen. The paper asked: "Are not thousands of these heroes still roaming about Lagos and the Provinces in search of the wherewithals of Life?"[53] This was not an exaggeration. In a letter to the editor of the *Nigerian Eastern Mail*, on February 26, 1946, one Echo of Obot-Nsit, Uyo Division, declared:

I have observed how little the authorities care for ex-solders here. They do not bother about their welfare, look down on discharged soldiers and do not seem to realise the sacrifices of boys from this district in the late war. Ex-servicemen in Uyo do not enjoy the same privileges that their comrades in other places are enjoying. The D.O. and the Resident Clerk neither listen to discharged solders nor pay any heed to their arrivals. In other districts about one-quarter of the available jobs are reserved for ex-servicemen, but in Uyo District this is not the case. ... The existing state of affairs is very likely to cause a riot if the authorities do not take steps instantly. The soldiers demand a square deal in this matter.[54]

As reflected in these petitions, the general economic conditions remained difficult in the postwar years. It was even tougher for some of the returning soldiers. The Nigerian soldiers, like their African counterparts who fought alongside the British and achieved distinguished records in combat, got a "raw deal," with most soldiers returning home to unemployment.[55] As historian Geoffrey Nwaka notes, "Nigerian ex-servicemen who served valiantly in the Middle East, Burma, East Africa and so on, saw themselves as victims of broken promises and injustice by the government."[56] Their expectations that they would have paid employment, war bonuses, big arrears of pay, tax exemptions, and other privileges upon their return home were dismissed by the government as "unrealistic and 'complete fabrication.'"[57] In fact, the official position was that Nigerian ex-servicemen were not professional soldiers. They were expected to

---

[52] Peter Rambler, "Here and There," *Nigerian Eastern Mail*, March 23, 1946, 17.

[53] *West African Pilot*, March 23, 1949.

[54] "The Authorities Neglect Ex-servicemen in Uyo District," *Nigerian Eastern Mail*, March 16, 1946, 11.

[55] Oliver Coates, "Narrative, Time, and the Archive in an African Second World War Memoir: Isaac Fadoyebo's *A Stroke of Unbelievable Luck*," *Journal of Commonwealth Literature* 51, no. 3 (2016): 371–386, at 376. See also Olusanya, *The Second World War and Politics in Nigeria*; C. N. Ubah, *Colonial Army and Society in Northern Nigeria* (Kaduna: National Defence Academy, 1998); Hamilton, *War Bush*.

[56] Geoffrey Nwaka, "Rebellion in Umuahia, 1950–1951: Ex-servicemen and Anti-colonial Protest in Eastern Nigeria," *Transafrican Journal of History* 16 (1987): 47–62, at 47.

[57] Ibid.

return to civilian life at the end of the war and were not regarded as a "separate or privileged group."[58]

The Employment of Ex-servicemen Ordinance, which provided for the reinstatement of men who voluntarily left their work to join the forces or who were conscripted into the army, also provided for the compulsory engagement of ex-servicemen (both disabled and able-bodied) in "filling all vacancies which may occur until such time as the quota determined by Government has been filled."[59] The reservation of these positions exclusively for ex-soldiers, however, was not welcomed by all sections of the population because of its long-term effect on Nigerian society. Some interpreted the policy as a government attempt to "coerce all departments to reserve all openings practically to the ex-servicemen." For Peter Rambler, a columnist for the in the *Nigerian Eastern Mail*, "sooner or later the Nigerian government will have to face the truth of these maxims."[60] The Employment of Ex-servicemen Ordinance No. 48 of 1945 could not address the resettlement question to the satisfaction of the ex-servicemen or those who believed that the ex-servicemen were being unduly favored at the expense of other sections of the population. Some questioned the moral and ethical fairness of the Employment of Ex-servicemen Ordinance. A source of discontent was the provision that required ex-servicemen of a lower qualification to apply for a job for which a higher qualification was required for other applicants. Rambler questioned the substitution of merit for the form of preferential treatment in employment reserved for ex-servicemen. Denouncing the Ex-servicemen Ordinance, Rambler wrote, "as tax-payers in Nigeria we feel that this Ex-servicemen Ordinance is lacking greatly (if not from its wording in its application in fair play and life ethics)."[61]

There were other problems of a general nature. The government was not able to meet the exaggerated promises made in the critical years of the war that helped to mobilize armies and recruit young men for service. After the victory over Germany, the government could not possibly keep its word over the provision of employment for all who had help save the empire.[62] Many returning soldiers remembered the broken promises and the lack of recognition they received for the contributions they made in helping secure victory over Japan. In the words of one veteran, "When we came back, what did they do

---

[58] Ibid. See also File C411/4 Rivprof: Speech of His Excellency the Governor at Oporoma, September 12, 1947. Of EP 22720, vol. I, CSE, Government Press Release on Ex-servicemen's Grievances, 1950.

[59] Nigeria, *Annual Report of the Department of Labour and on the Resettlement of Ex-servicemen, 1945*, 18.

[60] Rambler, "Here and There," 17.    [61] Ibid.    [62] Ibid.

for us?"[63] The bonuses promised were not given. Hassan Sokoto, another Nigerian veteran, recalled: "They treated us like children. In reality we were their slaves."[64] Usman Katsina, an African soldier who labored for the empire in Burma, echoed Sokoto: "We were under colonial rule, so we could not say anything to change it."[65] Although they were paid for their service, there is no evidence that soldiers came home wealthy or continued to receive support from the British. Some African ex-soldiers claimed they were promised allowances that were never paid, despite their repeated efforts over the years. One veteran, Dangombe, remarked: "We were supposed to get Long Service and British Empire Medals, but up until now – nothing."[66] Dangombe continued: "We wanted work. But what could we do? We were under colonial rule and we couldn't change anything."[67] Dangombe, who found himself without employment prospects at the end of the war, was not alone in decrying the unequal treatment that African veterans received and calls for equity were rife among ex-soldiers. And it was not only the money – there was a general lack of recognition at the end of the war.

As government promises of resettlement and support failed to materialize, ex-servicemen sought out civil work and regarded the right to work as an obligation owed to them by the government. Most of these men sought employment as prison wardens, police constables, fitters, and machinists. Ex-servicemen in Enugu, in the Eastern Region, complained of lack of civil employment. Many were disappointed that the army did not prepare them for the jobs they were seeking. Many had served in the army as members of the Labour Corps or Auxiliary Group but had never attended school and were unqualified for the positions they wanted, such as policemen. Despite their experience in the army, those without any technical training could not be employed as fitters, electricians, engine drivers, or as workers in any other technical field. The frustration of these ex-soldiers was expressed in a Department of Labour report that described the veterans as "rude in manner" and detailed threats and bullying of the clerks attached to the Labour Office:

That a man has been a soldier does not mean that such a man can do any job of which he has no knowledge and is consequently incapable of doing. It is therefore wrong to complain of not being offered civil employment when the ex-servicemen who served in the Auxiliary Corps refuse to be employed as coal miners or road

---

[63] "WWII's Forgotten Army."    [64] Ibid.

[65] Ibid. For more on the forgotten story of African soldiers, see Barnaby Phillips, *Another Man's War: The Story of a Burma Boy in Britain's Forgotten African Army* (London: Oneworld Publications, 2015).

[66] "Africa's Forgotten Wartime Heroes."    [67] Ibid.

laborers but rather choose to be employed as clerks or technicians, their incapabilities in doing such jobs notwithstanding.[68]

Hundreds of ex-servicemen, mostly those recruited from the rural areas where they were farmers, abandoned the countryside to seek employment in the cities.[69] The government predicted that unless these ex-servicemen "who do not like to be engaged according to their capacities in civil life change their present attitude towards those working in the Labour Department here, a serious fracas will take place one day."[70]

It was difficult to even keep track of the situations of most of the ex-soldiers, since many fended for themselves because state support was lacking. A 1947 report from the Asaba Division noted that the year began with a total of 800 unemployed ex-servicemen on the records at the Ogwashi-Uku and Agbo resettlement offices. By year's end, however, the numbers were 590 on the active live registers and 397 on the dead registers, including those who had left the division in search of employment at Lagos, Ibadan, Benin, and other centers.[71] A significant number of the ex-soldiers were unaccounted for, and the report assumed that many of these ex-servicemen had gone back to their farms and were doing well. However, this statement was qualified with the observation that "many now unemployed have spent all their savings and have not even enough money to buy seed-yams with which to begin farming."[72] It was estimated that between 100 and 150 demobilized soldiers returned to their homes in the Asaba Division during the year, and the majority of these men left the division in search of employment elsewhere.[73] The condition of Nigerian ex-servicemen was quite different from that of their European and American counterparts. Government expenditures and programs helped bring recovery in the postwar period. The G. I. Bill in particular helped lay the foundation for the United States' remarkable postwar expansion and the emergence of an enlarged middle class.[74] However, in Nigeria, when the war ended, the good fortunes and high incomes enjoyed by soldiers was in decline. African ex-servicemen were expected to return to their villages. Major James had warned the West African regiment to "take care of their money when they were paid off,"

[68] "Ex-servicemen in Enugu Wrongly Complain of Not Being Offered Civil Employment," *Nigerian Eastern Mail*, October 6, 1945, 9.
[69] Ibid.    [70] Ibid.
[71] NAI, ASA DIV 1–12, Annual Report of the Asaba Division of Nigeria for the Year 1947, Asaba Divisional Office, Ogwashi-Uku.
[72] Ibid.    [73] Ibid.
[74] On the New Deal, see, for example, William E. Leuchtenburg, *Franklin D. Roosevelt and the New Deal, 1932–1940* (New York: Harper and Row, 1963); and Arthur M. Schlesinger Jr., *The Age of Roosevelt: The Coming of the New Deal* (Boston: Houghton Mifflin Company, 1958).

encouraging them to put the greater part of their money in the Post Office Savings Bank.[75] For these soldiers, life was quite different after their demobilization, including a "change in the generous ration which they were receiving." While it appears that a small number of African ex-servicemen invested their savings in the retail trade and other income-generating activities, the bulk of these men returned to life in the villages and towns without any guarantee of an income for the future. Yet the low numbers of ex-servicemen absorbed into the civil service or other resettlement schemes continued to be a source of unrest, particularly in the eastern part of Nigeria, where there were about 22,751 ex-servicemen, including 2,566 from southern Cameroons.[76] While the government seemed satisfied with the achievement of the resettlement scheme, it blamed the ex-soldiers themselves for some of their problems. According to Nwaka, the public was expected to understand that:

most of the so-called "unemployed" ex-soldiers had no paid jobs before joining the army, and that the labor market had definitely became more competitive after the war than before it. Besides, the expectations of ex-soldiers were said to be unrealistically high, perhaps because of the extravagant promises, some of them unauthorized, made to them during the recruitment period or by field commanders to raise and sustain morale.[77]

Table 5.1 represents data up to February 28, 1946. In addition to the numbers placed on employment, sixty-three ex-servicemen were assisted to purchase sewing machines and thereby to establish private businesses as tailors.[78]

## Changes in Gender Relations and Masculinity

One distinct area of change after the war was gender relations and masculinity. Nigerian labor not only contributed to the Allied war effort but also in large measure led to the transformation of communities and of gender relations during and after the war. For World War II veterans, the construction of new identity and memory informed how they situated themselves within the colony upon their return. Both were intrinsically related to new conceptions of masculinity, and the value they attached to their new identity as soldiers of the empire. Historian Carolyn Brown's examination of labor history in the British colonies during World War II reveals that

[75] NA, CADIST 1/3/21, "West African Troops Abroad: Visit by Major H. P. James," 2.
[76] See figures for each province and southern Cameroons, which was a British mandate ruled from Nigeria after World War I, in Nwaka, "Rebellion in Umuahia, 1950–1951," 47.
[77] Ibid., 47.
[78] "Restitution of Ex-servicemen," *Nigerian Eastern Mail*, March 23, 1946, 20.

Table 5.1 *Restitution of ex-servicemen*

| Tradesmen | Total demobilized | Total registered for employment | Total placed in employment |
|---|---|---|---|
| Blacksmiths | 277 | 235 | 69 |
| Carpenters | 657 | 583 | 203 |
| Drivers | 3,504 | 2,088 | 436 |
| Electricians | 165 | 131 | 38 |
| Fitters | 204 | 136 | 93 |
| L/Workers (incl. trimmers) | 129 | 78 | 7 |
| Mechanics (incl. workshop assistants and engine hands) | 492 | 337 | 61 |
| Masons (incl. concreters) | 393 | 344 | 89 |
| Operators (incl. wireless switchboard and L/men | 460 | 256 | 84 |
| Painters | 68 | 62 | 30 |
| Plumbers | 96 | 66 | 4 |
| Signalers | 287 | 175 | 25 |
| Clerks (incl. store men) | 1,502 | 1,243 | 671 |
| Nursing orderlies (incl. laboratory assistants and dispensers) | 734 | 730 | 208 |
| Schoolmasters | 37 | 23 | 7 |
| Tailors (incl. textiles and refilters) | 181 | 147 | 13 |
| Miscellaneous | 560 | 464 | 378 |
| Total tradesmen | 9,556 | 7,080 | 2,404 |
| Total non-tradesmen | 29,232 | 11,280 | 3,433 |
| Grand total | 38,788 | 18,360 | 5,837 |

Nigerian workers "raised demands that articulated a blending of British working-class notions of masculinity and reformulated indigenous rural norms based on fatherhood and elite status."[79] As Brown notes, "African workers were conceptualizing their roles as men in the household, workplace and community."[80] Yet such subjective ideas about self and identity both had intrinsic value as these men sought new roles in the economy and public arena. Masculinity was articulated in terms of physique. While this may not have contributed to the impulse to enroll into the army, the army

[79] Carolyn A. Brown, "African Working Men, Racial Consciousness and the Imperial State during World War II: A History of Labour in the British Colonies," paper presented at the "Re-evaluating Africa and World War II" conference, Rutgers University, March 27–30, 2008.
[80] Ibid.

experience generated new enduring ideas. To the soldiers, the army was a ritual, like an initiation reserved for a few, which conferred new status and power on them. This was even more evident in societies such as the Igbo, where forms of centralized authority were less visible. The emergence and construction of individual and collective memory were influenced by the indigenous political and social constructions of identity. Although this may have differed from one ethnic group to the next, it was most visible among the Igbo, where ex-soldiers relied on their newfound wealth and status to challenge the gerontocratically based hierarchical order that privileged age and gave elders control over younger members of the clan.

Table 5.2 *The resettlement of ex-servicemen at the end of December 1948*

|  | Tradesmen | Non-tradesmen | Total |
|---|---|---|---|
| Total demobilized | 34,321 | 82,543 | 116,864 |
| Total registered | 29,575 | 50,166 | 79,741 |
| Total placed in employment | 15,829 | 20,939 | 36,768 |
| Reenlisted up to December 1948 | 1,300 | 3,167 | 4,467 |

*Source:* Nwaka, "Rebellion in Umuahia, 1950–1951," 56

Table 5.2 provides a summary of the resettlement data at the of 1948. As Table 5.2 shows, less than half of the demobilized soldiers were placed on any form of employment three years after the war. For the young men who had seen battle, their temporary soldiering experience was enough to challenge traditional forms of power. Linus Anabalam, who grew up in the 1940s, recalled: "Everyone wanted to be like the ex-soldiers. Their crisp starched dresses [and] their money made them very attractive as suitors."[81] Clearly many African civilian male workers who did not play combatant roles also conformed to hegemonic forms of wartime masculinity. This reconceptualization of male identity also took place at a different level. There was a clear association between joining the war and the emergence of a new form of masculine identity. The war experience afforded the men the opportunity to renegotiate hierarchies within their own locality and to develop new forms of masculinities. This sort of image was disseminated in military propaganda posters. The primacy of the "soldier hero" at the end of war was a new phenomenon that challenged the old social order. Isaac Iwuh, whose father was a World War II veteran, recalled stories of his father acting as debt collector and "a protector of members of his community." Those who felt

---

[81] Linus Anabalam (elder, former migrant worker), interviewed by Chima Korieh at Umuchieze, Mbaise, Nigeria, on December 24, 2000.

threatened "called upon him and those outside his community feared him."[82] Iwuh's father's wartime experience bestowed upon him a new sense of power and authority in his community.

The soldiers returned to their old world but as different individuals quite distinct from their life before the army. Their return was significant for the soldiers and for rural societies in general. The soldiers were entitled to substantial amounts of money after their prolonged period of active service abroad, with very restricted opportunities to draw or spend their pay.[83] Most soldiers had substantial arrears to their credit in addition to small gratuities, leaving many of them with £100 or more to come.[84] By Nigerian village standards, this was a small fortune. Therefore, while they did not get much for their service, they still nevertheless had more than the average Nigerian civilian. Such men included Pius, who served Major Cherns as an assistant. Following his demobilization, Pius acquired new wealth, including two expensive watches, a suitcase full of new European clothes, and other marks of "civilization."[85] Men like Pius returned to their villages as men of substance with enough resources to enable them to marry and help their families. As Major Cherns observed, many of the troops had lived a simple "African" way of life in remote places before they joined the army. They returned with substantial money and spending power and also a lifestyle far removed from their native origins – a new dress code and consumer culture having imbibed other trappings of "civilization." The ex-soldiers had traveled far and wide; the army had taught them special skills, such as truck driving and mechanics or clerical work or wireless maintenance. For many, their ambition was not to return to their rural "peasant" life but to get to the large towns where there were greater opportunities for mechanics and other forms of employment. Above all, as Cherns noted, "they have money in their pocket and have learned what it can buy, including drink and women."[86] Cherns's account is filled with stereotypical descriptions rested upon ambiguous use of ethnicity and race, but in this context with the characterization of the southerner as a less rational economic being bent on frivolous use of his earnings. But the postwar conditions do not bear this out. Many of the ex-soldiers of southern Nigerian origin invested wisely in business and became important leaders in their communities.

An important area affected by the war was marriage and the social obligations that structured it. In many African societies, bride-price payments were essential features of all recognized marriages. Often made in cash, the bride-price was necessary to establish that any children of the

[82] Isaac Iwuh (son of World War II veteran), interviewed by Chima Korieh at Umuchieze, Mbaise, Nigeria, on July 10, 2016.
[83] Cherns, "Walk through the Valley."    [84] Ibid.    [85] Ibid., 120.    [86] Ibid., 119.

union were their father's descendants and members of his patrilineage and also to maintain filial relationships. The sum was determined by negotiations between the two families involved. Significant changes occurred in local marriage practices because of the quick injection of money in the local economy by demobilized soldiers. One of the practices most affected was the bride-price paid for a wife, which rose significantly after the war. In eastern Nigeria, ex-servicemen, with increased incomes and severance payments, returned to the villages with substantial amounts of money and drove the bride-prices to a much higher level. E. W. Ardener, who carried out an ethnographic study of the Mbaise Igbo after the Second World War, noted that a high bride-price was being paid for the ideal girl. Ex-servicemen were driving "up the bride-price by the high amount they were willing to pay."[87] An ex-serviceman from Ezinihitte, Mbaise, paid £42 in 1943 as a bride-price. Ardener reported a second case of a man from Ogwama who had paid a down payment of £25 on a bride-price of £45 for a girl from Amuzi and had married the girl in church (also a heavy expense). Those who were not soldiers "resented this at the time."[88] For the soldiers, however, a high bride-price secured the respect of the wife. One ex-serviceman, who had paid upward of a £42 price for a wife, said "he would not marry for less again [for] no-one likes to think that the parents of the girl would have no trouble paying back the money."[89] Such heavy expenses earned the man respect from his in-laws, who may not have the capacity to repay in the case of the dissolution of the marriage. Bride-prices varied from community to community, which led to tensions, with some communities disparaging others where bride-prices were generally low. An informant told Ardener that in his place, if a man told his wife to stay in, she stayed in. In other places such as Isuobiangwu, a wife would "go all around, there being no respect for the husband."[90] The perception is that a higher bride-price earned the man respect and blind obedience from the wife. Such women would endure abusive relationships because leaving the husband would require a repayment of a substantial sum of money to the husband. The average dowries paid in Mbaise remained as high as £50. Although very few people could easily pay a £50 bride-price, the situation was paradoxical, for there were widespread complaints of the high level of the bride-price and yet it was regarded overall as a good thing because it led to greater respect.

The costs of marrying a wife were cause for concern for many, including local officials. There was discussion in the press about the bride-price

---

[87] NA, CO 927/158/3, E. W. Ardener, "Study of the Ibo People in Owerri Province (Nigeria), Field Notes."
[88] Ibid.    [89] Ibid.    [90] Ibid.

question in the 1940s and 1950s.[91] An attempt was made by one
J. A. Oparaji, a prominent man in Mbaise and a representative in the
councils, to introduce a proposal for fixing prices on an educational scale.
He argued "that a high bride-price did not ensure respect necessarily, as
he knew of many girls who had been married with large payments who did
not turn out to be good wives."[92] However, whatever the council members' motives, and whatever the bearing of the bride-price on respect, the
difficulty of enforcing such a measure would certainly be great, if it could
have been enforced at all.

In fact, the dramatic increase in the cost of dowry was widespread
among the Igbo of eastern Nigeria. In a letter to the editor of the
*Nigerian Eastern Mail*, C. A. Abangwu, a native of Nsukka, called attention to what he described as "the evil practice now in vogue in Nsukka
Division." He recalled that during recent years, "the amount of money
originally paid by a would-be husband on his intended wife has risen by
leaps and bounds."[93] Reflecting further on this social change as it relates
to marriage rites, Abangwu wrote:

With the advent of the war in 1939 and the employment of our sons in the
Government and NA Services, the entire communities of our division have seized
this chance to over-tax pockets of their sons abroad by raising the dowry very high.
By so doing, they are prostituting out good-old customs and encouraging a system
of "mild slavery" perhaps formally unknown. I have heard of more than two cases
of ex-service from the Middle East and Burma who were compelled to pay from
twenty-five to thirty pounds each on girls who have never been to school or had
any worthy domestic training.[94]

Abangwu reported the case of a young man who had worked for only two
years in the government service, but who was requested to "pay twenty
pounds plus a cow for a girl of ten and who was no better than nature left
her."[95] These changing social obligations had important consequences
for the local marriage system and a substantial economic cost.

Formally, the maximum dowry paid in any part of the division on any
girl was below £10 with a pig or a cow according to the locality. Such
a relatively low dowry served an important purpose. It meant that "girls
are not sold when married – the dowry being compensation to the parents
who for a time lose sight of their beloved daughter. In fact, some give their
daughter away without a payment of dowry – soliciting only the good
service of their in-law."[96] Consequently, when a woman felt she was being

---

[91] Ibid.     [92] Ibid.
[93] "Dowry-Mania in Nsukka Division," *Nigerian Eastern Mail*, February 12, 1946, 10.
[94] Ibid.     [95] Ibid.     [96] Ibid.

maltreated by her husband, she freely returned to her parents. She did not endure injustice and abuse, since she was not bought with money.[97]

## Postwar Economy

The effects of the Second World War shaped many aspects of life throughout the 1940s and 1950s. The postwar economic conditions were less than ideal for both Britain and its colonies. Consequently, there was an attempt by Britain to link its African colonies to economic reconstruction programs of the postwar period. The goal of promoting economic development centered on the agricultural potential for East and West African colonies and protectorates. Indeed, earlier attempts through the Colonial Development Act of 1929 and other subsequent legislation made provisions for the funding of development projects in African colonies, but their success was limited. The Second World War increased both the importance of the colonies to Britain and British commitment to the economic development of the African empire. The Colonial Welfare and Development Act of 1940 ended the development ideology of colonial self-sufficiency. Although wartime conditions produced an acute shortage of finance, Britain acknowledged the need for funds in 1945 when a substantial amount was allocated for development. Development schemes, however, were sometimes inappropriate or unsuccessful.

Despite the commitment of the Nigerian population to the war, its impact on their lives and economic activities suggests that rural survival remained a primary way of understanding the impact of the war on their lives. The end of the war created domestic labor problems. The cessation of hostilities made it necessary to "reduce the amount of labor in some industries."[98] Nigerians, like their African counterparts, were largely expected to fend for themselves at the end of the war. Many industries sustained production at "high pressure with a considerable labor force throughout the country."[99] Due to the magnitude of the work, a considerable quantity of unskilled labor was attracted to the mines during the war. However, a significant reduction in the labor requirement was expected as the war came to an end. According to the annual report of the Department of Labour for 1946, the total force in the mines for the first eight months of the year was an average of 60,000 per month. The number was

[97] Ibid.
[98] Nigeria, *Annual Report of the Department of Labour and on the Resettlement of Ex-servicemen, 1945*, 3.
[99] Ibid.

considerably reduced toward the end of the year.[100] Conditions for the less skilled seasonal labor drafted to meet the demands of the war were even worse. Most were Igbo from the Eastern Region who had been migrating in large numbers to the Northern and Western Regions. The first to lose their jobs were those who were less skilled, and who were more unlikely to find other jobs. Most cases of hardship, a government report stated, were "more acute among the Southern artisans and semi-skilled labor (almost exclusively the Ibo tribe) who found themselves without work."[101] Most were often heavily in debt, and with no means of repatriation.[102] The southerners, a labor report noted, "preferred to remain on the mine fields expecting better times and some of them became squatters and a nuisance to the mining communities."[103] Unlike the northerners (mainly Hausa), who often returned home to farming, and often with generous gratuities for good and long service, the southerners had a harder time making the transition. Nigerian soldiers who chose to continue their military careers went on to form the core of independent Nigeria's national army.

A Department of Labour report noted that an estimated 4,000 men, mostly Hausa and Igbos, would shortly be out of employment, since sleeper car production was almost completed.[104] The majority of them was feared would drift to Lagos and swell the ranks of the unemployed there.[105] There was some anxiety as to the future of a large labor force that had been employed since 1944 in Ondo Province on sleeper car production for the Nigerian Railway. With the cooperation of the Nigerian Railway and the Department of Forestry, transport warrants were issued to the men to enable them to return to the place of their original recruitment or to their homes.[106] But their future upon return was uncertain. In fact, colonial officials and European businesses regarded the Nigerian population as their personal serfs, who could be disposed of as soon as services were no longer required. The whole production system during the war was calculated to extract the highest amount for production as cheaply as possible. The laborers were paid very little or not even enough to support them and leave any savings.

Shortages experienced during the war continued in its immediate aftermath, and the cost of living continued to rise throughout the country, especially for local foodstuffs, imported merchandise, and rents.[107] In

[100] Ibid.
[101] Nigeria, *Annual Report of the Department of Labour, 1946* (Lagos: Government Printer, 1946), 3.
[102] Ibid.  [103] Ibid., 4.  [104] Ibid.  [105] Ibid.  [106] Ibid.  [107] Ibid., 8.

Lagos, the cost of living index shows a considerable increase from 164.19 in October 1944 to 175.92 in October 1945. As the *Annual Report of the Department of Labour* observed, the problem was compounded by the fact that the "anti-social practices of profiteering, hoarding and black market were stronger during the year than ever."[108] The monitoring of food prices by price inspectors did not bring relief to the urban population. In May 1945, the Department of Labour reported that some of the principal articles of native foodstuffs "were completely absent from the markets and the Lagos community had to rely on Government control centers where most of these commodities were retailed at prices below those prevailing in Lagos and at sources of supply." Large urban areas like Lagos, with its population of about 200,000 people, were not able to obtain enough food. The estimated 4,000 people who joined daily queues at the food centers every morning created so much disorder that it "became necessary to draft extra police constables to supervise sales at the control centres."[109]

By May 1948, local people were still required to obtain a permit in order to move food items from one part of the region to the other. Those mostly affected were traders of foodstuffs, especially garri and yams, which faced restrictions and controlled prices. The effect of the food shortages reverberated across the urban areas. Isichael Ume of Abakpa, Abakaliki, wrote the district officer on May 8, 1948, requesting a permit to transport his yams to Enugu for sale. He had written earlier in February but was apparently ignored. Ume faced losing his goods as they had started to decay. C. N. Onwuka confronted a similar situation. His appeal to the district officer in Abakiliki on May 7, 1948, is worth reproducing in detail:

I have the honour most humbly to approach you for assistance. My trouble is as follows: My customers had given 10,000 yams on a credit purchase system and that is to pay them after the selling of the yams at Enugu. Now you gave me a permit for one trip last month and that enabled me to carry 1000 half-rotten yams out of the above yams to Enugu. . . . I am not a dictator but an honest beggar who wishes to be faithful to his customers for future transactions if life stands.[110]

The continuation of a system of control of commodities, both by quota and by price, did not endear the empire to its subjects. The shortage of food and other essential items in Nigeria, meanwhile, had become so desperate that authorities imported food items like maize from Argentina

---

[108] Ibid.
[109] Ibid., 8. See also Wale Oyemakinde, "The Nigerian General Strike of 1945," *Journal of the Historical Society of Nigeria* 7, no. 4 (1975): 693–710.
[110] NAE, AIDIST 2/1/433, 450, C. N. Onwuka to District Officer, Abakiliki, May 7, 1948.

and garri from Ghana and the Gambia to augment the food supply in Lagos. These conditions were exacerbated by the general labor strikes going on in most parts of the country, as well as rising costs of manufacture and disruptions in shipping facilities under wartime conditions.[111]

There were additional economic factors. A significant amount of money was entering the economy as a result of the war. The Department of Labour commented on this situation: "Army allotments, separation allowances, and money from military contracts for buildings and food were steadily flowing into the hands of all classes, particularly the peasants."[112] Trading firms were paying higher prices for palm oil and nuts, groundnuts, cocoa, and rubber than in prewar times. Government and mercantile employees and missionaries "were receiving Cost of Living Allowances."[113] The West African currency in circulation at the beginning of war was £11,705,395. In December 1945, it had increased to £32,570,377. Indeed, more money was flowing into the economy under conditions of declining commodities. All these factors contributed to higher prices and inflation.

## Attempt at Reconstruction

The problem of postwar reconstruction in Europe brought changes in colonial policies and reorganization of the colonies' socioeconomic structures. It was envisaged that the colonies would play a significant role in postwar reconstruction through a more efficient exploitation of their resources.[114] Nigerian agricultural production was expected to contribute to the reconstruction effort. However, the postwar era also witnessed major depression following the decline in the prices of African agricultural produce. The agricultural schemes and development agenda of the postwar world in Africa did not achieve their desired objectives of leading the development of African societies and increased welfare. Ali Mazrui has noted the failure of the postwar groundnut scheme in Tanzania that had been conceived as an "appropriate strategy of interdependence between Africa and Europe."[115] In Nigeria, the economic crisis that emerged during the war brought the reality of the past agricultural policies to the attention of policy makers. The fall in exports undermined the main

[111] Nigeria, *Annual Report of the Department of Labour, 1946*, 9.   [112] Ibid.   [113] Ibid.
[114] See, for instance, British Central Office of Information, *Constitutional Development in the Commonwealth: United Kingdom Dependencies* (London: British Central Office of Information, 1955), Part 1.
[115] Ali A. Mazrui, "Africa and the Legacy of the Second World War: Political, Economic and Cultural Aspects," in *Africa and the Second World War: Report and Papers of the Symposium Organized by UNESCO at Benghazi, Libyan Arab Jamahiriya from 10 to 13 November 1980* (Paris: UNESCO, 1985), 17.

source of government revenue and threatened the rural economic
base.[116]

The wartime interaction between the metropole and the colony, as the
case of Nigeria reveals, led to new imperial formations that not only
affected the colonies but actually helped to fashion British society, its
peoples, and its political cultures. This was the case with other European
powers in the postwar period.[117] The governor of Nigeria, Lord
Milverton, described how attention turned to the immense task of postwar reconstruction:

> But as the war drew to a close, we began to plan for the peace, and so there came
> into being the 10-year Development and Welfare Plan. Briefly, it aims at spending
> £55,000,000, of which £23,000,000 are to be provided under the U.K. Colonial
> Development and Welfare Act, £16,000,000 by loans raised by the Nigerian
> Government, and the remainder from revenue. The plan covers all sides of the
> economic and social welfare of the people, but stresses in particular road devel-
> opment, water supplies, health and education.[118]

This step was an implementation of the policy of a shared responsibility
for the development of colonial dependencies between the mother country and its colonial subjects.[119] As reflected in Milverton's report, under
the Colonial Development and Welfare Act of 1945, the colonial authority introduced some innovation in the colonies. But these innovations
were presented within the context of an economically weak British
Empire, rising nationalism in the colonies, and a welfare-minded
Labour government. The combination of these factors shaped the nature
of the Colonial Development and Welfare Act and the Nigerian Ten-Year
Plan for Development. Postwar changes widened the range of techniques
implemented to overcome the constraints imposed by the war and
expanded the peasant economy. Government assistance increased

---

[116] See also Robert Shenton, "Nigerian Agriculture in Historical Perspective: Development
and Crisis, 1900–1960," in *State, Oil and Agriculture in Nigeria*, ed. Michael Watts and
Michael Hodd (Berkeley: University of California Press, 1987), 34–57, at 45.

[117] See Matthew G. Stanard, "Belgium, the Congo, and Imperial Immobility: A Singular
Empire and the Historiography of the Single Analytic Field," *French Colonial History* 15
(2014): 87–110; Antoinette Burton, ed., *After the Imperial Turn: Thinking with and
through the Nation* (Durham, NC: Duke University Press, 2003); Gary Wilder, "From
Optic to Topic: The Foreclosure Effect of Historiographic Turns," *American Historical
Review* 117, no. 3 (June 2012): 723–745, at 739. Ann Laura Stoler and
Frederick Cooper, "Between Metropole and Colony: Rethinking a Research Agenda,"
in *Tensions of Empire: Colonial Cultures in a Bourgeois World*, ed. Ann Laura Stoler and
Frederick Cooper (Berkeley: University of California Press, 1997), 1–56, at 4.

[118] Milverton, "Nigeria," 81.

[119] On the Colonial Development Welfare Act, see, for example, E. R. Wicker, "Colonial
Development and Welfare, 1929–1957: The Evolution of a Policy," *Social and Economic
Studies* 7, no. 4 (1958): 170–192.

under the Colonial Development and Welfare Act of 1945, which provided funds for long-term economic development in the colonies. The act
was seen as the means to increase the social and economic development of
the colonies and the welfare of their citizens, on one hand, and their
development as sources of supplies for Europe, on the other.[120] The
welfarist nature of development planning in this period was rationalized
by the argument that greater expenditure should be made on the welfare
of those who had contributed to the war effort.[121] The urgency of the
export scheme in Nigeria contrasted with the more systematic planning in
the war period, but much of this was specifically directed toward export
crops required for postwar reconstruction. Although demands for palm
produce increased significantly in this period, the rewards for producers
were not significant enough to encourage the expansion of production. As
scholar John Iliffe argues in the case of Tanganyika in the same period, it
was in these years of colonial rule that the complexity of the history of the
colonies became more apparent.[122]

The end of the war did not initiate a radical change in the colonial
emphasis on agriculture as the route to economic advancement and
colonial development. Ex-servicemen were to be integrated into the
Nigerian Department of Agriculture's education scheme as part of its
general development plan. The scheme in the northern provinces
included instructions to suitable men in mixed farming methods and
the provision of stock and equipment.[123] The men who had fought in
India showed considerable interest in farming following their experience
on the subcontinent. According to Major James, the men are "much
impressed with the Indian method of rice growing which is of course
dependent on the plentiful water supply in the area and this has made
them think of more scientific methods of farming in their own
country."[124]

The desire to improve the conditions in the colonies reflected the
ongoing debate within imperial circles concerning the need to enhance
the welfare of colonial subjects. However, this change was not often
reflected in the actions and opinions of the men on the spot. The government was not particularly enthusiastic about a proposal in September 1945
to grant credit services for farmers, rural industries, and demobilized

---

[120] On British policy in the postwar period, see, for example, Iliffe, *A Modern History of
Tanganyika*, 437; S. Anwarul Haque Haqqi, *The Colonial Policy of the Labour
Government, 1945–51* (Lahore: Aligarh, 1960), 128; David Goldsworthy, *Colonial
Issues in British Politics 1945–1961* (Oxford: Oxford University Press, 1971), 12.
[121] See Shenton, "Nigerian Agriculture in Historical Perspective," 48.
[122] Iliffe, *A Modern History of Tanganyika*, 437.
[123] NA, CADIST 1/3/21, "West African Troops Abroad: Visit by Major H. P. James," 3.
[124] Ibid.

soldiers. The colonial government gave some veterans land to begin new lives as farmers. Yet not all of them decided to pursue farming and instead these men "followed many paths after the war, returning to their villages, entering political life, or taking blue-collar jobs."[125] In reality, the project was in part a scheme to reduce their potential impact as a new political force.[126] However, L. T. Chubb, the secretary for the eastern provinces, noted in a letter to the chief secretary to the government that such schemes were likely to fail in the eastern provinces. Considering the difficult agricultural problems existing in the eastern provinces, which lacked the mixed farming system present in the northern provinces, the acting assistant director of agriculture for the province noted "that opportunities for constructive and economically sound assistance to peasant farmers in the form of credit facilities are likely to remain very limited until agricultural research has made more progress."[127] The enthusiasm toward agricultural development within the colonial government died down quickly after the war. On November 1, 1945, the colonial government in the eastern provinces disbanded the palm production team, and residents were requested to give a month's notice of termination to the African staff.[128] But peasants continued to produce palm oil and palm kernels in response to improved communications and higher prices in the postwar period. However, a new nexus of economic control was introduced through marketing control, creating a problem that rural producers could not easily circumvent.

On the global level, the Second World War led to the further incorporation of the Nigerian and other African economies into the global capitalist system. The most important structural change that occurred in postwar Nigeria was the establishment of produce marketing boards. The experiences of wartime marketing had demonstrated that statutory marketing organizations could achieve stability in seasonal prices and improve producer prices.[129] The origin of the marketing board system can be traced to the harsh global economic conditions of the late 1930s, which had triggered a wave of anticolonial protests.[130] These protests, historian Rod

---

[125] "Askari: Stories of African Veterans of World War II," Indiegogo, February 2, 2015, accessed January 20, 2019, www.indiegogo.com/projects/askari-stories-of-african-veterans-of-world-war-ii.

[126] "Africa's Forgotten Wartime Heroes."

[127] NAE, OP 2611, ONDIST 12/1/1737, "Credit Facilities for Farmers, Peasant Industries and Demobilised Soldiers," L. T. Chubb to Chief Secretary to the Government, Lagos, October 12, 1945.

[128] See NAE, 18038/38, vol. VII, C.S.E. 1/85/8584, C.S.E 1/85/8584, "Secretary, Eastern Provinces to Deputy Controller of Motor Transport, Aba," October 1946.

[129] H. A. Oluwasanmi, *Agriculture and Nigerian Economic Development* (Ibadan: Oxford University Press, 1966), 158.

[130] There was the 1929 Women's War in eastern Nigeria, the West African cocoa holdups, and riots in the West Indies. See Rod Alence, "Colonial Government, Social Conflict

Alence has argued, led "British officials to consider greater state involvement in colonial economies."[131]

With the outbreak of the Second World War, European businesses, including the United African Company (UAC), pressed for controlled marketing to reduce the risk of the West African trade, and the colonial office acceded.[132] The West African Cocoa Control Board and the West African Produce Control Board, set up in 1940 and 1942, respectively, formed the roots of the marketing board system.[133] The Nigerian Produce Marketing Company was incorporated in the United Kingdom in 1947.[134] The marketing boards were set up after the war to cater to each export item and its derivatives, starting with the Nigerian Cocoa Marketing Board in 1947 and followed by the Oil Palm, Groundnut, and Cotton Marketing Boards in 1949.[135] The boards were empowered to control and fix prices to be paid on the two most important products of the region – palm oil and palm kernels, which were still in high demand.[136] In the case of the Ghana Cocoa Marketing Board, Rod

[131] and State Involvement in Africa's Open Economies: The Origins of the Ghana Cocoa Marketing Boards, 1939–46," *Journal of African History* 42 (2001): 397–416, at 398. Ibid. See also J. M. Lee and Martin Peter, *The Colonial Office, War and Development Policy: Organization and the Planning of a Metropolitan Initiative, 1939–45* (London: Maurice Temple Smith, 1982); D. J. Morgan, *The Official History of Colonial Development, Vol. 1: The Origins of British Aid Policy, 1924–45* (London: Palgrave Macmillan, 1980).

[132] Alence, "Colonial Government, Social Conflict and State Involvement," 398. See also David Meredith, "The Colonial Office, British Business Interests and the Reform of Cocoa Marketing in West Africa, 1937–45," *Journal of African History* 29 (1988): 285–300; David Fieldhouse, "War and the Origin of the Gold Coast Cocoa Marketing Board, 1939–40," in *Imperialism, the State and the Third World*, ed. Michael Twaddle (London: British Academy Press, 1992), 153–182; David Fieldhouse, *Merchant Capital and Economic Decolonisation: The United African Company, 1929–87* (Oxford: Clarendon Press, 1994).

[133] The large surplus accumulated by the West African Produce Control Board played an important part in the decision to continue statutory marketing of export products after the war. For studies of the marketing boards, see, for example, H. M. A. Onitiri and D. Olatunbosun, eds., *The Marketing Board System: Proceedings of an International Conference* (Ibadan: Nigerian Institute of Social and Economic Research, 1974); P. T. Bauer, "Statistics of Statutory Marketing in West Africa, 1939–51," *Journal of the Royal Statistical Society* 117 (1954): 1–30; G. K. Helleiner, "The Fiscal Role of the Marketing Boards in Nigerian Economic Development, 1947–61," *Economic Journal* 74, no. 295 (1964): 582–610. For further comments, see David A. Iyegha, *Agricultural Crisis in Africa* (New York: University Press of America, 1988), 89–92; and Oluwasanmi, *Agriculture and Nigerian Economic Development*, 158–183.

[134] For the powers vested on the Nigerian Cocoa Marketing Board, see *Laws of Nigeria*, 1948, vol. V, Cap. 15, 37. See also Oluwasanmi, *Agriculture and Nigerian Economic Development*, 159–160.

[135] See *Laws of Nigeria, 1948–9* (Supplement), 237–286. Cited in Oluwasanmi, *Agriculture and Nigerian Economic Development*, 160.

[136] See *Laws of Nigeria, 1948–9* (Lagos: Government Printer, 1949). See also Oluwasanmi, *Agriculture and Nigerian Economic Development*, 160, Bede Onimode, *Imperialism and*

Alence has argued that "pressures on the government to mitigate domestic social conflict caused by volatility in the world economy are crucial to understanding the shift to controlled cocoa marketing."[137]

Marketing boards were charged with developing and improving the marketing of export products in addition to ensuring price stability. According to the secretary of state for the colonies, marketing boards were necessary to "maintain maximum possible production of palm oil and palm kernels."[138] The emergence of these boards expanded the involvement by European trading companies and the colonial authorities in local open economies.[139] The boards were also required to maintain and control efficient organizations of licensed buying agents to undertake the handling of produce and its delivery to the boards. They also helped to maintain legally prescribed grades and standards of quality, to improve the quality of export produce, and to allocate funds to the appropriate authorities by means of grants, loans, investments, and endowments for the purposes of economic development and research.[140] The actual purchasing of produce was left to licensed buying agents.[141] H. A. Oluwasanmi has described the system of licensing buying agents as a continuation of the "*status quo ante bellum.*"[142] In the case of palm products, prospective buying agents were required to show evidence that they could purchase with reasonable regularity at least 400 tons of palm kernels and 200 tons of palm oil in their first year of operation. In addition, licensed buying agents were required to produce "acceptable evidence of their ability to provide the necessary capital to finance their purchases."[143]

The boards were envisaged as buffers for African producers by ensuring the stability of producer incomes.[144] However, the marketing boards

*Underdevelopment in Nigeria: The Dialectics of Mass Poverty* (London: Macmillan, 1983), 165.

[137] Alence, "Colonial Government, Social Conflict and State Involvement," 397.

[138] NAE, 1642, Vol. II, ABADIST. 1/26/908, Secretary Eastern Province to Resident, Owerri Province, October 17, 1945.

[139] For the specific responses to the pressure toward greater state involvement in African economies, see Alence, "Colonial Government, Social Conflict and State Involvement," 400.

[140] On the role of the marketing boards, see Nigeria, *Handbook of Commerce and Industry in Nigeria* (Lagos, no date), 112.

[141] For the conditions for approval as a buying agent, see, for example, Nigeria Cocoa Marketing Board, Annual Report, 1947–48 (Lagos, 1949), 30; Eastern Regional Marketing Board, Annual Report, 1958, 93–95; Nigeria Groundnut Marketing Board, Annual Report, 1949–50, 29; and Northern Regional Marketing Board, Annual Report, 1954–55, 86–87.

[142] Oluwasanmi, *Agriculture and Nigerian Economic Development*, 163.    [143] Ibid., 164.

[144] See, for example, *Statement of Future Marketing of West African Cocoa*, Cmd. 6950. London, 1946, p. 8. See also Oil Palm Produce Marketing Board, *Statement of the*

became instruments of exploitation to siphon farmers' income. Jerome Wells has shown that the marketing boards diverted a quarter to a third of the gross income of farmers to finance development in infrastructure, plantations, farm settlements, and research.[145] Producer income continued to be lower than the world market price from the late 1940s into the 1950s.[146] According to economist P. T. Bauer, the differences between producer prices and market prices left the primary producers at roughly the same income level as they had been before the Second World War.[147] While the middlemen, the boards, and the trading firms made huge profits, farmers in Nigeria suffered from very low producer prices.[148]

The colonial authorities regulated the entrance of Nigerians into the economy. Setting the conditions through which one could become a broker ensured that the expatriate firms, both European and Levantine, remained dominant players in the produce trade from the postwar period into the 1960s, when the share of the expatriate firms declined due to the attainment of political independence.[149] The United African Company (the product of the merger in 1929 of the Niger Company and the African Eastern Trade Corporation) not only became the largest single firm in the West African import and export trade but dominated West African trade generally and Nigerian import–export trade in particular. According to Felix Ekechi, by 1940, the UAC controlled nearly half of the total West African trade and about 41.3 percent of Nigerian trade.[150] In the four major Nigerian primary products (palm

*Policy Proposed for the Future Marketing of Nigerian Oils, Oil Seeds and Cotton,* Sessional Paper No. 18 of 1948; and Nigeria Oil Palm Produce Marketing Board, *First Annual Report 1949* (Lagos, 1950), 5.

[145] Jerome C. Wells, *Agricultural Policy and Economic Growth in Nigeria, 1962–1968* (Oxford: Oxford University Press, 1974), 40, n. 5.

[146] The marketing board system throughout British colonial territories operated in a similar fashion. For the activities of the marketing boards in Jamaica in the 1960s, see, for example, Stephen K. Pollard and Douglas H. Graham, "Pricing Policy and Agricultural Export Performance in Jamaica," *World Development* 13, no. 9 (1985): 1067–1075.

[147] See P. T. Bauer, "Origins of the Statutory Export Monopolies of British West Africa," *Business History Review* 28 (September 1954): 197–213. See also Eno J. Usoro, *The Nigerian Oil Palm Industry: Government Policy and Export Production, 1906–1965* (Ibadan: Ibadan University Press, 1974), 111.

[148] See, for example, Iyegha, *Agricultural Crisis in Africa,* 89–90; Gerald D. Hursh, Arthur Niehoof, Neils Roling, and Graham Kerr, *Innovation in Eastern Nigeria: Success and Failure of Agricultural Programs in 71 Villages of Eastern Nigeria* (East Lansing: Michigan State University Press, 1968), 196.

[149] Iyegha, *Agricultural Crisis in Africa.*

[150] See Felix Ekechi, "Aspects of Palm Oil Trade at Oguta (Eastern Nigeria), 1900–1950," *African Economic History* 10 (1981): 35–65. C. C. Wrigley, "The Colonial Phase in British West Africa: Economic and Social Developments," in *A Thousand Years of West Africa History,* ed. J. F. Ade Ajayi and Ian Espie (Ibadan: Ibadan University Press and

oil, palm kernels, cocoa, and groundnuts) the company controlled 56.71 percent of the total exports by 1940.[151] Indeed, postwar economic planning was ambivalent in its goal of creating a viable economy and a productive peasantry. The interests of the British and the financial and political stability of the colonial state shaped colonial economic planning. The underlying philosophy of the development strategy pursued by the government generated rural poverty and underdevelopment despite the existence of a few wealthy middlemen. Related to this was a development policy that encouraged large-scale expansion of export crops but neglected other sectors.

The food sector suffered significant decline in the postwar era. In the Eastern Region, for example, the district officer for Eket in Calabar Province noted the alarming rate of agricultural involution. "I have very grave doubts," he wrote, "whether a drive for increased food production organized by local government bodies and Native Authorities would have any success in Eket, neither do I believe it would have much more success anywhere in the areas of the Eastern Provinces where there are substantial areas of oil palm."[152] But in spite of continually preaching the connection between a shortage of locally produced food and the increase in the cost of living, the district officer attested to the failure of the colonial campaigns as a result of the specific circumstances in the region:

I have failed entirely to detect any appreciation of this fact among the local bodies with which I have had dealings since the cost of living began to rise in the early years of the recent war. The realization of this fact might be brought home to the farmer in an area where there is plenty of spare land after the needs of the export crop and the food crops to feed himself and his dependents have been met, but in areas where there is little land surplus to the requirements of the export crop and the food locally consumed, even the liveliest propaganda cannot hope to succeed so long as the cash rewards for the export crop far exceed those to be expected from food crops.[153]

In some parts of Nigeria, however, the economy benefited from the growing expenditures on transportation and communication and rail and

Nelson, 1972), 423–439, at 432. According to Wrigley, the UAC was one of the seven large firms that controlled "roughly two thirds of the trade of West Africa as a whole." In 1976, the UAC boasted of a revenue of $1 billion. See James Flanigan, "Nigeria: Where the Real Action Is," *Forbes* 118, no. 11 (December 1, 1976), 51–61, at 58. Margery Ferham, ed., *Mining, Commerce and Finance in Nigeria* (London: Faber and Faber, 1948), 58.

[151]  Ekechi, "Aspects of Palm Oil Trade at Oguta (Eastern Nigeria), 1900–1950," 59–65; Charles Henry Wilson, *The History of Unilever: A Study of Economic Growth and Social Change*, 2 vols. (London: Cassell, 1954); F. J. F. Pedler, *The Lion and the Union in Africa* (London: Heinemann, 1974).

[152]  NAE, EKETDIST 1/2/50, File No. 499/96, "Food Production," District Officer, Eket to Resident, Calabar Province, Calabar, July 1951.

[153]  Nigeria, *Annual Report of the Agricultural Department, 1939–1940*, 1.

road development.[154] Between 1943 and 1946, the government allocated a substantial sum of money for the construction of rural roads to facilitate the evacuation of palm oil and palm kernels. The development of local feeder roads further integrated rural households into the colonial and war economy.[155] However, the development of roads and other forms of communication increased the capacity of rural peasants to leave the villages. They migrated to the towns, taking advantage of the opportunities in the construction industry and the expanding bureaucracy. Many Nigerian laborers were attracted to the opportunities offered by plantations in the mid-west and the timber industry in Benin and other parts of the region. Linus Anabalam, an Igbo migrant, recalled the opportunities and challenges posed by the postwar migration boom: "After the Second World War, the eye of the world opened and people started to migrate outside the rural area ... this was the beginning of labour scarcity for agriculture in this area. The expansion of educational opportunities took children away from the homes and farm work."[156] The increase in the migration of men and young boys tended to heighten frustration with the local economy, but migration provided a ready source of capital accumulation, a break from rural life, and increased opportunities that were absent in the countryside.

While the strategies adopted by rural peasants were diverse, they seem to have been overwhelmingly influenced by reduced producer prices, the increased cost of living, and a new lifestyle. But the urban areas did not often provide the means of survival. Yet postwar conditions generated a certain measure of socioeconomic progress and development. Higher prices introduced by the government for cash crops as well as improved processing techniques accounted for the boom.[157]

## The End of World War II and Political Developments

The political developments in the postwar period had their roots in the interwar years. There was already a general sense of disillusionment among the emerging educated elite by the 1930s. They channeled their

---

[154] Throughout Africa, the populations of major cities increased substantially. William M. Freund, *The Making of Contemporary Africa: The Development of African Society since 1800* (Bloomington: Indiana University Press, 1984), 169–170. See also Marvin Miracle, *Maize in Tropical Africa* (Madison: University of Wisconsin Press, 1966), 34–35.

[155] NAE, 18038/38, vol. VII, C.S.E. 1/85/8584, Resident, Onitsha Province to Secretary, Eastern Provinces, November 18, 1945.

[156] Linus Anabalam, interviewed by Chima Korieh at Umuchieze, Mbaise, Nigeria, on December 24, 2000.

[157] See Usoro, *The Nigerian Oil Palm Industry*, 74.

energy in the articulation of the future of the African continent through the founding of political parties and local print press.[158] The major attempt at political organization was initiated by J. C. Vaughn, Ernest Ikoli, H. O. Davies, and Samuel Akinsanya, who founded the Nigerian Youth Movement (NYM) in 1934. Although based in Lagos, the NYM had a national outlook that cut across ethnic lines. Following the Nigerian Youth Charter in 1938, which stressed national unity over ethnic divisions, notably between the Igbo and the Yoruba, the NYM, under Herbert Macaulay's[159] leadership, boasted a membership of 10,000 in 1938.[160] The NYM provided a platform for other emerging nationalist leaders such as Nnamdi Azikiwe, who was later to become the first indigenous governor-general of Nigeria. From 1937, Nnamdi Azikiwe used his newspaper, the *West African Pilot*, as an anticolonial voice for Nigerian nationalists. They challenged colonialism at three levels – political, economic, and sociocultural – in this period. In the political sphere, Nigerian nationalists essentially employed constitutional means to challenge the colonial occupation of their countries and the structures and institutions established by colonialism. The nationalist activities of this period were encouraged by the aftermath of several crucial developments during the interwar years, or the period of high imperialism. These included World War I, the Great Depression, and the rise of Soviet Communism, Italian Fascism, and German Nazism. In the interwar years, the nationalists were emboldened by the clauses in the Treaty of Versailles that outlined the new notion of colonies as a "Sacred Trust," and by President Woodrow Wilson's Fourteen Points that endorsed eloquently the right of small nations to self-determination.

The Second World War marked an important turning point in Africa's relationship with imperial powers. On a general level, the political impact of the war and the development of nationalism in the postwar period were

---

[158] Coates, "Nigeria and the World," 704.

[159] Herbert Macaulay is arguably the founder of modern Nigerian nationalism. He organized the first political party in Nigeria in 1922, known as the Nigerian National Democratic Party (NNDP), following a new Nigerian constitution introduced to provide for limited franchise elections in Lagos and Calabar. See Tekena N. Tamuno, *Herbert Macaulay, Nigerian Patriot* (London: Heinemann Educational, 1976); Isaac B. Thomas, *Life History of Herbert Macaulay, C. E.* (Lagos: Printed at Tika-To[r]e Press, 1946).

[160] Ibid. See also Richard L. Sklar, *Nigerian Political Parties: Power in an Emergent African Nation* (Trenton, NJ: African World Press, 2004), for political development in Nigeria. On the crisis that emerged within the NYM, see Quintard Taylor, "Contentious Legacy: The Nigerian Youth Movement and the Rise of Ethnic Politics, 1934–1951," in *Nigerian Studies in Religious Tolerance, Volume III, Ethnicity, Religion and Nation-Building*, ed. C. S. Momah and Hakeem Harunah (Lagos: University of Lagos Press, 1995).

far more enduring than its effect on other areas.[161] Remarkably, the war contributed to the political liberation of African societies "by undermining Europe's capacity to hold on to its empires."[162] The end of the war exerted an enormous influence on nationalist thought and on the development of counter ideologies to colonialist thinking. As A. Kum'a Ndumbe III has argued, "the good intentions outlined in Wilson's Fourteen Points did not materialize into self-determination for African countries."[163] In the First World War, Africans "came out of the war as they had gone into it – as colonized peoples."[164] As they had following the First World War, colonial powers did not consider Africans as part of the equation at the end of the Second World War.

Between 1939 and 1945, every part of the British empire in Asia and Africa underwent irreversible political transformations. Beginning in India, people all over the British colonies sought change that would eventually lead to independence. In *India's War*, historian Srinath Raghavan paints a compelling picture of how Indian participation in the war abroad and on the home front led to the end of colonial rule in South Asia.[165] The Indian example was mirrored in other parts of the British Empire, including tropical Africa. As Ian Kikuchi has shown, British domestic politics influenced the decline of the British Empire at the end of the war. The 1945 general election in the United Kingdom, which pitted the Conservative Party and its heroic wartime prime minister, Winston Churchill, against the Labour Party and its leader, Clement Attlee, was a defining moment for Britain in both its domestic and foreign policies and had important consequences for the colonies. The election was in many ways a struggle between those who wished to continue British imperial ambitions and those who wished to focus on Great Britain.[166] Britain's colonies were motivated by this struggle within British politics at home, and the success of the Labour Party over the Conservatives was not just a defeat for the wartime leadership but also resounding proof of the triumph of the vision and forces of

---

[161] See Olusanya, *The Second World War and Politics in Nigeria*; and James S. Coleman, *Nigeria: Background to Nationalism* (Berkeley: University of California Press, 1958).

[162] Mazrui, "Africa and the Legacy of the Second World War," 10, 12.

[163] Ndumbe, "Black Africa and Germany during the Second World War," 54.

[164] Ibid.

[165] Srinath Raghavan, *India's War: The Making of Modern South Asia, 1939–1945* (London: Penguin, 2017). See also Yasmin Khan, *India at War: The Subcontinent and the Second World War* (New York: Oxford University Press, 2015).

[166] See Thomas Merritt, "Britain and Post War Attitudes to Empire," Academia. edu, accessed January 19, 2019, www.academia.edu/34687086/Britain_ and_Post_War_Attitudes_to_Empire.

decolonization.[167] By 1945, colonies were an expensive liability for Clement Attlee's newly elected Labour government.[168] As Gerold Krozewski suggests, the relationship between British financial policy and political change in the colonial empire between 1939 and 1958, Britain's postwar recovery, changing economic priorities, and the structural transformation in the international economy and the sterling area all decreased the need for formal domination and eased the way toward decolonization in Africa.[169] Beyond the increasing view of empire as a burden was the changing international climate, which saw the United States, with its opposition to imperialism, as a rising global power, while Japan's wartime victories had destroyed Britain's imperial prestige.[170] As Ian Kikuchi has observed, the colonies "were not sacrificed to win the war, at least not in a deliberate, foreknown sense. They went away because they were already tottering, and Japanese triumph (and then failure to win the hearts and minds of their new conquests) just tipped the scale."[171]

The end of World War II coincided with the downfall of the British Empire that had started in India, where British imperial control faced its most viral challenge as the war came to an end.[172] Following Indian independence, the British government envisaged the gradual and ordered replacement of the empire. The empire would be replaced by a commonwealth of nations tied together by language, shared history, and economic interdependence.[173] Colonial administrators would hand over the reins to moderate local pro-British leaders. In practice, the road to independence was much quicker and rockier than British officials and politicians had initially planned. Indian independence created its own

---

[167] For more on the elections of 1945, see Gary McCulloch, "Labour, the Left, and the British General Election of 1945," *Journal of British Studies* 24, no. 4 (1985): 465–489. On the Conservative stance on the colonies, see Conservative Party Manifesto, 1945, "Mr. Churchill's Declaration of Policy to the Electors," Politics Resource United Kingdom Online, accessed September 20, 2016, www.politicsresources.net/area/uk/man/con45.html.

[168] Ian Kikuchi, "The End of the British Empire after the Second World War," Imperial War Museum, February 6, 2018, accessed January 19, 2019, www.iwm.org.uk/history/the-end-of-the-british-empire-after-the-second-world-war. See also Mark Phythian, *The Labour Party, War and International Relations 1945–2006* (London: Routledge, 2007).

[169] See also Gerold Krozewski, "Sterling, the 'Minor' Territories, and the End of Formal Empire, 1939–1958," *Economic History Review* 46, no. 2 (1993): 239–265.

[170] Kikuchi, "The End of the British Empire after the Second World War."    [171] Ibid.

[172] Das Taraknath, "India and the End of Empire," *Virginia Quarterly Review* 16, no. 1 (1940): 68–77.

[173] Central Office of Information for Commonwealth Office, "Nigeria: The Making of a Nation," 1960, National Archives, accessed January 19, 2019, https://media.nationalarchives.gov.uk/index.php/nigeria-the-making-of-a-nation-2.

momentum.[174] A White Paper (Cmd. No. 6599) was published on March 5, 1945, containing proposals for constitutional reform put forward by the governor of Nigeria. The major features of these proposals included: the representation of the native authorities in the legislature; the institution of regional councils for the northern, western, and eastern provinces; the revision of the membership of the Nigerian Legislative Council and the extension of its powers to cover the northern provinces; and the provision of African majorities in both the regional and the legislative councils. The governor's proposals were laid before the Nigerian Legislative Council at the opening of its budget session on March 5, 1945. The council passed a resolution signifying its approval and recommending the adoption of the proposals.[175]

Britain's African colonies drew inspiration both from India and from their own direct experiences of fighting abroad and the impact the war had at home. The perception of Africans as the degraded segment of humanity was challenged by their role in the war as well as the destruction of the notion of European superiority. As scholar Ali Mazrui has observed, "While the image of the African was humanized by being pulled up from equation with devils, monkeys and children, the image of the white man was humanized by being pulled down from equation with supermen, angels and the gods themselves."[176] So the war was a transforming experience for both the ex-servicemen and the Africans at home who had followed the progress of the war with keen interest. Propaganda and other wartime news formed an important educational experience for Africans in general and "increased their interest in world affairs and broadened their vision of human possibilities."[177] African societies tapped into this changing global environment in which power shifted from the hegemonic order that centered in Western Europe to the United States and the Soviet Union. The anticolonial stance of these two emerging world powers pressured old Europe to make concession to the liberation movements in Africa.

The weakened global stature of Britain after the war, the challenge to its superpower status, and the rise of the United States and the Soviet Union as superpowers with different political agendas put pressure on Europe to change. Despite its interests in exploiting African resources, the internal educational and political developments that took place in Africa and the were accelerated by the war made independence possible. Beginning with India, subject peoples all over the colonies began to challenge

---

[174] Ibid.
[175] NA, CAB/66/65/14, Report for the Month of March 1945 for the Dominions, India, Burma and the Colonies and Mandated Territories, April 20, 1945.
[176] Mazrui, "Africa and the Legacy of the Second World War," 14.     [177] Ibid., 15.

a weakened, impoverished, and humiliated empire. Thus, World War II favored the emergence of the kind of mass nationalism that was impossible a few years earlier.

Differences in the perception between Nigerian troops and other colonial troops are reflected in their anticipated role in postwar politics. Despite similarities in their wartime experiences, Nigerian troops were seen as more political in their general outlook. On his visit to West African troops in India in 1945, Major H. P. James observed in his report that a number of men, particularly Nigerian southerners, "are keenly interested in politics particularly the type that is presented by the Pilot and the Zik Press which are sent out to them."[178] Such men were also influenced by the Congress Party in India through its literature.[179] Although the extent to which such exposure led to subversive influence was unclear, the consciousness built during the period abroad was influential in local politics on their arrival back in Nigeria. However, the attitude of the soldiers on their return to civilian life was a concern to the authorities. James further observed that the "Nigerian Hausa and the men from the Northern territories of the Gold Coast will give little trouble."[180] Such could not be said of the southerners, who were seen as malcontents.[181] James's concern was well founded in a region where men and women worked valiantly to transform their societies at the end of the war. Southern Nigerians worked fervently in organizing anticolonial protests and other forms of social movement in the postwar period, as reflected in the rapid growth of organized labor in the 1940s.[182]

The different responses of the peoples of Nigeria have their roots in preexisting political and social structures. As Lord Milverton commented:

The people of the Northern Provinces, highly conservative in their outlook, predominantly Mohammedan, with all that that means in respect for tradition and authority, have a very different outlook to the people of the Eastern Provinces where individualism is the predominant characteristic and where the craving for Western education and individual advancement is most marked. The people of the Western Provinces on the other hand, though they have, like the Northern Provinces, a more developed system of Native Administration than the Eastern Provinces, have still a different outlook to the people of the other two sections.[183]

Nigerians, like people in other parts of Africa, intellectualized the global issues of liberty and freedom. In this intellectual world, Nigerians found

---

[178] NAE, CADIST, 1/3/21, "West African Troops Abroad," 5.    [179] Ibid.    [180] Ibid.
[181] Ibid.
[182] Amadi, "Political Integration in Nigeria, 1939–1945"; Coleman, *Nigeria*; Olusanya, *The Second World War and Politics in Nigeria*.
[183] Milverton, "Nigeria," 81.

a small window for rearticulating their category as imperial citizens. The connections between politics, economics, and the social world in postwar Nigeria were evident as both ex-soldiers and ordinary citizens navigated the complicated mosaic of local power, legitimacy, and authority. Nigerian demands for self-government and independence gathered steam under these prevailing conditions. Nigerian intellectual activities in the postwar period developed in a new direction, drawing from local social and economic conditions rather than the internationalism of the previous years. Two discernible periods – the period of troubles from 1944 to 1957, and the period of diarchy or cooperation between 1951 and 1959 – are evident. The period of troubles was characterized by the rise of militant party politics, particularly those of the National Convention of Nigerian Citizens (NCNC), the Zikist Movement, the Zikist National Vanguard, and the Action Group (AG). The postwar economic strains precipitated the General Strike of 1945, the Burutu Strike of 1947, and the Enugu Colliery Strike, which was brutally suppressed by the colonial administration. Nigerian politicians exploited every opportunity offered by these disturbances for effective propaganda against the colonial regime, attacking the colonial record on economic and social welfare.

Political consciousness was aroused among Nigerians because of widespread mass demonstrations, marches, walkouts, et cetera. This in part was facilitated by the rapid urbanization that occurred following the war, which led to growth in the number of wage and salary earners, and to its corollary, the spread of unionization. Workers' demand for cost-of-living allowances led to the promulgation, in 1942, of the Order General Defence Regulation, which declared strikes and lockouts illegal. A new nationalist era dawned, an era of fusion between the labor movement and political organizations, such as the NCNC, and of cooperation between unions and populist-inclined politicians. It was also an era characterized by the fusion of economic grievances with galvanized political issues and actions, all of which shook the foundations of British rule in Nigeria. Strikes by Nigerian workers fed the political agitation for greater autonomy. On June 22, 1945, African technical workers and laborers employed by the main government departments, including the railway, marine, public works, and printing departments, as well as the employees of the Lagos Municipal Council, came out on strike. The union to which the men belonged had been negotiating with the government for increases in basic wage rates and in cost-of-living allowances.[184] The government had refused to grant such increases, pointing out that they "would only result

---

[184] NA, CAB/66/67/38, "Report for the Month of June 1945 for the Dominions, India, Burma and the Colonies and Mandated Territories," July 1945.

in an inflationary spiral rise in prices." As an alternative measure to combat the admittedly increased cost of living, the government extended the existing scheme for marketing staple foodstuffs at controlled prices and increased supplies of other food imported by the government into Lagos, the center most affected by rising costs and political agitation.

While the strike was initially confined to technical workers, their actions accelerated political agitation as Nigerian nationalists seized the opportunity to raise the consciousness of Nigerian workers and to seek change.[185] Earlier during the strike, which lasted until August 7, 1945, the Nigerian government took action against certain local newspapers, following what the government described as "a series of misrepresentations of the facts regarding the strike."[186] The acting governor ordered the suspension of two newspapers, the *West African Pilot* and the *Daily Comet*, after they published a statement allegedly made by the government public relations officer, accusing the trade union leaders of "incapability and total inability to guide their followers along the right path."[187] Nationalist leader Nnamdi Azikiwe, who controlled both the newspapers concerned, had been sending telegrams to labor organizations throughout the world, appealing for support and alleging that the Nigerian government was considering his deportation and that his life was endangered.[188] Although the government stated that there was no substance in either of these allegations, Azikiwe's appeals evoked some response, "particularly from organizations in the United States sympathetic to Negro aspirations and from Labour organizations in the West Indies."[189] While the ban on the two newspapers was revoked after the strikers returned to work in August 1945, the strikes and attacks on nationalist leaders like Azikiwe accelerated the pace of the decolonization process in Nigeria.[190]

The fusion of revolutionary political leadership, radical trade unionism, ethnic associations, and the activism of the Nigerian Union of Students was consummated in 1943, when rallies and meetings were held to which political leaders of various persuasions were invited. This series of meetings led to the formation of the National Council of Nigeria and the Cameroons in 1944, later renamed the National Convention of Nigerian Citizens (NCNC) with Herbert Macaulay as president and Nnamdi Azikiwe as secretary. Although loose in structure and diffuse in

---

[185] Ibid., 13.    [186] Ibid.    [187] Ibid.    [188] Ibid.
[189] NA, CAB/129/1, Report for the Month of July 1945.
[190] NA, CAB/129/2, Report for the Month of August 1945 for the Dominions, India, Burma and the Colonies and Mandated Territories, October 2, 1945, 11.

goals, the NCNC provided leadership for the national cause through the adoption of an aggressive strategy against the colonial power.[191]

This period also coincided with a new constitutional proposal designed to promote unity and secure greater Nigerian participation in governance. This constitution was drawn by Sir Bernard Bourdillon and published by Sir Arthur Richards in 1944. Although the Richards Constitution promoted unity by bringing the North and the South together, it also promoted regionalism as provincial councils tended to divide more than unite Nigeria. The NCNC was critical of the Richards Constitution for a number of reasons, including its absence of consultation with the Nigerian public prior to its promulgation, the non-extension of the elective principles outside Lagos and Calabar, its failure to accord Nigerians greater participation in government and in administration, and the inclusion of chiefs who were puppets of the colonial administration as unofficial members to represent the interest of the Nigerian peoples. Consequently, the NCNC sent a delegation to the colonial office in London to seek revision of the Constitution but failed to achieve this goal. It lapsed into inactivity by 1947, and the Zikist Movement filled the vacuum by organizing demonstrations, strikes, and boycotts on Empire Day, by advocating the non-payment of taxes and publishing of anticolonial pamphlets and leaflets. The movement was declared illegal and prohibited in 1950.[192]

Postwar intellectualism drew immensely from discourses generated and developed during the war itself. Nigerian intellectuals had been an important voice in framing a new rhetoric of empire, imperial citizenship, and anti-Hitler propaganda. They exposed the inconsistencies of the colonial leaders. For example, in a nationwide radio broadcast in 1941, Bourdillon had declared that the British Empire was fighting for the "right of the ordinary man in every part of the world to live out his own life in freedom and peace."[193] Such views were notably echoed in the Atlantic

---

[191] James, I., "Nigeria: The Road to Independence," Online Nigeria, July 24, 2004, accessed January 19, 2019, http://nm.onlinenigeria.com/templates/default.aspx?a=137 &template=print-article.htm; "World War II and Post-War Trends," Online Nigeria, October 12, 2005, accessed January 19, 2019, www.onlinenigeria.com/independence/? blurb=635; Adiele E. Afigbo, "Indirect Rule in South Eastern Nigeria: The Era of Warrant Chiefs 1891–1929." *Tarikh* 4 (1974): 11–24, at 18; Robin Coren, *Labour and Politics in Nigeria* (London: Heinemann Educational Books, 1981); Michael Crowder, *The Story of Nigeria* (London: Faber and Faber, 1973), 243; Ezera K. Ezera, *Constitutional Development in Nigeria* (Cambridge: Cambridge University Press, 1964); Jean Herskovits, *Nigeria, Power and Democracy in Africa*. Foreign Policy Association Headline Series No. 257 (New York: Foreign Policy Association, 1982): 16; O. Nnoli, *Ethnic Politics in Nigeria* (Enugu: Fourth Dimension Publishers, 1978).
[192] "World War II and Post-War Trends."
[193] Ibhawoh, "Second World War Propaganda," 235.

Charter, in which both President Roosevelt and Prime Minister Churchill professed to respect the rights of all peoples to choose the form of government under which they will live and that they wished to "see sovereign rights and self-government restored to those who have been forcibly deprived of them."[194] The two leaders later contradicted this declaration and qualified that the Atlantic Charter was only for the European nations that were under the domination of Hitler's regime. These experiences compelled African elites to engage with wartime knowledge of universal rights, frame it within a certain context, and modify it to serve their own agendas.

Nationalist and trade unionists argued that the appropriation of the European assertion of self-determinism and the Eurocentric brand of nationalism was not in conflict with indigeneity and African self-assertion in the postwar world. For nationalist purposes, it was hard to see an alternative to this appropriation of a foundationally European ideal. Postwar media discourse focused on the extension of freedom and equality to Africans in recognition of their sacrifices during the war. Propaganda made an essential contribution to the liberation movements in postwar colonial Africa as a preparatory route to anticolonial activities. The involvement of Africans, specifically the Nigerian elites and media, in the production and dissemination of war propaganda in support of the Allies gave them a platform for anticolonial propaganda and had a significant influence on postwar political developments and nationalist discourses. The experiences in mass mobilization and information dissemination "strengthened the ability of the nationalist groups to mobilize mass action."[195] The role of Africans in anti-German propaganda provided a training of sort for organizing effective resistance forces by the African elite. Anticolonial propaganda instilled not only hope but faith and certainty in the eventual liberation of Africa from colonial rule. Nigerian nationalists drew upon Allied war propaganda and anti-German propaganda, which had stood on the moral ground of protection of individual liberty and extolled the tenets of self-determination, to challenge continued colonial domination. Indeed, Nigerians had supported the Allies materially and in manpower. They had endured untold hardship and lived frugally to support the war against Germany. For the Nigerians, it was time to reap the gains of the victory over totalitarianism and tyranny. They did not expect Britain to renege on the promises it made during the war.

African troops who fought alongside the British and French troops in the Second World War learned much from their wartime experiences,

---

[194] Ibid., 239.    [195] Ibid.

particularly about the discrepancies between policies and practices in European countries and those in the colonies. They saw how different social classes – the poor, the middle class, and the rich – were treated. They were treated as human beings with equal dignity. They also learned that the invincibility of the colonialist oppressors was a lie. They saw, for example, Japanese fighting the Europeans with equal might. Furthermore, they saw Europeans expressing actual human fear and being shot dead by black soldiers. In his memoir, Major Cherns recognized that "Africans are not fools." Of the Nigerian troops who had just returned from war, he observed that "they understand what 'Quit India' was about, and Nigeria already has a thriving nationalist independence movement. We are about to release a potential accretion to a rootless urban proletariat."[196]

When these soldiers came back home, they found life very difficult and lacked basic needs because of the colonial government's failure to pay them their entitlement for the war, pushing many to join the national movement for independence. African and Asian troops had served in European armies fighting a war against dictatorship and a form of military imperialism: the empire of Hitler in Europe and the empire of Japan in Asia. The war became a school of indoctrination for many colonial troops who witnessed the discrepancy between European colonial practices and European principles. Though their goals did not necessarily align with the political objectives of nationalists, their distinctive experiences and interests as ex-servicemen "proved powerful after the war, often informing ex-askari action" in Kenya and elsewhere.[197] Yet nationalist leaders tapped into the growing concerns of various classes, including ex-servicemen, in articulating a new agenda for popular participation in the politics of the postwar era.

Ironically, despite the changes in colonial society after the war, the demobilization of African soldiers had little direct impact on political development and the nationalist struggle. In Nigeria, their experiences did not translate into political action and agitation.[198] Indeed, Hal Brands has argued in the case of East Africa that although the release of 100,000 askaris from the King's African Rifles had widespread societal consequences in the social, economic, and political arenas, their demobilization "proved not to be the cataclysmic event that some had feared." Rather, they sought to maintain elite status within both the African community and the broader colonial sphere, and ex-servicemen pursued privileges for themselves and for their

---

[196] Ibid. Cherns, "Walk through the Valley."
[197] Ibhawoh, "Second World War Propaganda."
[198] For some exceptions, see David Killingray, "Soldiers, Ex-servicemen, and Politics in the Gold Coast, 1939–50," *Journal of Modern African Studies* 21, no. 3 (1983): 523–534.

former comrades rather than explicitly confronting the colonial state.[199] The ex-soldiers wanted to prove, as part of a class struggle, that they were part of the imperial structure while at the same time overtly challenging government expectations by "demanding a continuation of the privileges to which they had become accustomed."[200] Nigerian ex-servicemen were largely guided by the same principles. Despite the potentials that existed for political activism, ex-servicemen did not play a significant role in the political struggle in the postwar period.[201]

A few years after the end of the war, the general political and economic condition was mixed. Lord Milverton, governor of colonial Nigeria between 1943 and 1948, summarized the prevailing situation:

Over the past 8 years, Nigeria has seen its revenue more than doubled, and its expenditure constantly rising. Expanding trade and higher prices for its products have enabled the taxpayer to meet heavily increased taxation, and the country has not only balanced its budget since 1941, but has been able to strengthen its position by placing substantial sums to reserve. The cost of living has also steadily risen and has given rise to successive Commissions of Inquiry whose recommendations have been largely adopted by the Government. In common with the rest of the world the shadow of inflation haunts the country. The currency circulation shews a rise from £5 million in 1939 to £18 million in 1946. The difficulty of getting staff, the scarcity of consumer goods, and the impossibility of getting adequate supplies of capital goods, has made progress very slow at a time when speed is vital. And so the general impatience of the public is apt to focus on Government and to blame them for local difficulties which in fact are the result of world conditions.[202]

In the final analysis, the postwar period faded into the period of decolonization. The activities of the veterans were not a turning point in the nationalist movement, although the agitation surely played a key role in solidifying popular opposition to Britain's attempts to maintain its imperial possessions or slow down the pace of decolonization. But the goal of making the veterans a permanent feature of postwar society was not reached. The march toward political independence and the transition toward African control of politics and the economy was fundamental and beyond the scope of the ex-soldiers. The political transition changed the site of struggle for the ex-soldiers: they fought for the British Empire toward which they felt a sense of entitlement. They did not feel entitlement toward the emerging indigenous polity neither did the new Nigerian state have a sense of obligation.

---

[199] Brands, "Wartime Recruiting Practices, Martial Identity and Post–World War II Demobilization in Colonial Kenya."
[200] Ibid.    [201] Olusanya, "The Role of Ex-servicemen in Nigerian Politics," 224.
[202] Milverton, "Nigeria," 81.

In other areas of life, some of the social dynamics put in motion by the returning soldiers, such as the cost of marriage, among other transformations, continued to order life. On the political level, the sense of optimism that greeted the end of the war galvanized many parts of society and led to the emergence of radical nationalism that would push society toward independence. The nationalist movements of the postwar period pushed the colonial government and its Nigerian colonial subjects in different directions. In the economic sphere, the policy of the government demonstrated continuity with the incorporation of rural farmers as an essential part of postwar economic planning.

The end of the war brought important changes but also a degree of continuity. The economic conditions did not change significantly, and colonial intervention continued for most of the remaining years of British rule. The war, however, liberated the population, increased mobility and changed the social and economic dynamics of Nigerian societies. Other changes followed in the heels of increased political activities as Nigeria continually marched toward political independence.

# Conclusion

Pa Thaddeus Uwa, the last member of his age group in the village of Umuchieze, Mbaise, in eastern Nigeria, known as *ndi-French* (the French), died in 2016 at the age of 100 years. He was the last of the Second World War generation in this village. Among the Igbo-speaking people, each age group takes a name that reflects a unique identity or that commemorates special events in the history of the village or the group. *Ndi-French* was unique because it represented the group whose members had reached adulthood during a major global event and had fought in the war. Ironically, the group did not take its name after the British, its imperial masters, who most of the members served with in the war. The adoption of the name of *ndi-French* reflected the global scope of the war, the cooperation that developed between these two European colonial powers, and the projection of the Allies as a single front in the war against Germany. Remarkably, there is no memorial for these men who fought on behalf of the empire, and the memory of the war has vanished with the death of their group's last surviving member. Yet the war was Africa's world war too, though that fact is largely forgotten.

The Second World War was the greatest calamity to befall humanity in the twentieth century. An estimated 75 million people died – 3 percent of the world's population – including 25 million soldiers, sailors, and airmen.[1] While the war started in 1939, events in the earlier parts of the twentieth century transformed the political, social, and economic structures of the world in ways that no one could have imagined as the twentieth century ended. The world experienced a major conflict, the First World War, from 1914 to 1918, but the interwar years (1919–1938) were, indeed, a period of major uncertainty. The Treaty of Versailles, which ended the First World War, did not achieve its goal of guaranteeing peace.[2] While the era

---

[1] Neil Kagan and Stephen G. Hyslop, *Eyewitness to World War II: Unforgettable Stories from History's Greatest Conflict (Reader's Edition)* (Washington, DC: National Geographic, 2018), 7.

[2] Signed on June 28, 1919, the Treaty of Versailles ended the state of war between Germany and the Allies. For more information on the treaty, see, for example, Alan Sharp, *The*

witnessed the resurgence of German aggression, the victorious Allies did not abandon their goal of containing Germany and shifting public opinion against it. Neville Chamberlain, the British prime minister, pursued a failed policy of appeasement to curtail German aggression under the leadership of Adolf Hitler.[3] Chamberlain's hopes of avoiding war by signing the Munich Pact did not end German belligerence. With Hitler's invasion of Poland on September 1, 1939, the failure of diplomacy and reason gave way to the kind of antagonism Europe had not known since World War I, but German hostility assumed a global proportion that drew all parts of the world into the war. The war was an impetus for change in the context of local and global politics, culture, and social change, including the nature and contour of the political development of Europe in the postwar period.[4] Some of these changes built on transformations already affecting prewar Europe, while others, such as the Cold War, were the outcomes of postwar developments and alignments.[5] Just as the war itself had global spatial reach, its ending also reshaped other parts of the world in irreversible ways, triggering new responses and adaptation at the local level. Societies in Africa, Latin America, and Asia would all be drawn into the conflagrations of postwar global alignments. For African societies in particular, the war was a turning point in the emergence of long-term social, economic, and cultural developments that impacted postwar societies and politics.

The colonial effort during the war was coordinated from the highest levels of the imperial bureaucracy – from the Colonial Office in London to the colonial governors, from whom directives were passed to district officers down to African political leaders. British imperial possessions were divided into different zones for effective coordination. Special envoys were appointed in different parts of the empire to undertake the task of coordinating the war effort. Philip Cunliffe-Lister, 1st Earl of Swinton, was seconded to West Africa as the resident minister to

---

*Versailles Settlement: Peacemaking after the First World War, 1919–1923*, 3rd edn. (London: Red Globe Press, 2018); Sally Marks, "Mistakes and Myths: The Allies, Germany, and the Versailles Treaty, 1918–1921," *Journal of Modern History* 85, no. 3 (2013): 632–659; Marc Trachtenberg, "Versailles after Sixty Years," *Journal of Contemporary History* 17, no. 3 (1982): 487–506.

[3] On the policy of appeasement, see, for example, Frank McDonough, *Hitler, Chamberlain and Appeasement* (Cambridge: Cambridge University Press, 2002); David Faber, *Munich: The 1938 Appeasement Crisis* (New York: Simon & Schuster, 2009).

[4] A. W. Purdue, "The Transformative Impact of World War II," in European History Online (EGO), published by the Leibniz-Institut für Europäische Geschichte (IEG), Mainz, April 18, 2016, accessed January 9, 2019, www.ieg-ego.eu/purduea-2016-en.

[5] See, for instance, Arthur Marwick, *War and Social Change in the Twentieth Century: A Comparative Study of Britain, France, Germany, Russia and the United States* (London: Red Globe Press, 1974); and Walter Laqueur, *Europe since Hitler: The Rebirth of Europe* (London: Penguin Books, 1982).

coordinate all war-related activities in the four British colonies of Nigeria, Ghana, Sierra Leone, and Gambia. A similar strategy was adopted in eastern and southern Africa, where men such as Sir Phillip Mitchell and Charles Arden Clarke labored to support the empire's war efforts. Rather than setting up entirely new structures, the British authorities called upon existing colonial infrastructures, including the already established political structure of colonial rule.

Nigeria is indicative of the way participation in war both triggered new forms of relationships between metropole and colony and extended the frontiers of imperial control of Britain's disparate colonial possessions. This book has analyzed these complex interactions as they played out between Nigeria and the British Empire, focusing on peoples, commodities, and intangible outcomes – namely, social and political effects. I do not claim to cover all facets of this historical episode; rather, I have focused on neglected themes and sources that can cast new light on one of the most important episodes in the history of the twentieth century. During the Second World War, British and French African colonies received a new focus. Assessed through the lens of colonialism, Nigeria and several other European colonies provided essential human and material support to the Allies, relying on prewar colonial structures, networks, and political relationships with the indigenous chief class for the massive mobilization that occurred throughout Britain's African colonies. But Nigeria, like its African counterparts, provided more than material support. Through their role as individuals at home, soldiers on the war front, and producers of propaganda, Nigerians created opportunities for redefinition of the relationship between "metropole" and "colony."

Great Britain was by far one of the most successful imperial powers by the beginning of the twentieth century. Britain's colonies, and, to a lesser extent, the dominions, were at the center of Britain's external commerce.[6] They provided a steady source of raw materials for British industries, an outlet for British goods, and a fertile ground for the implementation of Britain's civilizing mission abroad. This relationship was often redefined by the two major global wars of the past century, entrusting the empire and its subjects to a far more complicated network. Even though Britain held many colonial dependencies differing widely in geographic location, racial composition, economic structure, and form of government, the empire increasingly pulled resources from such dependencies to meet its needs during periods of global crisis. This was the case during the First and Second World Wars. This truly global imperial outreach

---

[6] David Edgerton, *Britain's War Machine: Weapons, Resources, and Experts in the Second World War* (Oxford: Oxford University Press, 2011).

provided Britain with myriad resources from Asia, Africa, and the Middle East. Although British colonies had been woven into the fabric of the economic and social structures of the British Empire before the war, the war extended the integration of metropole and colony like never before. The war against Germany and its allies drew in several colonial territories, including Nigeria. Not only did Nigeria play a crucial ideological role in the war, its personnel, products, and finance gave Britain a much-needed boost. As European Fascism took hold and Europe went to war in 1939, it was inevitable, John Igbino has written in a recent book, "that Nigeria and its people would support Britain's war effort in return for Britain's commitment to political reforms."[7] Indeed, Nigerians of all classes, regions, and ethnicities, like many of their African counterparts, were involved in the struggle to defeat the Axis Powers, diligently sending soldiers, workers, and supplies to European and Middle Eastern theaters to aid the war effort.[8] Nigeria served the practical purpose of providing the manpower, funds, agricultural products, and other mineral resources vital to the war effort. As we have seen, the war changed the empire's relationship with its colonial subjects, challenging deeply held ideas that empires were tightly run by metropolitan elites, while providing opportunity for greater flow of people, goods, and ideas across the empire and on a global scale. Britain relied on the existing colonial relationship between the British Empire and its colonial subjects in Nigeria before the war.

Attention has been drawn particularly to the contributions of European colonies to the military effort. This military role, though employed on a massive scale in World War II, was not new. Colonial soldiers had been used in the establishment of European empires in Africa and Asia. From the Portuguese deployment of African soldiers in Taiwan in 1642 to the British use of Indian soldiers in the pacification of the subcontinent, African and Asian soldiers facilitated the conquest of what became European colonies in parts of Asia and Africa in the twentieth century.[9] The French extensively used conscripted West African troops in the expansion and maintenance of the French Empire. Local military forces were increased in strength due to the changing circumstances. Beginning with the Great War, the foremost global war of its time, European strongholds in Africa conscripted Africans as soldiers to meet their rising demands for manpower. They were an invaluable asset when France was

[7] Igbino, *Spidermen*, see especially chapter 1.
[8] Aderinto, "Isaac Fadoyebo and the Battle of Nyron," 109.
[9] David Killingray, "Parameters of the Second World War in Asia and Africa: Thoughts and Emotions," paper presented at the "Colonial Mobilization in Africa and Asia during the Second World War: Soldiers, Labourers and Women" conference, Kyoto, March 22–23, 2018.

desperately "short of men and did almost all her fighting on the Western Front."[10] Although Britain's colonial subjects were not allowed to fight in Europe, by 1916, African troops from the West fought valiantly in East Africa against Germany.[11]

The Second World War imposed even greater responsibilities on European colonies in Africa. A month after Britain declared war on Germany, the War Cabinet requested the Colonial and War Offices to prepare a report on how the colonial empire's manpower resources could best be utilized during the war.[12] The question was the subject of lengthy examinations and discussions between the War and Colonial Offices, and the colonial governments. Much thought was given to the contributions of the colonial dependencies under the circumstances. As Judith Byfield notes, "Britain and the United States would not have been able to produce the technology or provide the transportation their armies required."[13] British subjects served in the British imperial forces as soldiers in the King's African Rifles from East Africa alongside their West African counterparts in the Royal West African Frontier Force.[14] In East Africa, the number of men in the local forces in September 1939 was approximately 11,100 compared to 4,700 in August 1914.[15] The Royal West African Frontier Force recruited extensively from the British colonies in West Africa. Similar increases were witnessed in other parts of the British Empire like Trinidad, with 1,490 enlisted men compared to 260 in the Great War; 1,450 men in Hong Kong compared to 520 in the Great War; and 10,220 men in Malaya compared to 3,400 in the Great War.[16] During the war, the military forces trained in the colonial dependencies were more numerous and better equipped in September 1939 than in August 1914.[17] When France fell to Germany in June 1940, and Italian and German attacks in the Mediterranean made it difficult for supply ships to reach British forces in the Middle East, Britain "turned to an underdeveloped, 3,700-mile air route from Takoradi in the British colony of the Gold Coast to Cairo, Egypt."[18] Takoradi was bound to play a very significant role in the Allied trans-African supply line to Egypt that became officially known as the West African Reinforcement Route. Takoradi became one of the most important bases for Britain's Royal

---

[10] Paul Mulvey, "Mobilising Empires in the First World War," Academia.edu, accessed January 22, 2019, www.academia.edu/460820/Mobilising_Empires_in_the_First_World_War_lecture.
[11] Morrow, "Black Africans in World War II," 12.    [12] Ibid.
[13] Byfield, "Producing for the War," 24.
[14] Morrow, "Black Africans in World War II," 13.
[15] NA, CAB/67/4/15, "Utilization of the Man-Power Resources of the Colonial Empire," Memorandum by the Secretary of State for the Colonies, January 1940, 1.
[16] Ibid.    [17] Ibid.    [18] Quartey, "How West Africa Helped Win World War II."

Air Force and between August 1940 and June 1943, "over 4,500 British Blenheims, Hurricanes, and Spitfires were assembled at Takoradi and ferried to the Middle East."[19] Due to their roles in maintaining the colonial state and extending the frontiers, African soldiers were deployed much more extensively during the Second World War. Nigeria played a central role by providing soldiers. The West African regiments were made up of two battalions from Nigeria. The colonial mobilization of African soldiers for combat and noncombat roles achieved the Allied war objective of defeating the Axis, but it did much more than defeat the enemy. Nigeria's physical share in the war was huge. Nigeria, like other African colonies, assumed a significant and strategic role as a colonial subject of Britain and France in the two major conflicts of the twentieth century. Nigeria's participation in the war drastically changed its economy and increased British demands for "huge reserves of men, food, and raw materials."[20] Nigerians subsidized Britain by providing enormous quantities of agricultural products, thereby reducing the cost of waging the war on behalf of the British Empire at home.[21]

The process that culminated in Nigerians' support for Britain is not necessarily to be taken for granted. Rather the process that produced Nigeria's support for the war was partly a response to propaganda. Allied propaganda was a vital part of the conflict and central in shaping the response of Nigeria in the Second World War. Channels of propaganda, including the press and other print media, broadcasting, and film, employed extensively by colonial agencies that sought to garner the support of colonial subjects, curtailed anticolonial sentiments and generated patriotism toward the empire. Moreover, within the context of the war, a parallel space emerged for local articulation of anti-German propaganda. Aligning itself with the shifting pattern of morale during the war, Nigerian production of propaganda, which encouraged local support for the war, represents one of the ironies of the British–Nigerian encounter. While the propaganda was immediately successful in its main aim of drawing local support, its unintended consequences were significant. Nigerian production and consumption of propaganda produced the conditions that generated conflict at the end of the war as the local elite sought to liberate the country from colonial rule.

The war created many problems for Nigerians of different backgrounds, especially for ordinary farmers and traders in villages across the country. The greatest impact of the war on the Nigerian population was economic, much of which resulted from low levels of imports, scarcity

[19] Ibid.    [20] Mordi, "The Nigeria Win the War Fund," 88.
[21] Jackson, *The British Empire and the Second World War*, 171.

of essential goods, and trade regulations and restrictions imposed by the colonial government. Shortages of food items and higher prices for imported products, such as sugar, and for locally produced food items, forced colonial officials to introduce new regulations that transformed the lives of the farming population and traders. These regulations sought to address the crisis that emerged during the war, marked by direct intervention in the local economy that included control of food distribution within the country and the imposition of controlled prices on local and imported items. Although the nature of state intervention varied between and within colonies, the dictates of war imposed the need for "ordering" consumers into hierarchies based on their perceived "value" to the war effort. Within colonies, sectoral allocation accorded low priority to domestic civilian needs, placing them only after those of the military, the government, and commercial concerns such as the mines.[22]

The war had a significantly negative impact on prewar trading patterns. It particularly affected trade with Germany by disrupting the export of Nigerian palm products to the country. Nigerian traders faced the challenges of a contracted market when Germany cut off trade and supplies from the British Empire and other neutral countries. According to Uwakwe Esse, the small minority group dissatisfied with the Anglo-German war consisted of those "who had successfully established good business relations with the German businessmen in Nigeria." The few educated Nigerians in the coastal ports at Calabar, Port Harcourt, and Opobo had "not only benefited economically from such contacts, but had increasingly come to prefer German merchants, with their commercial liberalization and generous credit facilities, to British merchants."[23] The reactions of such elements in colonial Nigeria reveal that the Second World War, like many wars, was fought on several fronts and through different prisms. The war was largely fought in the battlefields but was also fought over ideologies, economics, and everyday survival. The intervention in the colonial economy in this period marked an "important transition in [the] British attitude to Africa."[24]

The end of the war created a vast number of unemployed ex-servicemen who created real and imagined problems for the colonial state. African ex-servicemen were left with experiences that changed

---

[22] Reginald A. Cline-Cole, "Wartime Forest Energy Policy and Practice in British West Africa: Social and Economic Impact on the Labouring Classes 1939–45," *Africa: Journal of the International African Institute* 63, no. 1 (1993): 56–79.

[23] Esse, "The Second World War and Resource Management in Eastern Nigeria," 20. See Jide Osuntokun, "Great Britain, Germany and War-Time Economy in Nigeria, 1914–1918," *Journal of African Studies* 2, no. 2 (July 1977): 29–59.

[24] Anderson and Throup, "Africans and Agricultural Production in Colonial Kenya."

their lives at the end of the war. The feeling among African troops that European colonial powers "owed them a great deal for the sacrifice they had made" was widespread. Many of these men "found themselves out of work when they returned home, and still, of course, under the rule of Europeans," leaving them with feelings of disappointment and disillusionment.[25] Although the ex-soldiers did not organize politically, the economic and social conditions and demands they made on the colonial states fed into the political atmosphere and encouraged anticolonial sentiments. Imbued with a new sense of entitlement, Nigerian veterans made demands upon the British colonial empire. Their demands for jobs and employment and other benefits were based upon their perceived contribution to the defeat of the Axis Powers and as "citizens" of the British Commonwealth who were entitled to the rewards accorded their European counterparts. Ex-servicemen saw themselves as victims of racism who were denied what was due to them and who were treated differently from their European counterparts. The attempts made by the government to reintegrate them into local society were not systematically pursued.

The war was gendered in many respects. All over the world, women were mobilized for wartime production, which offered new opportunities for them. David Killingray's claim that "women bore a heavy burden in wartime" is important in how I have evaluated the role of Nigerian women and the impact of the war on their lives.[26] Women engaged in trade and production, but they also faced challenges at the household level. Because combat duties were male dominated, women dominated the task of household management during the period of the war. Women sought participation in foodstuff trade, and perhaps an increasing role in regional trade, which was dominated by male brokers. The demand for food and the stringent regulation of life and livelihood was a burden for the local population, including women, who became victims of this regulation. Petty trading was dominated by women. So the small traders affected were disproportionately women and children who retailed for their mothers. Women's agency in the informal economy placed them in vulnerable positions in the wartime landscape. Like their male counterparts, women invoked British liberal ideas in their petitions. They equated women's interests with the broader goals of the war effort, but they also drew on their femininity in expressing their role in the war and in the household and to seek support for their request. While women negotiated

[25] "World War II," The Story of Africa: African History from the Dawn of Time, BBC, accessed January 23, 2019, www.bbc.co.uk/worldservice/specials/1624_story_of_africa/page20.shtml.
[26] Killingray, "Parameters of the Second World War in Asia and Africa."

the colonial space as independent actors, African men perceived them as different and as the weaker sex, revealing the persistence of gender ideology within the local society.

Much of the evidence about the impact of the war on African societies comes from sources generated by Europeans. At the county level, colonial sources describe the effort made by the government to garner the resources needed to support imperial war efforts. Additionally, the memoirs and reflections of colonial soldiers form the most important sources for gleaning the role of African soldiers in the war.[27] On the other hand, Nigerian petitions reveal the neglected but important impact the war had on the African population – such as the often severe instruments of colonial control and the capacity of the local populations to contest colonial orders, as well as their contributions to the British war effort. Nigerians expressed their disagreement with colonial regulations and restrictions by openly petitioning the authorities and appealing for interventions that would ameliorate their conditions. Petitions provided an opportunity for a surprisingly flexible power dynamic during the war. Petitioners deployed colonial institutions to address individual and group concerns to their benefit – gaining reprieve in some cases, and the opportunity to influence policy. Nigerian petitions provide a vehicle through which colonial subjects addressed the contradictions inherent in colonialism and the ideals of self-determination for which they were drawn into war with Germany. Such sites of power, as they emerged during the war, provided opportunities for ordinary people to operate across imperial boundaries. As Nigerian petitions reveal, rural farmers and traders used their power to provide support through the provision of resources to sometimes work against the grain of imperial policies. The microhistories of such ordinary people, who often were at the margins of colonial structures, provide a more nuanced understanding of how wartime policies were also constructed, co-opted, and curbed from below. Their accounts of the war, particularly its impact on their lives, and their demands for recognition and consideration of their importance in colonial society, place them at the center of imperial discourses of war and empire, and make them important actors and agents of change in wartime production, supplies, financial intermediation, and information flows.

The rhetorical language of petitions to colonial authorities in some cases embody both compliance and self-assertion in seeking to protect the interest of the local people. When E. O. Nwaogu, the secretary of the Aba Community League, wrote on June 28, 1943, the association was

---

[27] See, for example, Killingray and Plaut, *Fighting for Britain*; Clarke, *West Africans at War*; Kerslake, *Time and the Hour*; Osborne, *World War II in Colonial Africa*.

reacting to the prohibition of the order regulating the transportation of garri to northern Nigeria that the government had published three days earlier. The association asked the government to furnish the group with "reasons which have created the necessity for such a measure to be taken, along with particulars of, conditions required for, and any other information concerning, the permits to be issued." While the association noted that such information was necessary for the enlightenment of its members, its tone and framing reveal a subtle attempt to reckon its members' role in negotiating colonial wartime policy. The petition further revealed this perceived role, describing it this way:

It is presumed that by this measure your worship is endeavouring to ameliorate the plight of local garri consumers in connection with prices; but so that there may be no undue hardships and unnecessary confusion, I am directed to solicit your clemency, for an extension of the time limit to, the earliest, and of July, in order not only to allow traders to recover any cash or other advances they might have launched out to producers against deliveries, but also to afford both you and us the opportunity of meeting all interested sections in the garri business – cassava farmers, garri producers, local consumers and the various grades of traders – to discuss and stabilize price and to devise ways and means whereby any possible problem that may arise when permit or quota system actually comes into operation, may be neutralized.[28]

Each of these petitions is a witness to acts of deprivation, heroism, and survival in the midst of imperial control that are often ignored by the meta-narrative of World War II. They capture the economic and social consequences of wartime regulations and inflations that are not found in traditional sources available to historians. Petitions seeking amelioration of wartime challenges provide sufficient information on the petitioners that helps in drawing reasonable conclusions about the grief and despair Nigerian men and women endured in their service to and support of the British Empire. This reveals that Nigerians were not passive recipients of colonial regulations and control during the war. Still, while these petitions provide opportunity for the social historian to access voices from below, we must be "cautious of heeding these voices without a preliminary awareness of the letters' formal complexities," how these voices are mediated, and the powerful ways they speak to wider social, political, and economic contexts beyond the intent of the petitioner.[29] What we

[28] NAE, ABADIST 14/1/872, "Railing of Garri to North: Prohibition of," E. O. Nwaogu to District Officer, Aba, June 28, 1943. The League represented the majority of unions, "ethnic" groups, and communities in Aba Township in eastern Nigeria. Its motto, "Let all the ends thou aimest at be thy Country," certainly gave the impression that it wanted to present the association as patriotic.
[29] Coates, "The War, Like the Wicked Wand of a Wizard, Strikes Me and Carry Away All That I Have Loved," 75.

glean, however, from wartime petitions are incredible opportunities to reconstruct life, survival, and, in hindsight, the subversions of imperial policies in ways that illuminate how the war affected ordinary people's lives.

Class consciousness was not fully abated because of the cooperation between the British Empire and its colonial subjects. The accounts of African support in colonial sources conceal the overwhelming heterogeneity that forced Nigerians to at times circumvent the regulations imposed on them when those regulations threatened their survival. Refusing to sell at the controlled price or to report those who broke the law were tactics employed as subtle forms of resistance. The collaborative nature of the wartime organization of metropolitan and colonial resources created opportunities for decentering the sites of power. Industrial relations continued to be an area of conflict within the colony of Nigeria. Indeed, colonial reports as the war raged in 1940 noted that "the development of the trade union movement coupled with a growing sense of class-consciousness amongst the workers, has confronted the Colonial Governments concerned with a full range of new problems." The Colonial Office noted that "it was inevitable that the rather rapid development of this labour movement should be accompanied by difficulties and disturbances of various kinds."[30] The Colonial Office was aware of the new problem, although necessary measures were not put in place to redress any legitimate grievances or to effect amicable settlements of any disputes between employers and employees. This was an empire-wide problem for Britain. As it had predicted, the colonial government faced disturbances from self-conscious and class-conscious colonial labor groups.[31]

Significant transformations in the social and political arenas followed the war.[32] The war and its aftermath transformed people's lives and their societies as much as the relations between Britain and its Nigerian colonial subjects. The common goal of defeating Hitler and Nazi Germany led to the development of a symbiotic relationship that connected colonial subjects with the empire while at the same time providing Africans with a new platform for discourses on race, racism, and colonial ideology. Colonial officials encouraged Africans not only to appropriate the notions of liberty and self-determination as universal human rights but also to see the war as a global effort to stop Germany's tyrannical desire to control the world. In doing so, Britain attempted to convince Africans that their

[30] NA, CAB/68/6/17, "War Cabinet Report," April 1940, 11.     [31] Ibid.
[32] Ahmad Alawad Sikaing, "Conclusion: Consequences of the War," in *Africa and World War II*, ed. Judith A. Byfield, Carolyn A. Brown, Timothy Parsons, and Ahmad Alawad Sikaing (New York: Cambridge University Press, 2015), 501.

actions and support for the war against Germany were consistent with the global effort to protect freedom and liberty. These views influenced politics and society in the postwar period.

The intellectual discourses extended beyond the nationalist dimension to reveal the possibilities and the limitations of an imagined global empire during a period of social, economic, and political changes and of total war. War mobilization influenced postwar society in Nigeria, especially in the political and social arenas. The Nigerian political elite mobilized at this moment of great uncertainty for the empire. Seeking political independence for Nigeria and drawing upon the mood among workers, the postwar climate became a veritable tool for nationalism and decolonization. In a way, wartime mobilizations damaged the colonial state and weakened its hold on Nigerian society.

Clearly, the Second World War was also an imperial conflict from which two new imperial powers – Russia and the United States – emerged in a struggle for global power. Much discussion about African history in terms of its relations to empire during the period of world conflict was complex and ambivalent. In the final analysis, the Second World War posed an existential threat to empire; its global reach redefined the postwar world and offered unparalleled opportunities for self-determination. In the immediate aftermath of the Second World War, political battles fought over the relationships between empires and colonies within a new world order made it difficult to uphold prewar perceptions of the legitimacy of imperial hegemony as the natural state of affairs. While the developments and shifts of the war involved a rethinking of the place of colonies in the imperial system, they occurred within the framework of a hegemonic imperial ideology. Such ideology was at play in wartime policies even as imperial subjects created a closer bond with the metropole. Yet the successes recorded by imperial officials in the colonies were also dependent on the cooperation of African leaders, most of whom had become part of the colonial administration before the war. As they did in the past, African leaders mobilized their subjects and recruited the manpower required for the army and the construction industry.

This book has argued that the study of African and colonial history can make important contributions to the study of the world wars as global conflicts. It reveals how the relationship within the empire changed and shifted over the course of the twentieth century, as global conflicts changed the landscape in which the empire and its subjects had interacted. The complexity and diversity of the global experiences of the Second World War illustrate that there is no single experience, but many experiences. For Nigeria and other colonial territories, their peculiar experiences are linked and shaped by the hegemonic imperatives of colonialism as a source of identification with what Dwight Eisenhower called "the Great Crusade" as well as a tool for exploitation. African colonies provided part of the vital manpower in the global conflicts of the past century in two key areas: as soldiers and as labor. These two factors meant that Africans interacted with European soldiers on a level that did not exist before and in regions beyond their own societies. During these wars, imperial soldiers, sailors, and airmen took on active combat roles while those at home served in important noncombat roles. As Paul Mulvey has stated, "the contribution of the empire's dominions, colonies and territories was anything but nominal."[33]

As the Nigerian case suggests, the Second World War offered many opportunities and possibilities for the British colonies to identify with the war effort despite the contradiction or ambiguity that were inherent in colonial relations. For one, the war offered the opportunity to align with the empire in a crucial moment in history. Yet there is a tendency to view African contributions during the Second World War in terms of their produce and labor, rather than their humanity or the "home front," as has been the case with belligerent countries. Such neglect diminished Africans' contributions and the value attached to their association with the Allied war effort, but it did not diminish the impact of the war on their lives. In this way, Africans' contributions are not portrayed in terms of human cost. Sadly, while the heroic deeds of the millions of other veterans of the war, including those from the dominions, were feted over the following decades, the contributions of Africans to the war effort went largely unnoticed and ignored.[34] But Britain and its allies could not have sustained the war without significant reliance on their colonial outposts. In large part, this is a history from below that focuses on the entanglements of grassroots activism with the world of European colonialism, politics, and economics, specifically capitalism. As with major historical developments that impinged on the lives of peoples during the Second World War, rural and urban classes sought to play a role in shaping the structure of the worlds they had been forced into due to colonialism.

---

[33] Paul Mulvey, "'Their Finest Hour'? Britain and the Empire in World War Two" (Lecture), accessed September 21, 2019, www.academia.edu/444982/The_British_Empire_in_World_War_Two_lecture_?auto=download.
[34] "Askari: Stories of African Veterans of World War II."

# Bibliography

## Manuscript and Archival Sources

*Nigeria*

*National Archives of Nigeria, Calabar*

CALPROF 1–15, Calabar Provincial Office Records.
CSE 1/85/8614, vol. III.
ITUDIST, District and Divisional Office.
Reports of the Labour Department.

*National Archives of Nigeria, Enugu*

ABADIST, Aba District Office.
AIDIST, Abakiliki District Office.
CALPROF 17/1/154, File No. 2941 L, vol. 1. Application from Soldiers for Employment.
CALPROF 17/1/154, File No. 2941 L, vol. 2. Resettlement of Ex-soldiers for Employment.
CALPROF 17/1/154, File No. 2941 L, vol. 3. Resettlement of Ex-soldiers for Employment.
CALPROF 17/1/1542, File No. 2941 L, vol. 1. Postwar Reconstruction: Resettlement of Ex-soldiers.
CALPROF 17/1/1536, File No. 2941 E, vol. 1. Post-War Reconstruction – Land Utilization.
CALPROF 17/1/1539, File No. 2941 G. Post-War Reconstruction – Forestry.
CALPROF 17/1/1540, File No. 2941 H. Post-War Reconstruction – Housing.
CALPROF 17/1/1546, File No. 2941 M. Post-War Reconstruction – Economic Policy.
CALPROF 17/1/1546, File No. 2941 R. Postwar Recruitment – Credit for War Service.
CSO 26 File No. 02226/S.4. Accountant General's Department. Lagos. November 25, 1941.

OKIDIST 11/1/478 File. No. 1227, vol. 3. War Pensions and/or Gratuity.
OWDIST, Owerri District Office.

## National Archives of Nigeria, Kaduna

MINAGRIC I/I 3700, vol. II. Food Production Report, January 11, 1941.

MINAGRIC I/I, 3700, vol. III. Food Production Report, January 11, 1941.

MINAGRIC I/I 3700, vol. III. Food Production – General, Memo by AO, Kafinsoli, to ADA, NPs, "Food Production," January 30, 1941.

MINAGRIC I/I 3712: Food Supplies, Government Grain Reserves – Katsina Province.

MINAGRIC I/I 3712: "Grain Production and Consumption in Daura Emirate."

MINAGRIC I/I 31657/S3; Economic Organization of Grain Production in War Time.

## National Archives of Nigeria, Ibadan

ASA DIV I, No. A.D 881. Colonel I. C. Adm. Nigeria Area to Secretary, Eastern/Western Provinces: Recruiting, September 5, 1944.

ASA DIV I, No. A.D 881, Monthly Recruiting Bulletin, 1944.

ASA DIV I, No. A.D 881. Recruiting Policy, June 4, 1945.

CSO 6/1/9 Mimeo, 93–7. M. N. Hennessy, The History of the Royal West African Frontier Force (1st Draft 1948).

CSO 26/ 36229, File No. 112/0870, vol. V. Accountant – General to Chief Financial Secretary, Lagos, August 20, 1940.

CSO 26/ 36229, File No. 10310/8613. Director of Public Works, Lagos to Chief Secretary to Government, September 6, 1939.

CSO 26/36229, File No. 15924/28 & 30. Executive Council Minutes, October 25, 1941.

CSO 26/36229, File No. 17494/3/3. Secretary Western Provinces to Chief Secretary to Government, Lagos, July 3, 1941.

CSO 26/36229, File No. D.E.134/583. Director of Education, Nigeria to the Financial Secretary, Lagos, May 6, 1942.

CSO 26/36229, Secretary, Western Provinces to the Financial Secretary, Lagos, September 30, 1942.

CSO 26/36229/ S. I. Emmanuel Peter Thomas to Chief Secretary to Government, Lagos, June 3, 1940.

CSO 26/ 38215, vol. II. File No. SP/NDS/14/16. Acting General Manager, Nigerian Railway to Chief Secretary to Government, February 2, 1942.

CSO 26/42215, File No. 26194/16. Telegram, Chief Secretary, West African Council, Accra, Gold Coast to Governors, Nigeria, Gold Coast, Sierra Leone, Gambia, March 19, 1949.

CSO 26/ 50690/S I, MIMEO, 1–7. H. A. Lilley-Green Howards, "Brief History of R.W.A.F.F. in Mid East."

CSO 35541/S.3, File No. CR2E/860/222/70. A.A.G. Headquarters, East Africa, 2nd Echelon, Nairobi to the Regimental Headquarters, the Nigeria Regiment, Lagos, September 25, 1940.

CSO 38215, vol. II. File No. 2/7. Deputy Chairman, West African Governors' Conference to Chief Secretary, Lagos; Colonial Secretaries, Accra, Freetown, Bathurst, June 2, 1942.

CSO 38215, vol. II. File No. 38215/164. Chief Secretary to Government to Deputy Chairman, West African Governors' Conference, Lagos, February 10, 1942.

CSO 38215, vol. II. File No. 38215/218. Acting Financial Secretary to Secretaries Northern Provinces, Kaduna; Eastern Provinces, Enugu; Western Provinces, Ibadan, August 27, 1942.

CSO 38215, vol. II. File No. JRWA/143/A. Tradesmen's Rates of Pay, May 29, 1942.

OYO PROF 2/3 / C 227, vol. II. District Officer, Ibadan Northern District to Senior Resident, Oyo Province, Oyo, March 31, 1942.


*United Kingdom*

Information Department Records.
National Archives of the United Kingdom, Kew.
Records of the Colonial Office, Commonwealth and Foreign and Commonwealth Offices, Empire Marketing Board, and Related Bodies.
War Cabinet Records.


*Bodleian Library (Rhodes House), Oxford*

Bridges, A.F.B. *So We Used to Do*. Memoir. Mss Afr. S 1881 (1).

Broocks, Robert Bernard. Reports and Papers Revenue Commissioner. Mss Afr. s. 1873.

Bull, J. C. Part of the Diary of J. C. Bull, an African who worked for the Methodist minister in charge of the Oron Circuit, Calabar Province, Nigeria. Mss Afr. s. 1221.

Carr, Frederick Bernard (Sir) Reminiscences of Sir F. Bernard Carr – Administrative Officer, Nigeria 1919–1949. Mss Afr. s. 546.

Cookes, Nigel, *Empire in Decline: A Personal Experience*. Administrative Service Nigeria 1938–1962. Mss Afr. s. 2426.

Falk Edward Morris Papers as District Officer in Nigeria. Mss Afr. s. 1000.

Jacob, S. M. Former Government Statistician – Report on the Taxation and Economics of Nigeria 1934. Mss Afr. s. 16.

Kreiser, Nettie R. *Reminiscence of Life in Sierra Leone and Nigeria*. Mss Afr. S. 730.

Leith-Ross, Sylvia. The Small Coins Nigeria 1907–1969. Ms. of her reminiscence (unpublished) in seven parts with a forward and pre-scripts, also original longer version of part 6 and 7. Mss Afr. s. 1520.

Mackie, James Richard, Director of Agriculture (Retired in 1945) "Correspondence." Mss Afr. s. 2124.

Swaisland, H. Eastern Nigeria Papers. Mss Afr. S. 862.

*Imperial War Museum, London*

IWM 03/23/1: Private Papers of Major J. J. Cherns, "Walk through the Valley": With 6th (West African) Brigade in Arakan, 1943–1945.

IWM 62/193/1: Misc.: Lieutenant J. A. L. Hamilton papers.

Major Elvet D. Price papers.

"Media and War: The Battle for Hearts and Minds." Accessed September 15, 2010. www.iwm.org.uk/upload/package/29/media war/technolww2.htm.

## Oral Sources

Interview with Linus Anabalam, migrant worker, Umuchieze, Mbaise, Imo State, Nigeria, December 24, 2000.

Interview with Isaac Iwuh, Umuchieze, Mbaise, Imo State, Nigeria, July 10, 2016.

Interview with Eleazer Ihediwa Owerrenta, July 24, 1999, aged ca. seventy-one.

Interview with Gilbert Uzor, World War II veteran, Umuonom, Mbaise, Imo State, Nigeria, December 24, 2000.

## Unpublished Theses and Dissertations

Agber, K. S. "European Commercial Enterprise and Underdevelopment in Tivland." PhD dissertation, University of Jos, 1994.

Bogosian, Catherine Mornane. "Forced Labor, Resistance and Memory: The Deuxième Portion in the French Soudan, 1926–1950." PhD dissertation, University of Pennsylvania, 2002.

Bonat, Zuwaqhu Kalli-Abungwon. "The Colonial Phase of the Underdevelopment of Zaria Province, 1902–1945." MA thesis, Ahmadu Bello University, July 1985.

Coates, Oliver. "A Social History of Military Service in South-Western Nigeria, 1939–1955." PhD thesis, University of Cambridge, 2013.

Esse, O. Uwakwe. "The Second World War and Resource Management in Eastern Nigeria, 1939–1945." MA thesis, University of Nigeria, 1997.

"Road Transportation in Nigeria As a Private Enterprise among the Igbo, 1920–1999." PhD thesis, University of Nigeria, Nsukka, 2003.

Kamm, Emily. "Price Control, Profiteering, and Public Cooperation: The Lagos Market Women's Association and the Limits of Colonial Control." BA honors thesis, Paper 309, Portland State University, 2016.

Korieh, Chima J. "The State & the Peasantry, Agricultural Policy, Agricultural Crisis and Sustainability in Southeastern Nigeria, 1900–1995." PhD thesis, University of Toronto, 2013.

Onuoha, Okechukwu. "Food Production in Nigeria during the Second World, 1939–45." MA thesis, University of Nigeria, 2016.


## Official Publications and Government Sources

Broadcast by the Inspector of Prices. November 5, 1942. Lagos. Printed and Published by the Service Press Limited.

Eastern Regional Marketing Board, Annual Report, 1958 (1959).

"Mr. Churchill's Declaration of Policy to the Electors." Conservative Party Manifesto, 1945. Politics Resource United Kingdom Online. Accessed September 20, 2016.

Nigeria, *Annual Abstract of Statistics, 1960* (Lagos: Federal Government Printer, 1960).

Nigeria. *Annual Report of the Department of Agriculture, 1932*. Lagos: Government Printer, 1932.

Nigeria. *Annual Report of the Agricultural Department, 1939–1940*. Lagos: Government Printer, 1940.

Nigeria. *Annual Report of the Department of Agriculture, 1940–1941*. Lagos: Government Printer, 1941.

Nigeria, *Annual Report of the Department of Labour, Nigeria, for the Year 1942*, vol. 1. Lagos: Government Press, 1943.

Nigeria. *Annual Report of the Department of Labour and on the Resettlement of Ex-servicemen, 1945*. Lagos: Government Printer, 1946.

Nigeria. *Annual Report on Finance and Account for the Year 1942/43*. File No. 02226/S.4. Lagos: Government Printer, 1944.

Nigeria. *Colony Annual Report, 1939 Onward*. File No. 09512, vol. XII.

Nigeria. *A Colony's Effort*. Lagos: Government Printing Department, 1939.

Nigeria. *An Address by His Excellency the Governor, Sir Bernard Bourdillon to the Legislative Council, 4 December 1939*. Lagos: Government Printer, 1940.

*Nigeria General Defence Regulation, 1941*. Lagos: Government Printer, 1941.

Nigeria. *Laws of Nigeria*. Volume V. Cap. 15. 1948.

Nigeria. *Legislative Council Debates, 4 December 1939*. Lagos: Government Printer, 1940.

Nigeria. *Legislative Council Debates, March 17, 1941* (Lagos, 1941).

Nigeria. *Legislative Council Debates, Second Session March 1948, Vol. II*. Lagos: Government Printer, 1948.

Nigeria. *Memorandum on the Organisation and Control of War Time Trade and Production.* Lagos: Government Printer, 1943.

Nigeria. *Nigeria Defence (Compulsory National Service) Regulations 1940.* Lagos: Government Printer, 1940.

Nigeria. *The Nigerian War Relief Fund: Its Aims and Achievements.* Lagos: Government Printer, 1943.

Nigeria. *Report of the Commission of Inquiry Appointed to Inquire into the Disturbances in the Calabar and Owerri Provinces, December 1929.* Lagos: Government Printer, 1930.

Nigeria Cocoa Marketing Board, Annual Report, 1947–48. Lagos, 1949.

Nigeria Groundnut Marketing Board, Annual Report, 1949–50 (1951).

Nigeria Oil Palm Produce Marketing Board. *First Annual Report 1949.* Lagos: Nigeria Oil Palm Produce Marketing Board, 1950.

Nigeria Oil Palm Produce Marketing Board. *Statement of the Policy Proposed for the Future Marketing of Nigerian Oils, Oil Seeds and Cotton.* Sessional Paper No. 18 of 1948. Lagos: Nigeria Oil Palm Produce Marketing Board, 1948.

Nigeria Supply Board. "Memorandum, Economic Position in Nigeria."

Northern Regional Marketing Board, Annual Report, 1954–55 (1956).

## Periodicals

*Daily Service,* 1942.
*Eastern Nigerian Guardian,* 1938–1945.
*Nigeria Civil Servant,* 1944.
*Nigeria Magazine.*
*Nigerian Daily Times,* 1938–1945.
*Nigerian Eastern Mail,* 1939–1945.
*The Comet.*
*The Daily Service.*
*The Lagos Standard,* 1940.
*The Times* (London), 1938–1939.
*The Telegraph* (online).
*Washington Post,* 2018.
*West African Pilot,* 1938–1945.
*West African World.*

## Documentary Films

Central Office of Information for Commonwealth Office. "Nigeria: The Making of a Nation." 1960. National Archives. Accessed January 19, 2019. https://media.nationalarchives.gov.uk/index.php/nigeria-the-making-of-a-nation-2/.

"WWII's Forgotten Army: West Africa's Soldiers in Burma." *The Guardian.* August 14, 2015. Accessed December 1, 2017. www.theguardian.com/world/video/2015/aug/10/forgotten-army-world-war-two-west-african-soldiers-burma-video.

## Web Sources

"Africa in World War II: The Forgotten Veterans." Accessed September 13, 2019. www.dw.com/en/africa-in-world-war-ii-the-forgotten-veterans /a-18437531

"Africa's Forgotten Wartime Heroes." BBC News. August 14, 2009. Accessed September 12, 2018. http://news.bbc.co.uk/go/pr/fr/-/2/hi/africa/8201717 .stm.

"African Soldiers in World War II Asia: Battlefront for the Defense of the Commonwealth: Apology, Recognition and Reparation Do Matter." Africa and Science.com. Accessed November 14, 2016. http://africa-and-science.com/?p=2546.

Al Jazeera Correspondent. "The Burma Boy: Barnaby Phillips Follows the Life of One of the Forgotten Heroes of World War II." Al Jazeera. July 22, 2012. Accessed January 18, 2019. www.aljazeera.com/programmes/aljazeeracorre spondent/2011/08/2011828135228487172.html.

"Askari: Stories of African Veterans of World War II." Indiegogo. February 2, 2015. Accessed January 20, 2019. www.indiegogo.com/projects/askari-stories-of-african-veterans-of-world-war-ii.

Associated Press London. African Military Blog. June 23, 1942. Accessed December 2, 2017. www.africanmilitaryblog.com/2017/10/did-you-know-nigerian-chief-offers-his.html.

Charman, Terry. "What Life Was Like in Britain during the Second World War." January 8, 2018. Accessed February 2, 2019. www.iwm.org.uk/history/what-life-was-like-in-britain-during-the-second-world-war.

"Convincing the Colonies: How Did Britain Try to Keep the Support of the People of West Africa?" London, National Archives, 2008. Accessed January 9, 2019. www.nationalarchives.gov.uk/documents/education/ww2-propaganda.pdf.

James, I., "Nigeria: The Road to Independence." Online Nigeria. July 24, 2004. Accessed January 19, 2019. http://nm.onlinenigeria.com/templates/default .aspx?a=137&template=print-article.htm.

Kikuchi, Ian. "The End of the British Empire after the Second World War." Imperial War Museum. February 6, 2018. Accessed January 19, 2019. www .iwm.org.uk/history/the-end-of-the-british-empire-after-the-second-world-war.

Krinniger, Theresa, with Saleh Mwanamilongo. "Africa in World War II: The Forgotten Veterans." DW.com. May 7, 2015. Accessed August 15, 2017. www.dw.com/en/africa-in-world-war-ii-the-forgotten-veterans/ a-18437531.

Merritt, Thomas. "Britain and Post War Attitudes to Empire." Academia.edu. Accessed January 19, 2019. www.academia.edu/34687086/Britain_ and_Post_War_Attitudes_to_Empire.

Mulvey, Paul. "Mobilising Empires in the First World War." Academia.edu. Accessed January 22, 2019. www.academia.edu/460820/Mobilising_ Empires_in_the_First_World_War_lecture.

"'Their Finest Hour'? Britain and the Empire in World War Two" (Lecture). Accessed September 21, 2019. www.academia.edu/444982/The_British_ Empire_in_World_War_Two_lecture_?auto=download.

Nagawiecki, Mia. "American Women at War." National Endowment for the Humanities. February 2016. Accessed January 17, 2019. www.neh.gov/site s/default/files/inline-files/american_women_at_war.pdf.

Njoku, Onwuka N. "Nigeria: World War II." Worldhistory.biz. August 21, 2015. Accessed December 1, 2018. www.worldhistory.biz/sundries/44822-nigeria- world-war-ii.html.

Ogbechie, S. Okwunodu. "Remembering African Servicemen of WWII." May 31, 2010. Accessed April 30, 2019. http://aachronym.blogspot.com/ 2010/05/remembering-african-servicemen-of-wwii.html.

Plaut, Martin. "The Africans Who Fought in WWII." BBC News. November 9, 2009. Accessed December 6, 2018. http://news.bbc.co.uk/go/pr/fr/-/2/hi/afr ica/8344170.stm.

Purdue, A. W. "The Transformative Impact of World War II." In European History Online (EGO). Published by the Leibniz Institute of European History (IEG), Mainz. April 18, 2016. www.ieg-ego.eu/purduea-2016-en.

Quartey, Kwei. "How West Africa Helped Win World War II." Foreign Policy in Focus. June 6, 2012. Accessed January 22, 2019. http://fpif.org/ how_west_africa_helped_win_world_war_ii.

Salmon, Julie. "War Experiences in Nigeria and Burma." WW2 People's Year. BBC. November 9, 2004. Accessed January 2019. www.bbc.co.uk/history/ ww2peopleswar/stories/47/a3249047.shtml.

Sherwood, Marika. "Colonies, Colonials and World War Two." BBC. March 30, 2011. www.bbc.co.uk/history/worldwars/wwtwo/colonies_colo nials_01.shtml.

US Holocaust Memorial Museum. "Blacks during the Holocaust." Holocaust Encyclopedia. Accessed January 8, 2019. www.ushmm.org/wlc/en/article .php?ModuleId=10005479.

"VE Day Remembered." BBC. May 6, 2005. Accessed January 18, 2019. www .bbc.co.uk/history/ww2peopleswar/categories/c54817.

"World War II, the Story of Africa: African History from the Dawn of Time." BBC. Accessed January 23, 2019. www.bbc.co.uk/worldservice/specials/16 24_story_of_africa/page20.shtml.

"World War II and Post-War Trends." Online Nigeria. October 12, 2005. Accessed November 5, 2017. www.onlinenigeria.com/independence/? blurb=635.

## Secondary Books and Articles

Achebe, Chinua. *The Education of a British-Protected Child*. New York: Penguin Books, 2009.

Aderinto, Saheed. "Isaac Fadoyebo and the Battle of Nyron: African Voices of the First and Second World War, ca. 1914–1945." In *African Voices of the Global Past, 1500 to the Present*, edited by Trevor R. Getz, 107–138. Boulder, CO: Westview Press, 2014.

"'O! Sir I Do Not Know Either to Kill Myself or to Stay': Childhood Emotion, Poverty, and Literary Culture in Nigeria, 1900–1960." *Journal of the History of Childhood and Youth* 8, no. 1 (2015): 273–294.

Afigbo, Adiele E. "Indirect Rule in South Eastern Nigeria: The Era of Warrant Chiefs 1891–1929." *Tarikh* 4 (1974): 11–24.

*The Warrant Chiefs: Indirect Rule in Southeastern Nigeria, 1891–1929.* London: Longman, 1972.

Ajaegbu, H. I. *Urban and Rural Development in Nigeria.* London: Heinemann, 1976.

Akpen, Philip. "Forced Labor in Jos Tin Mines: The Psychological and Emotional Implications for Women in Tiv Society, Central Nigeria 1902–1945." Paper presented at the Second International Conference of the Transatlantic Group on "Gendering Global Transformations." Owerri. July 2006.

Alence, Rod. "Colonial Government, Social Conflict and State Involvement in Africa's Open Economies: The Origins of the Ghana Cocoa Marketing Boards, 1939–46." *Journal of African History* 42 (2001): 397–416.

Alexander, Martin S. "The Fall of France, 1940." In *The World War Two Reader*, edited by Gordon Martel, 7–39. New York: Routledge, 2004.

Amadi, Levi Onyemuche. "Political Integration in Nigeria, 1939–1945: The Role of Economic Development during the Second World War." *Transafrican Journal of History* 6, no. 7 (1977): 142–153.

Amdii, I. E. S. "Revenue Generating Capacity of the Nigerian Customs and Excise: 1875–1960." In *100 Years of the Nigerian Customs and Excise: 1891–1991*, edited by I. E. S. Amdii, 12–47. Abuja: Department of Customs and Excise, 1991.

Anderson, David and David Throup. "Africans and Agricultural Production in Colonial Kenya: The Myth of the War As a Watershed." *Journal of African History* 26 (1985): 327–345.

Anderson, Karen. *Wartime Women: Sex Roles, Family Relations, and the Status of Women during World War II.* Contributions in Women's Studies. Westport, CT: Praeger, 1981.

Aye, Efiong U. *Hope Waddell Training Institution: Life and Work, 1894–1978.* Calabar: Paico, 2012.

Baker, Anni P. "Daughters of Mars: Army Officers' Wives and Military Culture on the American Frontier." *Historian* 67, no. 1 (2005): 20–42.

Bandele, Biyi. *Burma Boy.* London: Jonathan Cape, 2007.

Bauer, P. T. "Statistics of Statutory Marketing in West Africa, 1939–51." *Journal of the Royal Statistical Society* 117 (1954): 1–30.

Bayly, Christopher Alan and Tim Harper. *Forgotten Armies: Britain's Asian Empire and the War with Japan.* London: Penguin, 2005.

Beck, Earl R. *The European Home Fronts, 1939–1945.* Wheeling, IL: Harlan Davidson, 1993.

Beckert, Sven. "American Danger: United States Empire, Eurafrica, and the Territorialization of Industrial Capitalism, 1870–1950." *American Historical Review* 122, no. 4 (2017): 1137–1170.

Boreham, Arthur C. *Saga of a Suffolk Soldier.* Worcester: Square One Publications, 1990.

Bourne, Stephen. *The Motherland Calls: Britain's Black Servicemen and Women 1939–45.* Gloucestershire: History Press, 2012.

Brands, Hal. "Wartime Recruiting Practices, Martial Identity and Post–World War II Demobilization in Colonial Kenya." *Journal of African History* 46, no. 1 (2005): 103–125.

British Central Office of Information. *Constitutional Development in the Commonwealth: United Kingdom Dependencies.* London: British Central Office of Information, 1955.

Brown, Carolyn A. "African Labor in the Making of World War II." In *Africa and World War II,* edited by Judith A. Byfield, Carolyn A. Brown, Timothy Parsons, and Ahmad Alawad Sikaing, 43–67. New York: Cambridge University Press, 2015.

   "African Working Men, Racial Consciousness and the Imperial State during World War II: A History of Labour in the British Colonies." Paper presented at the "Re-evaluating Africa and World War II" conference. Rutgers University. March 27–30, 2008.

Bryceson, Deborah. "Household, Hoe and Nation: Development Policies of the Nyerere Era." In *Tanzania after Nyerere,* edited by Michael Hodd. London: Pinter Publishers, 1989.

Burns, Catherine. "The Letters of Louisa Mvemve." In *Africa's Hidden Histories: Everyday Literacy and Making the Self,* edited by Karin Barber, 78–112. Bloomington: Indiana University Press, 2006.

Burton, Antoinette, ed. *After the Imperial Turn: Thinking with and through the Nation.* Durham, NC: Duke University Press, 2003.

Byfield, Judith A. "Producing for the War." In *Africa and World War II,* edited by Judith A. Byfield, Carolyn A. Brown, Timothy Parsons, and Ahmad Alawad Sikaing, 24–42. New York: Cambridge University Press, 2015.

   "Women, Rice, and War: Political and Economic Crisis in Wartime Abeokuta (Nigeria)." In *Africa and World War II,* edited by Judith A. Byfield, Carolyn A. Brown, Timothy Parsons, and Ahmad Alawad Sikaing, 147–165. New York: Cambridge University Press, 2015.

Calder, Angus. *The People's War: Britain 1939–45.* New York: Pantheon Books, 1969.

Campbell, Dan. *Women at War with America: Private Lives in a Patriotic Era.* Cambridge, MA: Harvard University Press, 1984.

Chetty, Suryakanthie. "Imagining National Unity: South African Propaganda Efforts during the Second World War." *Kronos* 38 (2012): 106–130.

Chuku, Gloria. "'Crack Kernels, Crack Hitler': Export Production Drive and Igbo Women during the Second World War." In *Gendering the African Diaspora: Women, Culture, and Historical Change in the Caribbean and Nigerian Hinterland,* edited by Judith A. Byfield, LaRay Denzer, and Anthea Morrison, 219–244. Bloomington: Indiana University Press, 2010.

   *Igbo Women and Economic Transformation in Southeastern Nigeria, 1900–1960,* New York: Routledge, 2005.

Clarence-Smith, William G. "Africa's 'Battle for Rubber' in the Second World War." In *Africa and World War II*, edited by Judith A. Byfield, Carolyn A. Brown, Timothy Parsons, and Ahmad Alawad Sikaing, 166–182. New York: Cambridge University Press, 2015.

Clark, F. A. S. "The Development of the West African Forces in the Second World War." *Army Quarterly* 55 (1947): 58–72.

Clarke, Peter B. *West Africans at War, 1914–18, 1939–45: Colonial Propaganda and Its Cultural Aftermath*. London: Ethnographica, 1986.

Cline-Cole, Reginald. "Wartime Forest Energy Policy and Practice in British West Africa: Social and Economic Impact on the Labouring Classes 1939–45." *Africa: Journal of the International African Institute* 63, no. 1 (1993): 56–79.

Coates, Oliver. "Narrative, Time, and the Archive in an African Second World War Memoir: Isaac Fadoyebo's *A Stroke of Unbelievable Luck*." *Journal of Commonwealth Literature* 51, no. 3 (2016): 371–386.

"Nigeria and the World: War, Nationalism, and Politics, 1914–60." In *The Oxford Handbook of Nigerian Politics*, edited by Carl Levan and Patrick Ukata. Oxford: Oxford University Press, 2018.

"'The War, Like the Wicked Wand of a Wizard, Strikes Me and Carry Away All That I Have Loved': Soldiers' Family Lives and Petition Writing in Ijebu, Southwestern Nigeria, 1943–1945." *History in Africa* 45 (2018): 71–97.

Coetzee, Frans and Marilyn Shevin-Coetzee. *The World in Flames: A World War II Sourcebook*. Oxford: Oxford University Press, 2011.

Coleman, James S. *Nigeria: Background to Nationalism*. Berkeley: University of California Press, 1958.

Cooper, Frederick. *Decolonization and African Society: The Labor Question in French and British Africa*. Cambridge: Cambridge University Press, 1996.

Coren, Robin. *Labour and Politics in Nigeria*. London: Heinemann, 1981.

Crowder, Michael. *Colonial West Africa: Collected Essays*. London: Frank Cass, 1978.

"The Second World War: Prelude to Decolonization in Africa." In *History of West Africa, II*, edited by J. F. Ade Ajayi and Michael Crowder, 8–50. London: Longman, 1974.

*The Story of Nigeria*. London: Faber and Faber, 1973.

*West Africa under Colonial Rule*. Evanston, IL: Northwestern University Press, 1968.

"World War II and Africa: Introduction." *Journal of African History* 26 (1985): 287–288.

Darwin, John. *Britain and Decolonization: The Retreat from Empire in the Post-War World*. London: Macmillan Education, 1988.

Das, Santanu, ed. *Race, Empire and First World War Writing*. Cambridge: Cambridge University Press, 2011.

Davidson, Basil. *Modern Africa: A Social and Political History*. 3rd edn. London: Routledge, 1994.

Daybell, James. *Women Letter-Writers in Tudor England*. Oxford: Oxford University Press, 2006.

Easterlin, Richard A. *Population and Economic Change in Developing Countries.* Chicago: University of Chicago Press, 1980.

Echenberg, Myron. *Colonial Conscripts: The Tirailleurs Sénégalais in French West Africa, 1857–1960.* Portsmouth, NH: Heinemann, 1991.

Edgerton, David. *Britain's War Machine: Weapons, Resources, and Experts in the Second World War.* Oxford: Oxford University Press, 2011.

Egboh, E. O. "The Nigerian Rubber Industry, 1939–1945." *Nigerian Field* 44 (1979): 2–13.

Eicher, C. K. "Facing Up to Africa's Food Crisis," *Foreign Affairs* 61, no. 1 (1982): 151–174.

Einzig, Paul. *Economic Problems of the Next War.* London: Macmillan, 1939.

Eisenhower, Dwight. *Crusade in Europe.* Baltimore, MD: Johns Hopkins University Press, 1997.

Ekechi, F. K. "Aspects of Palm Oil Trade at Oguta (Eastern Nigeria), 1900–1950." *African Economic History* 10 (1981): 35–65.

Emezue, Sydney. "Managing Wartime Shortages: The Salt Palaver in the Okigwe Division of Eastern Nigeria, 1939–1945." *Nsukka Journal of History* 2 (1990): 1–26.

Esse, O. Uwakwe, *Road Transport in Nigeria: The Development of Private Enterprise among the Igbo, 1920–1999.* Glassboro: Goldline and Jacobs, 2017.

Ezera, Ezera K. *Constitutional Development in Nigeria.* Cambridge: Cambridge University Press, 1964.

Faber, David. *Munich: The 1938 Appeasement Crisis.* New York: Simon & Schuster, 2009.

Fadoyebo, Isaac and David Killingray. *A Stroke of Unbelievable Luck.* Edited with an introduction by David Killingray. Madison: University of Wisconsin, 1999.

Falola, Toyin. "Cassava Starch for Export in Nigeria during the Second World War." *Journal of African Economic History* 18 (1989): 73–98.

"'Salt Is Gold': The Management of Salt Scarcity in Nigeria during World War II." *Canadian Journal of African Studies* 26, no. 3 (1992): 412–436.

Falola, Toyin and Adam Paddock. *The Women's War of 1929: A History of Anti-colonial Resistance in Eastern Nigeria.* Durham, NC: Carolina Academic Press, 2011.

Feierman, Steven. *Peasant Intellectuals: Anthropology and History in Tanzania.* Madison: University of Wisconsin Press, 1990.

Ferham, Margery, ed., *Mining, Commerce and Finance in Nigeria.* London: Faber and Faber, 1948.

Fieldhouse, David. *Merchant Capital and Economic Decolonisation: The United African Company, 1929–87.* Oxford: Clarendon Press, 1994.

"War and the Origin of the Gold Coast Cocoa Marketing Board, 1939–40." In *Imperialism, the State and the Third World*, edited by Michael Twaddle, 153–182. London: British Academy Press 1992.

Fitzpatrick, Sheila. *Everyday Stalinism: Ordinary Life in Extraordinary Times: Soviet Russia in the 1930s.* New York: Oxford University Press, 2000.

Flanigan, James. "Nigeria: Where the Real Action Is." *Forbes* 118, no. 11 (December 1, 1976), 51–61.

Food and Agriculture Organization. *Perspectives Study on Agricultural Development in the Sahelian Countries, 1975–1990*, 3 vols. Rome: Food and Agriculture Organization, 1976.

Foucault, Michel. *The History of Sexuality*. Translated by Robert Hurley. New York: Vintage Books, 1978.

Fourchard, Laurent. "Lagos and the Invention of Juvenile Delinquency in Nigeria, 1920–1960." *Journal of African History* 47 (2006): 115–137.

Fox, Jo. *Film Propaganda in Britain and Nazi Germany: World War II Cinema.* Oxford: Berg, 2007.

Francis, Martin. *The Flyer: British Culture and the Royal Air Force 1939–1945.* Oxford: Oxford University Press, 2008.

"Men of the Royal Air Force, the Cultural Memory of the Second World War and the Twilight of the British Empire." In *Gender, Labour, War and Empire: Essays on Modern Britain*, edited by Philippa Levin and Susan R. Grayzel, 197–218. New York: Palgrave Macmillan, 2009.

Freund, William M. *Capital and Labor in the Nigerian Tin Mines.* London: William Clowes [Beccles], 1981.

"Labour Migration to the Northern Nigerian Tin Mines, 1903–1945." *Journal of African History* 22, no. 1 (1981): 73–84.

*The Making of Contemporary Africa: The Development of African Society since 1800.* Bloomington: Indiana University Press, 1984.

Gardiner, Brian. *The African Dream.* New York: Putnam, 1970.

Goldsworthy, David. *Colonial Issues in British Politics 1945–1961.* Oxford: Oxford University Press, 1971.

Gorman, Daniel. "Wider and Wider Still? Racial Politics, Intra-imperial Immigration and the Absence of an Imperial Citizenship in the British Empire." *Journal of Colonialism and Colonial History* 3, no. 3 (2002): 1–24.

Grabowski, Jan. "German Anti-Jewish Propaganda in the General Government, 1939–1945: Inciting Hate through Posters, Films, and Exhibitions." *Holocaust and Genocide Studies* 23, no. 3 (2009): 381–412.

Grove, E. J. "The First Shots of the Great War: The Anglo-French Conquest of Togo, 1914." *Army Quarterly and Defence Journal* 106 (1976): 308–323.

Hamilton, John A. L. *War Bush: 81 (West African) Division in Burma 1943–1945.* Norwich: Michael Russell, 2001.

Hammond, R. J. *Food.* London: Her Majesty's Stationery Office, 1951–1962.

Hanson, Victor Davis. *The Second World Wars: How the First Global Conflict Was Fought and Won.* New York: Basic Books, 2017.

Haqqi, S. Anwarul Haque. *The Colonial Policy of the Labour Government, 1945–51.* Lahore: Aligarh, 1960.

Harris, J. S. "Some Aspects of the Economics of Sixteen Ibo Individuals." *Africa* 14, no. 6 (1944): 302–335.

Harris, Jose. "War and Social History: Britain and the Home Front during the Second World War." *Contemporary European History* 1, no. 1 (1992): 17–35.

Harrison, Mark. "Resource Mobilization for World War II: The U.S.A., UK, USSR and Germany, 1938–1945." *Economic History Review* (1988): 171–192.

Hartmann, Susan M. *The Home Front and Beyond: American Women in the 1940s.* Boston: Twayne Publishers, 1982.

Havens, Thomas R. H. *Valley of Darkness: The Japanese People and World War Two.* New York: University Press of America, 1986.

Helleiner, Gerald K. "The Fiscal Role of the Marketing Boards in Nigerian Economic Development, 1947–61." *Economic Journal* 74, no. 295 (1964): 582–610.

*Peasant Agriculture, Government, and Economic Growth in Nigeria.* Homewood, IL: Richard D. Irwin, 1966.

Herf, Jeffrey. "The 'Jewish War': Goebbels and the Anti-Semitic Campaigns of the Nazi Propaganda Ministry." *Holocaust and Genocide Studies* 19, no. 1 (2005): 51–80.

Herskovits, Jean. *Nigeria, Power and Democracy in Africa.* Foreign Policy Association Headline Series No. 257. New York: Foreign Policy Association, 1982.

Hinds, Allister E. "Government Policy and the Nigerian Palm Oil Export Industry, 1939–49." *Journal of African History* 38 (1997): 459–478.

Holbrook, Wendell P. "British Propaganda and the Mobilization of the Gold Coast War Effort, 1939–1945." *Journal of African History* 26, no. 4 (1985): 347–361.

Hursh, Gerald D., Arthur Niehoof, Neils Roling, and Graham Kerr. *Innovation in Eastern Nigeria: Success and Failure of Agricultural Programs in 71 Villages of Eastern Nigeria.* East Lansing: Michigan State University Press, 1968.

Ibhawoh, Bonny. "Second World War Propaganda, Imperial Idealism and Anti-colonial Nationalism in British West Africa." *Nordic Journal of African Studies* 16, no. 2 (2007): 221–243.

Idemili, Sam O. "What the 'West African Pilot' Did in the Movement for Nigerian Nationalism between 1937 and 1957." *Black American Literature Forum* 12, no. 3 (1978): 84–91.

Igbino, John. *Spidermen: Nigerian Chindits and Wingate's Operation Thursday Burma 1943–1944.* London: Author House, 2018.

Iliffe, John. *A Modern History of Tanganyika.* Cambridge: Cambridge University Press, 1979.

Imlay, Talbot. "Democracy and War: Political Regime, Industrial Relations, and Economic Preparations for War in France and Britain up to 1940." *Journal of Modern History* 79, no. 1 (2007): 1–47.

Iyegha, David. *Agricultural Crisis in Africa: the Nigerian Experience.* New York: University Press of America, 1988.

Jackson, Ashley. "African Soldiers and Imperial Authorities: Tensions and Unrest during the Service of High Commission Territories Soldiers in the British Army, 1941–46." *Journal of Southern African Studies* 25, no. 4 (1999): 646–665.

*The British Empire and the Second World War.* New York: Bloomsbury Academic, 2006.

*Distant Drums: The Role of the Colonies in British Imperial Warfare.* Eastbourne: Sussex Academic Press, 2010.

"Motivation and Mobilization for War: Recruitment for the British Army in the Bechuanaland Protectorate, 1941–42." *African Affairs* 96, no. 384 (1997): 399–417.

"New Research on the British Empire and the Second World War: Part I." *Global War Studies* 7, no. 1 (2010): 30–57.

"Supplying War: The High Commission Territories' Military–Logistical Contribution in the Second World War." *Journal of Military History* 66, no. 3 (2002): 719–760.

Jackson, Will. "The Shame of Not Belonging: Navigating Failure in the Colonial Petition, South Africa 1910–1961." *Itinerario* 42, no. 1 (2018): 85–101.

Jacobs, C. C. "Forced Labor in Colonial Nigeria." In *A History of Labor in Nigeria*, edited by M. Y. Mangvwat. Jos: University Press, 1998.

James, Lawrence. *Rise and Fall of the British Empire*. 3rd edn. New York: St. Martin's Press, 1997.

Jeffries, John W. *Wartime America: The World War II Home Front*. Chicago: Ivan R. Dee, 1996.

Jennings, Eric T. "Extraction and Labor in Equatorial Africa and Cameroon under Free French Rule." In *Africa and World War II*, edited by Judith A. Byfield, Carolyn A. Brown, Timothy Parsons, and Ahmad Alawad Sikaing, 200–219. New York: Cambridge University Press, 2015.

Kagan, Neil and Stephen G. Hyslop, *Eyewitness to World War II: Unforgettable Stories from History's Greatest Conflict (Reader's Edition)*. Washington, DC: National Geographic, 2018.

Kakembo, Robert. *An African Soldier Speaks*. Edinburgh: Edinburgh House Press, 1946.

Kallis, Aristotle A. *Nazi Propaganda and the Second World War*. New York: Palgrave Macmillan, 2005.

Kamtekar, Indivar. "A Different War Dance: State and Class in India 1939–1945," *Past & Present* 176, no. 1 (2002): 187–221.

Keegan, John. *The Second World War*. Sydney: Hutchinson, 1989.

Kehinde, Faluyi. "Nigeria's Contribution to the Second World War: The Production drive." *Nigeria Magazine* 57, nos. 3–4 (1989): 96–102.

"The Response of the People of Oyo Division of Western Nigeria to Cash Crop Development, 1935–1960: The examples of Ogbomoso and Ipetu-Ijesa." *Nigerian Journal of Economic History* 1 (1998): 41–56.

Kerslake, Trevor R. *Time and the Hour: Nigeria, East Africa, and the Second World War*. London: Radcliffe Press, 1997.

Khan, Yasmin. *India at War: The Subcontinent and the Second World War*. New York: Oxford University Press, 2015.

Khumalo, Vukile. "Ekukhanyeni Letter-Writers: A Historical Inquiry into Epistolary Network(s) and Political Imagination in Kwazulu-Natal South Africa." In *Africa's Hidden Histories: Everyday Literacy and Making the Self*, edited by Karin Barber, 113–142. Bloomington: Indiana University Press, 2006.

Killingray, David. "African Voices from Two World Wars." *Historical Research* 74, no. 186 (November 2001): 425–443.

"Parameters of the Second World War in Asia and Africa: Thoughts and Emotions." Paper presented at the "Colonial Mobilization in Africa and Asia during the Second World War: Soldiers, Labourers and Women" conference. Kyoto. March 22–23, 2018.

"Soldiers, Ex-servicemen and Politics in the Gold Coast, 1939–50." *Journal of Modern African Studies* 21, no. 3 (1983): 523–534.

Killingray, David, with Martin Plaut. *Fighting for Britain: African Soldiers in the Second World War*. London: James Currey, 2010.

Killingray, David and Richard Rathbone, eds. *Africa and the Second World War*. New York: St. Martin's Press, 1986.

Kitchen, Martin. *A World in Flames: A Short History of the Second World War in Europe and Asia, 1939–1945*. London: Longman, 1990.

Korieh, Chima J. *The Land Has Changed: History, Society, and Gender in Colonial Eastern Nigeria*. Calgary: University of Calgary Press, 2010.

*"Life Not Worth Living": Nigerian Petitions Reflecting an African Society's Experiences during World War II*. Durham, NC: Carolina Academic Press, 2014.

"'May It Please Your Honor': Letters of Petition As Historical Evidence in an African Colonial Context." *History in Africa* 37 (2010): 83–106.

"Urban Food Supply and Vulnerability in Nigeria during the Second World War." In *Nigerian Cities*, edited by Toyin Falola and Steven J. Salm, 127–152. Trenton, NJ: Africa World Press, 2003.

Krozewski, Gerold. "Sterling, the 'Minor' Territories, and the End of Formal Empire, 1939–1958." *Economic History Review* 46, no. 2 (1993): 239–265.

Kundrus, Birthe. "From the Herero to the Holocaust? Some Remarks on the Current Debate." *Africa Spectrum* 40, no. 2 (2005): 299–308.

Laakkonen, Simo and Richard Tucker. "War and Natural Resources in History: Introduction." *Global Environment* 5, no. 10 (2012): 8–15.

Lambo, Roger. "Achtung! The Black Prince: West Africans in the Royal Air Force, 1939–46." In *Africans in Britain*, edited by David Killingray, 179–196. London: Routledge, 1994.

Laqueur, Walter. *Europe since Hitler: The Rebirth of Europe*. London: Penguin Books, 1982.

Lee, J. M. and M. Peter. *The Colonial Office, War, and Development Policy: Organization and the Planning of a Metropolitan Initiative, 1939–1945*. London: Maurice Temple Smith, 1982.

Leuchtenburg, William E. *Franklin D. Roosevelt and the New Deal, 1932–1940*. New York: Harper and Row, 1963.

Liftoff, Judy Barrett and David C. Smith. *American Women in a World at War: Contemporary Accounts from World War II*. Wilmington, DE: SR Books, 1997.

Liftoff, Judy Barrett and David C. Smith, eds., *Since You Went Away: World War II Letters from American Women on the Home Front*. Lawrence: University Press of Kansas, 1991.

Lightfoot, Kent G. *Indians, Missionaries, and Merchants: The Legacy of Colonial Encounters on the California Frontiers*. Berkeley: University of California Press, 2004.

Lonsdale, John. "The Depression and the Second World War in the Transformation of Kenya." In *Africa and the Second World War*, edited by David Killingray and Richard Rathbone, 97–142. New York: St. Martin's Press, 1986.

Lowe, Keith. *Savage Continent: Europe in the Aftermath of World War II*. New York: St Martin's Press, 2012.

Luciana, Gabriel Olakunle. *The Second World War and Politics in Nigeria, 1939–1953*. London: Evans Brothers, 1973.

Lugard, Frederick. *The Dual Mandate in British Tropical Africa*. London: Frank Cass, 1965.

Lyne, R. N. "Germany's Claim to Colonies: The African Mandates." *Journal of the Royal African Society* 38, no. 151 (1939): 273–280.

Mackay, R., *Half the Battle: Civilian Morale in Britain during the Second World War*. Manchester: Manchester University Press, 2002.

Manserg, N. *Survey of British Commonwealth Affairs: Problems of Wartime Cooperation and Post-War Change, 1939–52*. London: Frank Cass, 1968.

Marks, Sally. "Mistakes and Myths: The Allies, Germany, and the Versailles Treaty, 1918–1921." *Journal of Modern History* 85, no. 3 (2013): 632–659.

Marwick, Arthur. *War and Social Change in the Twentieth Century: A Comparative Study of Britain, France, Germany, Russia and the United States*. London: Red Globe Press, 1974.

Matera, Marc, Misty L. Bastian, and Susan Kingsley Kent, *The Women's War of 1929: Gender and Violence in Colonial Nigeria*. New York: Palgrave Macmillan, 2011.

Mazrui, Ali A. "Africa and the Legacy of the Second World War: Political, Economic and Cultural Aspects." In *Africa and the Second World War; Report and Papers of the Symposium Organized by UNESCO at Benghazi, Libyan Arab Jamahiriya from 10 to 13 November 1980*, 13–25. The General History of Africa Studies and Documents 10. Paris: UNESCO, 1985.

Mba, Nina. *Nigerian Women Mobilized: Women's Political Activity in Southern Nigeria, 1900–1965*. University of California Institute of International Studies, Research Series, No. 48. Berkeley: University of California Press, 1982.

McCulloch, Gary. "Labour, the Left, and the British General Election of 1945." *Journal of British Studies* 24, no. 4 (1985): 465–489.

McDonough, F. *Hitler, Chamberlain and Appeasement*. Cambridge: Cambridge University Press, 2002.

McGuire, Phillip, ed. *Taps for a Jim Crow Army: Letters from Black Soldiers in World War II*. Lexington: University Press of Kentucky, 1993.

McLaine, Ian. *Ministry of Morale: Home Front Morale and the Ministry of Information in World War II*. London: Allen & Unwin, 1979.

Melber, Henning. "How to Come to Terms with the Past: Re-visiting the German Colonial Genocide in Namibia." *Africa Spectrum* 40, no. 1 (2005): 139–148.

Meredith, David. "The British Government and Colonial Economic Policy, 1919–39." *Economic History Review* 28, no. 3 (1975): 484–499.

"The Colonial Office, British Business Interests and the Reform of Cocoa Marketing in West Africa, 1937–45." *Journal of African History* 29 (1988): 285–300.

"State Controlled Marketing and Economic 'Development': The Case of West African Produce during the Second World War." *Economic History Review* 39, no. 1 (1986): 77–91.

Metz, Helen Chapin, ed., *Nigeria: A Country Study*. Washington, DC: Government Printing Office for the Library of Congress, 1991.

Milverton, Lord. "Nigeria." *African Affairs* 47 (1948): 80–89.

Miracle, Marvin. *Maize in Tropical Africa*. Madison: University of Wisconsin Press, 1966.

Moore, Aaron William. *Bombing the City: Civilian Accounts of the Air War in Britain and Japan, 1939–1945*. Studies in the Social and Cultural History of Modern Warfare. Cambridge: Cambridge University Press, 2018.

Mordi, E. N. "The Nigeria Win the War Fund: An Unsung Episode in Government–Press Collaboration in Nigeria during the Second World War," *Journal of Social Science* 24, no. 2 (2010): 87–100.

Morgan, D. J. *The Official History of Colonial Development, Vol. 1: The Origins of British Aid Policy, 1924–45*. London: Palgrave Macmillan, 1980.

Morrow, John H., Jr. "Black Africans in World War II: The Soldiers' Stories." *ANNALS of the American Academy of Political and Social Science* 632 (2010): 12–25.

Ndumbe III, Alexander Kum'a. "Black Africa and Germany during the Second World War." In *Africa and the Second World War; Report and Papers of the Symposium Organized by UNESCO at Benghazi, Libyan Arab Jamahiriya from 10 to 13* November *1980*, 51–75. The General History of Africa Studies and Documents 10. Paris: UNESCO, 1985.

Njoku, Onwuka N. "Burden of Imperialism: Nigeria War Relief Fund, 1939–1945." *Transafrican Journal of History* 6, no. 7 (1977–1978): 79–99.

"Export Production Drive in Nigeria During World War II." *Transafrican Journal of History* 10, nos. 1–2 (1981): 11–22.

Nnoli, O. *Ethnic Politics in Nigeria*. Enugu: Fourth Dimension Publishers, 1978.

Nwaka, Geoffrey I. "Rebellion in Umuahia, 1950–1951: Ex-servicemen and Anti-colonial Protest in Eastern Nigeria." *Transafrican Journal of History* 16 (1987): 47–62.

Ochono, Moses E. *Colonial Meltdown: Northern Nigeria in the Great Depression*. Athens: Ohio University Press, 2009.

"Conjoined to Empire: The Great Depression and Nigeria." *African Economic History* 34 (2006): 103–145.

Olorunfemi, A. "Effects of War-Time Trade Control on Nigerian Cocoa Traders and Producers, 1939–1945: A Case Study of the Hazards of a Dependent Economy." *International Journal of African Historical Studies* 13, no. 4 (1980): 672–687.

Olukoju, Ayodeji. "The Cost of Living in Lagos 1914–1945." In *Africa's Urban Past*, edited by David M. Anderson, and Richard Rathbone, 126–143. Oxford: Heinemann, 2000.

Olusanya, G. O. "The Role of Ex-servicemen in Nigerian Politics." *Journal of Modern African Studies* 6, no. 2 (1968): 221–232.

*The Second World War and Politics in Nigeria, 1939–1945.* Lagos: University of Lagos, 1973.

Oluwasanmi, H. A. *Agriculture and Nigerian Economic Development.* Ibadan: Oxford University Press, 1966.

Omu, F. "The Nigerian Press and the Great War." *Nigeria Magazine*, March/May 1968, 44–49.

O'Neill, William L. *A Democracy at War: America's Fight at Home and Abroad in World War II.* New York: Free Press, 1993.

Onimode, Bede. *Imperialism and Underdevelopment in Nigeria: The Dialectics of Mass Poverty.* London: Macmillan, 1983.

Onitiri, H. M. A. and D. Olatunbosun, eds. *The Marketing Board System: Proceedings of an International Conference.* Ibadan: Nigerian Institute of Social and Economic Research, 1974.

Opata, Christian C., and Apex A. Apeh. "In Search of Honour: Eya Ebule As a Legacy of Igbo Resistance and Food Security from World War II." *International Journal of Intangible Heritage* 13 (2018): 114–127.

Ortner, Serry B. "Resistance and the Problem of Ethnographic Refusal." *Comparative Studies in Society and History* 37, no. 1 (1995): 173–193.

Osborne, Richard E. *World War II in Colonial Africa: The Death Knell of Colonialism.* Indianapolis, IN: Riebel-Roque, 2001.

Osuntokun, Jide. "Great Britain, Germany and War-Time Economy in Nigeria, 1914–1918." *Journal of African Studies* 2, no. 2 (1977): 29–59.

Overy, Richard. "Front Line II: Civilians at War." In *The Oxford Illustrated History of World War II*, edited by Richard Overy, 293–321. Oxford: Oxford University Press, 2005.

*Why the Allies Won.* London: Random House, 2006.

Oyatoye, E. T. O. "The Administration of Agricultural Development in Nigeria: An Assessment of Past and Present Agricultural Policies." *Agricultural Administration* 14, no. 2 (1984): 101–113.

Oyemakinde, Wale. "The Nigerian General Strike of 1945." *Journal of the Historical Society of Nigeria* 7, no. 4 (1975): 693–710.

"The Pullen Marketing Scheme : A Trial in Food Price Control in Nigeria, 1941–1947." *Journal of the Historical Society of Nigeria* 6, no. 4 (1973): 413–423.

Parker, Pauline E., ed. *Women of the Homefront: World War II Recollections of 55 Americans.* Jefferson, NC: McFarland, 2002.

Parker, Robert Alexander Clarke. *Struggle for Survival: The History of the Second World War.* Oxford: Oxford University Press, 1990.

Parsons, Timothy H. *The African Rank-and-File: Social Implications of Colonial Military Service in the King's African Rifles, 1902–1964.* Social History of Africa. Portsmouth: Heinemann, 1999.

Pearce, R. D. "Violet Bourdillon: Colonial Governor's Wife." *African Affairs* 82, no. 327 (April 1983): 267–277.

Pedler, F. J. F. *The Lion and the Union in Africa.* London: Heinemann, 1974.

Phillips, Barnaby. *Another Man's War: The Story of a Burma Boy in Britain's Forgotten African Army.* London: Oneworld Publications, 2015.

Phimister, Ian. "Developing and Defending Britain and Her Empire: Montgomery's 1947 Tour of Africa." *Journal of Military History* 79, no. 3 (2015): 745–766.

Phythian, Mark. *The Labour Party, War and International Relations 1945–2006.* London: Routledge, 2007.

Pollard, Stephen K. and Douglas H. Graham, "Pricing Policy and Agricultural Export Performance in Jamaica." *World Development* 13, no. 9 (1985): 1067–1075.

Quintard, Taylor. "Contentious Legacy: The Nigerian Youth Movement and the Rise of Ethnic Politics, 1934–1951." In *Nigerian Studies in Religious Tolerance, Volume III, Ethnicity, Religion and Nation-Building,* edited by C. S. Momah and Hakeem Harunah. Lagos: University of Lagos Press, 1995.

Raghavan, Srinath. *India's War: The Making of Modern South Asia, 1939–1945.* London: Penguin, 2017.

Roodhouse, Mark. *Black Market Britain: 1939–1955.* Oxford: Oxford University Press, 2013.

Rose, Sonya A. "Race, Empire and British Wartime National Identity, 1939–1945." *Historical Research* 74, no. 184 (2001): 220–237.
*Which People's War? National Identity and Citizenship in Wartime Britain 1939–1945.* Oxford: Oxford University Press, 2003.

Rosenberg, William G. "Reading Soldiers' Moods: Russian Military Censorship and the Configuration of Feeling in World War I." *American Historical Review* 119, no. 3 (June 2014): 714–740.

Rosenblum, Shelly. "Review of Signatures of Citizenship: Petitioning, Antislavery, and Women's Political Identity, by Susan Ziska." *Canadian Review of American Studies* 36, no. 1 (2006): 117–121.

Samuel, Raphael. *Theatres of Memory, vol. I: Past and Present in Contemporary Culture.* London: Verso, 1994.

Schlesinger Arthur M., Jr., *The Age of Roosevelt: The Coming of the New Deal.* Boston: Houghton Mifflin Company, 1958.

Schneller, Robert J., Jr. *Breaking the Color Barrier: The U.S. Naval Academy's First Black Midshipmen and the Struggle for Racial Equality.* New York: New York University Press, 2005.

Scott, James. *Weapons of the Weak: Everyday Forms of Peasant Resistance.* New Haven, CT: Yale University Press, 1985.

Sharp, Alan. *The Versailles Settlement: Peacemaking after the First World War, 1919–1923.* 3rd edn. London: Red Globe Press, 2018.

Shenton, Robert. "Nigerian Agriculture in Historical Perspective: Development and Crisis, 1900–1960." In *State, Oil and Agriculture in Nigeria,* edited by Michael Watts and Michael Hodd, 34–57. Berkeley: University of California Press, 1987.

Sheppard, W. Anthony. "An Exotic Enemy: Anti-Japanese Musical Propaganda in World War II Hollywood." *Journal of the American Musicological Society* 54, no. 2 (2001): 303–357.

Shulman, Holly Cowan. *The Voice of America: Propaganda and Democracy, 1941–1945.* Madison: University of Wisconsin Press, 1990.

Sikaing, Ahmad Alawad. "Conclusion: Consequences of the War." In *Africa and World War II,* edited by Judith A. Byfield, Carolyn A. Brown, Timothy Parsons, and Ahmad Alawad Sikaing. New York: Cambridge University Press, 2015.

Sklar, Richard L. *Nigerian Political Parties: Power in an Emergent African Nation.* Trenton, NJ: African World Press, 2004.

Smyth, Rosaleen. "Britain's African Colonies and British Propaganda during the Second World War." *Journal of Imperial and Commonwealth History* 14, no. 1 (1985): 65–82.

"War Propaganda during the Second World War in Northern Rhodesia." *African Affairs* 83, no. 332 (1984): 345–358.

Spinney, Robert G. *World War II in Nashville: Transformation of the Homefront.* Knoxville: University of Tennessee Press, 1998.

Stanard, Matthew G. "Belgium, the Congo, and Imperial Immobility: A Singular Empire and the Historiography of the Single Analytic Field." *French Colonial History* 15 (2014): 87–110.

Stoler, Ann Laura and Frederick Cooper. "Between Metropole and Colony: Rethinking a Research Agenda." In *Tensions of Empire: Colonial Cultures in a Bourgeois World,* edited by Ann Laura Stoler and Frederick Cooper, 1–56. Berkeley: University of California Press, 1997.

Strachan, Hew. *The First World War in Africa.* Oxford: Oxford University Press, 2004.

Tamuno, Tekena N. *Herbert Macaulay, Nigerian Patriot.* London: Heinemann, 1976.

Taraknath, Das. "India and the End of Empire." *Virginia Quarterly Review* 16, no. 1 (1940): 68–77.

Thomas, Isaac B. *Life History of Herbert Macaulay, C. E.* Lagos: Printed at Tika-To[r]e Press, 1946.

Trachtenberg, Marc. "Versailles after Sixty Years." *Journal of Contemporary History* 17 no. 3 (1982): 487–506.

Travers, Daniel and Stephen Heathorn. "Collective Remembrance, Second World War Mythology and National Heritage on the Isle of Man," *National Identities* 10, no. 4 (2008): 433–448.

Ubah, C. N. *Colonial Army and Society in Northern Nigeria.* Kaduna: National Defence Academy, 1998.

Usoro, Eno J. *The Nigerian Oil Palm Industry: Government Policy and Export Production, 1906–1965.* Ibadan: Ibadan University Press, 1974.

UNESCO. *Africa and the Second World War: Report and Papers of the Symposium Organized by UNESCO at Benghazi, Libyan Aram Jamahiriya, from 10 to 13 November 1980.* Paris: UNESCO, 1985.

Varnava, Andrekos. "The Impact of the Cypriot Contribution during the Great War on Colonial Society and Loyalties/Disloyalties to the British Empire." *First World War Studies* 8, no. 1 (2017): 17–36.

Verner, Andrew. "Discursive Strategies in the 1905 Revolution: Peasant Petitions from Vladimir Province." *Russian Review* 54, no. 1 (1995): 65–90.

Weinberg, Gerhard L. *A World at Arms: A Global History of World War II*. 2nd edn. New York: Cambridge University Press, 2005.

Weitz, Eric D. "Review of Nazi Empire: German Colonialism and Imperialism from Bismarck to Hitler, by Shelley Baranowski." *Holocaust and Genocide Studies* 27, no. 1 (Spring 2013): 137.

Welch, David. *Persuading the People: British Propaganda in World War II*. London: British Library, 2016.

Wells, Jerome C. *Agricultural Policy and Economic Growth in Nigeria, 1962–1968*. Oxford: Oxford University Press, 1974.

Wicker, E. R. "Colonial Development and Welfare, 1929–1957: The Evolution of a Policy." *Social and Economic Studies* 7, no. 4 (1958): 170–192.

Wilder, Gary. "From Optic to Topic: The Foreclosure Effect of Historiographic Turns." *American Historical Review* 117, no. 3 (June 2012): 723–745.

Willmott, H. P. *The Great Crusade: A New Complete History of the Second World War*. New York: Free Press, 1989.

Wilson, Charles Henry. *The History of Unilever: A Study of Economic Growth and Social Change*. 2 vols. London: Cassell, 1954.

Winkler, Allan M. *Home Front, U.S.A.: America during World War II*. 2nd edn. Wheeling, IL: Harlan Davidson, 2000.

"World War II Homefront: A Historiography," *OAH Magazine of History* 16, no. 3 (Spring 2002): 5–8.

Witkowski, Terrence H. "World War II Poster Campaigns: Preaching Frugality to American Consumers." *Journal of Advertising* 32, no. 1 (2003): 69–82.

Wrigley, C. C. "The Colonial Phase in British West Africa: Economic and Social Developments." In *A Thousand Years of West Africa History*, edited by J. F. Ade Ajayi and Ian Espie, 423–439. Ibadan: Ibadan University Press and Nelson, 1972.

Yellin, Emily. *Our Mothers' War: American Women at Home and at the Front during World War II*. New York: Free Press, 2005.

Zeitlin, Irving M., with Robert J. Bryn, *The Social Condition of Humanity*. Canadian edn. Toronto: Oxford University Press, 1991.

Ziska, Susan. *Signatures of Citizenship: Petitioning, Antislavery, and Women's Political Identity*. Gender and American Culture Series. Chapel Hill: University of North Carolina Press, 2003.

Zweiniger-Bargielowska, Ina, *Austerity in Britain: Rationing, Controls, and Consumption, 1939–1955*. Oxford: Oxford University Press, 2000.

# Index